A Daily Devotional on the Song of Solomon

Beloved of Beloved, Bride of Brides, Song of Songs

Henry James Welch

BELOVED OF BELOVED, BRIDE OF BRIDES, SONG OF SONGS
A Daily Devotional of the Song of Solomon

Copyright © 2010 Henry James Welch

All rights reserved. No part of this publication may be reproduced, stored in a retrieval system, or transmitted in any form or by any means—electronic, mechanical, photocopy, recording, or any other—except for brief quotations in printed reviews, without prior permission from the publisher.

Unless otherwise indicated, all Scripture quotations are taken from the King James Version, which is in the public domain.

Scripture quotations marked RSV are taken from the Revised Standard Version of the Bible. Copyright © 1946, 1952, and 1971 National Council of the Churches of Christ in the United States of America. Used by permission. All rights reserved. Scripture quotations marked TEV are taken from The Good News Bible: Today's English Version. New York: American Bible Society. Copyright © 1992. Used by permission. All rights reserved.

ISBN-13: 978-1-77069-017-2

Printed in Canada.

Word Alive Press
131 Cordite Road, Winnipeg, MB R3W 1S1
www.wordalivepress.ca

With many thanks, I submit this work:

—To you, the chosen people of Jehovah.
—To the virgins and the daughters of Jerusalem.
—To the saints of the Most High God.
—To the spiritual Israelites of today.

Foreword

This book is a beautiful, day-by-day inspirational guide for God's dear children. Every page is a morning devotional that will uplift the soul and bring a ray of sunshine into the heart. It is a journey that goes step by step through a seldom understood but precious book of Holy Scripture. It reveals the love of God for His people from age to age and ends with precious promises to make you ready for the final events of earth's history. Surely, holy angels will stand by your side, and the Holy Spirit will direct your thinking as you absorb its messages of hope and cheer to lift you through the "daily grind." Never will you doubt the fact that you may be among the "chosen and faithful" who will meet the Heavenly Bridegroom as He comes to take His bride home with Him.

Marion Berry

THE AUTHOR'S INTRODUCTION

I acknowledge my thankfulness for the honour given to me of being introduced to the Song of Solomon some years ago. It was put into my thinking that some sort of reference book, like a morning devotional book, should be prepared to help God's people get ready for the bursting in the clouds.

Like Proverbs 30, I have seven reasons for preparing this work, yea eight (Proverbs 30:15,18,29).

1. to express my deep and elevated belief in my God, my church, my people.
2. to release and share some of the excitement experienced in my study of this book.
3. to aid others in declaring the very nearness of the Bridegroom to claim His bride.
4. to not only elevate the Bridegroom, but also His bride to her exalted and unique position.
5. to awaken the virgins and encourage them not only to trim their lamps, but to buy the necessary oil to keep their lamps burning brightly.
6. to awaken God's people to the historical, prophetic position of the most exciting bride ever to grace Planet Earth.
7. to establish the exalted nature and purpose of this song as it takes its rightful and honoured place among the inspired books of the sacred canon.
8. to feed, strengthen, confirm, and affirm my own soul,

The Song of Solomon is couched in figurative language of prophetic symbolism and can be decoded in a cross-referenced study of Scripture. It is a drama of church history which extends from the crucifixion at the cross to the second coming of Christ. Its drama provides a framework of historical and theological realities which identify God's people from the crucifixion to the final deliverance.

This thought, this nugget of understanding, that what you literally read is not which is literally meant, will be repeated, probably too many times, throughout the book. You will need to remember that.

As its name implies, the Song of Solomon is the superlative, the best, "the mostest of the most," expression of prophecy in poetic form, reserved for the last generation to lighten their way through the final crises which are a certainty, and the final deliverance, also a certainty.

Although I am encouraged to be an original thinker and not a reflector of other men's thoughts, I ask permission to simply reflect, many times word for word, many times the whole page, the ideas, thoughts, discoveries, and insights of Mrs. Marion Berry from her books on *The Song of Songs*. To tell it like it is, this daily devotional was simply a rearrangement of her books, so there is really nothing new by this author. Usually no credit is given at the time of using the material, so be aware that should there not be acceptable credit given, the material came from Marion Berry's *Song of Songs*, both the *Sabbath School Quarterly* and her accompanying *Workbook*.

One will notice that most of the Scriptural references in the top-right hand corner are from the Song of Solomon. Sometimes the same one is even repeated several days in a row through **Today's Thought**. This was done on purpose, as many texts have much wisdom and knowledge within them. Hopefully one will eventually memorize it.

One could also notice that there is some repetition, again done on purpose, for as a teacher I'm fully aware that to read something only once, one will retain a small portion of what is read. If I repeat it two or more times, the chances of retaining more is greater.

Concluding each day's reading will be a **Parting Gem:** a thought, an idea, a verse, to encourage you, to put you on your way for that day.

At the conclusion of each month's reading is a summary. This summary will have neither a **Today's Thought** nor a **Parting Gem.**

At the end of each month's readings there will be a poem, courtesy of the author. When Paul talks about gifts being given unto men (1 Corinthians 12:7-11,28 and Ephesians 4:8-13), the author was given a gift of poetry. He wishes to use it for the purposes Paul states.

In closing this introduction, I wish to encourage you to start looking at this drama, Song of Solomon, which is better known as Song of Songs, in an entirely different light. Not the sensuous, suggestive, below the belt idea, but as a prophetic outline of the Seventh-day Adventist Church, as an I.D. card for who you are, as a safeguard against offshoots, apostasy, discouragement, and a whole lot more.

Enjoy your walk to Emmaus.

Explanations of Citations

Some of the quotations found in this devotional have been gathered from the E.G. White writings as they occur in current books. The following abbreviations have been used to identify their source material. The full identity of these books can be found in the Bibliography.

AA	"Acts of the Apostles"
CM	"Colportor Ministry"
CD	"Councils on Diets and Foods"
COL	"Christ Object Lessons"
DA	"Desire of Ages"
Ed.	"Education"
EW	"Early Writings"
MH	"Ministry of Healing"
LS	"Life Sketches"
PP	"Patriarchs and Prophets"
SM	"Selected Messages" Book 1, 2, 3
SG	"Spiritual Gifts" Books 1, 2
TM	"Testimonies to Ministers and Gospel Workers"
MB	"Thoughts From the Mount of Blessings"
CSSW	"Councils on Sabbath School Work"

Table of Contents

Month	Passage	Description
January	Song 1:1 to 8:14	Introduction to Song of Solomon
February	Song 1:2 to 1:8 G. C. Ch. 2-3	Act I, Scene 1—*Calvary* Scene 2—*Apostasy* Scene 3—*Flight into Wilderness*
March	Song 1:8 to 2:7	Act I, Scene 4—*Description of the Bride in Wilderness*
April	Song 2:8 to 3:5 G. C. Ch. 4-15	Act I, Scene 5—*European Reformation*
May	Song 3:6 to 3:11 G.C. Ch. 16-17	Act II, Scene I—*Spiritual Stupor* Scene 2—*In City of Confusion, State of Nominal Christianity* Scene 3—*Exit from Wilderness, 1798* Scene 4—*Great Religious Awakening, 1800*
June	Song 4:1 to 4:16 G. C. Ch. 18	Act II, Scene 5—*Description of the Bride in the Great Religious Awakening, 1800, plus the Rise of the Millerite Movement (1833-1844)*

July	Revelation 10 Song 5:1 to 5:8 G. C. Ch. 19-23	Act II, Scene 6—*Experience of Ten Virgins* Scene 7—*The Great Disappointment of October 1844* Scene 8—*Disappointment Explained*
August	Song 5:9 to 5:16 G. C. Ch. 35	Act II, Scene 8—*A Description of the Beloved in Contrast to "Another Beloved"*
September	Song 6:1 to 6:13 G. C. Page 353	Act II, Scene 9—*Reason for the Disappointment, plus Bride's Description as per the Seventh-day Adventist Church*
October	Song 7:1 to 7:13	Act II, Scene 10—*Third Description of the Church Continued: Seventh-day Adventist Church*
November	Song 8:1 to 8:7 G. C. Ch. 36-40	Act III, Scene 1—*Bride's Lament* Scene 2—*Sealing of God's People* Scene 3—*Loud Cry of Third Angel* Scene 4—*Sealing of God's People in Arm*
December	Song 8:8 to 8:14	Epilogue

Appendices
1. Comparison of Song of Solomon with Revelation
2. What Happened Next?
3. The Seven Churches of Revelation in Light of Song of Songs
4. A Wedding Invitation
5. Recommended Books to Read
6. This Night of Nights
7. Synopsis of Song of Songs

Bibliography

January

January's Introduction and Aim

During January, you will be introduced to this book, Song of Songs. Each month, you will receive an assignment. Your assignment for this month is to read all 117 verses, eight chapters, of this drama in one sitting.

JANUARY

Day 1	Year of Years	Amos 4:12	4
Day 2	Launch of Launches	Luke 5:4	5
Day 3	Puzzle of Puzzles	Deuteronomy 29:29	6
Day 4	Baffle of Baffles	2 Timothy 3:16	7
Day 5	Thought of Thoughts	Song 1:1	8
Day 6	Enigma of Enigmas	Matthew 4:4	9
Day 7	Poem of Poems	Exodus 15:2	10
Day 8	Title of Titles #1	Song 1:1	11
Day 9	Sign of Signs	Luke 14:32	12
Day 10	Purpose of Purposes	2 Timothy 3:16	13
Day 11	Benefit of Benefits	2 Timothy 3:16-17	14
Day 12	Balance of Balances	Leviticus 19:36	15
Day 13	Drama of Drama	Psalms 95:1	16
Day 14	Hero of Heroes	Song 5:16	17
Day 15	Name of Names	Acts 4:12	18
Day 16	Heroine of Heroines	Matthew 11:28	19
Day 17	Mother of Mothers	Galatians 4:26	20
Day 18	Virgin of Virgins #1	Matthew 25:1-13	21
Day 19	Actor of Actors	John 14:29	22
Day 20	Charge of Charges #1	Luke 12:39	23
Day 21	Capsule of Capsules	John 14:29	24
Day 22	Surge of Surges #1	Revelation 22:20	25
Day 23	Hope of Hope	Lamentations 3:26	26
Day 24	Construction of Constructions	Isaiah 28:10,13	27
Day 25	Allegory of Allegories	Matthew 13:44	28
Day 26	Temptation of Temptations	Revelation 3:10	29
Day 27	Caution of Cautions	Acts 17:11	30
Day 28	Faith of Faiths	Romans 14:23	31
Day 29	Deceit of Deceits	1 Corinthians 3:18	32
Day 30	Result of Results	1 Corinthians 10:1	33
Day 31	Summary	PP 504:1	34

Poems of the Month: "I Knew That This Year" ... 35
   "His Promises Are Not for the Few" ... 36

JANUARY 1 — Year of Years — Amos 4:12

Today's Thought: *"Prepare to meet thy God, O Israel."*

God's people, that's you and me, are about to enter a new era of church history—an era where we see the closing of the judgment of the dead, and a switch to the opening of the judgment of the living. This point in time is heralded by the opening up of an entire book of the Bible—the Song of Solomon.

The book, Song of Solomon, is framed in figurative language of prophetic symbolism. To be correctly understood and decoded, one must let the Bible interpret itself through a cross-reference study of Scripture. This book is a drama depicting church history. It is Christ talking to His church. The curtain opens of Act 1, Scene 1, in Chapter 1, Verse 1 on a hill called Mount Calvary, and the final curtain is pulled closed in Chapter 8, Verse 7 at the sealing of God's people. The last few verses are an epilogue where the actors, coming out onto centre stage, depict what events are soon to follow.

In this book, God's people are identified. God's church is identified. This book is a gift from the Bridegroom to His bride, to prepare her for when He returns to claim her as His bride. It is a gift to edify, encourage, uplift, and prepare you and me to "Behold the Bridegroom," for He IS coming.

Therefore, prepare your minds, your hearts, arrange your time for this journey through the Song of Solomon, to gladden your hearts for this festive mood of a wedding between a lover and His love, between my fair, my love, and my Beloved May your hearts burn within you as you walk the "Emmaus Road" with my Beloved.

This book has strong parallelism with the book *The Great Controversy,* and one is encouraged to check this work with it. I would certainly encourage, yea urge, you to remember that many will stand in our pulpits with the torch of false prophecy in their hands, kindled from the hellish torch of Satan.

Parting Gem: *"These were more noble than those in Thessalonica, in that they received… and searched the scriptures daily."* (Acts 17:11)

JANUARY 2 — *Launch of Launches* — Luke 5:4

Today's Thought: *"Launch out into the deep, and let down your nets."*

You are about to set sail through this coming year on a 366-day journey. During this year, there are going to be fast, exciting experiences, offset by dull and slow frustrations, there will be easy sledding, as well as heavy slugging, easy to understand passages, followed by strange new concepts that will take strong, even white teeth to slowly chew some of this Word of God. Remember, just because you read it for morning worship, there has yet to be found reasons for not reading it several times until you finally and fully grasp its meaning and it becomes a part of your lifestyle, your strength, your being.

Welcome aboard this journey through the book near the middle of your Bible, commonly called Song of Solomon. The author's prayer is that you grasp, before December 31, the beauty of this book. The first assignment is that you read in one sitting the 117 verses that comprise this baffling, yet very exciting book. Do this many times, using as many different and varied translations as you can find. There will be many challenges throughout this year, challenges that will be met and appreciated when you have met them on your knees, in your secret chamber of prayer, in your daily communions with God, in your feasting on His Word. However, you are promised in Isaiah 55 that you will not only grow fat but that you'll delight thyself in that fatness.

"Ho, every one that thirsteth, come ye to the waters, and he that hath no money; come ye, buy and eat…. eat ye that which is good, and let your soul delight itself in fatness." (Isaiah 55:1-2)

When you arrive at the end of the year, you will have had answered many questions that now may very well baffle you. Stretch forth thy mind, thy faith, thy power. With excitement, prepare to step outside of your comfort zone into another zone to gain greater comfort.

Parting Gem: *To launch out into the deep, yet not let down your net, is nothing but a drift in the Lake of Life.*

January 3 — *Puzzle of Puzzles* — Deuteronomy 29:29

Today's Thought: *"Those things which are revealed belong to us."*

For those of you who have ever started a five thousand word jigsaw puzzle, you will be familiar with two aspects of solving that puzzle. Each piece of the puzzle has a specific and unique place in the overall puzzle. Each piece feels comfortable in the place allotted to it. If it was put into some other place, it just would not fit; it wouldn't feel comfortable even if it looked okay. The second aspect is that as you put the puzzle together, it becomes clearer when you compare it with the picture on the cover of the box.

So this enigma, or 117-word puzzle, this mystery in the midst of our Bible, will take shape as one piece after another is placed into its unique and selected spot. As each symbol is decoded, using the Bible as our interpreter, the overall emerging picture, as compared to the cover picture of history and Bible prophecy, confirms that the Bible student has done his homework. The overall picture then becomes clear and logical.

If the interpretation is correct, then not only will each and every verse takes its rightful place, but the entire book will assume its true, exalted position in Scripture. The message of this book will then edify the church and the individual faith of each one who looks for the coming Bridegroom.

When the Song of Songs is given its correct study, it is discovered that the sequential placement of verses throughout the entire Song provides a chronological outline of the history of the Christian Church. This neat alignment, this comfortableness, is undeniable proof of its prophetic nature, its correct interpretation, and its divine appointment.

The prophetic nature of Song of Songs is also identified by its alignment, both with Daniel in the Old Testament and with Revelation in the New Testament, as they outline church history. The figurative language of the three books is very closely entwined and the prophetic nature of all three books run parallel to each other.

Parting Gem: *This book belongs to you. Claim it and run with it.*

JANUARY 4   *Baffle of Baffles*   2 Timothy 3:16

Today's Thought: *"All scripture is given by inspiration of God, and is profitable for doctrine, for reproof, for correction, for instruction in righteousness: That the man of God may be perfect, thoroughly furnished unto all good works."*

After you have read the 117 verses of this book, Song of Solomon, and I trust that you have since assignment time yesterday, you'll be convinced that it is too complicated for human interpretation. This Song is so complicated in nature, in construction, in symbolism, and what have you, that since the days of its composition, some three thousand years ago, it seems to have defied understandable interpretation. This Scripture, which is given by inspiration of God, must also be interpreted by Him who wrote it. Its meaning, hidden for nearly three thousand years, must soon be decoded in order for it to fulfill the remainder of today's thought, that it is profitable for doctrine, reproof, correction, instruction, all in righteousness and all needed for men, women, boys, and girls to be properly equipped to handle the hassles of life.

As you read this book, notice that this Song has beautiful language, an honourable theme of love, a fast-forward movement of drama and suspense, yet also some deeper, hidden significance, some hidden meaning, some illusive something. In God's great plan of the play and the counterplay of men and nations, providence has preserved this love song for us in our modern day. As you read this fascinating and complicated account, be informed that, of all the Bible books, this one is the most difficult to interpret, the most embarrassing to read, yet one of the most rewarding, stimulating, and challenging. It is like a five thousand piece jigsaw puzzle with no picture on the box to follow.

Parting Gem: *We have launched out and, yes, it may be out into the deep. Yet one must remember that every day of our lives is a new launch. Every day we may have problems to solve, puzzles to decode, victories to claim, but the invitation to you is to launch out, cross over the border of your comfort zone. So, Reader, may this book be a gift to you for this year so that you may prepare to meet your Bridegroom, my Beloved.*

JANUARY 5   *Thought of Thoughts*   Song 1:1

Today's Thought: *"The song of songs, which is Solomon's."*

What a thought! How could such a thought as that thought be in our sacred canon all this time and we pass over it so easily or slip by it embarrassingly? Within the book itself, Chapter 1, Verse 1, by inspiration at that, the real title of this song is given—the Song of Songs. What a fantastic and awesome thought, a thought of all thoughts.

The titles given to the books of the Bible have been supplied by translators, tradition, or printers. The chapters and verse numbers were not inspired as well. The title of the books of the Bible fall into several categories. They may have been supplied according to the subject written, such as Genesis (the beginning), or Exodus (the moving out). According to the author of the book, such as Matthew and John. Or according to the person or place sent, such as Timothy, Philemon, Corinthians, Ephesians. A fourth category could be the main character, such as Esther, Ruth, Samuel, Job. Yet, a fifth category would be according to what they were, such as Psalms or Proverbs. So the title of this book, for this year, has been given the title *The Song of Solomon* by the translators and it has generally been accepted by the masses at large. Inspiration, on the other hand, has furnished us with the real, inspired name, *The Song of Songs*, the superlative of all songs.

Another book, a book of prophecy, given to God's people and having stupendous meaning to His people today, has experienced similar phenomena. According to Revelation 1:1, inspiration has put her stamp on the Revelation of Jesus Christ, whereas translators have given it the title of the Revelation of John the Beloved. It would appear that the Song of Songs is in good company.

The purpose of Revelation is similar to Song of Solomon in that it was written to tell us things shortly to come to pass. What a thought.

Parting Gem: *Higher than the highest human thought can reach is God's ideal for His children, God-likeness (ED 18). Are you ready to climb?*

JANUARY 6   *Enigma of Enigmas*   Matthew 4:4

Today's Thought: *"Man shall not live by bread alone, but by every word that proceedeth out of the mouth of God."*

Maybe you have also joined those who question whether this song even belongs in the sacred canon. Yet, in God's great plan of the play and counterplay of men and nations, providence has preserved this love song for us in our day. As you read this fascinating and complicated account, may you be informed that it has been declared, of all the books in the Old Testament, the most difficult to interpret. It has been called the "enigma of the Bible." It may also be declared to be the most embarrassing to read, some even declaring that it is too sensuous to be read. It has also been declared the richest and most rewarding. What a challenge lies before you this year. Rise up, grasp it, claim it as your own and make it a part of your own personal lifestyle.

Matthew 4:4 informs us that man shall not live only on bread and butter, but by EVERY word that comes from Him who supplied that bread and butter. This book should fit into that category of every word.

This book is a part of the inspired product of the prophets. As you read these thoughts each day this year, read them in cooperation with the Author of this Song written some three thousand years ago. Follow correct principles of decoding or interpretation of them. Watch this book come alive and your heart will burn within you.

Deuteronomy 29:29, John 15:4, and 1 Corinthians 10:11 give us permission to expect a solving of this enigma. They are a trilogy informing us that whatever was written before now was for our admonition, learning, comfort, hope.

This year, Reader, may the Song of Solomon be a gift to you to edify and prepare you to meet the Bridegroom, my Beloved. One of the things we people do when we receive a gift is to open that gift. An unwrapped gift is of no real value.

Parting Gem: *Sit up to the table for a feast on His Word and unwrap your gift.*

JANUARY 7　　　　　*Poem of Poems*　　　　　Exodus 15:2

Today's Thought: *"The Lord is my strength and song."*

> *Praise ye the Lord, Praise God in his sanctuary: praise him in the firmament of his power.*
> *Praise him for his mighty acts: praise him according to his excellent greatness.*
> *Praise him with the sound of the trumpet: praise him with the psaltery and harp.*
> *Praise him with the timbrel and dance: praise him with stringed instruments and organs.*
> *Praise him upon the loud cymbals: praise him upon the high sounding cymbals.*
> *Let every thing that hath breath, praise the Lord. Praise ye the Lord.* (Psalm 150:1-6)

The Bible has many places where poetry is written and expressed. A close look at them reveals that inspired writers and prophets like Moses, Miriam, Balaam, Mary, Elizabeth, and many others who gave utterances into the future placed their songs in poetic structure. It seems that poetry and prophecy go hand in glove. However, this poetry is usually, if not always, in the Hebrew structure.

In Genesis 3:14-19, the Creator, using poetic structure, outlines the curses to the serpent, woman and man, as well as gives the first promise of deliverance and total victory.

Exodus 15:1-18 is the victory song of Moses, the song of deliverance. Then, in verse 21, his sister Miriam prophesies in poetic structure her confidence in glorious triumph.

In Numbers 24:3-9 and 15-24, Balaam uses poetic utterance in his attempt to curse Israel, but instead he ends up blessing her, even prophesying of deliverance through the great Deliverer (verse 17).

In Luke 2, Mary, Elizabeth, then Zacharius prophesied and spoke praises in poetic structure when both John and Jesus were conceived in the womb. Mary was jubilant with praise to magnify her Lord.

It is estimated that 80% of the Old Testament is originally in poetic form—Hebrew poetic form—so the Song of Songs is in good company.

Parting Gem: *Pause just now and read aloud this poem of all poems.*

JANUARY 8   *Title of Titles #1*   Song 1:1

Today's Thought: *"The song of songs, which is Solomon's."*

The titles of our Bible books come from several sources. They could come from the reason for writing such as Genesis (the beginning), or Exodus (the exodus out of Egypt). They could come from the main character in the book, such as in Samuel, Job, or Nehemiah, or from the person who wrote the book, such as in Daniel, Matthew, Mark, Luke, and John. Some were named after the receiver, as in Romans, Hebrews, and Timothy. Remember, we mentioned that on January 5.

The title, the Song of Songs, is a Hebrew idiom which denotes a status similar to the King of kings, Lord of lords, the Holy of Holies. It denotes the superlative, the incomparable, the unsurpassable, the highest and best of any and all. Of all the kings ever to reign on thrones, there is an incomparable King, an unsurpassable King, high and lifted up, above and beyond any earthly king. So, by the same understanding, of all the songs ever written, of all the songs ever sung, this Song of Songs is the incomparable song, the unsurpassable song, the undeniable highest of any and all songs, high and lifted up beyond any earthly song. What a concept. What an awesome idea.

Anciently, the Jews presented this Song of Songs in colourful pageantry as the grand finale on the eighth day of the Passover. The Passover was a memorial of their deliverance from Egypt and a type pointing to their future deliverance which Christ was to accomplish in freeing His people from the bondage of sin. Their use of the book is a guide to us in understanding the nature of the book and its major emphasis. You'll discover that it is still a book of deliverance which applies to God's people in the very end of time.

So, throughout this year, because it sounds more romantic, because rightly understood in its fullness it has much more meaning, and because it is the title of inspiration, this book will be referred to as the Song of Songs, the song of my Beloved. To conserve mask-head, space we will simply refer to this drama as *Song*.

Passing Gem: *The Song of Songs, which is Solomon's; the Revelation of Jesus Christ which God gave.*

JANUARY 9 — *Sign of Signs* — Luke 14:32

Today's Thought: *Watch your heart today. Watch it or it may burst into flames like on the way to Emmaus.*

Many times, we read and study the signs of Christ's second coming as outlined in Matthew 24 and Luke 21, and get the idea that these are the most important or even the only signs to look for. Today, we look at the Methuselah of prophecy.

Methuselah, the son of Enoch, helped build the ark and preach of the coming flood. He died the year the flood occurred, because his name meant something like, "When I die, the end will come." As the preaching from Noah proceeded, the people must have watched Methuselah grow older and older. How their hearts must have pounded the day that they heard that he was sick in bed, or wounded. How did they really react when they were told that he was dead?

A closer look at the ark showed that it was completed. Then one day Noah makes his last appeal, the animals came in two by two or seven by seven, the birds fly in, all in an orderly manner. Suddenly, the ark's huge, massive door closed slowly so that any last decision could be acknowledged. Yet, with all of these signs, still only eight righteous souls were found inside safety. What a pity. What a seemingly waste of time and effort.

In the parable of the ten virgins of Matthew 25, the virgins "slumbered and slept" through the tarrying time. They could not be awakened until the "midnight cry" was made. So, in like manner, the sleeping church could not understand the meaning, the purpose, the scope of the Song of Songs until the time in history had come to sound the "midnight cry." Could it be that this Song is a vital part of the gospel to all the world, so that God's people could really know who they are?

The Song of Songs in its prophetic use is not given simply as a curiosity, or source of entertainment, but rather it is dedicated to the solemn intent of preparing a people for the final crises just ahead, a preparation of God's people in heart and mind to join the bridal procession to give that "midnight cry."

Parting Gem: *Behold, take notice, something is about to happen!*

JANUARY 10　　　　　*Purpose of Purposes*　　　　　2 Timothy 3:16

Today's Thought: *"All scripture is… profitable…"*

Did you wonder, as you read the 117 verses of this song, just what the purpose of this book is? Did you wonder why this embarrassing book was written, not only written but by inspiration, and why it has been incorporated and kept within the sacred canons?

Consider these nine reasons and apply them to our book for this year.

1. Prophecy is given so that after its fulfillment we may believe.
2. Prophecy is given to remind us, God's people, of the way the Lord has led His people and His teachings in their past history.
3. Prophecy assures us that there really is nothing to fear for the future, except that we forget.
4. Prophecy shines as a light in a dark place until the day dawns and the day star arise in your hearts (2 Peter 1:19).
5. Prophecy provides hope and understanding in times of crises and trial.
6. Prophecy provides a clear focus upon current issues.
7. Prophecy provides a focal point in history to tell God's people where, in history, they stand.
8. Prophecy highlights the important doctrines and concepts of salvation.
9. Prophecy glorifies Christ in His doctrines and glorious coming.

For nearly three thousand years, the Song of Songs, like all other prophetic books, surges forward towards the grand climax of history—the coming of the Bridegroom. The great message of this book is, *"Behold, the Bridegroom cometh"* (Matthew 25:6). It therefore has a very specific timing for its ultimate and effective proclamation, and that is just before the second coming of my Beloved. Go ye out to meet Him.

I wish you not to always agree, but to delve deep into the mineshaft of Scripture to find the gems of truth. Could it be, just could it be, that this Song is a part of the prophecy stating that this gospel must go to all the world before Christ can come? Could it be?

Parting Gem: *Therefore, the purpose we wish to place emphasis on this year is to prepare to meet our God, to prepare our hearts, our lives, our motives, our lifestyle, our families, to stand with rapt attention looking up into those clouds to exclaim, "This is our God."*

JANUARY 11 — *Benefit of Benefits* — 2 Timothy 3:16-17

Today's Thought: *"All scripture is given by inspiration… that the man of God may be perfect, thoroughly furnished unto all good works."*

It is impossible to list, on one page, all of the benefits one receives in a study of God's Word. Our thought tells us that all Scripture, including our Song, is inspired of God, and is profitable. Let's take the Bible at its word.

Counsel is given us to search the Scriptures, for in them we have eternal life, and they testify of Jesus Christ (John 5:39). These words are spirit and they are life (John 6:63).

The trilogy of Deuteronomy 29:29, Romans 15:4, and 1 Corinthians 10:11 tells us that whatever was written and given to us and our children was for our learning, our examples, our admonition, and to give us hope as they are revealed, to give us a precedent.

It's exciting to know that something positive is going to happen and that we are going to watch it happen. John 13:19 and 14:29 assure us of the possibilities of having our belief confirmed and belief in Jesus solidified as we see it happen.

We have been given the assurance in Ephesians 4:11-16 that gifts have been given to the church, each one of us getting certain gifts. These special gifts have been given to God's people so that they are equipped to do a better work for God, building up the church and encouraging His people to a position of strength and maturity, until finally they all believe alike about salvation and about our Saviour, and all become mature or fully grown up in Jesus Christ. Our methods of work and the use of our gifts may be different, but our basic belief and trust in salvation is one.

Our "faith in Jesus" will be fully understood, applied, and growing. We will be stable in our Shepherd as the winds of doctrine blow hither and yon across the pasture of life and as we consider the benefits of being an Israelite. Then offshoots are no more.

Parting Gem: *"Be ye therefore perfect."* (Matthew 5:48)

JANUARY 12 — *Balance of Balances* — Leviticus 19:36

Today's Thought: *"Just balances, just weights, a just ephah, and a just hin, shall ye have: I am the Lord your God, which brought you out of the land of Egypt."*

One needs to have balance, a true balance, in every aspect of life. There needs to be a balance between trust and obedience, between faith and works, between justification and sanctification.

Justification is what you receive when you are drawn to the Beloved, receive His forgiveness because you repent, confess, and acknowledge His authority. This happens in a moment, yet it is a daily experience, thus making it the work of a lifetime to stay justified.

Sanctification is a growth process, ongoing as you move "up the ladder" from faith to virtue, then on to knowledge and temperance, to patience and godliness, through brotherly kindness to charity or love. This growth process is called "growing up into Christ," is ongoing, yet at each level of the growth ladder, one is sanctified, so it too can be a work of a lifetime but as a daily, moment by moment joy.

So the Song of Songs presents a balanced view of justification and sanctification. True sanctification is a Bible doctrine. The Scriptures plainly show that the work of sanctification is progressive. When in conversion the sinner finds peace with God through the blood of the Atonement, the Christian life has but just begun. Now he is to *"go on unto perfection"* (Hebrews 6:1) to grow up *"unto the measure of the stature of the fullness of Christ"* (Ephesians 4:13).

Thus our heroine calls to her Hero, *"Draw me"* (Song 1:4). That way, we can run after and with Thee through the twin processes of justification reaching on to sanctification.

Paul puts his race and balance in life this way in 2 Timothy 4:7: *"I have fought a good fight, I have finished my course, I have kept the faith."*

Parting Gem: *Keep that balance between justification and sanctification; fight a good fight. Glorification comes next.*

JANUARY 13   *Drama of Dramas*   Psalms 95:1

Today's Thought: *"O come, let us sing unto the Lord."*

The Song of Songs is a drama because it has all of the makings of a drama.

One character is the Hero, Jesus Christ, the Bridegroom, most always referred to as my Beloved. A supporting actor is the heroine, the bride representing the corporate church in any particular period of time.

The bride has a mother, who plays a part in this drama representing the universal church. There are the daughters of Jerusalem, the virgins, the individual church members.

There are many supporting roles—these characters are sixty valiant soldiers, watchmen of the city, a chorus of voices, city inhabitants, street urchins, guests, relatives, and many others, each to be introduced in the drama as it progresses.

The stage settings and backdrops are composed of the historical progression of this "Drama of the Ages," in which God's people, struggling against evil, continue century after century to wait for His final deliverance in the coming of the Bridegroom.

Even an epilogue is present (Song 8:8-14). According to any dictionary, an epilogue is a speech... an address to the spectators, and spoken after the conclusion of the play; also, a concluding section... serving to complete the plan of the work.

The most conclusive evidence in the Song of Songs which establishes it as drama is found in 3:1-4 and 5:2-8. These two allegories are "happenings" in which the events occur in succession and are best acted out on stage.

This drama in Act 1, Scene 1 opens on Golgotha's Hill, where the Bridegroom pays the dowry for His bride. It closes after Act 3, Scene 5 with the epilogue.

Parting Gem: *In the Song of Songs, we hear the bride's voice saying, "My beloved is mine, and I am his" (Song 2:16). And He who is to her the "chiefest among ten thousand" (Song 5:10), speaks to His chosen one, "Thou art all fair, my love; there is no spot in thee" (Song 4:7).*

JANUARY 14   *Hero of Heroes*   Song 5:16

Today's Thought: *"This is my beloved and this is my friend."*

Solomon, in the Hebrew language, is composed of three consonants—S, L, M—and from which comes the Middle East greeting of "Salaam," or "Peace." Our Hero is the Prince of Peace. May we see Him as the Prince of Peace.

Solomon, the literal son of David, was the literal king of Israel, who ruled from Jerusalem, the earthly city of peace and was known as the prince of peace. Those who recognized Jesus of Nazareth as the Messiah addressed Him as the prophetic "Son of David," soon to reign from the heavenly city of peace—the New Jerusalem

Solomon, king of Israel, was a type of Christ in his kingly office, in his many attributes and accomplishments, especially in the establishment of the kingdom and in the completion of the building of the temple.

There are numerous Bible texts that say that a Son would be born who would be the Son of David, where children sang, *"Hosanna to the Son of David"* (Matthew 21:15) and where Jesus refers to Himself as the Bridegroom

In Matthew 25:1-13 is a story of Jesus the Bridegroom, ten virgins, five of them wise, five of them foolish.

Through the drama of the Song of Songs, our Hero is mentioned, uplifted, honoured. He is called Solomon in several places, but is usually referred to as "my Beloved." When the daughters of Jerusalem are challenged by the bride in chapter 5:9-16, regarding my Beloved, they respond, *"What is thy Beloved…?"* Following that question is a detailed description of just who my Beloved is (5:9-16).

Throughout this song is a Hero who is constantly mentioned, praised, adored, loved, and who is carried high and lifted up in all of the 117 verses. May you catch just a glimpse of Him and see Him as King of kings, Lord of lords, God of all gods, Hero of all heroes.

Parting Gem: *Notice, mostly, as you read these verses, the sheer confidence, the overwhelming theme of our bride-church. She mentions it several times, "I am His and He is mine." Amen and amen, end of discussion.*

JANUARY 15 — *Name of Names* — Acts 4:12

Today's Thought: *"There is none other name under heaven given among men, whereby we must be saved."*

Song of Songs 1:3 states, *"Because… the virgins love thee."* Throughout this love drama, the Hero, referred to as my Beloved, is uplifted. His name, His character, His climactic coming are stressed again and again and again and again.

In 1:3, His name is compared to ointment poured forth, and for this reason the church members, the virgins, love Him.

Paul, in Ephesians 5:2, compares Him to *"a sweetsmelling savor"* while Jeremiah 8:22 uses the phrase, *"balm in Gilead… physician…"*

We often sing praises to the name of our Hero, songs like:

--There is a Balm in Gilead,

--Precious Name, O How Sweet…

--Take the Name of Jesus With You.

Let us remember that this name is above all principalities, powers, all might and dominion, above every name ever named, not only on Planet Earth, but throughout the entire Universe (Ephesians 1:21).

Let us remember that God the Father and God the Holy Spirit have elevated that name and exalted Jesus, our Beloved, our Hero, and He has a name which is above every name.

That name, Jesus, has within it Wisdom, Love, Compassion, Honesty, Truthfulness, Omnipresence, Omnipotence, Uprightness, or in summary all of the fruit of the Spirit, in the singular for they are one.

It is at that name that every knee shall bow. It is to that name that every tongue shall confess that Jesus Christ is Lord (Philippians 2:10-11).

When you have been battered and bruised, when you feel worthless, you need a physician, a kind word, a song to sing, an ointment poured on your battered body and soul. That's what this song is about.

Is it any wonder then that the virgins love Him when He cares for them, gives them power through His name to repel demons, depressions, discouragement, and to rise victoriously through His name, a name above all names?

Parting Gem: *"Come unto me, all ye that labour and are heavy laden, and I will give you rest." (Matthew 11:28).*

January 16 — *Heroine of Heroines* — Matthew 11:28

Today's Thought: *"Come unto me, all ye that labour and are heavy laden, and I will give you rest."*

When Jesus spoke these words, He was addressing His people, His church, His bride. He returned to heaven; she remained on earth. She, therefore, the bride, the church, takes center stage in this drama of the Song of Solomon. She tells of her experiences, her blow by blow description of her history and growth, her heart's longing, her passion for being united with her lover.

Watch closely and you will notice that this bride-church speaks, on several occasions, her Beloved's passion, hunger, desire so that we, the readers, can catch a small glimpse of the homesickness this Beloved has for His bride His church, for you and for me. Fabulous thought.

The heroine of this drama is the bride, which represents the literal, corporate church of any particular age. This drama brings the bride, the literal church, Christ's true people who have been looking and longing for the coming of the Bridegroom, down through the ages

She does not, however, represent the individual church members, only the corporate church body. She does not represent the universal church of all ages, just the church during the particular period under discussion. The seven periods of church history are found in Revelation 2 and 3—Ephesus, Smyrna, Thyratira, Sardis, Pergamos, Philadelphia, Laodicean.

It is the bride, the true corporate church, who is continually taking center stage, continually describing her concerns, continually describing herself or her Beloved, continually expressing her joys, her sorrows, her frustrations, yet paramount is her unmovable confidence, her undying faith in Him and His return. Feel her passion and conviction when she declares, in various ways, *"I am his, he is mine"* (Song 2:16, 6:3, 7:10). She says, "I will be faithful to you, for you are coming for me."

Parting Gem: *"I know whom I have believed, and am persuaded that he is able to keep that which I have committed unto him against that day" (2 Timothy 1:12). Is this your claim?*

JANUARY 17   *Mother of Mothers*   Galatians 4:26

Today's Thought: *"But Jerusalem which is above is free, which is the mother of us all."*

In the Song of Songs, the bride—the organized corporate church—often refers to her mother. She does so in 1:6, 3:11, 6:9, and 8:2.

Using the Bible as its own interpreter, we find that the woman is a mother in Revelation 12:2, where it says, *"she being with child…"* In verse 4: *"…woman which was ready to be delivered."* In verses 5 and 13: *"she brought forth a man child."* And in verse 17: *"…the woman… the remnant of her seed."*

This "mother of us all" is above or in heaven, not on earth as the present, visible, corporate church. This mother represents God's people, but in a different way.

This mother represents the *universal church* of all ages. She is known as the *invisible church,* because most of her membership is waiting in the grave for the resurrection, and presently are seen neither in heaven nor on earth. Their names are registered in the Lamb's Book of Life in the capital city of the heavenly New Jerusalem.

The only exceptions would be Moses, who was resurrected; Elijah and Enoch, who were translated; and then those "first fruits" Christ took with Him to heaven at His ascension. They are not only registered in heaven, but reside there literally.

In Revelation 21, John uses two symbols together: *"New Jerusalem"* and *"prepared as a bride."* At the resurrection, when all of God's people are once again alive and active, they meet together in the sky. In the clouds, the living translated "church members" of the bride become the visible triumphant church.

So while the bride represents the visible corporate church age by age through the ages, the mother represents the universal church of all ages. One visible, the other invisible. One alive and active, the other resting in death.

Parting Gem: *Today, Lord, as we contemplate your church, help us to understand the "mother of us all."*

JANUARY 18　　　　*Virgin of Virgins #1*　　　　Matthew 25:1-13

Today's Thought: *"Then shall the kingdom be likened unto ten virgins, which took their lamps, and went forth to meet the bridegroom."*

A beautiful, yet sad, description of a wedding—an eastern wedding—is pictured. There, five of the virgins or bridesmaids are wise, having lamps and oil to keep the lamps glowing; the other five are foolish virgins have come with lamps but have no oil to keep their lamps glowing during the long delay.

The daughter of Jerusalem as in Song 1:5, or the daughters of Zion as in 3:11, or the virgins as in 1:3, are one and the same as the ten virgins in the above parable of Jesus.

We would call them today the bride's attendants, or bridesmaids, who are members of the wedding party. These virgins or daughters represent the individual church members, you, me, some wise, some foolish, but each one is looking for the coming of the Bridegroom. They are not hypocrites but members in good and regular standing. These individual church members, the virgins, are not to be confused with the bride, which is the corporate church, the heroine of heroines.

Yet, what is a virgin in this symbolic or spiritual sense of the word? Revelation 14:4 states, *"These are they who were not defiled with women for they are virgins. These are they which follow the Lamb whithersoever he goeth."*

"There is a difference also between a wife and a virgin. The [virgin] careth for the things of the Lord… she that is married careth for the things of the world, how she may please her husband" (1 Corinthians 7:34).

It appears that one who stays close to and involved with the Bridegroom, and who does not get involved with another beloved, does not get mixed up and involved with other churches, one who follows Him wherever He leads, is a virgin. His faith in Jesus is pure, undefiled, innocent, be they single or married.

Here are they that keep and have the faith of Jesus, that pure, innocent, undefiled faith that classifies them as virgins.

Parting Gem: *Lord, my aim and my prayer for today is, keep me pure, undefiled, with oil in my lamp burning, a spare flask on hand.*

JANUARY 19 — Actor of Actors — John 14:29

Today's Thought: *"When it is come to pass, ye might believe."*

Besides the Hero, heroine, Mother, virgins in this drama that is being played out in history, there are other characters who must take their place and walk across the stage. There are my mother's children.

My mother's children are found early in 1:6, and they are all of the "other churches" that make up the Christian family. They are not the ones the Bridegroom is concerned about or whom He is coming for. They actually give the bride a rough time.

There are the watchmen in 3:3 that go about the city. These are the "leaders" of the Christian community, the ministers who are supposed to be sounding the alarm on the city walls, but who have come down.

"There are threescore queens, and fourscore concubines, and virgins without number" (Song 6:8).

There are the foxes that spoil the vines in 3:15. Although these are mentioned briefly, they play a powerfully active role all through the drama. They are constantly hindering the advancement of the Bridegroom. Hhowever, as you will see, their part is not the concern of the bride. That's encouraging.

The Shulamite is mentioned in 6:13. This is the bride, given a name. She is not the literal wife of literal Solomon in this drama, even though she may have been in real life. Most, or at least a goodly number, of the commentaries do put this Shulamite woman as Solomon's actual wife. Did they miss the boat, or did they launch out into the deep?

In the epilogue, we meet "We," who has made a conditional promise to and for our bride. Other keepers of the vineyard are found in 8:11.

There is "our little sister," who is mentioned in 8:8. When we get to "our little sister," a thrill will go through you as you realize how she plays out in the drama.

Parting Gem: *You, as an actor in this great drama of the ages, are invited to take your place on the stage of life, proclaiming your love for your Bridegroom.*

JANUARY 20 — *Charge of Charges #1* — Luke 12:39

Today's Thought: *"And this know, that if the goodman of the house had know what hour the thief would come, he would have watched, and not have suffered his house to be broken through."*

A blessing is given to all servants who are found watching and waiting, longing for Christ the Bridegroom to come. They are urged to be ready at all times, for the Master will come when they think not.

At least three times in Matthew 24, it states that the time of Christ's coming is known only by the Godhead. However, lots of signs are given to let us know that the time is near.

Our bride in our Song told the church in her day at least three times not to get carried away with an expectation of the Bridegroom. They were charged on the three occasions not to *"awake my love, until he please"* (Song 8:4). In two of these charges—2:7 and 3:5—she bases her knowledge on the "roes and hinds"—on the Old Testament and the New Testament, on Daniel and Revelation.

She knew about the New Testament and Revelation because she was writing to people after the crucifixion, for us in these last days. She seems to be saying, "I know my Beloved is coming and that He's coming for me, but let us be patient and wait, let's not awaken Him. After all, He has a timetable, a day appointed."

On the third charge in 8:4, she omits the rows and the hinds as her backup. She seems to be telling us that she knows that most, "if not all," of the signs for the Bridegroom's return have been met. Our bride seems to have known something about when her Beloved would return for her. She states several times for Him to return, or to flee away, into the mountains until the day breaks and the shadows flee away (4:6, 2:7).

One of the prominent signs of His coming is when people of religious background are used by the evil one to state quite scientifically, environmentally, financially, governmentally, and whatever other way they can devise and make up, that "the sky is falling"—Chicken Little's scream when something fell on her head.

Parting Gem: *Our charge today, a challenge, is to "be ye also ready: for in such an hour as ye think not the Son of man cometh"* (Matthew 24:44).

JANUARY 21 — *Capsule of Capsules* — John 14:29

Today's Thought: *"I have told you before it come to pass, that, when it is come to pass, ye might believe."*

Encased in brackets as it were, are little gem-capsules of hope and assurance scattered throughout the Song. Here are some:

2:3—*"As the apple tree among the tree,"* to 8:5, *"I raised thee up under the apple tree…"*

2:6—*"His left hand is be under my head, and his right hand doth embrace me,"* to 8:3, *"His left hand should be under my head, and his right hand should embrace me."*

3:6—*"Who is this that cometh out of the wilderness,"* to 8:5, *"Who is this that cometh up from the wilderness…"* The Great Second Advent Movement is depicted here coming out from the wilderness.

5:9—*"What is thy beloved"* to 5:16, *"This is my beloved."* A description of the Beloved which, in turn, is contrasted to another beloved.

5:10—*"The chiefest among ten thousand,"* to 5:16, *"He is altogether lovely."* A description of Christ talking to His church.

6:11—*"… the pomegranates budded,"* to 7:12, *"… the pomegranates bud forth…"*

2:8—*"He cometh leaping upon the mountains, skipping upon the hills"* and 2:17, *"… be thou like a roe or a young hart upon the mountains of Bether,"* to 8:14, *"… be thou like to a roe or to a young hart upon the mountains of spices."* Here is Christ's second coming announced, preached and finally urged to come, Lord Jesus.

2:10—*"Rise up… and come away,"* to 2:13, *"Arise, my love, my fair one, and come away."* Here is depicted the Sardis Church during the Reformation, being urged to rise up against the controlling powers and break from them. *"Come out of her, My people"* (Revelation 18:4). Come out, come out…

Parting Gem: *As the material between the two slices of a sandwich is the good part, so within these capsules are little and great gems of wisdom and truth.*

JANUARY 22   *Surge of Surges #1*   Revelation 22:20

Today's Thought: *"Even so, come, Lord Jesus."*

That's John the Revelator adding his personal testimony to the visions, dreams, challenges, and the warnings of his book, Revelation.

Now, however, times have moved on and we are nearer the second coming than our bride was at the writing. The passion and hunger for her Beloved to come ends the drama in 8:14. At the end of the Song, there is this very unique change in the references to the roes and the hinds. No longer is it, "Do not wake Him," but, "Make haste, my Beloved, make haste. Come, come, come quickly; the world is now ripe, cups of iniquity are now full, your people are now sealed, so there's really nothing standing in your way. Make haste, make haste, make haste."

There is a similarity between Revelation's close and that of the Song of Songs' close. Both are saying exactly the same thing, yet using different words. "Come, make haste, hurry, delay no longer."

Our bride is urging her Beloved to be quick, like nimble-footed roes and sure-footed young harts skipping over the mountains of time. She is now urging her Beloved to surge ahead, without any more delay as her passion and hunger for Him to be united with her increases.

Early in this year, I wish to turn to the back of our drama to find the outcome of just what happens and who "wins." It's a sneak preview, and maybe cheating a bit, but you need to know the outcome sooner rather than waiting in suspense.

Revelation 22:20 says, *"Even so, come, Lord Jesus."*

John 14:2-3 says, *"I go to prepare… and if I go… I will come again, and receive you unto myself; that where I am, there ye may be also."*

This theme, this passionate concern, this hungering longing, started back in the Garden of Eden, runs throughout the entire Bible and ends triumphantly in the Book of Revelation. Here, however, in our drama, it appears to be the main emphasis of the book. It is the bride's desire as she states it several times, as well as the Groom's desire as we will notice throughout this year. May it be your burning desire.

Parting Gem: *Remember, please remember, Genesis 3:15. The serpent has already bruised the heel of the woman; now it's the woman's turn to have her Seed crush the serpent's head.*

JANUARY 23　　　　*Hope of Hopes*　　　　Lamentations 3:26

Today's thought: *A man should both hope and quietly wait.*

What has been the hope of the Christians since the Garden, but the Messiah? Ever since the promise in the Garden of bruising and crushing, the women of the followers of Christ have hoped that their son would be that promised One. Now, in order for that prophecy to be fulfilled, Christ must come. This theme of the second coming of the Bridegroom is the overriding, ever present, all consuming passion of the Song of Songs.

Each of the Old Testament prophets spoke of the coming of Christ, for Jesus opened their understanding on the way to Emmaus. Paul states, in 1 Corinthians 15:19, *"If in this life only we have hope in Christ, we are of all men most miserable."*

He further showed us a mystery in that not everyone will die, but those who do die will be resurrected to join those who did not die. Yet they kept their faith, so that together we will rise up to meet Christ in the cloud. He closes with the thought that our labour is not in vain in the Lord (1 Corinthians 15:51-58).

Of all of the promises and hopes recorded in the Bible, none is more precious, more inspiring, and more relevant than that of the promise of His coming, this hope of all hopes. So, fellow journeyers, *"be ye also patient and stablish your hearts, for the coming of the Lord draweth nigh"* (James 5:8). Let us keep our conversation fixed on heaven, *"from whence we look for the Saviour, the Lord Jesus Christ"* (Philippians 3:20).

Then, we shall all be changed from our vile body, at the sound of the last trumpet; we shall receive the gift of immortality, permanently, unchangeable, all in the twinkling of an eye, as quick as it takes to blink. What a hope. What a promise.

One question that keeps swirling within my cranium is, if we are changed at the sound of the last trumpet, do we hear the first trumpet?

Parting Gem: *Take the help of angels that heaven has promised to you through your daily experiences. Abide in Him, having His word abiding in you, so that you give Him permission to transform and keep you until that day when hope turns into reality.*

JANUARY 24　　　*Construction of Constructions*　　　Isaiah 28:10,13

Today's Thought: *Precept upon precept; line upon line; here something, there something; a capsule here, another one there; a starting bracket and a closing bracket.*

The Song of Songs has two peculiar characteristics in this drama. One employs two prophetic symbols, again and again, to reinforce a concept. Should one miss the meaning the first time, then the second can supply it. By this manner of repetition, the Bible scholar is less apt to make a mistake if he has done his research carefully. Some examples are the following.

2:1—"*I am the rose of Sharon, and the lily of the valleys.*"

2:17 and 4:6—"*The Mountains of Bether*" and "*the mountains of myrrh, and to hills of frankincense.*"

2:9—"*He standeth behind our walls, he looketh forth at the windows, shewing himself through the lattice.*"

3:6—"*Who is this that cometh out of the wilderness,*" to 6:10, "*Who is she that looketh forth as the morning, fair… clear… terrible.*"

5:7—"*The watchmen that went about the city… the keepers of the walls.*"

The parallel construction of Hebrew poetry uses a second statement to further verify the concept of the first statement.

Yet the second characteristic provides insights into the meanings in which certain sections are bound, at the beginning and the end, by similar statements. In this way, those section dealing with a specific event in history are set apart, and are thereby recognized as a unit. We mentioned this in Capsule of Capsules. Here are five examples:

2:8 to 2:17—encloses the European Reformation.

2:10 to 2:13—embraces the call of the Reformation to come out and join.

4:1 to 4:7—portrays the Advent Movement.

3:4 to 8:2—bundles up the Investigative Judgment.

5:2 to 5:8—encases the great 1844 disappointment.

Parting Gem: *A challenge for you today is to look for these two characteristics. The first is the repetition of an important point. The second, those capsules encased at the beginning and the end to form a unit, as you read again the 117 verses of our song.*

JANUARY 25 — *Allegory of Allegories* — Matthew 13:44

Today's Thought: *"The kingdom of heaven is like unto…"*

There is a tendency, in my experience, to notice people rejecting the Song of Songs as church history because they call it an "allegory," meaning a fable or a myth. Although it is not an allegory in that sense of the word, it is allegorical in nature, written in symbols and figurative language, similarly to Daniel and Revelation.

The allegorical interpretation has been common among the Jews since earliest times, and from them it has passed over into the Christian Church. The Jews regarded the Song as expressing the love relationship between God and His chosen people, as does the church.

Like every other one of God's good gifts entrusted to the keeping of humanity, marriage has been perverted by sin; but it is the purpose of the gospel to restore its purity and beauty. In both of the Testaments, the marriage relationship is employed to represent the tender and sacred union that exists between Christ and His people, the redeemed ones whom He has purchased at the cost of Calvary. He says, *"Fear not… thy Maker is thine husband; the Lord of hosts is his name; and thy Redeemer the Holy One of Israel"* (Isaiah 54:4-5). In the Song of Songs, we hear the bride's voice saying, *"My beloved is mine, and I am his"* (Song 2:16). And he who is to her *"the chiefest among ten thousand"* (5:10) speaks to His chosen one, *"Thou art all fair, my love; there is no spot in thee"* (4:7).

The most conclusive evidence in this Song, which establishes it as a drama, is found in 3:1-4 and 5:2-8. These allegories are "happenings" in which events occur in succession and are best acted out on stage. There is a mysterious knocking at the door, sleepy confusion in trying to answer the door only to find no one there. The bride understands that it was the Bridegroom who has passed by to take her to the marriage, but she cannot find Him, and goes out into the streets to look for Him. There is danger and suspense as the bride runs up and down the streets of the city in the dark of night, and then an encounter with those who mistake her identity and beat up the victim.

Parting Gem: *Try not to throw the baby out with the bath water.*

JANUARY 26   *Temptation of Temptations*   Revelation 3:10

Today's Thought: *"Because thou hast kept the words of my patience, I also will keep thee from the hour of temptation, which shall come upon all the world, to try them that dwell upon the earth."*

When Jesus in His model prayer stated, *"Lead us not into temptation,"* do we understand what temptation He had in mind? Was it just any and every temptation or was it the *temptation* of all temptations, that of yielding up our confidence, trust, faith, belief that He is able to save us amply, fully, entirely, that of trying to live some other way or do some other thing than that which God could approve, by ourselves?

Was it the *temptation* to disobey His very simple and clear commands, which is the result of rejecting His authority in place of some other authority?

There are two types of *temptations* that are greater than any other temptations. One is a great and wonderful temptation, while the other is exactly the opposite, the wildest and the worst.

The one temptation is to turn your back on anything holy, sacred and right; to give our trust and confidence to someone other than the Bridegroom, someone like another beloved. It is to show our lack of confidence by disobedience to His simple commands, which in turn shows our rejection of His authority. It is this temptation that needs to be repented of. It is this temptation that leads into sin and death, and is Christ's concern.

The other and better temptation to accept Jesus Christ as one's personal, intimate, and only Saviour. This leads to eternal life in the long run, yet leads to peace and security in this life. It gives us a more abundant life, one well worth living, It leads our bride-church to exclaim several things: *"I am His; He is mine."* End of story. Period. No more questions on that. Not only is the Word of God settled in heaven, but this relationship with the Bridegroom is settled here on earth, within my heart, my life, my very being. This "repentance" is the repentance that needs not to be repented of; no change needs to be made here.

Parting Gem: *Memorize Revelation 3:10, "Because thou hast kept [my] word... I also will keep thee from the hour of temptation."*

JANUARY 27 — *Caution of Cautions* — Acts 17:11

Today's Thought: *As an airplane "seems" to pick up speed and the ground "seems" to be spinning past the windows faster as the plane comes down to a landing, so the world and the happenings of last day event "seem" to be spinning past us faster. Yet, the last movements will be rapid ones.*

Paul the Apostle was a tremendous preacher, even a chosen vessel, chosen by God Himself, to take the gospel to far-flung regions of the then-known world. Yet, there was a certain group of people who, when they listened to Paul, had an open mind and received what Paul had to say, then went home, got out their reference books, and searched the Scriptures to see if what Paul was preaching was what they should be following. They have often been called "The More Noble Club," because they were more noble than those in Thessalonica. That's how to "have the preacher home for dinner," and there are several blessings in receiving, then searching.

Acts 17:12 states that, *"Therefore many of them believed…"* For good reason. One has to study in order to learn, understand, and believe; God's people can perish for lack of this knowledge.

Isaiah 55:8-11 says, *"For my thoughts are not your thoughts, neither are your ways my ways, saith the Lord. For as the heavens are higher than the earth, so are my ways higher than your ways, and my thoughts than your thoughts. For as the rain cometh down, and the snow from heaven, and returneth not thither, but watereth the earth, and maketh it bring forth and bud, that it may give seed to the sower, and bread to the eater: so shall my word be that goeth forth out of my mouth: it shall not return unto me void, but it shall accomplish that which I please, and it shall prosper in the thing whereto I sent it."*

Parting Gem: *As we get closer to the time for the Bridegroom to come, we must be prepared for false prophecies kindled from the hellish torch of Satan being preached from our pulpits, printed in our publications. We must be prepared for the rapidity of the ground moving under us as we fly low.*

JANUARY 28 — Faith of Faiths — Romans 14:23

Today's Thought: *"Whatsoever is not of faith is sin."*

Throughout this Song of Songs, one will notice the tremendous confidence this bride has in her coming Bridegroom. Her faith is solid, well anchored, living. I am His; He is mine.

Faith is that confidence one has in his God; it is his trust, belief, hope, his assurance that his God is able, willing, and eager to save not only to the uttermost, but amply, fully, entirely. That's the bride.

In my thesaurus, faith is deemed to be "confidence," which in turn is deemed to be, "assurance, conviction, credence, credit, dependence, reliance or trust."

Faith needs to occupy in our lives the prominent position in which it was presented to John the Revelator and which is expressed by the bride-church. If faith is lacking in our daily religious experience, then Paul states that it is sin.

The bride-church in our drama was confident of her Lover, and of His soon coming. She trusted in His promises which she knew very well. She trusted in His ability to deliver her from sin; yea, more than deliver but to save her from succumbing. She put that confidence into play by obeying His every word, thus showing Him, and the rest of the world, that she accepted His authority over every other authority. See if you can find this in the Song as you read it.

When John the Baptist exclaimed, *"Behold the Lamb of God, which taketh away the sin of the world"* (John 1:29), do we understand what the sin of the world happens to be? Could it be the *sin* of all sins, the rejection of His ability to save to the uttermost, the rejection of His authority in our religious experience as well as our entire life which leads to the rejection of His commands and will in our lives? In other words, it leads to disobedience. Put these three rejections together and that quality called faith seems to disappear.

Your faith and confidence, whatever word you wish to use, grows daily as you react thankfully and positively to your daily experiences.

Parting Gem: *Remember that this bride-church is spoken of in Revelation 14:12 as "... they that keep ... the faith of Jesus."*

JANUARY 29　　　　*Deceit of Deceits*　　　　1 Corinthians 3:18

Today's Thought: *"Let no man deceive himself."*

According to Collins Essential Canadian Dictionary, the word *deceive* is a verb meaning to "mislead by lying." In other words, to cause someone to believe that which is not true."[1] That's why we say Eve was deceived; she was led to believe something that was not true. She believed the serpent when he said:
1. "Has God really said that you shall not eat of every tree in the garden?" A sneak, a twist of what God really did say.
2. "You shall not surely die should you eat of this fruit," thus making God a liar.
3. "God knows that when you eat this fruit, your eyes will be open, you shall be as gods, and you will know both good and evil."

Adam, on the other hand, was not deceived. He knew what he was doing. He deliberately chose to follow where his wife did not know she was going, all because of his great lack of faith in his Creator-God and his great love for Eve, not because of appetite.

Could it be said that deception follows a lack of faith and knowledge? Because Adam and Eve both failed in three areas spoken of in Genesis 3:6, and 1 John 2:16—the lust of the flesh, the lust of the eyes, the pride of life—they naturally sinned. The sin was not merely eating the fruit; that was simply the point of no return.

Both Eve, and then Adam:
1. did not believe nor trust their Creator to get them out of any bad situation; Eve from the tree, Adam from losing his mate. Their trust was in the serpent.
3. did not accept the authority of the Creator, but that of the serpent.
2. did not obey the simple request of their Creator not to eat. Instead Eve accepted the serpent's suggestion to eat. Adam accepted Eve's request to taste and see, this for fear of losing Eve.

Check out the reasons one sins and you just might find that they do not believe what they need to believe, that they do not accept the authority that they need to accept, thus leading to not obeying that which they ought to obey. Simple, yes?

Parting Gem: *When one loses these three aspects of the Christian life, there is a powerful affinity to be deceived, thus to sin.*

---

[1] *Collins Essential Canadian English Dictionary & Thesaurus* (Toronto, ON: Harper Collins), 2006, p. 36.

JANUARY 30 　　　　　*Result of Results* 　　　　　1 Corinthians 10:1

Today's Thought: *"I would not that he should be ignorant…"*

For every action, there is an equal and opposite reaction. That's a scientific law taught in science class. When the Creator told Adam that in the day that he ate that fruit, he would surely die, He meant just that. Be it called a promise or a threat, it came true. There was an equal and definitely opposite reaction.

According to Genesis 2:16-17, should man eat of the forbidden tree, he would die that day. Yet today we disobey God on a daily basis and are still alive. So, consider this possibility.

We hear some talk about being born again, born of water and blood, the second birth. We hear some talk about two deaths, two resurrections, the natural death given to all of us because of Adam's sin, and of the spiritual death given only to those not born the second time.

Christ warned us not to fear those that could kill us physically, the natural body, but fear him who could kill both body, natural life, and soul, spiritual life. Paul tells us that there is a natural body as well as a spiritual body (1 Corinthians 15:44).

The natural body of Adam died after 950 years, yet the spiritual body died that very day he ate the fruit. Genesis 2:25 states that both Adam and Eve were naked, yet not ashamed. They were not ashamed, because they were covered with the Robe of Christ's Righteousness. Then in 3:10, after partaking of the fruit, Adam admits that he was ashamed because he was naked. He was naked because his Robe of Righteousness was gone.

We today are trying to reverse Adam's decision and get back eternal life. When a Christian dies, our natural, physical bodies are dead, but our spiritual bodies are alive and well, just asleep, waiting to be resurrected, for *"he that hath the Son hath life"* (1 John 5:12).

One aim this year is for you to have the action (you reading this book) and to get the reaction (You've met the Beloved).

Parting Gem: *We have come to the end of January's reading; we have looked at various aspects of our drama. Knowing all about this fabulous book will do us no good unless we encounter the Bride-groom, our Beloved, in our journey this year*

JANUARY 31 *Summary* PP 504:1

Today's Thought: *Greater attention should be given to instructing.*[2]

At the close of each month's reading, we will stop and summarize that particular month's discoveries. This will be in conjunction to some good advice given to us in 6T 56 and PP 504, as well as the examples given to us in the Song of Songs. At least three times, the bride mentions something about "He is mine and I am His." At least three times she reviews with us the fact that we should not awaken her Beloved. Three times she is described in all her beauty and innocence. So that example will be followed.

During January, we covered the aim that was set out for us. We discovered that the name of the book is the Song of Songs, not Song of Solomon; that it is a drama, complete with actors, both leading and supportive; and that this entire drama is surging forward to the climactic conclusion of the coming of the Bridegroom. We concluded also that it is inspired.

We became aware of the elevated scope and language of the book, that it was a love song, written in poetry, of course, between the Beloved Jesus Christ and His church, the apple of His eye.

We read that poetry is the sublime, elevated mode of communication. Song of Songs is an enigma, a mystery, to a large extent unsolved and avoided. The church in the wilderness understood it as far as it was fulfilled to their time.

We were made aware of the purposes of the book and the high, elevated status that it should have.

We saw that it was a drama, complete with backdrops and characters, especially the Hero and the heroine.

We heard that even though it is an enigma, a puzzling puzzle, even a time-worn embarrassment, it is an unrolling of the scrolls now that the time for its understanding has arrived.

We noticed some characteristics of Hebrew poetry, the repetition in various terms, and the periods of emphases encased in brackets.

Parting Gem: *This superlative gem of inspired Scripture, when viewed in correct manner, has all its pieces fit together like our jigsaw puzzle.*

---

[2] White, E.G. *Patriarchs and Prophets* (Nampa, ID: Pacific Press), 2005, p. 504.

I Knew That This Year

I looked behind me as I stood at the door,
    To the way I had come, to the labours I bore;
To the mountains of trial I'd gotten around;
    To the deep valleys of grief I had somehow found;
To the jobs I'd done and to those I'd refused;
    To the days of certainty, to days when confused;
To the battles I'd won with the Lord by my side;
    To my Lord in His glory as He walked as my Guide

Then I turned around so that the future I faced,
    I saw not a thing for that view was erased;
I saw not the joys nor the trials in my way;
    Yet, I saw that same Guide as my Rock and my Stay.
I stood and I saw Him beckoning me on;
    So I entered the new year with a smile and a song.
I saw that His hands were outstretched for my grip,
    I knew that this year would be a victory-trip.

His Promises Are Not For the Few

'Twas the midst of the week
     when I sat down to seek,
         some time to rekindle my soul.

I had come a good piece,
     now, my soul sought release,
         so I laid out a plan and a goal.

With no pressure at hand,
     and this unexplored land,
         what a chance to relinquish my scars.

So I sought for some sights
     out under the night lights,
         and plastered my eyes on the stars.

Soon my soul was revived,
     my spirit came alive,
         my outlook on life rose anew.

What a thrill to be here,
     knowing God is so near,
         His promises are not for the few.

February

February's Introduction and Aim

During the month of February, we will go from the kiss of reconciliation on the cross in 1:2 to the Shepherd's tent in 1:8, in Scene 1, Act 1.

Scene 1, in AD 27. On Golgotha's Hill, the paying of the dowry on the cross by Christ, the setting up of His church, covered by the Ephesus Church (AD 31 to AD 100). This period is also represented in Revelation as the white horse of Revelation 6:2, a period of guidance from the Holy Spirit as the early church went forth conquering and to conquer.

Scene 2, in Jerusalem in AD 34, shows the angriness of the mother's daughters while still in the Ephesus period, with the stoning of Stephen, the apostasy, and going through the Smyrna period (AD 100 to AD 323). This is the period of persecution depicted with the red horse (Revelation 6:4). Great persecution existed only from AD 303 to AD 313 (Revelation 2:10). Remember that Constantine joined the church, becoming a "Christian," in AD 313.

Scene 3. During the fourth century and the period covered by the Pergamos Church (AD 323 to AD 538) to the setting up of the Papacy. The time that intervened between the reign of Constantine and the establishment of the Papacy in AD 538 may be justly noted as the time when the darkest errors and grossed superstitions sprang up in the church.[3]

The changing scenes and the moving drama of this Song are rapid, and provide a historical framework of the major experiences of the Christian Church. It advances from the crucifixion to a transition from the Jews to the Gentiles, and

---

[3] Smith, Eriah. *Daniel and Revelation* (Washington, DC: Review & Herald), 1944, p. 428.

then continues on into the apostasy resulting in the establishment of the Papacy, given as AD 538. This caused the true church, our bride in this Song, to be driven into the wilderness for some 1,260 years.

The prophetic Song of Songs presents, in the historical progression, a "timeline" of church history, very similar to those of Daniel and Revelation, which also use symbols. These three books cover the same historical events and are linked together, running parallel to each other. A correlation with *The Great Controversy* is also present.

L.E. Froom, in *The Prophetic Faith of our Fathers* (Vol. 1, p. 640, 641, 884), mentions how great expositors as early as AD 1153, and in the sixteenth century in England, were linking the timelines of Revelation with the drama and timelines of the Song of Songs.

FEBRUARY

Day 1	Him of Hims	Song 1:2	41
Day 2	Kiss of Kisses	Song 1:2	42
Day 3	Love of Love	Song 1:2	43
Day 4	Wine of Wines	Joshua 24:15	44
Day 5	Savour of Savours	Song 1:3	45
Day 6	Ointment of Ointments	Song 1:3	46
Day 7	Event of Events	John 3:16	47
Day 8	Pouring of Pourings	Song 1:3	48
Day 9	Dowry of Dowries	Song 1:2-3	49
Day 10	Draw of Draws	John 12:32	50
Day 11	Race of Races	Hebrews 12:1	51
Day 12	Chamber of Chambers	Song 1:4	52
Day 13	Remembrance of Remembrances	Song 1:4	53
Day 14	Black of Blacks	Song 1:5	54
Day 15	Comeliness of Comelinesses	Song 1:5	55
Day 16	Tent of Tents	Song 1:7	56
Day 17	Curtain of Curtains	Song 1:5-6	57
Day 18	Sun of Suns	Song 1:6	58
Day 19	Anger of Angers	Song 1:6	59
Day 20	Detour of Detours	Song 1:7	60
Day 21	Keeper of Keepers	Song 1:6	61
Day 22	Vineyard of Vineyards #1	Song 1:6	62
Day 23	Pasture of Pastures #1	Psalms 23:2-3	63
Day 24	Rest of Rests	Song 1:7	64
Day 25	Noon of Noons	Song 1:7	65
Day 26	Flock of Flocks #1	Song 1:7	66
Day 27	Fairest of Fair #1	Song 1:8	67
Day 28	Kid of Kids	Song 1:8	68
Day 29[4]	Summary	Song 1:2-8	69

Poem of the Month: "There's Always Something Worse Than Death"   70

---

[4] Given in the event that you use this devotional during a leap year.

| FEBRUARY 1 | *Him of Hims* | Song 1:2 |

Today's Thought: *"Let him kiss me with the kisses of his mouth: for thy love is better than wine."*

Who is this "him" that kisses with his mouth? Notice the pronouns in verses 2-4. They are all about that same Person, our Beloved, our Hero, the Bridegroom.

In verse 3, the perfume-like fragrance of His good ointment; the name of Jesus is so sweet the virgins love Him. In verse 4, *"Draw me, [Christ,] we will run after thee: the king [Jesus] hath brought me into his chambers; we will be glad and rejoice in [Christ]."*

In Exodus 3, this Person is identified as *"I AM THAT I AM"* (Exodus 3:14). Moses was to inform his fellow Israelites that *"I AM hath sent me unto you"* (Exodus 3:14). That's at the beginning of God's Word.

In the middle of God's Word, John 10, this "him" of Song 1:2 is, *"I AM the door of the sheep"* (John 10:7, emphasis added) and *"I AM the good shepherd"* (John 10:11, emphasis added). In John 9, He is identified as *"the light of the world"* (John 9:5).

"I AM the resurrection, and the life" (John 11:25, emphasis added). See August's poem.

At the end of God's Word, Revelation 2 and onward, *"I AM Alpha and Omega, the beginning and the end, the first and the last"* (Revelation 22:13, emphasis added).

"I AM he that holds the seven stars in my hand" (Revelation 2:1, paraphrased). He is the Son of God who has eyes like flames of fire and feet like unto brass (Revelation 2:18).

He is the one that is holy, true and that has the keys of David (Revelation 3:7).

He is the *"Amen, the faithful and true witness, the beginning of the creation of God"* (Revelation 3:14).

In Song 5:16, in August, he is, the one *"altogether lovely."*

Throughout the year you have chosen to read this book, may you daily find this "him" of Song 1:2. May you come face to face with Him, confront Him, encounter Him, wrestle with Him. Yet more than that, accept Him, not only as your personal Saviour, but as your personal Lord and King in your daily life.

Parting Gem: *In thinking how to leave today, I found John 21:25: "And there are also many other things which Jesus did, the which, if they should be written every one, I suppose that even the world itself could not contain the books that should be written. Amen."*

FEBRUARY 2   *Kiss of Kisses*   Song 1:2

Today's Thought: *"Let him kiss me with the kisses of his mouth…"*

When the father saw his prodigal son returning, he ran to him, fell on his neck and kissed him, a kiss of forgiveness and reconciliation (Luke 15:20).

When Esau came to meet Jacob, he fell on his neck and kissed him, again a kiss of reconciliation (Genesis 33:4).

David suggested that one "kiss" the Son, be reconciled to the Son, lest one suffer the consequences (Psalms 2:12).

In Luke 7:45, Jesus tells Simon that this woman, Mary Magdalene, has not stopped kissing His feet. As well, she has anointed His head, then states that although her sins were many, she has been forgiven, been reconciled to Him.

Before you finish today's reading, take time to read aloud Psalms 85, where the revelation of God's salvation is described as reconciling righteousness and peace so that they are figurative pictured as kissing each other (SDA Dictionary; "Kiss").

A kiss is a sign or symbol of friendship. The Christian marriage ceremony seals the legal vow or marriage with a kiss.

When Paul was about to leave Ephesus, and the Ephesians knew they would not see him again, they *"fell on Paul's neck, and kissed him"* (Acts 20:37). They blessed him and showed that all was well with their relationship between them and him.

Paul requested that the Christians greet each other with "a holy kiss." Greet each other by telling them that all is well between them, they have nothing to hide (Romans 16:6, 1 Peter 5:14).

In the Wild West, a handshake with the right hand implied a friendship and an agreement not to draw the colt-pistol that hung on the right hip. It's difficult to shake hands and at the same time draw your weapon.

Solomon here is requesting that reconciliation be forthcoming. For four thousand years, they were waiting for the Messiah to come and bring in reconciliation. Notice this plea for reconciliation throughout the Song, expressed quite passionately, as this concept of reconciliation and atonement by the death of Jesus on the cross is the fundamental doctrine of salvation.

Parting Gem: *This drama begins at this point in history, "kiss the Son."*

FEBRUARY 3 — *Love of Loves* — Song 1:2

Today's Thought: *Let him kiss me with the kisses of his mouth: for thy love is better than wine.*

Figuratively, wine can indicate "doctrine." It would therefore tell us that a love relationship is of more importance than doctrine, even when the doctrine is true and uplifting. A personal relationship, one that brings commitment and a walk with Jesus Christ, is of first importance in the act of reconciliation.

This relationship, based on love, would encourage and urge us on up the growth ladder as we grow in grace and in a knowledge of Jesus Christ, as we give diligence and add to our faith virtue, to virtue knowledge, then temperance, patience, godliness, brotherly kindness, climaxing in true love (1 Peter 5:5-7).

1 Corinthians 13 tells us that *"though I speak... thou I have the gift... [thou I] understand all mysteries... thou I bestow... thou I give my body... and have not charity, it profiteth me nothing"* (1 Corinthians 13:1-3). This is one chapter we should read every day.

1 John 4:8 says, *"God is love."* Love suffers long, is kind, envies not, boasts not, is not puffed up, does not behave itself unseemly, is not easily provoked, thinks no evil, and does not rejoice in iniquity but rejoices in the truth. If we were to read 1 Corinthians 13 every day, by beholding these gems of truth and wisdom, we would become more loving, kind, patient; we would not boast as we do, nor would we covet nor think evil.

For God so loved the world and His church, that He gave. He gave us victory over sin and temptation, He gave us a way of escape that we might be able to bear temptation, He gave us eternal life for the life is in the Son, He gave Himself a ransom for many, specifically for me. He gave us all things that pertain to life and godliness that we might be partakers of the divine nature, and that we might be presented to Himself pure, and wrinkle-free (2 Peter 1:4).

Parting Gem: *We are so valuable in His sight that the Father gathered everything in heaven that He could possibly gather so that He could put this up for collateral in the joint venture to save us. Had Christ failed, all of the universe would have been lost.*

FEBRUARY 4 — *Wine of Wines* — Joshua 24:15

Today's Thought: *"Choose you this day whom ye will serve."*

I've been told that only in Christian nations or churches do people have the power of choice, the privilege to choose for themselves just what they want to happen.

There are several ways of looking at our wine this day. They all apply, they all work, and they all give us a pause to reflect.

We have looked at Love of Loves and found that God so loved the world, He gave. We were challenged to have that same quality of love in our daily life.

Love is contrasted to wine in that they both permeate to the very springs of attitudes and emotions, affecting the thinking process and motor skills as they both enter the brain. May God's love permeate our lives.

Wine in Revelation pertains to doctrine. *"She made all nations drink of the wine of the wrath of her fornication"* (Revelation 14:8). Love would be better than this wine, which leads to fornication and a broken relationship with the Beloved, while love leads to a strong, saving relationship, a commitment, a burning faith.

Henceforth, anyone who drinks that wine of Roman doctrine will also *"drink of the wine of the wrath of God, which is poured out without mixture"* (Revelation 14:10). Love, in this case, is also much better than this wine, which leads to total annihilation.

Whether we use wine here as literal, fermented wine, wine of the Roman doctrine, or wine as the wrath of God, love is better in every case.

We are urged to touch not the wine that moves itself in the glass, but to study the doctrines, the *"whatsoever I have said unto you"* (John 14:26), and emulate the love found in the Bible, to flee from the wine of Babylon, as well as confirm daily our saving, passionate relationship with our Bridegroom.

Yet, wine in the Bible means more than fermented wine; in many cases, it means grape juice. While fermented wine is definitely not encouraged as a drink of any kind, that is not true of grape juice. That is encouraged to be taken. As a matter of fact, we use it at communion.

Parting Gem: *Come ye apart and rest awhile, become acquainted with the Bridegroom, walk with Him as He ministers with you.*

FEBRUARY 5   *Savour of Savours*   Song 1:3

Today's Thought: *Because of the savour of thy good ointments thy name is as ointment poured forth.*

One can look at the Atonement in seven stages, each leading to the next and each necessary. The total makes up the seven wonders of heaven.

Phase one is when God became one with us, or even one of us; when He became flesh and dwelt among us, the "Incarnation." One of His names is Emmanuel… or "God with us." As one of us, He knows us.

Phase two is Christ's "Sinless Life," by which he left us an example. He acquired the necessary experience we have so that He could understand and intercede for us. He has "been there, done that."

Phase three was on the cross where the dowry was paid. The cross must occupy the central place, because it is the means of man's salvation. This is called the "Vicarious Death."

Phase four is the "Resurrection," for we serve a risen Lord. He is the God of the living and not of the dead.

Phase five is His "Ascension," where Christ goes back to heaven to begin the next phase of His ministry (Acts 1:11).

Phase six is His "Intercession" for us on our behalf. "The Day of Atonement," or the "Investigative Judgment," is that time when Christ stands before the Father and the universe to give legal witness in application of His blood sacrifice, where He makes up His jewels (Malachi 3:17).

The word "Investigative Judgment" very often brings curdles to the blood, a scariness to the mind. This Song removes this feeling, giving in its place a joyful and happy celebration in Song 3:11 where the Beloved is crowned on the day of His marriage.

Phase seven occurs when the King of Kings returns and we shall *"ever be with the Lord"* (1 Thessalonians 4:17). This is the reason for the first six phases, to climax the marriage ceremony and to make this whole journey through life meaningful. This culminates His passion, His desire.

Parting Gem: *It will help if one could remember that the Investigative Judgment is the time Christ sits down to make up His invitations to His wedding. His "PS" has a notation: The wedding reception is to follow immediately after the gathering ceremony, plus the necessary, required wedding garment is freely supplied.*

FEBRUARY 6 — *Ointment of Ointments* — Song 1:3

Today's Thought: *There is a balm in Gilead to heal the sin-sick soul.*

The bride declared that *"because of the savor of thy good ointments thy name is as ointment poured forth, therefore do the virgins love thee"* (Song 1:3).

Let us repeat what Acts 4:12 states: *"There is none other name under heaven given among men, whereby we must be saved."*

Philippians 2:9-10 says, *"Wherefore God hath also highly exalted him, and given him a name which is above every names: that at the name of Jesus every knee should bow."*

Ephesians 3:14-15 says, *"For this cause I bow my knees unto the Father of our Lord Jesus Christ, of whom the whole family in heaven and earth is named."*

Make your covenant this day to practice bowing your knee unto the Father and the Son, so that when the final time comes when this is fulfilled, you will have practiced so habitually that this event will be done with enthusiasm, praise, and eager willingness.

Atonement and reconciliation occurs in that process known as "Justification by faith alone in Jesus Christ" and there is no other name whereby this can be done.

Someone has said that justification is the work of a moment but is done every day of life, whereas sanctification is the work of a lifetime but done day by day as we go through that lifetime.

Is there any reason then why the virgins should not love that name, that name that brings to them justification, reconciliation, redemption, purity of heart and mind and soul, not to mention eternal life, which just happens to be glorification?

Parting Gem: *Faith has many definitions. The best one yet: Faith in the ability of Christ to save us amply and fully and entirely is the faith of Jesus. That means that our faith is expressed in our belief, our trust, our hope, our confidence in our God that He can and will save us amply and fully and entirely, and no doubt do it with exceeding great joy and jubilation (Jude 24).*

FEBRUARY 7   *Event of Events*   John 3:16

Today's Thought: *"For God so loved… he gave."*

There are few events in history that are as long lasting as the crucifixion. In most parts of the world, we start counting our years and our dating from the crucifixion. The Babylonian empire existed from 606 BC until 539 BC.

This system of dating from the crucifixion did not get set up until a sixth century scholar, Dianysius Exeguus, put it together. He was out four years in his reckoning, yet the system works. Christ was born in 4 BC.

This was the great event Jesus spoke to Nicodemus about that night they met. *"If I be lifted up from the earth, [I] will draw all men unto me"* (John 12:32). This was the event that stirred Nicodemus when Christ was lifted up and crucified, pulling him out of secrecy into the limelight of helping bury his newfound Lord.

This is the event Paul so confidently proclaimed. *"But we preach Christ crucified, unto the Jews a stumblingblock, and unto the Greeks foolishness; but unto them which are called, both Jews and Greeks, Christ the power of God, and the wisdom of God"* (1 Corinthians 1:23-24). Paul understood that the cross must occupy the central place in life, for it is the means of man's redemption.

Furthermore, Paul was also adamant that he was *"not ashamed of the gospel of Christ: for it is the power of God unto salvation to every one that believeth; to the Jew first, and also to the Greek. For therein is the righteousness of God revealed from faith to faith"* (Romans 1:16-17).

This event is mentioned in 1 Corinthians 15. If there is no event of events, then Christ Himself is not risen, preaching is in vain, faith is also in vain, we are still in our sins. If this is the only life we have hope for, we are of all men most miserable.

It is this event that brings to us immortality and incorruption. It really is some event. This event accomplished the "kiss of reconciliation."

Parting Gem: *Remember that it was necessary for Christ to come as a Babe in a manger in order for Him to die on the cross, "for this reason was I born and for this reason did I come" (John 18:37, paraphrased). It was necessary for Him to come the first time in order to come the second time.*

FEBRUARY 8 — *Pouring of Pourings* — Song 1:3

Today's Thought: *"… thy name is as ointment poured forth…"*

Pause just where you are, and meditate. Think in your mind of a great dam holding back a lake full of water. The mountains are continually pouring more water into the lake. The flood gates are open and the water is pouring downstream to the people and industries there. Water is rushing, unstoppable, so it seems. So, God in His great mercy and love is pouring His ointment of His good name over us.

Yet the lake of God's great ointment is never dry; it is continually being filled by the mountain streams. What an awesome God, don't you just love Him?

Many are the stories of people in trouble who have breathed that name silently and trouble disappears. Many have breathed that holy name in prayer, and life became bearable.

Paul, writing to the Ephesians (3:8), tells them that he has been given grace so that he could preach the unsearchable riches of Christ. This corresponds to the statement that, "There is no limit to the usefulness of one, who putting self aside, make room for the workings of the Holy Spirit upon his heart and lives a life wholly consecrated to God" (DA 250).

Here is a question to ponder and trouble you today. Is it possible, even feasible, that those you know who are powerfully useful in most ways have put self aside and made room for the working of the Holy Spirit upon their hearts?

Consider what grace is; it is the character of Jesus Christ. The dictionary gives several definitions of grace: elegance, indulgence, goodwill, honour. These all fit the picture of Jesus Christ in relation to us as sinners. It is through His indulgence, if you please, His goodwill, to His honour that He saved us. The elegance of grace is the loveliness, pleasantness, attractiveness, poise, and polish in His saving us. What an awesome thought.

Parting Gem: *For God so loved you and me that He gave to us His only Son, to die in our place so that we might enjoy the pleasures of eternity. He died for us because He loved us; He didn't love us because He died for us. Please get that difference.*

FEBRUARY 9 — *Dowry of Dowries* — Song 1:2-3

Today's Thought: *"Let him kiss me with the kisses of his mouth; for thy love is better than wine. Because of the savour of thy good ointment thy name is as ointment poured forth, therefore do the virgins love thee."*

The drama of the Song of Songs begins at the crucifixion, where the Bridegroom gave the dowry price for His bride. He then returned to heaven to prepare a place for her (John 14:1). The drama reveals her experiences between the crucifixion and His return. *"I go to prepare a place for you… I will come again and receive you"* (John 14:2-3).

In the film *Johnny Lingo*, the title character, to the utter surprise of his entire island, gave his bride's father eight cows as his dowry. Eight cows as a dowry was never heard of before, and no doubt the one most surprised was the shy, low-esteemed bride herself. Yet, it changed the island, and it changed the bride. Now she was the most expensive bride around. Now she had status. Now the island looked up to her as somebody, like Johnny Lingo's wife.

The dowry given at Calvary tells us emphatically that Christ saw so much value in us that He spent all of heaven to redeem us. We insult Him when we claim we are worthless, not worthy of His love, and that He is foolish in spending all that He spent to redeem us (7T 214:3,4).

If and when we realize the expensiveness of our redemption, we too will be changed. When we realize that we are the universe's most expensive piece of "real estate," or purchase, then our self-esteem will rise, our self-worth will grow, our self-image will explode. When we understand that we are royalty, that we have royal blood within our veins, it just makes us humbly lift our heads and open our hearts to a realization that we are the sons and daughters of the Creator of the Universe. We are the most expensive piece of real estate possible to find.

Parting Gem: *We are sons and daughters of God, the King of Kings. We were created in His image after His likeness, after the likeness of the Creator of the universe. Who do you think you are, anyway? I don't think, I* know *who I am the son of the God of Heaven and a younger sibling of Jesus Christ.*

February 10   *Draw of Draws*   John 12:32

Today's Thought: *"And I, if I be lifted up from the earth, will draw all men unto me."*

Some days ago we read, in "Event of Events," just how this kiss of reconciliation was to be accomplished. Our glimpse today shows us that it was to be accomplished by the lifting up from the earth, to hang between heaven and earth, that reconciliation was accomplished.

Just think of Christ hanging between heaven and earth because the world rejected Him and wanted nothing to do with Him; that was the farthest and best way to demonstrate His love: and heaven could not have Him because He was *"sin for us"* (2 Corinthians 5:21).

However, just listen to the bride: "Draw me, I will come, Draw me to You. Hug me and place your arms around me. O, how I love Thee, how all the virgins just love Thee." Can you hear her, in her despair and anguish?

James, the brother of Jesus, tells us to *"draw nigh to God, and he will draw nigh to you"* (James 4:8).

No man can come unto Jesus except the Father draws him. When Jesus draws us and we do not resist, we will be raised at the last days (John 6:44).

Jeremiah knew what this drawing meant when he said, *"The Lord hath appeared of old unto me, saying, Yea, I have loved thee with an everlasting love: therefore with lovingkindness have I drawn thee"* (Jeremiah 31:3). Notice that love of loves mentioned here.

The bride is certainly aware of the promise recorded years later in Matthew 11:28-29. *"Come unto me, all ye that labour and are heavy laden, and I will give you rest."* It is like he is saying, "I will draw you to Myself. I will encircle you with a canopy of peace and rest."

It has been found that one can actually lose that close one-on-one relationship when he does not spend that time alone with Him. Group fellowship, be they small groups or camp meeting groups, is not enough. It is in the secret chambers, where one spends time on one's knees with open Bible, with open heart, where one's heart burns within him.

Parting Gem: *May the bride's plea be your plea just for today: "Draw me, just draw me and keep me close."*

FEBRUARY 11 — *Race of Races* — Hebrews 12:1

Today's Thought: *"Let us run with patience the race that is set before us…"*

In ancient Greece, there was only one winner in the race and he received a wreath of flowers for his reward. They practiced daily with heavy weights attached to their bodies. Now at the starting line, they have stripped themselves of any unnecessary weights and, even in some cases, the very clothes they wore. Now these were all laid aside.

Now, let us lay aside any weight, any sins that so easily beset us that we may run with patience that race, knowing that we do not receive a withering wreath of flowers but a golden crown with precious gems.

Paul, the apostle, knew that only one person, the winner, even though they all ran, got the laurel wreath. Yet he states that every man that strives to be a winner is temperate in all things, so he ran, certain of his reward and he fought and kept his body and all temptations in their proper place.

This race is a strange race, in that, at a time when you are done with life, say on your death bed, or like the thief on the cross, as you are about to breathe your last, you can still get a crown of life.

In Matthew 20 there is the parable of the vineyard where a householder went out early in the morning to hire workers. After they agreed on wages, he went out again at the third hour, again at the sixth hour, still again at the ninth hour, and finally at the eleventh hour. Yet, all received the same wage. Those who bore the burden and heat of the day didn't think the distribution of wages was all that fair. Maybe even those at the eleventh hour didn't think so, but they didn't complain.

The wage, really gift, that our householder is going to give to those who *"have borne the burden and heat of the day"* (Matthew 20:12), as well as those who come in just as their day is done, in the eleventh hour, are all going to receive the gift of eternal life. What higher or better wage could you get for working in the vineyard, or in our case for today, in running the race of life?

Parting Gem: *Have you ever contemplated, imagined, or daydreamed just what it will be like to walk in eternity? Can you picture in your mind the beauty, aroma, atmospheric pressure of heaven?*

FEBRUARY 12 — *Chamber of Chambers* — Song 1:4

Today's Thought: *"The king hath brought me into his chambers."*

As we will repeat later in "Wedding of Wedding," all legal signatures and procedures in an eastern wedding are done only by the male members at the city hall or court house. The bride remains at home, until all legal matters, signatures, and dowry transactions are cared for, and then, at last, the bridegroom returns to pick up his bride and take her to the house which he has prepared for her. The marriage supper and festivities then follow.

Read the story of the ten virgins in Matthew 25, and you will see these portrayed beautifully.

The bride, in a marriage, usually takes the husband's name. The husband takes the new bride to his house (chambers) he has prepared for her. They enter into an intimate relationship, growing closer together until they are one, because they are one.

So, the new convert takes upon himself the Master's name, Christian. They enter into a growing life together. They become more and more alike, until at last the image of Christ is perfectly reproduced in the human soul. The Christian has the same mind as was in Christ. His character is perfectly reflected in his daily life, all through abiding with Him in His secret chambers.

Enoch, in his secret and private chamber, as well as daily in his walk and work of life, would often go into the audience chamber of his Lord and God to get strength, courage, and grace as well as his directions for the day.

Christ would often be found in the audience chamber of His Father, sometimes all night, as He, too, gathered grace and strength for the activities of the coming day and for the will of His Father. For Jesus this was necessary, for it has been found that without this chamber experience, one loses the one-on-one relationship. If it was necessary for Jesus, how much more for us?

Parting Gem *One purpose of "His chamber" is to spend some quality, intimate, meaningful time together, not as in a group, but on a one-on-one basis.*

FEBRUARY 13 *Remembrance of Remembrances* Song 1:4

Today's Thought: *"We will remember thy love more than wine…"*

The fourth commandment starts out by saying, *"Remember the sabbath day to keep it holy"* (Exodus 20:8). Solomon informs us to *"Remember now thy Creator in the days of thy youth"* (Ecclesiastes 12:1). Paul talks to the Galatians about remembering the poor (Galatians 2:10), coupling it with advice to the elders: *"I have shewed you all things, how that so labouring ye ought to support the weak, and to remember the words of the Lord Jesus, how he said, It is more blessed to give than to receive"* (Acts 20:35).

In one of David's pinnacle points, he stated, *"Some trust in chariots, and some in horses: but we will remember the name of the Lord our God"* (Psalms 20:7). Powerfully good confession.

Jeremiah 9:23 puts it nicely: *"Thus saith the Lord, Let not the wise man glory in his wisdom, neither let the mighty man glory in his might, let not the rich man glory in his riches: But let him that glorieth glory in this, that he understandeth and knoweth me, that I am the Lord which exercises lovingkindness, judgment, and righteousness, in the earth: for in these things I delight, saith the Lord."* Powerfully good advice to remember.

We need to remember that God's love, that love of the Beloved, is so strong and so powerful that it will draw us out of the mire of sin and degradation and place us on solid ground, if we do not resist.

As good and important as wine is, wine being doctrine, if it lacks love, it is worthless. Keeping the Sabbath day, although an excellent practice, if done out of the wrong reason, without love, and with wrong motives, lacks credence.

To you married people, remember today the choice of your life-partner and declare unto him or her that you still love them even now with the accumulation of the years of marriage.

Parting Gem: *Remembering to love the Lord our God with all of our hearts, all of our minds, all of our soul, all of our breath, all of everything we have is of more value than knowing everything there is to know.*

FEBRUARY 14 — *Black of Blacks* — Song 1:5

Today's Thought: *"I am black, but comely."*

To start this day's reading, let us be aware that it has nothing to do with the colour of the skin. This is speaking symbolically.

In Revelation 6, there is a prophetic symbol for apostasy. Armed with the Word of God, and guided by the Holy Spirit, the early church went forth. *"And behold a white horse: and he that sat upon him had a bow; and a crown was given him"* (Revelation 6:2). This represents the Ephesus Church from AD 34 to AD 100.

"And there went out another horse that was red… and there was given unto him a great sword" (Revelation 6:4). A lot of persecution. This is the Smyrna Church from AD 100 to AD 323.

In Revelation 6:5, we find the appearance of a black horse, a period from AD 323 to AD 538 where the church has apostatized into a period of great darkness. How quickly the work of corruption progresses! A period of great darkness and moral corruption must be denoted by this symbol (Smith, D & R 428).

The reason for the apostasy is plainly stated. The bride-church is black because the sun hath looked upon her. Christianity, the church, has become corrupted by forms of sun-worship. As civilization moved westward in its expansion, pagan forms of worship reached Rome, which became the capital of Christianity.

To attract these pagans, the church mixed her pure religion with the impure practices of the pagans in an attempt to Christianize them—practices like art forms, doctrines, and the day of worship which originated in Babylon.

Greek and Roman sun gods were carved from stone and set up in the Pantheon in Rome, and were renamed in honour of the apostles. Thus the veneration of images was incorporated into the church. The doctrine of the immortality of the soul was accepted. The Babylonian structure of the priesthood, monasteries, nunneries, rosaries, incantations, candles, indulgences, and many more, were incorporated into the Christian teachings.

Parting Gem: *As a result of the apostasy, "Babylon," the false system of religion, brought forth her "man-child," another beloved.*

FEBRUARY 15   *Comeliness of Comelinesses*   Song 1:5

Today's Thought: *"I am black, but comely."*

Enfeebled and defective as it may appear, the church is the one object upon which God bestows in a special sense His supreme regard.

Even though the church, as an organization, fell into apostasy, yet there were and still are many individuals to whom Christ gave commendation. In each of the three churches in Revelation covered by this period—Ephesus, Smyrna, Pergamos—the Lord stated, *"I know thy works…"* (Revelation 2:2) and gave commendations and rebuke.

Let us be encouraged with Jeremiah 6:2, *"I have likened the daughter of Zion to a comely and delicate woman."*

When the bride states that she is black but comely, she is not saying that apostasy is beautiful. Like the parable of the ten virgins, there were some wise and some foolish, there were "some black, some comely." When we read about the ten virgins, let us remember that these were all members in good and regular standing within the church.

It is that same period in our Song that is depicted in Revelation 6 of the black horse, a period of tremendous spiritual darkness and moral corruption. Accept or be killed were the alternatives; yet the true bride found another solution in Revelation 12:14, *"And to the woman were given two wings of a great eagle, that she might fly into the wilderness, into her place, where she is nourished for a time, and times, and half a time, from the face of the serpent."*

That was her way out. If you can't fight them, flee; especially when you read that this power will prevail over the saints of God for some 1,260 years. It just might be that should you flee and remain alive, you can do more good than if you stayed and were killed.

Uriah Smith states that, "The time that intervened between the reign of Constantine and the establishment of the Papacy in AD 538 may be justly noted as the time when the darkest errors and grossest superstitions sprang up in the church" (Daniel & Revelation 428).

Parting Gem: *Christ will present His bride to Himself "a glorious church, not having spot, or wrinkle, or any such thing; but… holy and without blemish" (Ephesians 5:27). This is a great promise to remember.*

FEBRUARY 16 *Tent of Tents* Song 1:7

Today's Thought: *"Tell me, O thou whom my soul loveth, where thou feedest, were thou makest thy flock to rest at noon."*

The bride's question is, where should the flocks feed and where should they eat during the 1,260 years of papal supremacy? Where is the flock to rest at noon?

During this 1,260 year sojourn in the wilderness of Europe, there were times when the almost overwhelming onslaught of the papal armies caused the bride to flee yet again. This would be especially true at the high noon point, the zenith, of papal rule.

The picture emerges of a Christian community in the rocky recesses of Europe constantly alert for advancing papal armies, so that in the event of discovery, they could pick up their tents, their moveable habitation, and move on to other territory.

While the papacy was at its highest, most brutal point, this small band of saints kept alight the torch of truth. In every age, noticeably this 1,260 year period, God has had His faithful followers. In lands beyond the jurisdiction of Rome, there existed for centuries bodies of Christians who remained almost wholly free from papal corruption. They continued to feed on God's Word, taking it as their only rule of faith and practice.

Although there were many Christians in Central Africa, Ethiopia, Armenia, the Waldenses stand out. They determined to maintain their allegiance to God. They were among the first of the peoples of Europe to obtain translations of Scripture in their native tongue. These they copied and scattered through the regions. They denied papal supremacy, rejected image worship as idolatry, kept the true Bible Sabbath, held the Bible as the only supreme infallible authority. Their pastors led the flock of God, leading them to the green pastures and living fountains of water found in God's Holy Word.

Parting Gem: *The 23rd Psalm mentions being led beside the still water, in green pasture, all to have our souls refreshed. But, then again, we must follow the Shepherd.*

FEBRUARY 17   *Curtain of Curtains*   Song 1:5-6

Today's Thought: *"I am black… as the tents of Kedar, as the curtains of Solomon… because the sun hath looked upon me."*

Tents were used by patriarchs during their sojourn in Palestine, and also by Jews in their wilderness wanderings and early history in Canaan. Of various sizes and shapes, they usually had a covering over them. This covering was generally made of cloth woven of black goats' hair. The Bedouins still use them to this day.

The "curtains of Solomon" is, in the original language, derived from the Hebrew root "to tremble" or "to glitter in the sun." The reflective power of the sun is tremendous enough to darken the skin. Symbolically, this could reflect the pervading influence of sun-worship with all of its glitter and splendour. This sun-worship has encircled the globe, penetrating even into the worship of Christian churches.

Those who brought such errors into the church are identified in the messages to the seven churches of Revelation 2. Three, namely: *"them which say they are apostles, and are not, [are]… liars"* (2:2); *"them which… are [of] the synagogue of Satan"* (2:9); and those who are *"where Satan's seat is"* (2:13).

It is in the two church periods, that of Smyrna and Pergamos, that is covered from AD 100 to AD 538. It is also in this period between the reign of Constantine and the establishment of the Papacy that the darkest and grossest superstitions sprang up in the church (Uriah Smith, D & R 428).

It is helpful to compare that with Revelation 6, where in verses 5-8 it speaks of a black horse, a period of AD 313 to AD 538, then of a pale horse and Death followed, a period from AD 538 to AD 1517. They seem to agree. The Reformation "officially" got started with Luther in AD 1517.

Parting Gem: *Should we depart on these curtains, we could request that the Lord place a hedge around us and our children and to lay over us a blanket, both to protect us from the evils and heresies coming upon the world.*

FEBRUARY 18   *Sun of Suns*   Song 1:6

Today's Thought: *"I am black, because the sun hath looked upon me."*

We open this Act 1, Scene 3 during the fourth century. The Christian church, with headquarters in Rome, was distracted by the counterfeit system of sun-worship. As she gradually lost sight of the true *"Sun of righteousness"* (Malachi 4:2), the counterfeit usurper or antichrist-Papal sun was rising toward a zenith of politico-religious domination over Europe. The Christian church gradually became corrupted by forms of Babylon sun-worship. So the bride states that she is corrupt, because sun-worship has burned her.

"Little by little, at first in stealth and silence, and then openly as it increased in strength and gained control of the minds of men, the mystery of iniquity carried forward its deceptive and blasphemous work. Almost imperceptibly the customs of heathenism found their way into the Christian church... Paganism... Controlled the church. Her doctrines, ceremonies, and superstitions were incorporated into the faith and worship of the professed followers of Christ" (GC 49, 50).

By the fourth century, the Christian church had incorporated many of the practices, art forms, doctrines, and the day of worship which originated in Babylon.

The first day of the week, named by sun worshippers, in honour of the sun, was Sunday. Amid declining spirituality, Christian worshippers gradually came to favour Sunday observance in place of the seventh-day Sabbath of the Ten Commandments. This was a slow and gradual change and acceptance.

Christians were forced to select either their integrity or accept papal ceremonies and worship to wile away their life in dungeons, suffer death by the rack, the fagot, or the headman's axe, or flee (GC 54, 55).

Some simply chose to flee into the wilderness, the mountain recesses of several countries like France, Italy, Switzerland, even faraway Scotland.

Parting Gem: *Yet, the woman fled. Her desire to remain faithful, comely, and unadulterated, was more important to her than acceptance, peace, and easy living. I trust that that is the way it is with us as we await the Bridegroom.*

FEBRUARY 19 — *Anger of Angers* — Song 1:6

Today's Thought: *"My mother's children were angry with me…"*

The Jewish nation had been chosen by God, not by favouritism, but by their stated willingness to be His missionaries, to take the gospel of salvation to all the world, and as such they were known as "the keepers of the vineyard."

In the figurative language of the parable in Matthew 21:33-41, Jesus told the Jews that He would *"let His vineyard unto other husbandmen"* (21:41)—the Gentiles. As the Jews rejected the promised Messiah and began to persecute His missionaries, they "made" the Gentiles the "keepers of the vineyard." The Jews were angry with the newly formed Christian Church and persecuted them.

To paraphrase it, the Gentile church—the bride—says, "My mother's children (Jews) were angry with me. They made me the keeper of the vineyard to take the gospel to all the world. They were so angry with her that they stoned one of their young believers, Stephen." This was in 34 A.D.

This is the transition of the vineyard, from the literal, geographical Jews to the newly formed Christian Church, being spiritual Jews or spiritual Israel. This was done "officially" by the Jewish people. The Hebrew nation met in "council" and that legal decision was the "voice of the nation." The act of putting Stephen to death put to an end the seventieth week of Daniel 8, and put to an end the Jewish nation as being "the "keepers of the vineyard." It was now transferred to the newly formed Christian Church to carry to the world the everlasting gospel.

Just exactly where this Christian Church was formed and founded may not be known, yet in the upper room when the Holy Spirit came down upon that group like tongues of fire was an important start.

Parting Gem: *Anger many times is a cause of rejoicing. When Paul and Barnabas disagreed about Mark, it caused the workforce to double. When the Jews got angry to the point of stoning Stephen, it resulted in the later conversion of Saul. Bad things do happen to good people.*

FEBRUARY 20   *Detour of Detours*   Song 1:7

Today's Thought: *"Tell me, O thou whom my soul loveth…"*

Today, let us detour for a short history lesson. From *Builders of the Old World* (on pages 236 and 192), it states that the pagans had many gods that they regularly worshipped. On the day of the sun, now called Sunday, they worshipped the sun. In Bible times, this was called the first day of the week. On Monday, they worshipped the moon, or moon's day. The god, Tiew, had his day on Tuesday.

More of these Germanic gods gave us Wednesday, the god of Woden's day. Woden, or Odin as he was sometimes called, was the chief of all gods. He ruled and directed the affairs of the earth.

Thor was Odin's eldest son. His day for worship came on Thursday, called Thor's Day. It is believed that Thor had a great hammer, with which he slew giants, wore a belt which doubled his strength, wore a pair of steel gloves, and when it thundered, Thor was throwing his hammer across the heavens. Freya's Day, now called Friday, came from a worship of Freya, the Norse goddess of love and beauty. This Friday was the "Preparation Day" in Bible times.

Julius Caesar gave us the principles of our present Julian calendar to help bring order out of chaos. January is named for the god Janis. February comes from a Roman name for feast. March is named in honour of Mars, the god of war. April is Latin, meaning "to open," like in spring when flowers open. May is from Maia, a Roman goddess. June is from Juno, the wife of Jupiter. July is from Julius himself, his first name. August is in honour of the emperor Augustus. Latin words for seven, eight, nine, ten give us September, October, November, December (the Roman year started in March, not January).

One of the popular events in the Canadian year is the night on which the Juno Awards are given, so we still use some of these names.

In many parts of the world, the Bible's seven day, the Sabbath Day is still called Sabbath. Look on many calendars. It also was chosen to be the planet Saturn's day.

Parting Gem: *It's amazing how much paganism rules our world and our day. You can't change it, so enjoy this day God has given you.*

FEBRUARY 21 — Keeper of Keepers — Song 1:6

Today's Thought: *"They made me the keeper of the vineyards."*

Although the vineyard was transferred from the Jews to the newly formed Christian Church, the bride of the church laments, *"Mine own vineyard have I not kept."* (Song 1:6). Here is a very clear acknowledgement of the apostasy. The church which fell into apostasy was the Pergamos Church, which means "watchtower." Ironic, is it not, that the watchtower did not keep watch against the enemy? When she failed in her task, she began the long decline into the Dark Ages, and only the long dark night stretched ahead.

Very slowly the prophetic period, both in Daniel and the Revelation, would begin in which the church would *"flee into the wilderness"* from great persecutions to be lost from human sight for 1,260 years. Looking back into history, one sees the point where there was a fork in the road of the Christian Church. Some changed as these errors crept in, accepting and changing the true doctrines to fit into the pagan culture and customs. The other fork being the "comely ones," who had to flee. They fled into the wilderness prepared for them (Revelation 12:6).

Do not miss that gem of this verse 6, *"And the woman fled into the wilderness where she hath a place prepared of God."* Before one calls on the name of the Lord, He already has an answer. Before the saints fled into the wilderness, the Lord already had places for them to hide.

Although the church, as an organization, fell into apostasy, the Son of God states to the Thyratira Church that, *"I know thy works, and charity, and service, and faith, and thy patience, and thy works; and the last to be more than the first"* (Revelation 2:19). The church in the wilderness is growing.

Paul the apostle saw at an early date errors creeping into the church that would prepare the way for the setting up of the papacy (GC 49).

As a result of this apostasy, "Babylon," the false system of religion brought forth her "man-child," the usurper, antichrist.

Parting Gem: *One needs to remember that the pure church changed from being pure as the apostolic church to the point that the comely ones had to leave, or were forced out, by this apostasy that was creeping in. They went into hiding for 1,260 years.*

FEBRUARY 22   *Vineyard of Vineyards #1*   Song 1:6

Today's Thought: *"... but mine own vineyard have I not kept."*

Here is a very clear acknowledgement of her apostasy. Previously, she stated that she was black because the sun had looked upon her. Thus, in Hebrew poetic style, two chances are given to understand what is being said.

Although the vineyard was transferred from the Jews to the Gentiles, the Gentile church laments that she did not take care of it. The church which fell in apostasy, the Pergamos Church, which means "watchtower," should have kept watch against the enemy. When she failed in her purity, she began the long descent into the Dark Ages. The long 1,260 year night stretched out ahead of her (Song 1:13, Jeremiah 6:4).

Isaiah 5:1-7 elaborates on this transfer of the vineyard. *"Now will I sing to my wellbeloved a song of my beloved touching his vineyard. My wellbeloved hath a vineyard in a very fruitful hill: and he fenced it, and gathered out the stones thereof, and planted it with the choicest vine, and built a tower in the midst of it, and also made a winepress therein: and he looked that it should bring forth grapes, and it brought forth wild grapes... I will tell you what I will do to my vineyard: I will take away the hedge thereof, and it shall be eaten up; and break down the wall thereof, and it shall be trodden down"* (Isaiah 5:1-2,5)

We pick up the story in Mark 12:9. *"What shall therefore the lord of the vineyard do? he will come and destroy the husbandman, and will give the vineyard unto others."*

It is true that Christ wished the gospel to be taken to the Gentiles, but it was through the Jews that this was to be done. They refused, so the next alternative was to give it to the Gentiles and let them take care of His vineyard.

Although it might seem that the Old Testament dealt with the gospel staying fairly close to the Israelites, Christ in the New Testament put strong emphasis in getting the gospel to the Gentiles. Read from Acts onward to get the picture.

Parting Gem: *"Also I heard the voice of the Lord, saying, Whom shall I send, and who will go for us? Then said I, Here am I; send me." (Isaiah 6:8)*

FEBRUARY 23 — *Pasture of Pastures #1* — Psalms 23:2-3

Today's Thought: *"He maketh me to lie down in green pastures: he leadeth me beside the still waters. He restoreth my soul."*

The bride's question is, *"Tell me, O thou whom my soul loveth, where thou feedest, where thou makest thy flock to rest at noon"* (Song 1:7). This noon is the noon of the papacy, which is also the midnight for the bride-church. It is the work of the church to feed the flock. Three times Jesus gave to Peter the commission to feed His lambs, feed His sheep, feed His ship. It seems the bride's question is not only, where should I feed them, but what should I feed them with?

The neat answer comes back to her to take her flock to the tent of the shepherd during this troublesome time of 1,260 years. It is the responsibility of the shepherd to feed the flock, so feed the flock as all good shepherds have always done, feed them on the Word of God.

Those were difficult times during the wilderness wanderings and hidings. Try living on a hillside, in a so-called house made of boulders and stones, put together in some manner of form, always on the lookout for Papal soldiers. Always subject to the winds, rains, and elements of nature. According to stories, the pastors did a good job.

Parents needed to train their children to live and to stay alive. In their precarious conditions and times, what would you teach your children that was not specifically dovetailed into this aspect of staying alive? Then there was the need, actually the urgency, to carry the good news that forced you up into these hills, to those still in the valleys and the towns and hamlets.

Should you be familiar with farming, the pasture is not always out there waiting for the animals to feast on. The winter hay, put up while the sun shone, is brought to the animals. That's the idea that these people in the mountains had. Who will feed the flock down below? Who will search out the other sheep not of this fold down there in the valley? It was no easy sacrifice, yet the pasture had to be shared. Why should one have all of the benefits while others are unaware of the blessings and promises of eternal life?

Parting Gem: *Let's try not to put the responsibility all onto the pastor's table. We, too, are ministers of the gospel. Let us feed the flock.*

FEBRUARY 24 *Rest of Rests* Song 1:7

Today's Thought: *"Tell me, O thou whom my soul loveth, where thou feedest, where thou makest thy flock to rest at noon."*

When true Christians think of rest, they think Sabbath. Yet, this term is used variously. God offers to all an inward rest of soul, not dependent on outward conditions, but on a supreme trust in Jesus. There is an outward rest from wandering as a people, a Christian community, without a country, a rest from persecution, from running, hiding. Then there is a rest from persecution itself, from sin, troubles, even life that the Christian receives at the second coming of Christ.

During this 1,260 year period, the bride needed rest. She needed the weekly Sabbath rest. The weekly Sabbath rest was one of the main reasons she was hiding in the mountains of Europe. Had she followed the Sunday requirements instead of keeping the seventh-day Sabbath, she would not be found in the recesses of those mountains.

She needed the inner peace of the soul, that peace that passes all understanding, that awareness and inner confidence in one's God. For without that inner rest, life in those mountain hideaways would be unbearable. She needed the rest of understanding that she was doing the will of God and that she was not up here in these mountains because of some whim of hers.

She needed outward rest, that rest from aimlessly, fugitively wandering from persecution, from hunger and protection, from the elements.

She also needed that spiritual-physical rest to be instituted at Christ's second coming.

Death may well have been a welcome experience, for it brought the first three rests and guaranteed the fourth and final eternal rest, which could be called the real rest, the rest of all rests.

As one person said, *"There are a lot of things worse than death, and one of them is living."* (See poem at the end of February.)

One needs to remember that our bride-church is asking where she should feed the kids at noon. Tomorrow, we look at the noon she speaks of.

Parting Gem: *Good advice would be to come apart and rest awhile, so come apart.*

FEBRUARY 25 — *Noon of Noons* — Song 1:7

Today's Thought: *"Tell me, O thou whom my soul liveth, where thou feedest, where thou makest thy flock to rest at noon."*

Where should she feed her flocks at noon? The noon of the Papacy was the midnight of the world (GC 60). European reformers referred to the Pope as the "noonday demon" and historians of the centuries described this "midnight of the world" as "The Dark Ages." While the Papacy denied the Scriptures to the people, what could she feed the flock, remembering that during these 1,260 years persecution was rampant, where hiding places were scarce, where danger and death lurked around every corner?

This noon time period, like ours today, indicates that the afternoon and evening is coming. Later in Song 2, we will read about the coming springtime, indicating that this is the midwinter season as far as the 1,260 year period is concerned.

While it is the noon, and probably high-noon, for the persecutors and the midnight for the persecuted, the daybreak is coming. We get that picture in 2:17, *"until the day break, and the shadows flee away."*

In AD 538, the Pope of Rome obtained the police powers of the states of Europe to enforce the dogmas of the church. By establishing the Courts of the Inquisition, and the confessionals, directed by the order of Loyola, the Pope was able to reign over all of Europe. It was this "Papal Reign" that drove the true church into the wilderness. It was a long noon hour, "lunch break."

It may seem that a very long scope of church history has been covered in so short a time. The Song of Songs 1:5-8 provides a historical unit which is all connected in cause and effect relationships: (1) the Christian church receives the commission to be "Keepers of the vineyard," but (2) she does not keep it and thus falls into apostasy. (3) That very apostasy establishes the Papacy and that Papacy is the power which drove her into the wilderness!

Parting Gem: *Soon the clouds will part, the sun will shine, the flowers will blossom and bloom, spring will be here. It's coming. Patience.*

FEBRUARY 26 — *Flock of Flocks #1* — Song 1:7

Today's Thought: *"Tell me, O thou whom my soul loveth, where thou feedest, where thou makest thy flock to rest at noon."*

Jesus remarked in John 10:11 that He was the Good Shepherd, and that the Good Shepherd gives His life for the sheep, His flock.

Psalm 23 tells us that the Lord is our Shepherd so then there is no need to fear or want. He leads us to still waters and green pastures. Sheep drink from still waters, not from flowing streams—or so I understand it.

The bride's major question is where and what should she feed the flock, especially at noon, high noon, heat-of-the-day-noon. Now, remember that this noon is the high noon of papal supremacy and persecution, which at the same time is the midnight for the followers of the Good Shepherd. So this flock, the apple of God's eye, this object of supreme regard, in the heat of the day's persecution needs a place to rest and to feed, let alone to hide.

This flock is called the daughter of Zion and is likened to a comely and delicate woman (Jeremiah 6:2). Check back to Song 1:5 and repeat what the bride states: *"I am black, but comely."* This flock is the bride of Christ (Ephesians 5:22-32). It is the church of God which has been purchased with the blood of Christ (Acts 20:28).

As you go through your activities today, contemplate Luke's counsel in 12:32, *"Fear not, little flock; for it is your Father's good pleasure to give you the kingdom."* We repeat Song 2:16, 6:3, 7:10, where the bride states her trilogy that, *"I am his and his desire is towards me."* This is expressed by Luke in the above words, and we repeat, *"It is your Father's good pleasure to give you the kingdom."* It is your Father's burning desire to gather together His flock so He can lead them where the water flows gently and the grass grows green.

John 10:14-16 says, paraphrased, *"I AM the good shepherd, and I know my sheep, and they know me, but I have other sheep which are not of this flock. They too must hear, understand, and join me, so that there will be only one fold, only one flock, only one shepherd"* (emphasis added).

Parting Gem: *"He shall feed his flock like a shepherd: he shall gather the lambs with his arm, and carry them in his bosom, and shall gently lead those that are with young."* (Isaiah 40:11)

FEBRUARY 27　　　　*Fairest of Fair #1*　　　　Song 1:8

Today's Thought: *"If thou know not, O thou fairest among women, go thy way forth by the footsteps of the flock, and feed thy kids..."*

This description of the bride, the bride-church, is an important one, one that each one of us needs to know, understand, and respect. We are actually talking about the "First Lady of the Universe." As we go through the year, we will find several more descriptions of the bride. The neat thing about it is that each description of the bride gets more elaborate, more exciting, more meaningful. Adjectives increase.

This description is of the bride while in the wilderness for 1,260 years. At this era of time, it would be the Church of Thyatira, found in Revelation 2:18-29, the age of Adversity and Papal Supremacy. According to Revelation 2:19, it was a growing church in that there were more members at the close of its period than at its beginning.

There are several descriptions of the church in its respective period as we go on through the year. Each time we will repeat some moving statements about these churches.

Some of these descriptions are: "...enfeebled and defective as it may appear, the church is the one object upon which God bestows in a special sense His supreme regard" (AA 12).

"It [the church] is the case which contains His jewels" (6T 261).

"His church... His own fortress which He holds in... a revolted world" (TM 16).

"Nothing else in this world is so dear to God as His church" (6T 42).

That's what the Lord states through His messenger, E.G. White. Now let's look at the Word itself.

2 Corinthians 11:2 says, *"For I am jealous over you with godly jealousy: for I have espoused you to one husband, that I may present you as a chaste virgin to Christ."*

Ephesians 5:25,27 says, *"Husbands love your wives even as Christ loved the church and gave himself for it... that he might present it to himself a glorious church, not having spot, or wrinkle, or any such thing; but that it should be holy and without blemish."*

Parting Gem: *What an awesome thought that the church is the First Lady of the Universe.*

FEBRUARY 28 — *Kid of Kids* — Song 1:8

Today's Thought: *"...feed thy kids beside the shepherds' tent."*

It takes only a very few short chapters to cover the events from the seven-day creation week in Genesis 1 to the flood in Genesis 6. So, from the crucifixion of Christ where He pays the dowry (Song 1:2) to the sojourn into the wilderness in AD 538, there are only eight verses.

A long scope of Church history, covered in Song 1:1-8, depicts the Ephesus Church period from AD 31 to AD 100, as well the Smyrna Church period from AD 100 to AD 323, followed by the Pergamos Church period from AD 323 to AD 538, pushing up into the Thyratira Church period of AD 538 to AD 1563 when the Reformation breaks loose.

These verses are all linked together in a cause and effect relationship. First, Christ pays the dowry. The Christian Church receives the commission to be *"keepers of the vineyard,"* but does not keep it and therefore falls into apostasy. That very apostasy establishes the Papacy, and this Papacy is the power which drove them into the wilderness.

The history of God's people during these days that followed the Roman supremacy is written in heaven, as well as this drama we are reading. Few traces of Rome's activities during this period can be found. It was the policy of Rome to obliterate every trace of dissent.

During this period of time, pastors faithful to their duty seriously taught the flock. The Waldenses trained their youth and required them to memorize large portions of Scripture, learn a trade, and then sent them willingly down into the valley and towns to peddle their wares, and when some interest seemed present to open to them the Word of God.

These "kids" were to be trained and fed in the tents of these pastors. They were to keep the truth of God's Word unadulterated, and to pass it on to the next generation. They were to feed thy kids beside the shepherds' tent.

Parting Gem: *What a challenge for moms and dads of today to train their children. As Moses spent only a few years before being ushered into Pharaoh's courts, and as Samuel was just weaned before given to Eli, what can Mom and Dad do today to train their children?*

FEBRUARY 29　　　　　　　*Summary*　　　　　　　Song 1:2-8

After reading through the month of February, we have found in very few verses:

- Christ paying the price for our salvation on Calvary's cross.
- The bride acknowledging that love is much better than doctrines.
- The virgins love the name and man called the Bridegroom, Jesus.
- The bride declaring to her Lover to draw her to him, and she will follow wherever He leads her.
- The Bridegroom takes into His Chamber of Truth His chosen bride, the church.
- The bride is excited and glad that she has found Him and she rejoices in this finding.
- It is much more important to remember the love of God in all of its facets than it is to know all about the wine or doctrines of the Bible. Doctrines will not "save" one, but the Bridegroom can and will.
- In verse 5, the bride admits that she has apostatized and become overwhelmed with the sun-worship of her day, but nevertheless she still claims to be comely. She still admits that she is His chosen and nothing can change that. This is a message to all married couples, similar to that episode in the Bible about Hosea and his unfaithful spouse, which in turn depicts how our Beloved yearns for us even though we have apostatized and gone astray from Him.

We found that there is one event, above all other events ever to grace this globe, that is the longing, desire of the Beloved's heart. This is what this whole drama is leading up to and is emphasizing. We will take a closer look at this event in Song 7:10.

We looked at the dowry that Christ paid to redeem His people back from the abyss of despair. A closer look at that dowry will surprise us. That dowry is one reason why the virgins love Him.

We considered the race and the time spent in the vineyard, whether we started out in early dawn (as a youth) or whether we went out at sunset (on the death bed), we all get the same reward, which just happens to be eternal life. Nothing is greater than that.

Then the 1,260 year period was introduced, and we learned why the church was in the wilderness. We compared the noon to the midnight. We close this summary with a request that you consider the fairest of the fair, only the first of several, actually many, such descriptions.

There's Always Something Worse Than Death

There's always something worse than death,
    Worse than the grave where there is no breath,
Worse than the absence of loved ones gone,
    Worse than one lying beneath the sod.

What's worse, you say, with a smirk on your face?
    Just being a part of this sickly race,
Just being aware of the crooks and their crime,
    Just being awash with their grease and grime.

What's worse, you say, with a sickening dread,
    As you mill away on your daily tread;
As you try to find enough to eat;
    As you try to cover your swollen feet?

What's worse, you say, as you walk the street,
    As you gather your rags around you for heat,
As your stomach grinds and your body groans,
    As you look to the future and sickly moan.

What's worse, you say, as you lay in bed,
    With a mind quite active, yet, your body so dead.
What's worse than death? Is that what I hear.
    Get ready for death for its nothing to fear.

March

March's Introduction and Aim

The aim this month of March is to look at the description of the bride while in the wilderness, from AD 538 to AD 1563; from Song 1:8 to 2:7. This is Act 1, Scene 4. There are two more descriptions of the bride in different areas of time. This period of church history is covered in Revelation 2:18-29, or the Thyratira Church. We finished off February on Song 1:8, because it answers a question from verse 7. We also start March on Song 1:8 because it is the start of the description of the bride.

It is important to remember that in symbolism, which the Song of Songs is written in, what is stated does not mean in the literal sense what it says. It is in this misunderstanding that many people find the sensuous portion embarrassing, thus puzzling why this book would be including in the canon, as well as its meaning. So, let us not try, even a little bit, to uncover, explain, nor understand the wisdom and the planning of the Almighty Beloved.

We start the month with another expressive adoration of the bride. She is in the wilderness for that period of time which used to be called "The Dark Ages." Read our coverage, Song 1:8-2:7, as well as Revelation 2:18-2:29, the Thyratira Church period.

We meet the embarrassing portion, the breasts, only if you look at it from the sensuous side. Look at it from the spiritual symbolic and they take on a whole new and different meaning. Enjoy.

We get a new picture of the Rose of Sharon and the lily of the valleys, which again may cause us to look at things in a different light. Enjoy this as well.

We know of the symbolism for Christ as the Bread and Water of life, the Good

Shepherd, the Word, so be prepared for a new symbol—the roe.

A small glimpse of the Bridegroom comes this month. A more detailed description comes later in Song 5:9-16.

A second charge is given, a charge to not yet expect Christ to come.

Your poem for this month is "The Bullock—Between the Plough and the Altar," taken from *Ministry of Healing,* page 502.

Enjoy your readings for the month.

MARCH

Day 1	Fairest of Fair #2	Song 1:8	75
Day 2	Comparison of Comparisons #1	Song 1:9	76
Day 3	Cheek of Cheeks #1	Song 1:10	77
Day 4	Neck of Necks #1	Song 1:10	78
Day 5	Border of Borders	Song 1:11	79
Day 6	Myrrh of Myrrh	Song 1:13	80
Day 7	Breast of Breasts #1	Song 1:13	81
Day 8	Camphire of Camphires	Song 1:14	82
Day 9	Fairest of Fair #3	Song 1:15-16	83
Day 10	Bed of Beds #1	Song 1:16-17	84
Day 11	House of Houses	Song 1:17	85
Day 12	Rose of Roses	Song 2:1	86
Day 13	Lily of Lilies	Song 2:1	87
Day 14	Apple Tree of Apples Trees	Song 2:3,5	88
Day 15	Thorn of Thorns	Song 2:2	89
Day 16	Beloved of Beloved #1	Song 2:3	90
Day 17	Shadow of Shadows	Song 2:3	91
Day 18	Taste of Tastes	Song 2:3	92
Day 19	Banquet House of Banquet Houses	Song 2:4	93
Day 20	Banner of Banners	Song 2:4	94
Day 21	Flagon of Flagons	Song 2:5	95
Day 22	Apple of Apples	Song 2:5	96
Day 23	Comfort of Comforts	Song 2:5	97
Day 24	Lovesick of Lovesick	Song 2:5	98
Day 25	Right Hand of Right Hands	Song 2:6	99
Day 26	Embrace of Embraces #1	Song 2:6	100
Day 27	Embrace of Embraces #2	Song 2:6	101
Day 28	Charge of Charges #2	Song 2:7	102
Day 29	Roe of Roes	Song 2:7	103
Day 30	Stirring of Stirrings	Song 2:7	104
Day 31	Summary	Song 2:8-3:5	105

Poems of the Month: "Between the Plough and the Altar"   106
                 "The Vine That's True"   107
                 "In the Morning"   108

MARCH 1 — Fairest of Fair #2 — Song 1:8

Today's Thought: *"O thou fairest among women."*

This is the first of four descriptions of the bride-church. This one goes from Song 1:9 to 2:7, and describes the church while in the wilderness, covering the Thyratira Church, AD 538 to the Reformation.

This phrase, *"O thou fairest among women,"* is repeated several times throughout this drama. It gets more adjectives as the centuries go on. Each church as it comes onto the stage is similarly depicted as *"O thou fairest among women,"* or a similar affection address.

A woman in the Bible depicts a church, so this description of the bride-church is saying, of all the churches on the stage at this period of time, the one described here is the fairest, the best, the ultimate, the comeliest.

The bride-church is the only object upon earth upon which Christ bestows His supreme regard, even if it is enfeebled and defective (AA 12). It is His fortress which He holds in a polluted and revolting world (TM 16). It is His showcase which contains His jewels (6T 261). There is nothing else in the entire world that is as dear to Christ as His church. (7T 242).

It may be for that reason that God has always had His church down through the centuries as recorded in Revelation 2-3. Each church in its own period of time on the stage is the fairest of the fair. Of all the churches that are planted and operating around the world, God's true church that keeps His commandments, has His faith, and has His messengers is always very dear to Him, the fairest and the best of all the churches around at that period of time.

Parting Gem: *To put it in modern terms, the ark of Noah may have been cramped for space, noisy with the scream of animals, foul smelling with all of the waste material, but when one considers the alternative, it was a pretty neat place. So in Jericho, of all the places one thought unsafe, or even undesirable to be found in, the house of Harlot Rahab on the walls themselves would be it. One should always consider the alternate, especially when it comes to eternity.*

MARCH 2   *Comparison of Comparisons #1*   Song 1:9

Today's Thought: *"I have compared thee, O my love, to a company of horses in Pharaoh's chariots."*

Looking at Exodus 15:19. *"For the horse of Pharaoh went in with his chariots and with his horsemen into the sea, and the Lord brought again the waters of the sea upon them; but the children of Israel went on dry land in the midst of the sea."*

What happened to those horses and chariots and horsemen? They were swept away into the sea, they were lost, gone, disappeared. No one could find them. So the church was driven into the wilderness for 1,260 years when she was gone, lost, disappeared, so no one could find them.

The church was swept away with the persecutions of the papal powers up into the wilderness. Across the waters onto the British Isles, safety was found. Scotland was one place found when England began to persecute. Although the Waldenses are the better known "company of horses," there certainly were others.

The Albigenses and the Huguenots were others who were swept up in the mass migration to places of safety. They were gone, lost from sight just as Pharaoh's horses, chariots, and warriors were swept away by the onrushing of the Red Sea and were gone, lost from sight.

Pharaoh's onslaught was in persecution. The serpent cast water out of his mouth as a flood of persecution after the woman so that he might cause her to be carried away by the flood (Revelation 12:15). The papal persecution caused God's church to be swept up and away from the outside world, to places up in the mountains of Italy, Switzerland, Austria, even across the waters to the havens of Scotland.

Parting Gem: *It seems that Satan isn't too fussy as to how he persecutes us, just so long as we succumb to his devises and traps. I've found that one needs to slip away into the inner resources of his closet to spent time with the Bridegroom before starting the excitement of the day. Have you been into the inner closet to commune with the Bridegroom today, before you start you activities?*

MARCH 3   *Cheek of Cheeks #1*   Song 1:10

Today's Thought: *"Thy cheeks are comely with rows of jewels."*

In Biblical symbolism, cheeks represent abuse, affliction, persecution.

"They have smitten me upon the cheek reproachfully" (Job 16:10).

"He giveth his cheek to him that smiteth him: he is filled full with reproach" (Lamentations 3:30).

"For thou hast smitten all mine enemies upon the cheek bone" (Psalms 3:7).

"I gave my back to the smiters, and my cheeks to them that plucked off the hair" (Isaiah 50:6).

"But I say unto you, That ye resist not evil: but whosoever shall smite thee on thy right cheek, turn to him the other also" (Matthew 5:39).

Here is a bride-church who is familiar with being smitten, abused, persecuted, yet also comely, good-looking, attractive, beautiful, pleasing in the eyes and in the mind of her Beloved, being decked with precious stones and jewels.

For 1,260 years, from AD 538 to AD 1798, this bride is in the wilderness, the desolate places, the forest valleys, the mountain peaks. Year after year, generation after generation, she perseveres, holding onto the truths of the Bible, constantly keeping one eye open to advancing Roman soldiers, while the other eye is on God's Word. Throughout the 1,260 years, she clung to the Bible as the only rule of faith and doctrine.

Notice that the cheeks are mentioned only in this first description of the bride who is persecuted, not in the other descriptions, although when the Beloved is described we meet them again.

The church in times of persecution generally grows not only in numbers but in spirituality, and these verses were written in the times of trouble. The mighty Angel states of the Thyratira Church in Revelation 2:19, *"… and the last [is] more than the first,"* indicating a growth in membership.

Thus, this church-bride being in the rocky recesses of Europe, being persecuted and hunted down like game, continues to glisten and glitter with the beauty of richness.

Parting Gem: *"And they shall be mine, saith the Lord of hosts, in that day when I make up my jewels; and I will spare them, as a man spareth his own son that serveth him."* (Malachi 3:17)

MARCH 4   *Neck of Necks #1*   Song 1:10

Today's Thought: *"... thy neck with chains of gold."*

As checks are symbolic of persecution and being smitten, so its partner, the neck, is symbolic of power, strength, and endurance.

Isaiah 48:4 says, *"Because I knew that thou art obstinate, and thy neck is an iron sinew, and thy brow brass."*

Jeremiah 17:23 says, *"But they obeyed not, neither inclined their ear, but made their neck stiff..."*

Proverbs 1:8-9 says, *"My son, hear the instruction of thy father, and forsake not the law of thy mother: for they shall be an ornament of grace upon thy head, and chains about thy neck."*

Job 39:19 says, *"... hast thou clothed his neck with thunder?"*

Gold symbolically represents great worth and value, as well as spiritual riches or *"faith which worketh by love"* (Galatians 5:6). Gold does not necessarily always represent money or financial riches.

Chains were worn either for ornamentation or as symbols of honour and dignity, or used to restrain prisoners. Both Joseph (Genesis 41:42) and Daniel (Daniel 5:1,29) had chains placed around their necks upon their elevation to higher office.

Although this bride-church is noted for her persecutions, she is also elevated to a high and powerful position. Her strength (neck) is adorned with ornamental honour and dignity, showing her tremendous worth, value, and *"faith which worketh by love"* (Galatians 5:6).

Once again, we hear that enfeebled and defective... the church is still the one object upon earth which God bestows His supreme regard (2SM 396).

Remember, "His church... is His own fortress, which He holds in a revolted world" (TM 16), and that "it is the case which contains His jewels" (6T 261).

Parting Gem: *Should you not yet be a jewel in His case, today would be an excellent time to just bow your head and say to the Great Master Jeweller, "Master, I am yours, please be mine, so that I may have the experience like the bride."*

MARCH 5 — Border of Borders — Song 1:11

Today's Thought: *"We will make thee borders of gold with studs of silver."*

We, speaking of the same *"We"* in creation where it states, "Let us make man"—this is the Trinity describing the bride-church and how They will prepare her for the work before her and the day she shall be spoken for (Song 8:8).

Here, *"We will make her borders of gold with studs of silver."* Later, when she is to be spoken for, *"we will build upon her a palace of silver… we will inclose her with boards of cedar"* (Song 8:9).

We will surround her, We will empower her, We will do for her what is needed to be done so that she can be a picture of expensive beauty. We will decorate her with studs and beads made of silver. She will be something the king can set back in reflective contemplation and enjoy.

The king, in thoughtful repose, while setting at his table, is engulfed in the fragrance and bouquet perfume of this highly expensive item of commerce, usually kept in a sealed alabaster box and brought forth only on very special occasions or for the wealthy.

Just as Mary anointed the feet of Jesus with this ointment of Alabaster scent brought forth exclamations of "ah" and wonder, so this bride-church sends forth her perfume thereof.

It's neat to sit back and contemplate the value we are in His sight. We are the most expensive piece of real estate ever to be purchased. God the Father gathered all of heaven, the suns, moon, galaxies, solar systems, created beings of other worlds, and brought them to Jesus, saying something like this, *"I'm putting all of the multiverse that I can gather up for collateral in our bid to redeem Planet Earth."*

Parting Gem: *While the bride-church may be slapped in the face, abused, persecuted, she is strong, determined, well-grounded. We have our eyes on her and will reward her with a beauty and fragrance of the highest calibre. She brings honour, glory, majesty to God when she values herself according to the price He has placed upon them. The converse is also true; we insult Him and He is disappointed when the church, you and me, place a low estimate upon itself (DA 668 1/ RH 1897-06-29).*

MARCH 6 — *Myrrh of Myrrh* — Song 1:13

Today's Thought: *"A bundle of myrrh is my wellbeloved unto me; he shall lie all night betwixt my breasts."*

Myrrh is a pleasant-smelling substance reaching from six feet to fifteen feet, depending on where it is growing. It has an odoriferous bark through which a gum exudes naturally. A more pronounced flow can be made by making an incision in the bark, considered by Eastern people to be both a perfuming agent and a medicine.

Myrrh was an ingredient of the holy anointing oil used by priests; as well, it served as a purifying agent for women. Both garments and beds were perfumed with myrrh. A nice sensation as the Beloved lies all night between the bride's breasts. A tremendous sense of hope, encouragement, power, victory, and what have you came to the church in the wilderness as they cradled themselves in the Word of God, the Old Testament, and the New Testament, here figuratively spoken as *"betwixt my breasts."*

A gift from the wise men at the birth of the newborn Christ child, it was also used as an embalming agent at His death. It was considered of sufficient value to be used as a gift to a dignitary.

Between spikenard, myrrh and camphire, one gets the idea that this *"fairest among women"* is someone very special. It is powerfully difficult to explain in human language just what the Beloved thinks of her.

But then again, there is a verse in the Bible found in 1 Corinthians, taken from Isaiah 64:4, *"Eye hath not seen, nor ear heard, neither have entered into the heart of man, the things which God hath prepared for them that love him"* (1 Corinthians 2:9).

Parting Gem: *The Lord Jesus regards us of infinite estimation. He left His royal throne, His royal courts, the adoration of the host of heaven. He clothed His divinity with humanity which He will keep forever, and He experienced a shameful death upon the cross of Calvary, just so that you and I can be saved. What an awesome God; don't you just love Him? (RH 1897-06-29)*

MARCH 7 — *Breast of Breasts #1* — Song 1:13

Today's Thought: *"A bundle of myrrh is my wellbeloved unto me; he shall lie all night betwixt my breasts."*

There are several occasions in this drama where breasts are mentioned. This is the embarrassing portion for some people. However, we need to remember that we are talking figuratively, not literally. Understood figuratively, we have a beautiful picture of a church whose constant reliance is upon the "breasts," where the milk of the Word is upon a *"Thus saith the Lord"* found in both the Old Testament and the New Testament.

Here in 1:13, we are looking at the church in the wilderness, who lies all night between the Old and the New Testament. For 1,260 years while in the wilderness, this church bases her every act or thought upon the Word of God, the Bible, from whence she could get the milk of the Word. Deep theological discourses may not have been what this church needed, but rather the simple and plain steps to Christ as found in the simple, clear Word of God. This bride-church stayed within the confines of the Old and the New Testament, figuratively between the breasts.

In Song 8:1, it says, *"O that thou wert as my brother, that suckled the breasts of my mother!"* Nothing is as sweet as a newborn babe nursing. So, these Christians in the wilderness, some of strength yet all struggling, satisfied their hunger with the milk of the Word. Their whole night of 1,260 years was held together by the Word, symbolically the breasts.

In 4:5 of this song, the breasts are compared to two young roes which feed among the lilies. In 2:16, my Beloved is feeding among the lilies, while in 6:2-3, my Beloved is gone down into His garden to feed and gather lilies. Here the meat of the Word is symbolized by the clean meat of the deer. Notice the strong attempt to convey this symbolic meaning of breast as the Word of God.

Parting Gem: *Laying aside the political correct procedure, be aware that men notice a woman's breasts first when looking at a woman. Notice also that these breasts are mentioned some eight times in one way or another. Why? Could it be that this drama wants to get across the idea that the Word of God is uppermost and out front with this bride-church? The Bible and the Bible only is the bride's motto and call.*

MARCH 8 — *Camphire of Camphires* — Song 1:14

Today's Thought: *"My beloved is unto me as a cluster of camphire in the vineyards of Engedi."*

Camphire, or henna, is an Old World tropical shrub bearing cruciferous flowers. The shrub ranges from four to twelve feet tall and bears yellow and white flowers of great fragrance. The ground plant and flowers were often used to stain the palms of the hands and the souls of the feet, complete with fingernails and toenails. A bouquet of henna flowers is regarded by young Eastern women as a most generous token of love (SDA Bible Dict).

Engedi, meaning "spring of the Kid," is a fertile place on the Dead Sea. A hot spring feeds into this wilderness area. It is an oasis that is rich in palm trees, vineyards, and balsam.

David used these wild surroundings as a hiding place from Saul. In one of the caves, he cut a piece of Saul's robe off.

So, my Beloved is to me a fragrance of love, a token given to me to demonstrate His love for me. My Beloved is an oasis in the wild and barren wilderness where I can come to at the close of my day, where I can feast on the vineyard, rest under the palm trees, and bathe in the hot springs. All this time, there is this rich poignant fragrance that soothes the nerves. There is this fountain filled with blood that flows from Emmanuel's vein. There is this steadfast source of strength filled with eternal life that is given to us through the precious blood of Jesus.

Parting Gem: *Is your Beloved such a cluster of camphire as to have given your daily life and lifestyle a rich poignant fragrance that soothes the nerves of those you come in contact with? Are you an oasis in this wild and turbulent world where people can come to and find rest under your "palm tree" or bath in your "hot springs?" Remember yesterday's parting gem to spend time in your inner resources of your closet? Put these thoughts together and see what God will do for you today.*

| MARCH 9 | *Fairest of Fair #3* | Song 1:15-16 |

Today's Thought: *"Behold, thou art fair, my love; behold, thou art fair, thou hast doves' eyes. Behold, thou art fair, my beloved, yea, pleasant."*

Is the point made? It is repeated three times. *"Behold, thou art fair."* As stated in various places, the church is the one object upon earth that Christ bestowed His supreme regard. She could be called "The First Lady of the Universe." Remember, this is the God of Abraham, Isaac, and Jacob talking about and to His bride, His church.

Looking at the often repeated word "behold" in the dictionary and thesaurus, we interpret it to mean "observe, perceive, regard, survey, watch, witness, look at." It is an Old English word hardly used in modern speech.

Genesis 41:32 gives us an understanding of why in Hebrew poetry such words and ideas are repeated. That is, *"because the thing is established by God, and God will shortly bring it to pass."*

Another reason, noticeable in our drama, is that if after you missed it the first time around or didn't get the meaning on the first pass, the second pass should help you.

Our first example of this was 1:5-6: *"I am black... look not upon me, because I am black, because the sun hath looked upon me."* That's the first time. The second is, *"My mother's children were angry [mad] with me; they made me the keeper of the vineyards; but mine own vineyard have I not kept."* I am black with apostasy and have not kept my first love, nor looked after my vineyard.

Behold or take a look at this, My Bride. Just stop and get a load of her beauty. She is fair to look upon; she is pleasant to be around. She is the multiverse's First Lady, and that is a powerfully high position in the sight of her Beloved.

Parting Gem: *No man enjoys having his wife slandered, ridiculed, nor derided, no matter how true it may seem. So the King of the multiverse does not approve of His First Lady being treated that way either.*

MARCH 10 — *Bed of Beds #1* — Song 1:16-17

Today's Thought: *"Behold, thou art fair, my beloved, yea, pleasant: also our bed is green. The beams of our house are cedar, and our rafters of fir."*

When one is fleeing for his life, there isn't much he would take. As persecution crept closer, the Christian community did not have much time to do some planning for this event. Although they may not have known just how long this evacuation from home would last, they took some essentials that they could safely carry and would sneak away at night.

Beds in those days would be simple, a mat on the floor which could be easily picked up and carried (John 5:8). Going up into the mountains, they would, if fortunate, take their sleeping mat. If unfortunate, then the green carpet of nature would have to suffice.

When one puts this green carpet of nature's grass with verse 17, where *"the beams of our house are cedar, our rafters of fir,"* a picture emerges of the Christian community living in similar conditions to Adam and Eve in Eden's Garden. Of course there are many differences to consider.

Roman soldiers were constantly searching out this community; the weather was not always ideal. Snowstorms, rain downpours, violent winds, all caused havoc with this house. Having a constant need of shelter would generate stone shelters and dug-out caves. All this Adam and Eve missed out on.

Yet, the bride has stated that they had made their bed and now they must sleep in it. They had made a decision some days ago and this is the direct result of such a decision. Their decision, using their power of choice, to reject the papal creed and to follow the Bible and the Bible only, is taking them to the other side of the fence where the grass is greener, like it always seems to be. Yet, in this case they are willing to sleep on the green grass, wherever they can lay down their bed, as long as they have the Bridegroom powerfully close.

Parting Gem: *When you make your bed and are aware that you must sleep in it, figuratively speaking, be sure the Bridegroom is close by.*

MARCH 11 — House of Houses — Song 1:17

Today's Thought: *"The beams of our house are cedar, and our rafters of fir."*

Our drama from Song 1:9-17 and 2:1-5 is one continuous detailed description of the bride-church in the wilderness. It takes a thorough, detailed cross-referencing to describe and decode the symbols used to describe this bride, and not all symbols have been in any way fully and accurately decoded. It's another reason why it must not be taken literally as King Solomon and his favourite wife.

One of the leading doctrines of Rome is that the pope is the visible head of the universal church, that he is Deity on earth, that he demands homage of all men. The pope came to be almost universally acknowledged as the vicar of God on earth, endowed with authority over church and state. "In the sixth century the papacy had become firmly established… Now began the 1,260 years of Papal oppression foretold in the prophecies of Daniel and Revelation" (GC p. 50/54). The pope became the representative of sun worship in modern form—a blend of Christianity and sun worship, the Sunday as the Mark of her authority (Berry, Quarterly, P26).

For hundred of years, the church of Christ found refuge in seclusion and obscurity. "The woman fled into the wilderness, where she had a place prepared of God that they should feed her there a thousand and two hundred and three-score days" (GC. P 54/55). She fled into the mountains of Europe, into Switzerland, Germany, Italy, even as far away as Scotland to find safety. Please do not skip over the awesome fact that God had prepared for this church of His a place, seclusion, safety, away from the direct influence of the Papacy.

Thus we have our bride-church in a rural wilderness setting and our thought for today simply states that, *"The beams of our house are cedar, and our rafters of fir."*

Parting Gem: *Several thoughts come to my mind as I read about this place that God had prepared for His bride. Thoughts like, "Before they call, I will answer; and while they are yet speaking, I will hear" (Isaiah 65:24). What an awesome, loving God we serve.*

MARCH 12 — *Rose of Roses* — Song 2:1

Today's Thought: *"I am the rose of Sharon and the lily of the valleys."*

Isaiah 65:10 says, "And Sharon [the church] shall be a fold of flocks… a place for the herds to lie down in, for my people that have sought me."

It is implied in 1T 19 that the prophet of the Lord in her youth compared the rose of Sharon to all the beautiful creatures of God.

Although traditionally the *"rose of Sharon"* has been considered an appellation for Christ, the construction of the passage indicates this verse to be a statement of the bride, the church.

In Isaiah 35:1, the word *chabasseleth* (Hebrew for "rose") is used to picture a land that blooms again after being redeemed from its enemies. How fitting that we will blossom when we have been redeemed.

The dictionary (Vol. 8 SDABC) describes the rose as a shrub, possessing prickly stems and bearing a sweet-smelling, five-pedaled, or double-pedaled blossom prized for its beauty and its fragrance

So, what is the bride saying? "I am sweet-smelling incense; I am prized for my beauty and my fragrance. Although I have prickly characteristics, I am still sweet incense to my Beloved. I am that pasture, that fold of flocks, that place where God's people may lie down in and be safe. Yes, I may be "black" and prickly, yet I am still comely, I am still the apple of God's eye, I am still the only object upon earth that receives His supreme regards, I am the First Lady of the multiverse. I am the Rose of Sharon, the rose of all roses, the church of all churches." There is nothing else in the entire world more precious to the Beloved than His bride, the church, His jewel case containing all of His precious, valuable, unique gems, you and me.

Parting Gem: *When one considers the prickly characteristics of the rose and compares them to the same characteristics of the church, then looks at the family-cramped apartment of Rahab, that apartment that acted as a prison on the walls which were soon to crumble, remembering that Rahab was a harlot, one needs to understand that this apartment was the only safe place to be in all of Jericho. The alternative, well, we won't go down that street.*

MARCH 13   *Lily of Lilies*   Song 2:1

Today's Thought: *"I am the rose of Sharon, and the lily of the valleys."*

According to the SDA Bible Dictionary, the lily, that long-stemmed, star-like field flower we know as the lily, may be any one of many species called lily in the Bible. The lotus, tulips, anemone, autumn crocus, Turk's cap-lily, ranuncules, iris, and gladiolus may all fall within the meaning of the Hebrew and Greek word translated "lily." It was a common flower of the field, possessing a lovely fragrance and an artistic form which is copied in architecture.

Could this be one reason for the lily being used to symbolize the church? The church has so many architectural formats, from small, simple, plain structures to large magnificent cathedrals. The services range from a very simple and congregational-based form of worship where the few members are compelled to participate because of their smallness, to the large multicultural, multi-pastoral performances. From the small church that shares a pastor with several other churches to the bigger, college base churches where there are more than one pastor.

So, not only is this bride-church saying that she is a sweet-smelling, yet prickly rose, she's also saying that she is a church for all peoples with artistic and a structural worship program for all to meet the needs of people. Like the rose, this lily-of-the-valley church possesses a lovely fragrance.

Even the apostle Paul agrees and writes in 1 Corinthians 12:12, *"For as the body is one, and hath many members, and all the members of that one body, being many, are one body: so also is Christ."*

Again we notice the Hebrew poetry. If you missed it the first time around, you should get it the second time. The first time she is the rose of Sharon, and now the lily of the valley.

Parting Gem: *Many times the sweet fragrance of a flower is not noticed until it is touched (like a geranium), or picked (like mint), or crushed (like mint again), or even when the night comes on (like lady nicotine). Thus the beautiful and neat allusion to the Christian Church.*

MARCH 14 — *Apple Trees of Apple Trees* — Song 2:3,5

Today's Thought: *"As the apple tree among the trees of the wood, so is my beloved among the sons. I sat down under his shadow with great delight, and his fruit was sweet to my taste… Stay me with flagons, comfort me with apples: for I am sick of love."*

God found Jacob in a desert land, in a waste howling wilderness, led him about, instructed him, kept him as the *"apple of his eye"* (Deuteronomy 32:10).

"A word fitly spoken is like apples of gold in pictures of silver" (Proverbs 25:11).

Support me, comfort me with Thy holy law as well as with good encouraging words, words which build up, support, lift up, feed me.

"By contemplation of God's matchless love, we take upon us His nature. Christ was a representative before men and before angels, of the character of the God of heaven. He demonstrated the fact that when humanity depends wholly upon God, men may keep God's commandments and live, His law will be as the apple of His eye" (TM 226:2).

The command of Christ is of the highest importance and should be strictly obeyed. It is like apples of gold in pictures of silver (4T 310:1).

Our bride requests that she be steadied, held up, guided with flagons or "a cake of raisons" (SDABC) and to be comforted with "apples." The Law of God is as a rock in a stormy situation, as an anchor to the soul, as a light shining from the lighthouse, to direct the ways of man. This is the request of the bride.

God has His measurement of character, those who obey Him that live, who keep His law as the apple of their eye that He preserves (Ev. 244:1).

As our day goes onward from here, may we speak words of comfort, patience, and love, so that we may support and build up those that are our significant others, as well as the stranger that is within our gates.

Parting Gem: *Here are some neat words that will boggle your mind. They are found in* In Heavenly Places: *"Those who believe on Christ and obey His commandments… who rely of His keeping power… who resists temptation and… copies the pattern given… will through faith in the atoning sacrifice become partakers of the divine nature… Every one who by faith obeys God's commandments will reach the condition of sinlessness in which Adam lived before his transgression" (IHP 146).*

March 15 — Thorn of Thorns — Song 2:2

Today's Thought: *"As the lily among thorns, so is my love among the daughters."*

I have been told many times in growing up that the Bible doesn't hide the bad and negative experiences and characteristic traits of a person, giving only the good and positive. So we see that today.

Both the rose and the lily are being portrayed as the bride-church. The rose has thorns connected with it. The church has thorns among its members, or as the Gospels calls them, "tares." That's one thing that makes the church so developmentally friendly. Should you allow these thorns to dig you, bite you, hurt you, then that's one experience. Should you allow these thorns to develop character in you, then that's altogether a newer and brighter experience for you.

Another way of looking at these thorns is that the lily, the bride-church, is among much persecution. This lily in its white purity and beauty is under tremendous persecution. It stays, however, in its purity and comeliness. Now, not all lilies are pure white; some are streaked with pinks and reds, which could indicate the persecution the church is undergoing.

Thorns, and thistles, symbolically represent annoyances, infirmities, spiritual obstacles (SDA Dictionary, Thorns). Do we have here a picture of a pure church complete with the many annoyances, infirmities, hardships, obstacles, and whatever else you wish to put in there, including the persecutions and constant harassments of the papal powers? Yet, remember she states that *"I am comely."*

As the "lily among thorns" versus the "apple tree among the trees of the woods," that is my Beloved among the sons.

Parting Gem: *It's neat to remember that these thorns will be gathered up and burned at the very end of time. Therefore, we will have no more annoyances, no more infirmities, no more hardships, nor obstacles, even persecutions. What a day, think on these things.*

MARCH 16 — *Beloved of Beloved #1* — Song 2:3

Today's Thought: *"As the apple tree among the trees of the wood, so is my beloved among the sons."*

In our Song, please notice that our bride-church is very eager to talk about her Beloved, about how He belongs to her and she belongs to Him. She seems to take every opportunity she can get to boast, brag, and proclaim their love for each other. Did not our Friend Jesus do this, take every opportunity He could to tell everyone of His Father and how His Father loved them?

An apple and an apple tree appears to be the ultimate in fruits and trees. Among all of the other trees in the forest, they do not bear edible fruit, whereas the apple tree does bear edible fruit. We, His children, are the "apple of His eye." Notice, it does not say that we are the "orange" of his eye or the "banana" of His eye, but the "apple of His eye," So the apple has a favoured place in God's fruit.

The very same thing goes for the bride's relationship to her Beloved. Of all the trees in the forest, of all the fruit in the orchard, the apple holds the highest, the mostest of the most, the position of positions as far as the bride is concerned. How is it with you, Reader?

Let's go to that time when Christ asked His disciples who men were saying He was. Peter, bold, upfront Peter, blurts out that they said Jesus was a prophet risen from the dead. When Christ wanted to know who they, His disciples, thought He was, again Peter blurted out, and rightly so, *"Thou art the Christ, the son of the living God"* (Matthew 16:16).

When many of His disciples were leaving Him for not fulfilling their tremendous wish to be free from the Romans, Christ asked His disciples, *"Will ye also go away?"* (John 6:67) Again, our friend Peter blurts out, without any thinking on his part because Christ meant so much to Peter, *"To whom shall we go? Thou hast the words of eternal life"* (John 6:68).

When one considers the many things one receives by being a follower of Christ, where else can one go? He is the Bread and Living Water of life, He is Life itself, and that's eternal life. He is the Resurrection, the Great I AM, He is the One altogether lovely.

Parting Gem: *Meet Him today at your every turn and in all of your conversations. Feast on this Beloved of all beloveds.*

MARCH 17　　　　　*Shadow of Shadows*　　　　　Song 2:3

Today's Thought: *"I sat down under his shadow with great delight, and his fruit was sweet to my taste."*

Let us look at some verses, such as Psalms 17:8, *"Keep me as the apple of the eye, hide me under the shadow of thy wings."*
Psalms 91:1 says, *"He that dwellest in the secret place of the most High shall abide under the shadow of the Almighty."*
Psalms 121:5 says, *"The Lord is thy keeper; the Lord is thy shade upon thy right hand."*
Isaiah 4:5-6 says, *"And the Lord will create upon every dwelling place of mount Zion, and upon her assemblies, a cloud and smoke by day, and the shining of a flaming fire by night: for upon all the glory shall be a defence. And there shall be a tabernacle for a shadow in the daytime from the heat, and for a place of refuge, and for a covert from storm and from rain."*
Isaiah 25:4-5 says, *"For thou hast been a strength to the poor, a strength to the needy in his distress, a refuge from the storm, a shadow from the heat, when the blast of the terrible ones is as a storm against the wall. Thou shalt bring down the noise of strangers, as a heat in a dry place; even the heat with the shadow of a cloud: the branch of the terrible ones shall be brought low."*
Isaiah 32:2 says, *"And a man shall be as an hiding place from the wind, and a covert [concealed, secret hiding place] from the tempest; as rivers of water in a dry place, as the shadow of a great rock in a weary land."*
Isaiah 49:2 says, *"In the shadow of his hand hath he hid me…"*
Isaiah 51:16 says, *"And I have… covered thee in the shadow of mine hand…"*
Hosea 14:7 says, *"They that dwell under his shadow shall return… revive… grow…"*
We get this picture of our bride-church, there in the wilderness prepared for her. She sits in the shadow, the protection of her Lover, unafraid, enjoying the benefits of being who she is, the apple of His eye.

Parting Gem: Hymn #303 of the S.D.A. Church Hymnal has taken some of these ideas, *"Beneath the cross of Jesus, I fain would take my stand. The shadow of a mighty rock, within a weary land; A home within the wilderness, a rest upon the way, From the burning of the noon-tide heat, and the burden of the day."* It would be great if today we would spend more time under the shadow of the Almighty.

MARCH 18 — *Taste of Tastes* — Song 2:3

Today's Thought: *"I sat down under his shadow with great delight, and his fruit was sweet to my taste."*

There are several texts pertaining to taste, but the best known one is probable found in Psalms 34:8, *"O taste and see that the Lord is good."* That would be a wise experience for us today. Peter expresses a similar thought in 1 Peter 2:3, *"Like newborn babes, long for the pure spiritual milk, that by it you may grow up to salvation; for you have tasted the kindness of the Lord"* (RSV).

Psalms 119:103 states, *"How sweet are thy words unto my taste! Yea, sweeter than honey to my mouth!"*

Jeremiah 15:16 says, *"Thy words were found, and I did eat them; and thy words was unto me the joy and rejoicing of mine heart: for I am called by thy name, O Lord God of hosts."*

Coming in from a different angle, we read in John 8:51-52, *"Verily, verily, I say unto you, If a man keep my sayings, he shall never see death. Then said the Jews unto him, Now we know that thou hast a devil… thou sayest, If a man keep my sayings, he shall never taste of death."*

Try to picture in your mind being under the shadow or protection of the apple tree symbolized as Jehovah God, your Beloved, and enjoying the fruit of His attention and protection. The fruit, benefits, are sweet to your taste.

The benefits of sitting under the protection of the Beloved are so very numerous. One can have his sins forgiven, cast into the depth of the sea, thrown behind God's back, covered over as a thick, black cloud, wiped out, thrown as far as the east is from the west. That's a powerfully sweet taste. It results in freedom from guilt and shame.

Then there is the benefit of never dying. That's living forever, which again is a tremendously long time. Enjoying the benefits of heaven with one's best Friend is nothing to sneeze at, either.

Parting Gem: *Pause throughout today to ponder the many benefits you will receive when you slow down and gather under the apple tree to bask in its shade. You'll no doubt find that the Lord is good and greatly to be praised.*

MARCH 19   *Banquet House of Banquet Houses*   Song 2:4

Today's Thought: *"He brought me to the banqueting house, and his banner over me was love."*

I know we all know what a banquet or a banqueting house or hall is, yet let me run this idea past you. A banquet is a feast, a dinner, a meal, a repast, a revel or a treat. Then again, a revel is to enjoy, to bask in, delight in, gloat about, indulge in, lap up, luxuriate in, rejoice over, savour, take pleasure in, to celebrate, to make merry, and a whole lot more. The picture wanting to be portrayed here is that in that banquet hall, all of the above verbs apply. So, Friend, gloat in it and lap it up.

Verses 3 and 4 have one of those Pass #1, Pass #2 arrangements. Should you miss the first pass, the second one is there. Notice Pass #1 in verse 3, *"I sat down under his shadow with great delight, and his fruit was sweet to my taste."*

Pass #2 reads, *"He brought me to the banqueting house [where I sat down under his shadow], and his banner over me was love [where his fruit was sweet to my taste]."* This is Hebrew poetry, maybe even at its best. Ever wonder why?

Allow me to take a short detour to explain one reason why in Hebrew poetry they repeat things in two passes. I found the answer in Genesis 41:32, *"And for that the dream was doubled unto Pharaoh twice; it is because the thing is established by God, and God will shortly bring it to pass."* Is that not awesome to you? He wishes to establish the fact that when He says something, He means it and it will come to pass.

In case you're wondering about today, we say the same thing and mean the same thing. "You can say that again."

Starting with verses 1 and 2, where this church is the rose of Sharon and the lily of the valleys, then having the tree of trees, the apple tree to feast on, the bride is brought into the banquet room where all manner of fruits are, all manner of love, hope, assurance, wines of doctrines, meat and milk to feast on. This is a banquet one can feast on every Sabbath at church.

Parting Gem: *Yet, as good as this banquet is, the one I'm going to enjoy as I sit down at my nameplate will be the Marriage Supper of the Lamb. What a banquet. You are invited to join me.*

MARCH 20 — *Banner of Banners* — Song 2:4

Today's Thought: *"He brought me to the banqueting house, and his banner over me was love."*

There are only two camps in which you can pitch your tabernacle. One is in the violent, unruly camp of the arch-enemy. The other is in the camp where the blood-stained banner of Prince Emmanuel flies.

That banner soaked in blood brings victory. Period. End of discussion. The first banner, that of Satan, brings... well, we won't go down that road today.

A banner is a standard, such as an ensign or a flag, under which one marched as in a parade or to a war. It was something identifiable with those who marched under that banner.

This banner which is over the bride is LOVE. Now understand that love can be a tremendous good thing, as well as an utterly tremendous nebulous thing. It is powerful, as one would find out by reading 1 Corinthians 13, which would help us a great bit if we would also read that on a daily basis.

Love, this banner over the bride-church, is the topic for discussion, of scholars and illiterate alike, of saints, throughout eternity, which they tell me is a powerful long time. How is it that Christ suffered, not only and just on the cross, not for those three and a half years in ministry, nor the thirty-three years of earthly life, but from eternity in the past for some gobs of clay called mankind? What an awesome God; don't you just love Him?

This banner of love over the bride kept the bride fully aware that she was and is the most valuable piece of real estate in the multiverse. That should be our prayer of thanks that over you and me is this blood-stained banner of Prince Emmanuel.

Parting Gem: *We have been admonished in the book* Desire of Ages[5] *that it would be well for us if we would spend a thoughtful hour each and every day contemplating the life of Christ. Especially is this true when it comes to the closing scenes of His life. Should we do this, one would come away from those scenes with a tremendous burden, which is a theme of a speech or the chorus of a song. What an awesome burden.*

---

[5] White, E.G. *Desire of Ages* (Nampa, ID: Pacific Press), 2005. *Desire of Ages* is a book covering the gospels, emphasizing the life of Jesus Christ, who is the Desire of Ages.

MARCH 21 — Flagon of Flagons — Song 2:5

Today's Thought: *"Stay me with flagons, comfort me with apples: for I am sick of love."*

To "stay" is to remain, hang around, stand by, yet also it means to support, reinforce, brace, or fortress.

A flagon is a vessel for liquors, with a handle and a spout, as well as the contents within.

Our bride, then, is requesting that she be steadied, supported, reinforced with wines and liquors; as well she is requesting that she not be left alone but that she have someone stand by her, and hang around. Wine symbolizes doctrines. In these mountain recesses, they have had and continue to have the breast milk of the Word; they also have the meat of the Word in the roes and the hinds. Now she is requesting the deeper theological aspects of the wine, those doctrines upfront in the Bible. This gives them an understanding of their belief system.

She also requests that she be comforted with apples, no doubt from the apples tree of verse 3. She needs to be supported by all aspects of God's Word, the thoughtful hour each day contemplating the life of Christ, the in-depth analysis of the character of her Beloved.

She needs this support, this reinforcement, and this comfort because she is waiting for the return of her Beloved, which seems a long way off. This causes, in turn, her love sickness.

She desires to claim Jeremiah 15:16, *"Thy words were found, and I did eat them; and thy word was unto me the joy and the rejoicing of mine heart: for I am called by thy name, O Lord God of hosts."*

This bride in the mountain crevasses knew that "no other Book is so potent to elevate the thoughts, to give vigour to the faculties, as the broad ennobling truths of the Bible." She knew that "if the Bible was studied as it should be studied, she would have a breadth of mind, a nobility of character, and a stability of purpose that is rarely seen in any day" (ST). Thus she makes this serious request.

Parting Gem: *"Thy word have I hid in mine heart, that I might not sin against thee… Open thou mine eyes, that I may behold wondrous things out of thy law." (Psalms 119:11,18)*

MARCH 22 — *Apple of Apples* — Song 2:5

Today's Thought: *"Stay me with flagons, comfort me with apples: for I am sick of love."*

Proverbs 25:11 says, *"A word fitly spoken is like apples of gold in pictures of silver."* So, Friend of mine, what does it mean to have apples of gold in pictures of silver? Notice the word "pictures;" it does not say "pitchers of silver."

Stay me, support me, comfort me with the holy law as well as with good encouraging words, words that build up, support, lift me up.

"The command of Christ is of the highest importance and should be strictly obeyed. It is like apples of gold in pictures of silver" (4T 310:1)

In TM 226, we read, "By contemplation of God's matchless love, we take upon us His nature. Christ was a representative before men and before angels, of the character of the God of heaven. He demonstrated the fact that when humanity depends wholly upon God, men may keep God's commandments and live, and His law be as the apple of the eye."

We know that the eye is one of the most sensitive and most vulnerable parts of the body. It needs protection. The eye reflects what it sees. When God looks at us, He sees in His eye our reflection.

We also know that the apple is one of earth's superior fruits (CD 312). We have all heard the saying that "an apple a day keeps the doctor away." Why is it always an apple and not a banana or peach or pear, grapefruit or orange? Why always the apple? Ponder this question as you go about your daily activities today. See if you can come up with a reasonable answer. Why always the apple?

Parting Gem: *May the Lord find us in our desert land and waste-howling wilderness. May He lead us about, instruct us, and keep us as the apple of His eye, deemed to be the most highly protected part of the human body.*

MARCH 23 — *Comfort of Comforts* — Song 2:5

Today's Thought: *"Stay me with flagons, comfort me with apples: for I am sick of love."*

Stay me, or steady me. Solidify my stand and doctrine with flagon, the wine of prophecies. Throughout the 1,260 years of papal domination, I have enjoyed the sincere milk of the Word from the breast of the Old and the New Testament; I have eaten the meat of the Word from the twins fawns, the roes and the hinds, and now it is time to dig much deeper into the prophecies, into the heavy doctrines of the wine of God's Word. I want to squeeze the sweet juice from the rich clusters of grapes to get all of the prophecies possible. I need to know just where we stand in the stream of church history, and just how close is the time for my Beloved to come.

I wish to be comforted with the precious promises of my Beloved's return, to know the signs of His nearing. Comfort me with the fruits of righteousness, for I am sick of love. I'm sick just waiting for my Beloved to come bounding over the mountains to claim me as His bride.

Yes, I know that He, my Beloved, supports me, that He is constantly near me, and that I can rely on Him to wrap His arms around me. I need that comfortable assurance, and I get it from these flagons, as well as the elementary facets of salvation in the breast. Then also, I know I get support and comfort from the meat of His Word, and now that I'm really interested in studying God's Word as far as the prophecies are concerned, I wish for my faith to be realistic. I need to reaffirm my decision to come way up here in these mountains to get away from the papal authorities who try to get me to choose that "other beloved."

So, as I think of all that is happening and where I am, I get comfort from knowing that my Beloved's arms are wrapped around me. I can lean on His broad shoulders.

Parting Gem: *What an awesome God we serve. Don't you just love Him? There are various ways the Scriptures tell us that our God lives and is very near to us. Here, His arms support us and embrace us. For today, rest assuredly in His arm, and stop now and again to contemplate His Presence.*

MARCH 24 — *Lovesick of Lovesicks* — Song 2:5

Today's Thought: *"Stay me with flagons, comfort me with apples: for I am sick of love."*

This looks like one of those capsules we mentioned. This one starts with, *"for I am sick of love,"* as above. It ends at 5:8, after the great disappointment. *"I charge you, O daughters of Jerusalem, if ye find my beloved, that ye tell him, that I am sick of love."*

This first utterance of "Lovesickness" is when the church was in the wilderness. They were tired, homesick for heaven, could hardly wait for this drastic 1,260 year period of papal supremacy to close. They felt that they needed to have a shoulder to cry on. They needed comfort, they needed to be steadied in faith or doctrines or even in perseverance. Have you ever felt that way?

I believe it would be hard, but put yourself in the place of one of the saints, one of the believers up in the mountains. Your home is not sure, neither your food nor safety. You are constantly on the lookout for the papal authorities, the Roman armies, the enemies of your Beloved that continually harass you. How would you feel?

There are times in life when death looks very inviting. Being in those mountains may very well have been one of those times. Yet, you must hold the fort, the torch, the faith, to pass it on to your children, but O how you long and hunger for these 1,260 years to be finished. You want to go home. Do you, by the way, feel that way as you read this? Do you feel that you are homesick for heaven?

Yet, as great as that feeling is that you have, there is One who has a heavier, stronger, hungrier desire for His children. We've looked at that hunger several times. It is a indescribable ache in the heart. I might add that it has been there for a mighty long time; it is not going away but is getting stronger and more urgent as time moves onward.

Parting Gem: *Try to contemplate as you go about your day that there is One who has a tremendous hunger, a passion, even a desire for His children to be with Him where He is.*

MARCH 25 — Right Hand of Right Hands — Song 2:6

Today's Thought: *"His left hand is under my head, and his right doth embrace me."*

After declaring, *"I am sick of love,"* lovesick just waiting for my Beloved to come, she realizes that her Beloved, through His various agencies, is supporting her. There are a large number of texts where this support is prevalent.

Deuteronomy 26:8 says, *"And the Lord brought us forth out of Egypt with a mighty hand, and with an outstretched arm, and with great terribleness, and with signs, and with wonders."*

Jeremiah 21:5 says, *"And I myself will fight against you [the king of Babylon] with an outstretched hand and with a strong arm, even in anger, and in fury, and in great wrath."*

Nehemiah 1:10 says, *"Now these are thy servants and thy people, whom thou hast redeemed by thy great power, and by thy strong hand."*

Exodus 6:6 says, *"Wherefore say unto the children of Israel, I am the Lord, and I will bring you out from the burdens of the Egyptians, and I will rid you out of their bondage, and I will redeem you with a stretched out arm, and with great judgments."*

Jeremiah 32:17 and 21 says, *"Ah Lord God! behold, thou hast made the heaven and the earth by thy great power and stretched out arm, and there is nothing too hard for thee... And hast brought forth thy people Israel out of the land of Egypt with signs, and with wonders, and with a strong hand, and with a stretched out arm, and with great terror."*

Psalms 37:24 says, *"Though he fall, he shall not be utterly cast down: for the Lord upholdeth him with his hand."*

Do you get the point that we need to get?

Parting Gem: *Thus we have a picture of a mighty God, her Beloved, supporting her, comforting her, protecting her during this long 1,260 year period. Her confidence in His ability and willingness to do this is very evident. Now, today, let us apply that to ourselves. Are we as confident as the bride-church is that our Beloved has us wrapped around Him, that His arms support us? As you go about your excitement today, stop now and again and request your Beloved to engulf you in His arms.*

MARCH 26 — *Embrace of Embraces #1* — Song 2:6

Today's Thought: *"His left hand is under my head, and his right hand doth embrace me."*

Talk about an embrace. The Scriptures are full of such embracing experiences. Read Joshua 1 to find out how Joshua was embraced. *"Have not I commanded thee? Be strong and of a good courage; be not afraid, neither be thou dismayed: for the Lord thy God is with thee whithersoever thou goest"* (Joshua 1:9).

"I will never leave thee, not forsake thee. So that we may boldly say, The Lord is my helper, and I will not fear what man shall do unto me" (Hebrews 13:5-6).

"Submit yourselves therefore to God. Resist the devil, and he will flee from you. Draw nigh to God, and he will draw nigh to you" (James 4:7-8).

"I have set the Lord always before me: because he is at my right hand, I shall not be moved" (Psalms 16:8).

Remember that we are in discussion over the bride-church, so these passages apply to her, this bride-church, this apple of God's eye, this jewel case containing all of His precious jewels and gems. In the wilderness for such a long time, this bride, who realizes that she is the rose of Sharon as well as the lily of the valley, still requests that she be supported and comforted. This is something each one of us need to realize in our daily walk with our Beloved. Our thought for today is an answer, her answer, her realization to her need. She fully realizes that He supports her in the wilderness, and that He wraps His loving arms around her.

Is it possible that should we really realize that His right arm is under our head, where our decisions are made, and His left hand embraces us, a token of His acceptance, that we would be better prepared to handle the day's activities and our mental state would be firmer?

Parting Gem: *David wrote in Psalms 107 several times, "Then they cried, he saved them." Does that sound like the Lord is close by, ready with His right hand to support your head and His left hand to wrap around you arms of love? Does it seem that even when you "rebel," He is still there with His right and left hand? Think in these lines.*

MARCH 27　　　*Embrace of Embraces #2*　　　Song 2:6

Today's Thought: *"His left hand is under my head, and his right hand doth embrace me."*

Here is the beginning of one of those capsules within capsules previously mentioned. The other end of this capsule is in Song 8:3. The next text following both of these capsule ends is a charge: *"I charge you, O ye daughters of Jerusalem… that ye stir not up, nor awake my love, till he pleases"* (Song 2:7). Notice that *"the roes, and the hinds of the field"* are not in the end of the capsule.

This first part of the capsule is in the wilderness, just before the breaking of the Reformation when she was told to *"rise up… and come away"* (Song 2:10). The end of the capsule is near the end of the drama, which means, to me, that the Beloved has had his left hand under our heads all the time and His right hand has always been embracing us.

Talk about protection! We are in the hollow of His hands, and that is tremendous protection. Revelation 1:16 states, *"And he had in his right hand seven stars…"* These seven stars are the seven churches of Asia, and He has them cupped securely in His right hand. The right hand, or right side in ancient Israel, was a position of safety and approval.

Looking at Psalms 18:35, *"Thou hast also given to me the shield of thy salvation: and thy right hand hath holden me up, and thy gentleness hath made me great."* Let's look at the next text, verse 36: *"Thou hast enlarged my steps under me, that my feet did not slip."* This is tremendous assurance that we are protected and cared for; the bride-church was fully aware of this embrace and she expresses it several times in several different ways.

2 Samuel 22:2, *"The Lord is my rock, and my fortress, and my deliverer."* Acts 2:25 quotes from Psalm 16:8, which says, *"I have set the Lord always before me: because he is at my right hand, I shall not be moved."*

Contemplate what it means to be in His embrace today.

Parting Gem: *So, Friend of Mine, what is the Lord to you? To our bride, He is a support always there, a rock, a tower, a Shepherd of the sheepfold, with His left hand under her head and His right hand embracing her.*

MARCH 28 — *Charge of Charges #2* — Song 2:7

Today's Thought: *"I charge you… by the roes, and by the hinds,,, that ye stir not up, nor awake my love, till he please."*

This charge is given to the church during the 1,260 years of their mountain retreat, from AD 538 to AD 1563, during the Thyatira Church period. It is the first of three charges before the last and final charge.

In Matthew 25:13, Christ speaks in the parable of the ten virgins, *"Watch therefore, for ye know neither the day nor the hour wherein the Son of man cometh."*

In Matthew 24:4-5, it says, *"Take heed that no man deceive you, for many shall come in my name, saying, I am Christ; and shall deceive many."*

In verse 26, He again cautions us, *"Wherefore if they shall say unto you, Behold, he is in the desert; go not forth: behold, he is in the secret chambers; believe it not."*

Verse 36 says, *"But of that day and hour knoweth no man, no, not the angels of heaven, but my Father only."*

Verse 42 states, *"Watch therefore: for ye know not what hour your Lord doth come."*

Verse 44 says, *"Therefore be ye also ready: for in such an hour as ye think not the Son of man cometh."*

The second coming of Jesus has been the "blessed hope" of the church of all ages. The church of the Dark Ages, suffering centuries of persecution, longed and prayed for His coming and deliverance. But, according to the time prophecies, the church was to remain in the wilderness for 1,260 years.

"I charge you…" A charge is an official admonition, as issued from a court. God's official communication to man is through His Holy Word, the Bible.

"By the roes, and by the hinds… that ye stir not up, nor awake my love, till he please." Look at the Old Testament and the New Testament, look at Daniel and Revelation, and you will see that it is not yet time for my Beloved to arise and gather me, His bride, home.

Parting Gem: *When the fullness of the time arrives, it will be time for my Beloved to come. Keep that in mind.*

MARCH 29 *Roe of Roes #1* Song 2:7

Today's Thought: *"I charge you, O ye daughters of Jerusalem, by the roes, and by the hinds... that ye stir not up, not awake my love, till he please."*

Taking another piece of this enigma puzzle, we have the roes and the hinds of the field. We will come across these two animals several times in our drama of the song, so let us put one or two more pieces of this puzzle into place.

In John 1:1 and 14, it says, *"In the beginning was the Word, and the Word was with God, and the Word was God... and the Word was made flesh, and dwelt among us."* A clear identification of the Word is given—Jesus.

In John 6:35 and 51, Christ is identified not only as the Bread of Life, but the Living Bread, whereas in 4:10-15, He tells the woman at the well that He is the Living Waters that removes all thirst.

1 Corinthians 3:2 states, *"I have fed you with milk, and not with meat."* Peter tells us to desire the sincere milk of the Word, especially as a newborn babe in Christ. This, in our drama, is spoken of some eight times as the breast of the woman.

Here now, in our song, we encounter the meat of the word spoken of in 1 Corinthians 3:2, *"I have fed you with milk, and not with meat: for hitherto ye were not able to bear it."* And John 6:27 and 55 says, *"Labour not for the meat which perisheth, but for that meat which endureth unto everlasting life... For my flesh is meat indeed, my blood is drink indeed."*

Isaiah 55:1 and Matthew 20:1-16 speak figuratively of wine and milk as the word that you may grow thereby.

When we come to Song 2:9, *"My beloved is like a roe or a young hart,"* there is a clearer picture of Jesus as the Word, leaping across the mountain tops, skipping over the hills. The word of God spoken figuratively as roes and hinds give us the Old Testament, specifically Daniel, and the New Testament, specifically Revelation in the New Testament. It is these two books that outline most perfectly the settings in which the Bridegroom can come.

Parting Gem: *The progression of growth for a child of God is spelled out. First the milk of the Word, then the meat and potatoes of the Word, and finally the heavier prophecies of wine, as in roes and hinds.*

MARCH 30 — *Stirring of Stirrings* — Song 2:7

Today's Thought: *"I charge you, O ye daughters of Jerusalem… that ye stir not up, nor awake my love, till he please."*

There are a few phrases in Scripture used to indicate a coming to power or an awakening. Michael will stand up to deliver His people (Daniel 12:2). The most exciting is in Daniel 11:44, *"But tidings out of the east and out of the north shall trouble him."*

2 Timothy 1:6 says, *"Wherefore I put thee in remembrance that thou stir up the gift of God."* Similarly, 2 Peter 1:13 states, *"Yea, I think it meet, as long as I am in this tabernacle, to stir you up by putting you in remembrance."*

To stir means to mix or agitate, or arise, get moving, or hasten, according to the thesaurus. Here the bride is saying very clearly not to agitate or stir up the idea of the coming of the Bridegroom. There are still many years of our sojourn here in the wilderness. We cannot expect Him to come until after the 1,260 years are over in 1798. After that time, yes.

According to the prophecies of both Daniel and Revelation, as well as other Scripture, no one knows the day nor the hour. This hope of the second coming of Jesus Christ has been the hope of God's people since He ascended on Mount Olive.

A major stirring took place between 1833 and 1844, as will be expressed in our drama in Song 5. It has been proclaimed by numerous denominations, by numerous peoples down through the ages. Yet, this verse and similar ones in our drama state that at this time, while the church is hiding in the wilderness, please do not get excited about His near coming, because it is not yet time for Him to come.

Parting Gem: *This phrase is a recurring one. At various periods in church history, the 1,260 year sojourn in the wilderness, the 1844 period, the Investigative Judgment period, all say the same thing. The last charge is much different, however. So remember that the best is yet to come.*

MARCH 31 — *Summary* — Song 2:8-3:5

- March brought to us to the first description of our bride-church; this was during the 1,260 year sojourn in the wilderness. This was Act 1, Scene 4, the Thyratira Church period, AD 538 until AD 1563, when the Reformation started.
- Again, we wish to emphasize that this is all symbolic language written here. No young lady, or older one either, would feel that she has been complimented if her lover should use these words to describe her beauty.
- Both 1:8 and 15 speak of *"My beloved, my fairest of the fair."* A very simple expression of love for the bride. Watch them grow throughout the year.
- Her strength and beauty are mentioned after she has been swept, like Pharaoh, into the wilderness. Her cheeks, symbolic of her sufferings and persecutions due to her stand on her Beloved, are mentioned. Don't miss this point. This is a suffering church, fleeing her persecutors who are relentless in her destruction.
- A brief description of the rocky building erected for shelter is given. They are made out of whatever they had, which was not a whole lot.
- In a very simple and quiet way. she states that she, the church, is the lily of the valleys, as well as the rose of Sharon, that prickly sweet-smelling flower of the field. Yes, it does have some thorny characteristics, but she is safe to abide in it. During Noah's time, there was only one safe place, and that was in the smelly, cramped, noisy, fowl-aired place called the ark. The alternative was something else. Should you not like Noah's example, consider Rahab and her on-the-wall apartment. That was the only safe place. It, too, was crowded, very restricted, under strict orders, but again, should you consider the alternative, that also was something else.
- During these 1,260 years, the bride knew that she was supported, comforted, fed, protected by her Lover. Yes, she very well may have been home-sick for heaven, but she was well aware that her Beloved was not due to come for many years. She informed us by the prophecies of Daniel and Revelation, the Old Testament and the New Testament, not to push his coming by setting dates. When the fullness of the time is come, He'll come.

Between the Plough and the Altar
(Ministry of Healing 502:5)

There stands the bullock, strong, massive, muscular,
    With his feet firmly planted on the turf, his shaggy head down.
He's muzzling for the green growth beneath him,
    Simply doing the duty that lies closest at hand, grazing.
He's eager, very fully charged with desire, great with passive haste.

Off to one side is the plough, sharp, shiny, new.
    Ready to bit deep into the prairie sod, to turn virgin turf, expose it to the skies.
Ready to expand the homestead bread basket, the growing tasks, the endless chores.
    Ready, waiting, just waiting for a bullock to take its place,
In front, between the traces.

Off close to another side lies an altar,
    freshly erected, stately constructed, yet simple in design.
Ready to receive its daily sacrifice, the morning oblation, noting the act of surrender.
    Ready, in all of its splendour, to proclaim to the world, to angels and to men, its greatest gift.
Ready, waiting, just waiting for the bullock to take its place, on top, amidst the flames.

There stands the Christian, man, woman, growing child.
    Deep in thought, in contemplation, with perplexed anticipation.
Listening for the call of duty, of sacrifice, of surrender for a mighty cause.
    Deaf to the lure of wealth, of power, of worldly fame, there is a pause.

To one side he sees the plough, to the other he sees the altar.
    He is ready, ready to venture out, explore and expand for the mighty cause of God.
Ready to bit deep into heathenism, erect churches, find God's children.
    Ready to call the youth to service, to show to them the plough, the altar.

Ready, too, to take his place beside the bench, the scaffold, the engine.
    Ready to pound nails, turn wrenches, yes, even to plough fields.
Like the bullock between the plough and the altar, he too is ready.
    Ready for the joy of the plough, the heat of the altar, be what they may, but ready for both.

The Vine That's True
(DA 675:2)

On the gorgeous hills of Palestine, a goodly vine was sowed.
    Planted by the heavenly One, the Husbandman of old.
Its beauty was attractive to the common passer-by,
    Its origin was well declared that its roots were from on high.

Yet this goodly vine was misconceived, like a root from ground that's dry.
    Unholy feet upon it stamped each time they passed it by.
The Husbandman lost not His sight of this plant they wished to kill,
    But took the plant and placed it o'er the wall beside the hill.

No longer there to stamp and crush, but hidden from their view,
    This vine draped fruit up o'er the wall, fruit luscious, fresh and new.
I saw this vine climb o'er the wall, a vine of awesome sight.
    Its branches laden down with fruit, rich clusters full and bright.

Once more I thought within my mind, once more I chose to pick.
    This fruit I thought, would give to me much grace and power to lick,
That enemy with all his woes and all his wily darts.
    Then as I looked upon that fruit I longed within my heart,

To pick that precious fruit of love, of joy and peace,
    Of charity and patient trust thus all His joy release.
I wish to leave to every mind an influence to save,
    Cling to that Vine, that Vine that's true, the One He freely gave.

In the Morning

In the morning it is quiet,
    much less rushed,
        and I am fresh.

It's a time I meet my Saviour,
    plan my day,
        so He can bless.

Through the day I've many duties,
    things to do,
        and I get tired.

Through the day there are these chances,
    nerves get frayed,
        And I come unwired.

It's a time to stop and ponder,
    for I'm pushed,
        my nerves get frayed.

When I meet my God each morning,
    things go well,
        I'm glad I prayed.

April

April's Introduction and Aim

This month of April will cover Song 2:8-3:5.

Song 2:8-2:17 depicts the beginning and growth period of the Protestant Reformation from AD 1563, when the Reformation started, to AD 1798, during the Sardis church period when the church came out of the wilderness. This is found in Revelation 3:1-3:6

Song 3:1-3:5 will cover the period after AD 1798, when the church came out of the wilderness to start the Great Religious Awakening. This would be the Philadelphia Church period, AD 1798 to AD 1844. This is found in Revelation 3:7-3:18.

We will look at how the Bible depicts a blurred vision, how we can't quite see everything as we would like. The Reformation is pictured in a springtime, so look closely at the symbolism. Try to see the big picture. We will meet the beginner of the Reformation, John Wycliffe, as the Morning Star of the Reformation, which he is deemed to be. This indicates that there will be more stars appearing, and there were.

It is hoped that you catch the confidence of our bride-church as she screams out across the stage of her time that which she repeatedly screams out. You can easily make this your favourite hymn, #511, titled "I Know Whom I Have Believed."

We are going to meet briefly the ministers and leaders of the nominal Christian churches, but just briefly, because she doesn't spend a whole lot of time after she found her Beloved.

We will spend three days listening to our bride declare not to expect Christ to come during her time in history, which causes a question to appear. What would have happened if the Millerites had know of this verse, or the three verses? But then again, this book is a mystery kept secret until it had reached its fullness of time.

Of course, your assignment for the month of April is to read the entire 117 verses of this drama again, especially in one sitting the April coverage of 2:8-3:5. Our reading for April covers Act 1, Scene 5.

Extra reading to go with this portion can be found in *The Great Controversy*, Chapters 4 through 15. The regular reading assignment is Song of Songs 2:8-3:5, as well as Revelation 3:1-3:6, the Sardis Church.

APRIL

Day 1	Awakening of Awakenings #1	Song 2:8	113
Day 2	Voice of Voices #1	Song 2:8	114
Day 3	Roe of Roes #2	Song 2:9	115
Day 4	Wall of Walls #1	Song 2:9	116
Day 5	Lattice of Lattices	Song 2:9	117
Day 6	Springtime of Springtimes	Song 2:10-13	118
Day 7	Hiding of Hidings	Song 2:14	119
Day 8	Fox of Foxes	Song 2:15	120
Day 9	Intrigue of Intrigues	Song 2:13,15	121
Day 10	Morning Star of Morning Stars	Revelation 2:28	122
Day 11	Confidence of Confidences #1	Song 2:16	123
Day 12	Retreat of Retreats	Song 2:17	124
Day 13	Movement of Movements	Song 2:17	125
Day 14	Stupor of Stupors	Song 3:1	126
Day 15	Alarm of Alarms	Song 3:1	127
Day 16	Conclusion of Conclusions	Song 3:1	128
Day 17	City of Cities	Song 3:2	129
Day 18	Failure of Failures	Song 3:2	130
Day 19	Watchman of Watchmen	Song 3:3	131
Day 20	Token of Tokens	Song 3:3	132
Day 21	Study of Studies	Song 3:4	133
Day 22	Passing of Passings	Song 3:4	134
Day 23	Success of Successes	Song 3:4	135
Day 24	Holding of Holdings	Song 3:4	136
Day 25	Chamber of Chambers	Song 3:4	137
Day 26	Finding of Findings	Song 3:4	138
Day 27	Charge of Charges #3	Song 3:5	139
Day 28	Charge of Charges #4	Song 3:5	140
Day 29	Charge of Charges #5	Song 3:5	141
Day 30	Summary	Song 2:8-3:5	142

Poems of the Month: "Midst" 143
"The Wastefulness of God" 144

APRIL 1 — Awakening of Awakenings #1 — Song 2:8

Today's Thought: *"The Christian Church was formed by Jesus, deformed by apostasy, and reformed by the European Reformation, or the Protestant Reformation. The Waldenses planted the seeds of the Reformation that began in the time of Wycliffe, grew broad and deep in the days of Luther, and is to be carried forward to the close of time by those who are willing to suffer all things for the Word of God and for the Testimony of Jesus Christ"* (GC 61-78).

The Word of God had for centuries been locked up in the languages known only to the learned: but the time had come for the Scriptures to be translated, and given to the people of different lands in their native tongue. The world had passed its midnight. The hours of darkness were wearing away, and in many lands appeared tokens of the coming dawn. The minds of men were directed to the long-forgotten Word of God. A divine hand was preparing the way for the Great Reformation. "It was the work of the Reformation to restore to men the Word of God" (GC 388).

Within the description of the church in the wilderness, known as Thyatira, the statement which refers to the work of the European Reformation towards the end of the 1,260 year period is found in Revelation 2:19, *"I know thy works, and charity, and service, and faith, and thy patience, and they works; and the last to be more than the first."* The church was increasing.

The Second Coming of Jesus has been the "Blessed Hope" of the church in all ages. The church of the Dark Ages, suffering centuries of persecution, longed and prayed for His coming and deliverance. But according to the time prophecies, the church was to remain in the wilderness 1,260 years (Revelation 12).

The church in the wilderness is charged by the Scriptures—specifically the time prophecies of Daniel and Revelation (the roes and the hinds)— that she *"stir not up, nor awake [the Deliverer] till he please"* (Song 2:7).

Parting Gem: *May we, here in these last days, have the same fervent desire to do our portion to finish the work.*

APRIL 2   Voice of Voices #1   Song 2:8

Today's Thought: *"The voice of my beloved! behold, he cometh leaping upon the mountains, skipping upon the hills."*

"The voice of my Beloved" refers to God's Word (One cannot speak without words). The time had come for the European reformers to translate the Bible into the languages of the people of Europe.

"Behold, he cometh leaping upon the mountains." Bible commentators have concluded from the context that these "mountains" represent obstacles and difficulties. There were indeed "mountains of difficulties" which faced the reformers who attempted to translate the Bible. Rome had forbidden the translation and circulation of the Scriptures. Among the people there was ignorance, superstition, fanaticism, and there was persecution from politico-religious machines inspired by satanic opposition.

Through these, His servants, God was leading the people out of the darkness of Romanism; but there were many great obstacles for them to meet, and He led them on, step by step, as they could bear it (GC 103).

But over and above all these obstacles, the translators, with the help of the newly-invented printing press—the Gutenberg press of 1456—surmounted these difficulties and unlocked the Scriptures from the dead languages of the people of Europe. Christ, embodied as the Word, came, *"like a roe or a young hart"* (Song 2:9), *"leaping and skipping"* over the mountains and valleys, to the countries of Europe, to the world beyond.

Then John the Baptist came as the *"voice of one crying in the wilderness, Make straight the way of the Lord."* In these modern days, we have the voices of the three mighty angels who fly in the midst of heaven crying with a loud voice. The many airwaves are abuzz with the three angels' message of Revelation 14:6-12 being broadcast globally, 24/7. Praise God.

Parting Gem: *Have you noticed how when God needs a man, woman, or invention, it seems to come at just the right time? In this period of time, we have the invention of the printing press. Crude and cumbersome, maybe, but it was effective to do God's work. Notice today the technology so prevalent that it's coming just when it is needed.*

APRIL 3   *Roe of Roes #2*   Song 2:9

Today's Thought: *"My beloved is like a roe or a hart: [skipping, leaping, standing]."*

The sacrificial aspect of Christ was revealed in type by a lamb. *"Behold the Lamb of God"* (John 1:29). *"And I beheld, and lo… stood a Lamb…"* (Revelation 5:6).

Christ's kingly office was prophesied by the symbol of the lion. *"Behold, the Lion of the tribe of Juda, the Root of David…."* (Revelation 5:5).

Christ's military aspect is usually depicted by His name "Michael." Michael is always and only used when discussing the conflict with Lucifer. Jude 9 is an example.

Yet the doe, the roebuck, or the hart seems to be of the Word, or the spoken Word of the Scriptures. Watching this symbolism will establish the certainty of the immediacy of the Second Coming of Christ.

The Song of Songs is a mosaic of prophetic symbolism, some of which has been hidden or lost from view, needing to be rediscovered and viewed in all of its beauty. One such symbol is that of the deer. In the Song of Songs 2:9, the bride exclaims, *"My beloved is like a roe or a young hart [a deer]"* (emphasis added). This direct analogy is self-explanatory—that Christ is represented symbolically as a deer. This is a key text. But the question is this: The deer symbol represent Christ in what capacity? As a lamb, He is our sacrifice. As a lion, He is our King of Kings. But what clue is given in Scripture as to the meaning of the deer? It is found in the Hebrew language itself. The Hebrew word "emer" has two meanings: it can mean "deer" or it can mean "word." Compare Genesis 49:21 in the KJV and the RSV:

"Naphtali is a hind let loose, he giveth <u>goodly words</u>" (KJV).

"Naph'tali is a hind let loose, that bears <u>comely fawns</u>" (RSV).

Now we can read our Thought for Today as, *"the Word is skipping, leaping, spreading across the mountains."*

Parting Gem: *We have references to the milk of the Word, to the wine of prophecy, and now here we have the meat of the Word. Thy words were found and I did eat.*

APRIL 4   Wall of Walls #1   Song 2:9

Today's Thought: *"My beloved is standing behind the walls, just on the other side; you can hardly see him" (paraphrased).*

He standeth behind our walls. The "wall" is translated from the Hebrew "kothel," or "kothel mar avil"—the wall of trouble. The western wall of Jerusalem today is known as "the wailing wall" or "the wall of trouble," called "kothel mar avi." This wall of trouble is synonymous with the "mountains of difficulties."

The Song of Songs has a peculiar characteristic in that it employs two symbols, again and again, to reinforce a concept. Should you miss one, the second is there to catch your attention. By this manner of repetition, the Bible scholar is less apt to make a mistake if he has done his research carefully. Yes, I know, I've said this before.

The very next statement reveals a success of the reformers' work. *"He looketh forth at the windows, shewing himself through the lattice"* (Song 2:9). The prophecies of the Word of God… pierced the centuries, laying out the conflicts and martyrdoms of our bride-church, the true church, and declared her final triumph. These prophetic texts were looked upon as WINDOWS, letting in eternal light, showing what was going to come, into their dungeons, (Prophetic Faith of our Father V. 11, p.102).

In 2:9, the Word of God is pictured as showing through a lattice—partially obscured. "Though they did not see all things clearly, they were enabled to perceive many long buried truths… From century to century, other faithful workers were to follow, to lead the people still further in the path of reform… Martin Luther had a great work to do in reflecting to others the light which God had permitted to shine upon him; yet he did not receive all of the light which was to be given to the world. From that time to this, new light has been continually shining upon the Scriptures and new truths have been constantly unfolding" (GC 148-9).

Daniel 12:9 verifies that the time had not yet come for a full revelation of truth, *"Go thy way, Daniel: for the words are closed up and sealed till the time of the end."*

Parting Gem: *May we in our daily lives continually uncover for ourselves the wonderful words of truth and light.*

APRIL 5 — *Lattice of Lattices* — Song 2:9

Today's Thought: *"My beloved is standing behind the lattice work so I can't fully see him" (paraphrased).*

In Northern Europe, the Reformation took hold, but in much of southern Europe, Romanism retained its power. Furthermore, the full truths and reforms of Scripture were not realized in the European Reformation. It was not a culminating movement. It was a fundamental structure upon which the remnant church should be built. Therefore, the Word of God is pictured as a deer, shewing himself through a lattice—partially obscured—not able to make a full and complete entrance into Europe, that "house of many rooms,"[6] not able to make a full restoration of all the truths yet to come to God's people, who would finally be ready to meet the Bridegroom. Yet, like the rising sun before the full dawn, like the end of a long night, or the warming trend after a cold and darkened winter, the European Reformation gave promise of spring, by the rising of the Sun of Righteousness, who would finally provide the full seasons of summer and final harvest.

The "lattice" gives an impression of an obscured view. The "windows" and the "lattices" give the impression of being inside of a house.

Europe is a house of many rooms (countries), some bright and some dark. The light of the gospel in the Reformation of the sixteenth century sought to penetrate everywhere, but it was shut out (as though by a lattice) here and there (Christ's Last Legion, Spalding, A. W. p 31).

"The prophecies of Daniel, Paul and John, whose inspired vision pierced the centuries, marked out the conflicts and martyrdoms of the true church, and declared her triumph. These prophetic texts became their stay and comfort. They were looked upon as windows letting in eternal light" (Prophetic Faith of Our Fathers. v2. 102).

Parting Gem: *After centuries of being in the darkness of falsehood, the bright light of complete truths would have been too much for the world. Although the reformers may have known about the truths of the Sabbath or state of the dead, the most important present truth at that time was the Bible and the Bible only.*

---

[6] Berry, Marion G. *The Prophetic Song of Songs, Resource Book* (Albia, IA: The Prophetic Song of Songs, Inc.), 1969, p. 35.

APRIL 6   *Springtime of Springtimes*   Song 2:10-13

Today's Thought: *Are you ready for a Biblical picture of a prophetic springtime describing the European Reformation?*

The Song of Songs 2:10-13 is a unit which begins and ends with the same phrase: *"Rise up… and come away."* It was a two-fold call to arise up to a new study of the Word of God in order to find Christ and His salvation; it was also a time to "come away" from the Papacy and from Rome, the beginning of the Protestant Reformation.

It is a description of a springtime scene. In the apostasy and following Dark Ages, men had lost sight of the Son of Righteousness and His salvation. The European Reformation, through a concentration on the written Word, once again discovered Christ and justification by faith. Their recovery of the Son of Righteousness was as a springtime after a cold, dark winter.

It was a happy time. It was a time to gather the flowers of truth. It was a time for the congregations to express their joy in song. To this very day, our hymn books carry many of those hymns written and sung at this time. It was a time for the "turtle dove" to be heard in the land. It was springtime.

John 1:32 says, *"… I saw the Spirit descending from heaven like a dove, and it abode upon him."* The European Reformation was led out and directed by the Holy Spirit of God, bringing light upon the Holy Scriptures.

The fig tree putteth forth her green figs, a reference in symbolism of the signs of the times, giving a signpost as to where one was in the timetable to eternity. The Reformation was the beginning or sign of a great movement to follow which would proclaim the time of the end.

A similar call to the churches in the Laodicean period that the Laodicean Church will give to the world under the power of a fourth angel of Revelation 18:1-4 is, *"Come out of her, my people…"* (18:4)

Parting Gem: *The invitation is extended to "rise up and come away." Rise up from our lax lifestyle and come away into our private closet and worship area to confront and encounter this fabulous Bridegroom.*

APRIL 7 — *Hiding of Hidings* — Song 2:14

Today's Thought: *"O my dove, that art in the clefts of the rock… let me hear thy voice; for sweet is thy voice, and thy countenance is comely."*

The lofty bulwarks of the mountains of Europe, the Piedmont Valley of France, the Mountains of Italy, and the mountains and valleys of Switzerland were hiding places for the church during these 1,260 years of Roman domination. They were hiding in the clefts of the rock literally, as well as the song implies in the Rock of our salvation.

These secret places in the mountain peaks and valleys were the headquarters for the Waldenses, in the very land where popery was fixed. They were to spread out over Europe with the Scriptures they had so laboriously written out, and to tell others of Jesus the Rock of Ages being the only Advocate between man and God, as well as the Sabbath truth so hated by the Roman powers. The Waldenses were among the first of the peoples of Europe to obtain a translation of the Holy Scriptures even hundreds of years before the Reformation.

In the secrecy of these hills, small towns, and private domains across Europe, men like Wycliffe (1324-1384) in England, the morning star of the Reformation, the beginning light was soon to break forth with each new step of the stairs being built by such reformers as John Huss (1370-1415), Jerome (1380-1416), both from Bohemia; Ulric Zwingle (1484-1531), born in a herdsman's cottage in the Alps of Switzerland; Martin Luther and Melanchthon (1522) out of Germany; and others, extended upon the rising movement of the Reformation.

A platform in the stairs was solidified in 1529 when the Christian princes of Germany offered their Protest at the Diet of Spires. The courage, faith, and firmness of these men of God, gained for succeeding ages liberty of thought and of conscience. Their Protest gave to the reformed church the name Protestant; its principles are the very essence of Protestantism.

Parting Gem: *Thus Christ could say, "Let me hear thy voice; for sweet is thy voice, and thy countenance is comely"* (Song 2:14). He could say, "Let Me hear of your progress and see your advancement."

APRIL 8 — Fox of Foxes — Song 2:15

Today's Thought: *"Take us the foxes, the little foxes, that spoil the vine: for our vines have tender grapes.*

"Foxy," according to the thesaurus, means crafty, artful, astute, cunning, devious, guileful, sharp, shrewd, sly, tricky, wily. That's quite a description to be applied to the Roman authorities, yet that was how the early Christian Church in the wilderness saw them.

William Moreland, in the 1600s, as he combined the prophetic symbolism of Revelation with that of the Song of Songs, wrote: "…the woman fled when she was persecuted by the Dragon… where she had a place prepared of God, that they should feed her one thousand two hundred and sixty daies; (sic) That here it was that the Church fed, and where she made her flocks to rest at noon, in those hot and scorching seasons of the ninth and tenth centuries… it was in the clefts of these Rocks, and in the secret places of the stairs… that the Dove of Christ then remained, where also the Italian foxes then began to spoil the Vines with their tender Grapes, although they were never able utterly to destroy or pluck them up by the roots" (Prophetic Faith of our Fathers, Froom V 1, p. 884).

The Reformers' preaching excited great interest, but the priests from Rome followed with threats and misrepresentations. Persecution without and fanaticism from within nearly spoiled the "tender vines."

William Tyndale grieved this: "What is to be done? While I am sowing in one place, the enemy ravages the field I have just left…" (GC 246)

In bitterness of soul, Martin Luther sometimes asked, "Can such then be the end of the great work of the Reformation?" (GC 188)

Rome was up against the wall, the Reformation was wreaking havoc to her, and she had to come up with some devising to stop this movement or Rome would be brought to her knees.

In Luke 13:31-32, when some Pharisees urged Christ to leave, for Herod was going to kill Him, His reply was to go back and tell that old fox what He should do in the next three days.

Parting Gem: *Understand that the major thrust of the Reformation was not merely an emphasis on a certain doctrine, but rather a renewed interest in the Word which brought various doctrines into focus.*

APRIL 9　　　　　　*Intrigue of Intrigues*　　　　　　Song 2:13,15

Today's Thought: *"The fig tree putteth forth her green figs, and the vines with the tender grapes give a good smell... for our vines have tender grapes."*

"Throughout Christendom, Protestantism was menaced by formidable foes... Rome summoned new forces. At this time, the order of the Jesuits was established. The time was 1534; the founder was Ignatius of Loyola, his real given name being Inigo Onaz Lopez de Loyola.

"The Jesuits were the most cruel, unscrupulous, and powerful of all the champions of popery. Vowed to perpetual poverty and humility, it was their studied aim to secure wealth and power, to be devoted to the overthrow of Protestantism, and the reestablishment of the papal supremacy.

"To give them greater power, a bull was issued reestablishing the Inquisition... This terrible tribunal was again set up by popish rulers, and atrocities too terrible to bear the light of day were repeated in its secret dungeons. Thousands... were slain, or forced to flee to other lands.

"Such were the means which Rome had invoked to quench the light of the Reformation, to withdraw from men the Bible, and to restore the ignorance and superstition of the Dark Ages" (GC 234-236).

The wording, the Dark Ages, has tremendous meaning, yet it seems to have been removed from modern history books, thus from the mind of modern man. For those of you who have not heard of or know about the Dark Ages, it is because the words and the actions during the Dark Ages are no longer in history books like they were when the author was young.

Check the internet for "Jesuits" and/or "Ignatius of Loyola" to get another view of this man. It may surprise you.

Parting Gem: *An intriguer is one who beguiles, compels, diverts, connives, conspirers, plots, double-deals, and what have you who is evil. You can fill in your own adjectives. That's what the Reformers had to deal with, and that from a so-called Christian Church.*

APRIL 10   *Morning Star of Morning Stars*   Revelation 2:28

Today's Thought: *"And I will give him the morning star."*

Still in the Thyatira Church period from AD 538 until AD 1563, the start of the Reformation appears just over the horizon.

In the fourteenth century arose in England "the morning star of the Reformation." John Wycliffe (1324 to 1384), was the herald of reform, not for England alone, but for all Christendom. The great protest against Rome which it was permitted him to utter, was never to be silenced. That protest opened the struggle which was to result in the emancipation of individuals, of churches, and of nations (GC 80). It was solidified in the Diet of Spies, in 1529.

The world had passed its midnight. The hours of darkness were wearing away, and in many lands appeared tokens of the coming dawn (GC 79, 80). The tide began to turn for the Reformation.

Slowly the gleams of day appeared and while the lowlands were yet in partial shadow, the earliest beams of the yet unseen sun began to touch the distant peaks, with roseate hue in promise of the sun yet to come (Froom, Prophetic Faith of Our Fathers. V1, p.902).

As the great work of the prophets in days gone by was to give to mankind the Bible, the great work of Wycliffe was to translate that Bible into the English language, the language of the people.

All over Europe, God raised up fearless men of intellectual competence who were so educated as to be able to translate the Bible into the language of the people. Gutenburg's invention of the printing press in 1456 multiplied their efforts and the Word of God was on its way to all the world, leaping, skipping over the mountains of difficulty.

What a lesson of beauty of the descriptive poetry of the Song of Songs as it predicted the nature and purpose of the European Reformation in the prophetic symbolism of a glorious springtime, after a long dark winter of persecution.

Parting Gem: *If there was a morning star, would there be more stars to follow? The simple answer is yes. Could it be that you, the reader of this devotional, could be a star in your neighbourhood?*

APRIL 11 — Confidence of Confidences #1 — Song 2:16

Today's Thought: *"My beloved is mine, and I am his." Amen. Period.*

O that God's people could have the confidence and trust in their Saviour God, in their Creator God, that is expressed here in the Song 2:16, to see that her Beloved has but one church He is interested in.

There are three occasions where the bride expresses this strong passion conviction, a trilogy of passion, desire, longing; a confession that her Beloved has no other.

In this one here, *"My beloved is mine, and I am his: he feedeth among the lilies"* (2:16), the church is in the wilderness for those 1,260 years. The foxes of Italy are persecuting her, yet her confidence is in Him. She has no other lover, no other interests outside of her marriage relationship with her Beloved. She knows also that her Beloved has no other lover, no other church that can be called the apple of His eye. She knows where her Beloved is, out among the lilies feeding, taking pastoral care of His churches.

In 2:1, the bride declares that she is the lily of the valleys. The church is being added to day by day, as her beloved works among the churches.

There is one in 6:3. *"I am my beloved's, and my beloved is mine: he feedeth among the lilies."* Again the bride knows where her Beloved is. The bride makes this passionate confession just after the 1844 disappointment, when the question was asked, "If He didn't come to cleanse the earth, where did He go?" He went into the Most Holy Compartment of the heavenly sanctuary to start the Investigative Judgment portion of His ministry.

Another one is found in 7:10. *"I am my beloved's, and his desire is toward me."* If her Beloved could ever get homesick for His people, this verse shows it. His desire, His longing, His passion is to be with His people.

Parting Gem: *There is a beautiful song in the SDA Hymnal, #511, named, "I Know Whom I Have Believed," inspired from 2 Timothy 1:12, which states, "For the which cause I also suffer these things: nevertheless I am not ashamed: for I know whom I have believed, and am persuaded that he is able to keep that which I have committed unto him against that day." O, that our passion could be so strong.*

APRIL 12 — Retreat of Retreats — Song 2:17

Today's Thought: *"Until the day break, and the shadows flee away, turn, my beloved, and be thou like a roe or a young hart upon the mountains of Bether."*

This Song of Solomon is primarily a song between the bride-church and the Beloved, Jesus Christ, and the climactic event in the book is His second coming. Yet, chapter two, which deals with the Reformation, closes with the bride lamenting that according to the *"roe and hinds"* (2:7), the time prophecies of Scripture, specifically of Daniel and the Revelation, the day breaking at His Second Coming was still some centuries away.

So, because there were still mountains of time and difficulties, still many prophecies yet unfulfilled, separating the bride from her Beloved, her request is for Him to flee across Europe, the Americas, the islands of the sea taking His good news to the world.

The name "Bether" in the original language means "separation." Between the Reformation and the coming of Christ the second time were some four centuries separating the two.

As great as the Reformation was, still it was not the time for the Bridegroom to come and claim His bride.

The deer is a symbol for the Word of God, particularly the prophecies pertaining to the coming of the Bridegroom. The prophecies of Daniel and the Revelation did not indicate that the Bridegroom should come during the 1,260 years but just the opposite, that many events must yet occur in history before the Second Coming.

Our aim for today is to, *"do well that ye take heed, as a light that shineth in a dark place, until the day dawn, and the day star arise in your hearts"* (2 Peter 1:19).

Parting Gem: *It is now the time when the ten bridesmaids slumber and sleep, all ten of them. Soon there will be a grand and glorious awakening in the hearts and experience of at least the five wise bridesmaids. Our joy is to keep our lamps trimmed and burning.*

APRIL 13 — *Movement of Movements* — Song 2:17

Today's Thought: *"Until the day break, and the shadows flee away, turn, my beloved, and be thou like a roe or a young hart upon the mountains of Bether."*

In the earliest days, Abram was called out of Ur of the Chaldees, a Sumerian city in Lower Mesopotamia, the modern site of *el-Mugaiyar*, about 150 miles southeast of old Babylon and about 150 miles northwest of the Persian Gulf, all in modern Iraq.

From this cradle of civilization, Abram was called by God to the land of Canaan, into Palestine, the crossroads of the world. One purpose was to teach all travellers going through these crossroads of the saving God of the Israelites.

From this area, the Judo-Christian religion was set up by Christ; His disciples carried the message to the world. As Christianity progressed westward, the main thrust seems to have centered in Rome. From Rome the "Christian religion" moved across Europe, down to Africa.

Around AD 1000, Leif Erickson and his Vikings "discovered" the eastern coast of North America, sailing from Iceland to Greenland, settling in Newfoundland, on down around Massachusetts. They set up some colonies; however, "the fullness of time had not yet come." The colonies were abandoned.

In 1492, Columbus discovered the new land of America. Magellan sailed around the world. For various reasons, explorers from Spain, France, England, Portugal, Holland set sail, setting up colonies, trading posts, mission stations, bringing the vigour, energy, and strength of pioneers to this new land.

Huguenots, Puritans, Pilgrims, and other colonists from European countries sought religious freedom from the earth which opened up her mouth to help the woman (Revelation 13:16). Once again the center of God's work shifted westward into the new land of America. The Reformation which started in Europe had now shifted for the final Reformatory Movement centred in America.

Parting Gem: *From Abraham through Leif Erickson, passing the Pilgrims and early colonists to our day, let us get involved with this movement of movements.*

APRIL 14   *Stupor of Stupors*   Song 3:1

Today's Thought: *"By night on my bed, I sought him…"*

From the Thyatira Church, the scene comes to Act 2, Scene 1, as this drama now enters into the Sardis Church from the Reformation time to 1798.

In Revelation 3:1, the condition of the church is clearly stated, *"I know thy works, that thou hast a name that thou livest, and art dead."* The church claimed to be Protestants, yet what were they protesting against?

This drama states, *"By night on my bed…"* A state of stupor and lethargy does not encourage deep study nor commitment. The Protestant churches of America—and those of Europe as well—so highly favoured in receiving the blessings of the Reformation, failed to press forward; there was almost as great a need of reform in the Protestant churches as in the Roman church in the time of Luther. There was the same worldliness and spiritual stupor (GC 297/8).

It was needful that men should be awakened to the danger: that they should be aroused to prepare for the solemn events connected with the close of probation (GC 310).

To prepare a people to stand in the day of God, a great work of reform was to be accomplished. God saw that many of His professed people were not building for eternity, and in His mercy He was then to send a message of warning to arouse them from their stupor, and to lead them to make ready to meet their Bridegroom (GC 311).

The bride-church could not discover the Bridegroom in "Present Truth" of prophecy concerning the time of His coming while in this spiritual stupor *"on my bed."* Therefore, she concluded and said that, *"I found Him not"* (Song 3:1) She must arise and awaken to search the Scriptures and prophecy. This awakening and arising came to be known as "The 1800 Awakening."

Parting Gem: *What brought about the great 1800 Awakening? There were two major, major, major events. Think on this point until tomorrow.*

APRIL 15 — *Alarm of Alarms* — Song 3:1

Today's Thought: *"By night on my bed I sought him whom my soul loveth: I sought him, but I found him not."*

The alarm clock went off; the world was in shock; the churches awoke. What had happened?

From France, the baby of the papacy, known as the "daughter of Rome," Napoleon sent General Berthier into the Vatican and took Pope Pius VI captive, because the pope would not approve of Napoleon's hunger to rule the world. The date was February 10, 1798; that pope died in captivity on August 29, 1799. The church was suddenly jarred awake. Their eyes were opened and they saw the Papal Supremacy end. They knew that the 1,260 year prophecy of Daniel and Revelation had met its fulfillment. They knew that the deadly wound of Revelation 13:3 had been inflicted, and inflicted right on time, and possible inflicted twice. Listen!

Had someone pushed the snooze button? The alarm went off again. In 1812, the new pope, in agreement to be released from captivity, surrendered Vatican control of the Papal States. They were absorbed into the United Kingdom of Italy. General Pepin had captured these Italian states from the Lombards, an Arian nation, and when he destroyed the Lombards in AD 756, he gave the states to the Pope in what has been termed "The Donation of Pepin."

As this tyranny of papal suppression ended, and the awareness that prophecy had been fulfilled, then Protestantism suddenly became aware of its new freedom as well as obligations to the rest of the world.

This awakening, called the Great Religious Awakening of 1800 both in the Old World of Europe and in the New World of America, caused a spiritual influence to be spread to many islands and lands. That was the first reason for the awakening.

Parting Gem: *When the fullness of the time comes, be ready. For your serious consideration today has the deadly wound been healed, or is it in the long process of being healed? Do these entire Papal States need to be restored to Vatican control in order for the wound to be completely healed? Watch for this in the close future. It'll come.*

APRIL 16   *Conclusion of Conclusions*   Song 3:1

Today's Thought: *"By night on my bed I sought Him… [I needed Him]."*

In 1798, the church in spiritual stupor was suddenly awakened and her spiritual eyes opened as she saw the Papal Supremacy ended with the capture of Pope Pius VI, recognized by Bible expositors as the end of the 1,260 day-year prophecy of Daniel and Revelation. Previously, between November 26, 1793 and June 17, 1797, the French Revolution had just taken place. This was three and a half years, as depicted in Revelation 11:1-14.

As the Protestant churches became aware of their influence and their freedom, as well as their desperate need spiritually, God worked to cooperate with them. New inventions made it possible so that transportation and communications technology could be used to reach out into the world with a strong missionary program. In North America, theological seminaries sprang up, these later to become well-known universities and colleges. Tract societies, Sunday schools, missionary societies, and great public revivals took place. More than one million were added to the different churches. Great reformatory movements were in evidence, such as temperance societies, anti-slavery agitations, women suffrage, all between 1800 and 1840. New countries were thought of as mission lands.

One of the greatest accomplishments of the Great Religious Awakening of 1800 was the formation of the American Bible Society in 1816, the British and Foreign Bible Society in 1804, which have since published and distributed the Bible to many languages and dialects, all to awaken the message of the coming Bridegroom.

This Great Religious Awakening of 1800 prepared the way for the Great Advent Movement of 1831 to 1844. Upon the crest of the tide of the 1800 Awakening, "The Great Advent Movement" occurred with its astonishing announcement of the coming of the Bridegroom, expected sometime between 1843 and 1844.

This caused Bible students in different lands and denominations to simultaneously concentrate on a study of the 2,300 day prophecy of Daniel 8:14, all coming to the same conclusion that the Bridegroom was expected sometime between 1843 and 1844.

Parting Gem: *"Thy words were found, and I did eat them." (Jeremiah 15:16)*

APRIL 17   *City of Cities*   Song 3:2

Today's Thought: *"I will rise now, and go about the city in the streets, and in the broad ways..."*

Unfortunately, this generation has nearly forgotten the 1800 Awakening. The 1800 revivals added over a million converts. It founded theological seminaries, which later became universities and missionary societies which sent men and women to the far corners of the world. One hundred twenty-five education training institutes were founded by 1840 in which pagan classics were banned and manual labour required in a work-study program. It worked for political and religious liberty, anti-slavery, temperance, even vegetarianism and health reforms.

On the massive crest of this tide, William Miller and other Advent pioneers initiated "The Great Advent Movement," a proclamation from the 2,300 day-year prophecy of Daniel 8 and 9 that the coming of the Bridegroom should be in or about 1843 or 1844.

The 1800 Awakening occurred in many denominations, but they did not agree in doctrine. Their varied positions were often opposite to each other and even the Bible itself. This state of confusion is described in prophetic symbolism as *"Babylon... that great city"* (Revelation 14:8). One could say that the Advent Movement began in "The City." "

"... *in the streets, and in the broad ways I will seek him...* " Babylon is that great city of many "streets" and "broad ways." Although many believe that each denomination is just another road to heaven, Jesus warned: *"Narrow is the way, which leadeth unto life, and few there be that find it"* (Matthew 7:14).

It was in the United States that the Advent message was most widely proclaimed and received. As Bible prophecies relating to the return of Jesus were accepted by able men and women of many religious faiths, a large following of earnest Adventist believers resulted; however, no separate and distinct religious organization was formed. This hope led to deep revivals benefiting all churches, leading many sceptics and infidels to publicly confess their faith in the Bible and in God.

Parting Gem: *Who is this great city, to be shadowed by a greater?*

APRIL 18 — *Failure of Failures* — Song 3:2

Today's Thought: *"I will rise now, and go about the city in the streets, and in the broad ways I will seek him whom my soul loveth: I sought him, but I found him not."*

In all of the Protestant Churches of this time, not one had any belief in the Advent doctrine. Christ admonished us to *"Enter ye in at the strait gate: for wide is the gate, and broad is the way, that leadeth to destruction, and many there be that go in thereat; Because strait is the gate, and narrow is the way, which leadeth unto life, and few there be that find it"* (Matthew 7:13-14).

Jeremiah 29:13 says, *"And ye shall seek me, and find me, when ye shall search for me with all of your heart."*

Depicted here in few verses is a picture of one who is seeking for some answers and no one is willing or capable of giving a good answer. Early Adventist history tells the story of young people, Robert and Ellen Harmon to be specific, who went to their church for prayer meeting but were not encouraged but discouraged in speaking about this hope of a second coming. No one seemed to know anything about it nor did they wish to discuss it.

Our bride-church is seeking her Beloved. She goes to the churches of that time seeking for the message of a soon-coming Bridegroom, her Beloved, her Saviour, Jesus Christ; but, alas, she does not find this saving message. *"I found him not,"* is wrenched from her heart.

Yet, notice the determination of this bride, *"I will rise, go about the city streets and by-ways I will seek."* Notice also that she knows just what she is seeking for—*"Him whom my soul loveth."*

Parting Gem: *Today, as you go about your joys and perplexities, make it a point to seek Him whom your soul loveth, talk to Him as you drive, wait, walk, listen, look, and reflect on just who this Beloved is. This is part of the way that Enoch walked with God.*

APRIL 19 — Watchman of Watchmen — Song 3:3

Today's Thought: *"The watchmen that go about the city found me."*

At the time of Christ's first advent, the priests and scribes of the holy city, to whom were entrusted the oracles of God, might have discerned the signs of the times, and proclaimed the coming of the Promised One. The prophecies of Micah designated His birthplace; Daniel specified the time of His advent. God gave these prophecies to the Jewish leaders; they were without excuse if they did not know and declare to the people that the Messiah's coming was at hand. Their ignorance was the result of sinful neglect. Absorbed in their ambitious strife for place and power among men, they lost sight of the divine honours proffered them by the King of heaven (GC 313).

Prophecy not only foretells the manner and object of Christ's coming, but presents token by which men are to know when it is near… These signs were witnessed before the opening of the nineteenth century, in the opening of the sixth seal of Revelation. In fulfillment of this prophecy there occurred in the year 1755 the most terrible earthquake, in Lisbon, Portugal. Twenty-five years later appeared the next sign mentioned in prophecy—the darkening of the sun and moon… on the 19th of May, 1780. Christ had bidden His people to watch for the signs of His advent (GC 312).

In 1798, the Pope was taken captive, thus establishing the exact date of the end of the 1,260 years of Papal supremacy. According to the prophecy, this was the date when the church should come *"out of the wilderness"* of hiding—these were surety of fulfilling prophecy and surety of the nearness of the coming Bridegroom.

Yet, the scholarly theologians, the *"watchmen of the city,"* refused to acknowledge these signs and closed their minds to a study of the prophecies of Scripture concerning the coming of the Bridegroom. They not only denied the doctrine of the literal soon coming of Jesus, but began to oppose and ridicule those who preached it. Those who held fast to the Scriptures soon discovered that Present Truth was not to be found with the popular clergy.

Parting Gem: *The watchmen may not have found Him, but I will, just you wait and see. Will you find Him, whom to find is life eternal?*

APRIL 20   *Token of Tokens*   Song 3:3

Today's Thought: *"The watchmen that go about the city found me: to whom I said, Saw ye him whom my soul loveth?"*

"The watchmen that go about the city found me." The scholarly theologians of Christendom suddenly "found," or became aware of, a rising movement in all their churches.

Humble, "faithful men, who were obedient to the promptings of God's spirit… who (took) heed to the sure word of prophecy" (GC 312) sounded out a warning: *"Fear God, and give glory to him; for the hour of his judgment is come"* (Revelation 14:7). These men were warning the world of the soon Second Coming of Christ, at which time must occur the judgment of all men.

They preached the "judgment message," upon the basis of prophecy and prophecy fulfilled:

"Prophecy not only foretells the manner and object of Christ's coming, but presents tokens by which men are to know when it is near… These signs were witnessed before the opening of the nineteenth century. In fulfillment of this prophecy there occurred in the year 1755, the most terrible earthquake (Lisbon). Twenty-five years later appeared the next sign mentioned in prophecy--the darkening of the sun and moon… On the 19th of May 1780. Christ had bidden His people to watch for the signs of His advent" (GC 304-308).

The watchmen on the walls… should have been the first to lift their voices to proclaim Him near, and the first to warn the people to prepare for His coming. But they were at ease, dreaming of peace and safety. Yet sometimes, just sometimes, people in authority, as well as not in authority, are reluctant, hesitant, leery of taking advice from others.

Parting Gem: *Today as you go about your joys and excitements, consider not necessarily the sun, moon, star, earthquakes, but the famines, floods, fires, hurricanes, cyclones that are happening around you now. Then be ready to give to every man a reason why these things are happening, especially when they ask ""Where is God in all this?"*

APRIL 21 — *Study of Studies* — Song 3:4

Today's Thought: *"I found him whom my soul loveth."*

As the movement neared its high point in the early 1840s, several hundred ministers united in proclaiming the message. In the lead was William Miller, who lived in the eastern edge of New York State. He was a man of prominence in his community and engaged in farming for a livelihood. In spite of a rich religious background, he had grown sceptical in his youth. He lost faith in the Word of God and adopted deistic views. While reading a sermon in the Baptist Church one Sunday morning, the Holy Spirit touched his heart, and he was led to accept Jesus Christ as his Saviour. Miller set about to study the Word of God, determined to find in the Bible a satisfactory answer to all his questions, and to learn for himself the truths set forth therein.

For two years, he devoted much of his time to a verse-by-verse study of the Scriptures. He determined not to take up the next verse until he felt he had found a satisfactory explanation of the one he was studying. He had before him only his Bible and a concordance. In time, he came in his study to the prophecies of the literal, personal, second coming of Christ. He grappled also with the great time prophecies, particularly the 2,300-day prophecy of Daniel 8 and 9, which he linked with the prophecy of Revelation 14 and the message of the angel proclaiming the hour of God's judgment (Revelation 14:6-7).

At the conclusion of this two-year study, he wrote out his confession of beliefs, which fell far short of being anywhere similar to the beliefs of the Protestant churches of his time, one of which was the distinct assurance of the nearness of Christ's second coming. Thinking he may have been wrong in his conclusions, he spent another four years of intense review, and another written confession of faith. He had an overwhelming conviction to tell what he had discovered to the world that Christ was expected within twenty-five years. Even Martin Luther in his time predicted Christ to come within four hundred years, or near 1844.

Parting Gem: *By a study of God's Word, one has a reward of finding Him who is the one altogether lovely.*

APRIL 22 — *Passing of Passings* — Song 3:4

Today's Thought: *"It was but a little that I passed from them, but I found him whom my soul loveth: I held him, and would not let him go, until I had brought him into my mother's house, and into the chamber of her that conceived me."*

Robert Harmon and Eunice Gould had eight children, the last of them being twin girls, Ellen Gould and Elizabeth. Robert Harmon Jr. and his sister Ellen were close in nature and often went to spiritual meetings together. They discussed the religious times taking place.

There was a six-month period of time when Ellen, at age fifteen, had not a cloud of darkness passed over her mind. Daily her soul was drinking rich draughts of salvation, and she felt she must tell everyone about her hope of Christ's second coming. When she gave her testimony, the class leader interrupted saying, "through Methodism"; but she could not give glory to Methodism when it was Christ and the hope of His soon coming.

Most of Robert Harmon's family were full believers in the advent, and for bearing testimony to its glorious doctrine seven of them, including Ellen, were at one time cast out of the Methodist Episcopal Church where they had been members labouring for the conversion of souls for some forty years (LS 17; EW 13).

William Miller came to Portland, Maine in June 1842 for the second time. The first time he came was in March 1840. His lectures at that time produced a great sensation, and the Casco Church was crowded day and night… But this second time in the same church, a greater excitement was raised. With few exceptions, the different denominational churches closed their doors against him.

Yet, the bride-church said that she left them and then found her Beloved. The scholarly theologians, the Protestant Churches of the 1840s, did not have this hope of a very soon coming Saviour. They spurned the very idea of such an event so soon, so visible.

Parting Gem: *But she found him, she found the hope, she found the assurance of the soon-coming King, her Beloved. Stop, right where you are. Have you found Him?*

APRIL 23 — Success of Successes — Song 3:4

Today's Thought: *"It was but a little that I passed from them, but I found him whom my soul loveth: I held him, and would not let him go, until I had brought him into my mother's house, and into the chamber of her that conceived me."*

Can you hear the excitement of the bride as she lets the world know that success has been hers? She has found the one thing she has been looking for, similarly to finding the pearl of great price, or the treasure in the field of Matthew 13. She sold everything she had. History backs that up.

It was not the scholarly theologians of Christendom who had an understanding of the prophetic symbolism for their day. "Had these been faithful watchmen diligently and prayerfully searching the Scriptures, they would have known the time of night" (GC 312). Humbler, faithful men, obedient to the promptings of God's spirit who searched the prophetic Scriptures, comprehended the message for their day and comprised God's true church, represented by the bride, in the drama of the Song of Songs.

She says, *"It was but a little that I passed from them [the scholarly theologians], but I found him"*—a message of His soon second coming. *"As soon as I left them, I found him"* (TEV). God's people could not identify with Babylon, for they were to be identified with Jerusalem—God's universal church of all ages which proclaims the Present Truth for each age of earth's history.

Others in past history found out that they too had to *"pass from them"* the churches which they belonged to, in order to fully follow the Beloved. Luther was "forced" to leave Catholicism, even against his desire, yet he too was successful.

In the last part of verse 4, the bride identifies herself with the Universal Church of all ages as she proclaims the prophetic message concerning the coming of the Bridegroom: *"my mother's house."*

Parting Gem: *Heavenly Father, through my Beloved, help us to identify with your people of all ages, holding firm to the faith once delivered to the saints, and to bring all of this into our house, our repertoire of beliefs.*

APRIL 24 — *Holding of Holdings* — Song 3:4

Today's Thought: *"I held him, and would not let him go, until I had brought him into my mother's house, and into the chamber of her that conceived me."*

Can you catch the picture here? The bride had found something, something powerfully important to her. She has found a truth that Jesus Christ, her Beloved, is soon to come. "Soon" meaning within years, months or weeks, not centuries or even decades.

She wants to hold onto this truth so that no man will take her crown. She needs to not only hold it and not let it go, but she needs to go into her mother's house, into the place where truth is conceived, and compare, compare, compare. She needs to take Isaiah 28:10, and put it to the test. *"For precept must be upon precept, precept upon precept; line upon line, line upon line; here a little, there a little."* Not only must she hold onto this truth, but she must not let anyone, preacher, church, tradition, or family detour her from her belief.

As this bride-church discovers truth that she did not previously have, she wants to take it, analyze it, delve into what Mother has to say about it and make sure that Mother agrees with this gem of truth. If Mother agrees with her finding, she will already have it in her possession; it will be in her repertoire of knowledge. If that is the case, then this bride-church will hold onto it, possess it, make it her own personal belief and standard of conduct and add it to her repertoire of beliefs.

If it does not agree with what her mother already has in her possession, then this bride-church drops this idea of truth.

That has been the philosophy of this bride-church. If she cannot find Jesus Christ in each and every doctrine she has in her repertoire, then that doctrine is not allowed to take up valuable space.

Parting Gem: *Have you ever thought of going through your house of truth to see if what you believe now is still up to date with what you believed when you first discovered this truth. Review and update, shake off the dust and rededicate yourself to your Beloved. As you go about your activities today, contemplate the vast store of Bible verses you know, as well as line them up under their respective doctrine. Have a joyous and healthy day.*

APRIL 25 — Chamber of Chambers — Song 3:4

Today's Thought: *"... until I had brought him into my mother's house, and into the chamber of her that conceived me."*

The universal church is represented by the prophetic symbol of a "mother" (Revelation 12). In each age, she has been granted her portion of Present Truth, imparted as the "Wisdom of God". As it has been revealed from age to age, she has been erecting an edifice which has been likened to the building of a house. *"Wisdom hath builded her house, she hath hewn out her seven pillars... Whoso is simple, let him turn in hither: as for him that wanteth understanding, she saith to Him, Come, eat of my bread, and drink of my wine... The fear of the Lord is the beginning of wisdom"* (Proverbs 9:1,4-5,10).

The Advent Movement presented the Present Truth of the First Angel's judgment-hour message, entered into that "house" and continued to build the "House" of Truth, joining themselves into the family of the universal church of all ages. Present Truth has always been a fuller revelation of Jesus Christ. Therefore, the Advent Movement says, "I found him, and would not let him go, until I had brought him into my mother's house." They preached that the hour of his judgment of Revelation 14 is come.

The Lord has many ways to achieve His goal. There was that great disappointment of October 22, 1844 in which thousands of people waited for the Bridegroom to come. Of course, He didn't come. This forced the early pioneers to dig deep into the Word to find the cause of this bitter experience. As they dug to find reasonable answers, they found the truth about the sanctuary, the pre-millennium judgment, the work of the High Priest officiating in the Most Holy compartment for the sins of spiritual Israel.

Consider what would have been the result should there have been no disappointment? Jesus states in John that He was to go and prepare a place for us that where He was, we may be also. Just how long does it take to prepare those mansions? Especially in the light of Psalm 33:9, where *"he spake and it was done; he commanded, and it stood fast."*

Parting Gem: *Have you started to build your house of wisdom for your daily life?*

APRIL 26 — *Finding of Findings* — Song 3:4

Today's Thought: *"It was but a little that I passed from them, but I found him whom my soul loveth: I held him, and would not let him go, until I had brought him into my mother's house, and into the chamber of her that conceived me."*

Do you recall some of those Bible verses depicting people who have found great findings?

Jeremiah 15:16 says, *"Thy words were found, and I did eat them; and thy word was unto me the joy and rejoicing of mine heart; for I am called by thy name, O Lord God of hosts."*

Psalms 119:72 says, *"The law of thy mouth is better unto me than thousands of gold and silver."*

Psalms 119:103 says, *"How sweet are thy words unto my taste! yea, sweeter than honey to my mouth."*

Psalms 119:11,105 says, *"Thy word have I hid in mine heart, that I might not sin against thee… Thy word is a lamp unto my feet, and a light unto my path."*

Luke 24:32-34 says, *"And they said one to another, Did not our heart burn within us, while he talked with us by the way, and while he opened to us the scriptures? And they rose up the same hour, and returned to Jerusalem, and found the eleven gathered together, and them that were with them, saying, The Lord is risen indeed…"*

Proverbs 3:13-18 says, *"Happy is the man that findeth wisdom, and the man that getteth understanding. For the merchandise of it is better than the merchandise of silver, and the gain thereof than fine gold. She is more precious than rubies: and all the things thou canst desire are not to be compared unto her. Length of days is in her right hand; and in her left hand riches and honor. Her ways are ways of pleasantness, and all her paths are peace. She is a tree of life to them that lay hold upon her: and happy is every one that retaineth her."*

Parting Gem: *Lord, help us today to find the treasures of Your word and put them into our minds, our lives, our lifestyle.*

APRIL 27 — *Charge of Charges #3* — Song 3:5

Today's Thought: *"I charge you, O ye daughters of Jerusalem, by the roes, and by the hinds of the field, that ye stir not up, nor awake my love, till he please."*

Slipping back to Song 2:7, we find the exact same charge, word for word, comma for comma, depicting the 1,260 year wilderness sojourn. This is the second time this charge is given. The occasion for this charge is during the loud cry, *"Behold the bridegroom cometh; go ye out to meet him"* (Matthew 25:6) in the 1840s.

The bride-church has awakened from her bed, gone through the city seeking him whom her soul loveth, and finding Him, holding Him, not letting Him go. Yet, the charge is given not to go setting times and dates for His return, for no one knows the day nor the hour, not even the month nor the year.

This verse is a recurring refrain. It is repeated at significant historical periods of church history. As each surge of spiritual awakening caused the church to expect the coming of the Bridegroom, this refrain is repeated in its historical setting.

Even the apostle Paul said the same thing back in 2 Thessalonians 2; he stressed that they be not shaken nor disturbed by the coming of the Lord, because that day cannot come until there is a falling away first, and that the man of sin be revealed.

When Christ was upon earth and men tried to take Him, *"no man laid hands on him... because his hour was not yet come"* (John 7:30). So it seems to be that there is a timetable set up that Christ is following, and when it is time, it is time. *"When the fullness of the time was come God sent forth his Son..."* (Galatians 4:4).

So, when the fullness of the time is come, when the cup of iniquity of the nations is full, when the gospel goes to all the world, when everything that can be done has been done, when everyone who can be saved is ready to be saved, then my Beloved will awake, stir up, and come for me; for you?

What an awesome God we serve, don't you just love Him?

Parting Gem: *Be ye also ready: for in such an hour as ye think not the Son of man cometh.*

APRIL 28 — *Charge of Charges #4* — Song 3:5

Today's Thought: *"I charge you, O ye daughters of Jerusalem, by the roes, and the hinds of the field, that ye stir not up, nor awake my love, till he please."*

The Great Advent Movement (1831-1844) proclaimed that Jesus would return to receive His bride in 1843 or 1844. They based this announcement on the 2,300 day-year prophecy of Daniel 8:14—*"Unto two thousand and three hundred days; then shall the sanctuary be cleansed."* (See Appendix 2.)

The historical references and the mathematical calculations were indeed correct, but their understanding of the prophetic symbolism of the term "sanctuary" was not correctly decoded by Scriptural cross-references. They assumed that the "sanctuary" to be cleansed represented this earth, and the cleansing was to be at the coming of the Bridegroom, Jesus Christ, in the clouds. Had they interpreted the symbols of all of the time prophecy correctly, they would not have suffered the great disappointment of 1844.

Remember, however, that the Bridegroom works in strange and mysterious ways, many times confusing His people. He had his hand over their mistake, and worked it out in such a way that the bride came to know about the heavenly sanctuary doctrine as well as a whole host of other gems from His treasury.

The Advent Movement fully expected the immediate coming of the Bridegroom in 1844. However, they are cautioned in this verse that they are not to awake Him to the deliverance of His people at that time! In reality, the prophetic Scripture, the roes and the hinds of the field, did not declare His immediate coming.

The texts of Daniel 8:14, Matthew, and Joel were to usher in "The Time of the End"—the Investigative Judgment, not the second coming.

Parting Gem: *Father in heaven, help us as the daughters of Jerusalem, as the virgins of your kingdom, to be ready for the time when you do finally come, like when we your people believe you enough to be ready, as well to help get others ready for that climactic event.*

APRIL 29 — Charge of Charges #5 — Song 3:5

Today's Thought: *"I charge you, O ye daughters of Jerusalem, by the roes, and the hinds of the field, that ye stir not up, nor awake my love, till he please."*

A blessing is given to all servants who are found watching and waiting, longing for Christ to return. They are urged to be ready at all times, for the Master will come when they think not (Luke 12:37-40).

At least three times in Matthew 24, it states that the time for Christ's coming is known only by the Godhead (Matthew 24:36,42,44). There are certain signs, lots of them, given to let us know that the time is near.

Our bride has at least three times told the church in her day not to get carried away with an expectation of the Bridegroom coming. In two of these charges, 2:7 and 3:5, she bases her knowledge on the *"roes and the hinds,"* the Old Testament and the New Testament, even Daniel and Revelation. According to these, there were still prophecies to be fulfilled before the Bridegroom could come.

The bride was not to expect her Beloved to come while she was in the wilderness. The wilderness experience would end in 1798, and there were many prophecies yet to be fulfilled, such as the dark day/night, falling of the stars, a great earthquake, not to mention the wars, the floods and droughts, the weather turmoil. She was not to expect her Beloved to come during the Millerite Movement, yet she did and she drank of that bitter cup depicted in Revelation 10, and subsequently suffered a great disappointment.

On the third charge, Song 8:4, she omits the *"rows and the hinds"* as her backup. She seems to be saying, "I know my Beloved is coming and He's coming for me, but let us be patient and wait. Although all the prophecies have been fulfilled, let's not wake Him up. After all, He does have a timetable, a day appointed." So, what is He waiting for? Could it be that He is waiting for you and me, His people, to reflect His image? Yet, it's more than that. He is waiting for His people to trust Him, accept and obey His authority, which will in turn change God's people. so that they are ready, waiting, for Him.

Parting Gem: *"Be ye also ready: for in such an hour…"* (Matthew 24:44)

APRIL 30   *Summary*   Song 2:8-3:5

We've covered from Song of Songs 2:8-3:5.

Chapters 1 and 2 of the Song of Songs are actually one historical unit covering nearly seventeen centuries of church history. Its poetic facade gives abundant evidence of God's love for His church while its decoded symbolism focuses directly upon those major historical and doctrinal milestones which identify the true church through the centuries. These first two chapters lay the foundation for the remainder of the Song of Songs, which deals with those events which prepare the way for the coming of the Bridegroom. It is a characteristic of prophecy to lay a prophetic timeline of events which are past, so that the present and the future can then be set into meaningful position.

It is characteristic of prophecy that it opens up at the time of fulfillment. As Rome saw the reformation advancing, a counter reformation was organized to destroy the work of the reformers, described as the "foxes" in 2:15. Although the reformers were able to understand and apply the Song of Songs as far as chapter 2, they could not understand the remainder of the book for they were "prisoners of history".

This month, we were introduced to the Word of God peaking through the lattice of time and difficulty. We met the Morning Star, John Wycliffe, as well as those foxy "foxes" of Rome, the Counter Reformation. We caught a glimpse of the springtime breaking through the tough winter as new songs appeared, as flowers of promises came. We heard the call to come out of her my people through the words, *"Rise up… and come away."* The vines were flourishing, yet Rome was there to tear up the tender vines, the new converts not yet settled into the truth.

Then, starting in 3:1, we were flung into the Philadelphia Church period, 1798 to 1844. This is the start of the Great Religious Awakening of the 1800s in America. This is the time when our bride-church is looking for her Beloved to come, a message of His soon return. She doesn't find that message in any of the churches of that day.

We met William Miller and his in-depth study of Scripture, specifically the 2,300-day prophecy, coming to the conclusion that Christ would appear about 1844. Our bride declares that *"I found him whom I sought."* She leaves her churches of the day and holds on to this second coming doctrine, and added it to her repertoire of doctrines.

Midst

Out of the wilderness, a woman came,
    Midst pillars of smoke, midst lightnings, midst flame,
Midst the cry of Battle both fearful and stark,
    With sun and moon both bloody and dark

Midst stars that fell; midst an earth that quaked;
    Midst banners unfurled; midst a terror' fierce wake,
Midst a rising sun, midst a moon that's fair,
    Midst a sun that's clear, midst that army beware.

Midst the blow-up in France as she took to the streets
    As she casts the Word down to be trampled with feet.
Midst the wound with the sword and the pope in exile,
    This woman came out with a broad, vibrant smile.

Then all of a sudden, just out of the blue,
    The world came awake and with assurance they knew,
That this was the end of the woman's sojourn,
    We'll see if the church did a complete about turn.

The Wastefulness of God

My Lord is such a wasteful God,
    He has so much to give.
That ball of flames out there in space
    Gives us heat and light to live.
Just think how much this earth receives
    Compared to open space.
That teeny bit that earth receives,
    Is all the rest just waste?

Let's take a look at the gospel seeds,
    And how many really grows.
Yet, all the rest seems all but lost,
    But, continually He sews.
The seeds are found on many grounds.
    Some grows, but most feed birds.
But it must go to all the world
    For not all the world has heard.

God's love with all its massive strength
    Is freely splashed about.
No matter who or what you are,
    No one by Him's left out.
On Calvary's tree He poured it out,
    The flood-gates of His love.
Freely drenched on all mankind,
    The vultures and the dove.

May

May's Introduction and Aim

The month of May will cover Song of Songs 3:6- 3:11, from the coming out of the wilderness in 1798 to the rise of the Great Religious Awakening in the 1840s, which just happens to be the Philadelphia Church period (Revelation 3:7-13). This will cover Acts 2, Scenes 1-4. Corresponding to this will be *The Great Controversy*, Chapters 16-17.

We cover the question, "Who is this that is coming out of the wilderness?" and a description of same. As well, we look at how she came out of the wilderness.

We are given an invitation that hopefully removes all your anxiety, fear, trepidation pertaining to the "judgment." To me, this portion of our drama is one, and only one, of the exciting parts, and one that has helped me to understand the fearful "J" word.

We will look at the coming out of the wilderness and the reason for the going into the wilderness. It is hoped that you catch the excitement and the glamour of this bride coming out.

You shall meet several warriors, brilliant and articulate; they are called the "valiant of Israel." See how they did some mathematical footwork that awed the world.

The foundation of the Seventh-day Adventist Community is uncovered complete with one man who helped uncover it,

Hopefully your fear of the "J" word will vanish when you look at the seven phases of it. The last one should cause you to rejoice.

A brief introduction to a weak girl of about age 17 years will be your privilege. She was used by God and proof of her position in God's army will be given. There are four main and five minor proofs. Remember them, appreciate them.

Your assignment for this month of May is to read, again, the full 117 verses, eight chapters of our drama. As you do so, put into place and in your thinking the meaning of this drama that you have had uncovered so far. Does this drama start to make much more sense? Read also of the Philadelphia Church period in Revelation 3:7-3:12.

Try to use a different version of the Bible than the one you are used to. Especially read our portion for May, Song 3:6- 3:11. A question to ponder, are you remembering TM 409-410 and Acts 17:11? I hope so.

Ponder also just how much time can be covered in so short a period. Creation is covered in very few verses. This drama wastes no time in covering a long stretch of history.

MAY

Day 1	Exit of Exits	Song 3:6	149
Day 2	Blowing of Blowings	Song 3:6	150
Day 3	Entrance of Entrances	Revelation 12:14	151
Day 4	Pillar of Pillars	Song 3:6	152
Day 5	Perfume of Perfumes	Song 3:6	153
Day 6	Powder of Powders	Song 3:6	154
Day 7	Bed of Beds #2	Song 3:7	155
Day 8	Men of Men	Song 3:7	156
Day 9	Israelite of Israelites	Song 3:7	157
Day 10	Sword of Swords	Song 3:8	158
Day 11	Expert of Experts	Song 3:8	159
Day 12	Calculation of Calculations	Revelation 9:13	160
Day 13	Night of Nights	Song 3:8	161
Day 14	Chariot of Chariots	Song 3:7,9	162
Day 15	Wood of Woods	Song 3:9	163
Day 16	Support of Supports #1	Song 3:10	164
Day 17	Gripping of Grippings	Revelation 10:9	165
Day 18	Awakening of Awakenings	Song 3:6	166
Day 19	Relief of Reliefs	Jeremiah 20:9	167
Day 20	Encounter of Encounters	Isaiah 65:24	168
Day 21	Venture of Ventures	Song 3:7	169
Day 22	Warrior of Warriors	Song 3:7-8	170
Day 23	Messenger of Messengers #1	Song 3:10	171
Day 24	Espousal of Espousals	Song 3:11	172
Day 25	Atonement of Atonements	Song 3:11	173
Day 26	Change of Changes	Song 3:11	174
Day 27	Investigation of Investigations #1	Daniel 7:10	175
Day 28	Marriage of Marriages	Song 3:11	176
Day 29	Mood of Moods	Song 3:11	177
Day 30	Crowning of Crownings	Song 3:11	178
Day 31	Summary	Song 3:6-11	179

Poem of the Month: "A Tree of Life"   180

MAY 1   *Exit of Exits*   Song 3:6

Today's Thought: *"Who is this that cometh out of the wilderness…?"*

This starts Acts 2, Scene 3, in both the old world and the new world.

"Who is this that cometh out of the wilderness…?" Let's look at who fled into the wilderness.

Revelation 12:6 says, *"And the woman fled into the wilderness, where she hath a place prepared of God, that they should feed her there a thousand two hundred and threescore days."*

Revelation 12:14 says, *"And to the woman were given two wings of a great eagle, that she might fly into the wilderness, into her place, where she is nourished for a time, and times, and half a time, from the face of the serpent."*

Revelation 12:16 says, *"And the earth helped the woman, and the earth opened her mouth, and swallowed up the flood which the dragon cast out of his mouth."*

The woman that fled into the wilderness for 1,260 prophetic-symbolic days, and who had a place prepared for her, represents God's people—His church. She was there for 1,260 literal years, from AD 538 to AD 1798, through two church periods, the Thyatira Church from AD 538 to AD 1563, and by the Sardis Church from AD 1563 to AD 1798.

The wilderness represents a forsaken, empty place, such as the mountains of Europe, divinely appointed. The earth, representing dry, sparsely populated areas—as contrasted to "seas," which represents populated areas—that opened up her mouth to swallow the woman, was North America and the Protestant nations of Europe.

Just why should the church-bride flee into the wilderness and be there 1,260 years? What happened in or near AD 538 to send the woman into hiding?

Parting Gem: *A question for you to ponder today is, how would you react should you have some, many, or all of your freedoms taken away unless you complied with the ruling powers? Is there such an idea of peaceful coexistence when that power is determined to bring you and your thinking under its power and influence?*

MAY 2   *Blowing of Blowings*   Song 3:6

Today's Thought: *"Who is this that cometh out of the wilderness like pillars of smoke, perfumed with myrrh and frankincense, with all powders of the merchant?"*

In Revelation 8:7 and onward is the description of the trumpets, which are symbols of war. It would be profitable to read about these trumpets in 8:6- 9:21. These four trumpets were against Rome.

Trumpet #1 was the attack of Alaric of the Visigoths against Rome for Rome's first fall in AD 410. This set the stage for all other barbaric tribes to rebel against Rome. The Visigoths later settled in Spain.

Trumpet #2 was the attack against Rome by Generic of the Vandals, when Rome was looted for some two weeks. Vandals were Arians who settled in North Africa around Carthage. These were uprooted in the African campaign from AD 533 to AD 534.

Trumpet #3 was under Attila of the Huns. Rome was challenged by Attila and Rome complied. After Attila died, the Huns passed away.

Trumpet #4 was when Odoacer of the Arian nation Heruli ruled Rome from AD 476, when Rome fell, until AD 493, when another Arian tribe under Theodoric of the Ostrogoths drove the Heruli out of Rome and then ruled Rome from AD 493 to AD 538. Both the Heruli tribe and the Ostrogoths tribe were uprooted in the Italian Campaign from AD 534 to AD 538, as both of these tribe were Arians tribes, and had settled in Italy

Now that the Arian nations were uprooted, the Edict of Justinian, Emperor of Eastern Rome, which was issued in AD 533, could take effect. This edict gave to the Bishop of Rome the "authority" and the "right" to have complete and unchallenged rule over all of the "Christian Churches." Those who did not submit to this new Roman Bishop's authority had but few options. There could become slaves, they could be killed, or they could flee.

Many choose to flee. In our drama, they are called "the comely ones."

Parting Gem: *Lord, help us to be truly prepared to make such a sacrifice as did these comely one of our drama.*

MAY 3   *Entrance of Entrances*   Revelation 12:14

Today's Thought: *The woman, church, with the speed of a great eagle with powerful wings, fled into the wilderness, to a place prepared for her, where she remained for 1,260 years.*

What happened in AD 538 to send the woman fleeing into the wilderness, so that now she can come out?

Daniel 2 tells of ten toes of the great metallic image; Daniel 8 tells of ten horns, three of which were "uprooted." These ten tribes were either pagan or Arian in religion. All but three "converted" to "Christianity."

Very briefly then, to "uproot" these unwilling nations, Emperor Justinian issued the "Edict of Justinian" in AD 533. This gave the Bishop of the Church in Rome supreme authority over all churches in the empire, and was issued to get the church's permission to attack these three nations so that Aryanism could be wiped out.

When the edict was passed and the emperor got his permission, the African Campaign (AD 533-534), then the Italian Campaign (AD 534-538), wiped out these three remaining Arian nations. From that date of AD 538, the church took universal rule over all the people's mind, thoughts, life. Those not willing to submit to the church were either killed or they had to flee. So the church, the faithful ones, the comely ones, who still gave their allegiance to Almighty God, were forced to flee into the recesses of the surrounding mountains.

According to Revelation 12:14, the women fled into the wilderness where a place had been prepared for her. Now she was coming out. I like how John states that the place of refuge had been prepared for her. Surely the Lord God of Israel takes care of His people.

We should be aware, and positively so, that God also has a place for us, not only in the New Earth or Heaven, but also here upon Planet Earth. He wishes us to do His bidding, whether that's pulling wrenches, ploughing fields, teaching, preaching, or being a stay-at-home mom training the next generation to take their place in the earth made new.

Parting Gem: *Notice that the woman does not come out quietly, but like pillars of smoke, perfumed with myrrh and frankincense, with all powers of the merchants. What an awesome sight to behold.*

MAY 4 — *Pillar of Pillars* — Song 3:6

Today's Thought: *"Who is this that cometh out of the wilderness like pillars of smoke, perfumed with myrrh and frankincense, with all powders of the merchant?"*

This phrase, *"pillars of smoke,"* is used only twice in Scripture, and both times it refers to the church which comes out of the wilderness.

Joel 2:30-32 says, *"And I will shew wonders in the heavens and in the earth, blood, and fire, and pillars of smoke. The sun shall be turned into darkness, and the moon into blood, before the great and terrible day of the Lord come."*

The *"pillars of smoke"* appear to refer to the glory of God and the outpouring of His Holy Spirit. Who is this that comes up out of the wilderness, "the remnant whom the Lord shall call?" (V 33) The remnant came out of the wilderness under the signs in the heavens and the shakings of the earth. This remnant-bride was to come forth *"perfumed with myrrh and frankincense, with all the powders of the merchant,"* expecting to meet the Bridegroom.

The three and a half year French Revolution, from November 26, 1793 to June 17, 1797, was followed the next year by the startling capture and imprisonment of Catholic Church Pope Pius, which was enough to awaken the world to the fact that things were happening with speed. This immediately caused a renewed interest in the study of Scriptures, resulting in "The 1800 Awakening," which was the springboard that moved quickly into "The Great Second Advent Movement"

Amid the signs and wonders, the Philadelphia Church took the stage when the church came out of the wilderness in 1798 at the end of the Dark Ages. It came out with a sweet, appealing and feeling-aroused message, *"Behold the bridegroom cometh; go ye out to meet him"* (Matthew 25:6).

Consider Isaiah 6:2-4, *"Above it stood the seraphims... And one cried to another, and said, Holy, holy, holy, is the Lord of hosts: the whole earth is full of his glory. And the posts of the door moved at the voice of him that cried, and the house was filled with smoke."*

Parting Gem: *How appropriate that our Song of Songs, which is a song about the Bridegroom and His bride, should focus on that proclamation of His Second Advent.*

MAY 5 — Perfume of Perfumes — Song 3:6

Today's Thought: *"Who is this that cometh out of the wilderness like pillars of smoke, perfumed with myrrh and frankincense, with all the powder of the merchant?"*

Our drama is replete with descriptions of the bride-church, symbolized by perfumes, myrrh, pomegranate, apples, garden of nuts and spices, and all the chief spices. One could and should get the idea that this bride-church is pleasant to the eye, harmonious to the touch, melodious to the ear, sweet-smelling to the nose, sweet to the taste.

Yet, while she is all this, she is also a church militant coming up out of wilderness with a mighty display of power and activity. Song 8:5 tells us that she comes up out of the wilderness *"leaning upon her beloved."* This is the Philadelphia Church coming on stage. The Philadelphia Church was a church that did not receive a *"I have somewhat against thee"* in Revelation 3. The Sardis Church was the other.

Life Sketches states, "We have nothing to fear for the future except as we shall forget the way the Lord has led us and our teachings in our past history"[7]

The "coming out of the wilderness" period speaks of the time from 1798 to 1844, into the Awakening and the Great Advent Movement, and all the powders of the merchant. This merchant is the same one who sells His goods in Revelation 3:18. He sells His righteousness, the Holy Spirit, faith, eye salve, white raiment, so that the buyer may see, be rich, not be ashamed of being naked.

Notice Song 4:3-6, where she is categorized with orchards of pomegranates, with pleasant fruits, camphire, spikenard, as well as saffron, calamus, cinnamon.

Parting Gem: *Back in 2:1, the bride states that she is the rose of Sharon. Roses have thorns, so although this bride of ours is "The First Lady of the Multiverse," she still may have prickly characteristics as in a rose, but still the only object upon which God bestows His highest and supreme regard. What an awesome and sobering thought.*

---

[7] White, E.G. & C.C. Criter & W.C. White. *Life Sketches* (Boise, ID: Pacific Press), 1915, p. 196.

MAY 6 — *Powder of Powders* — Song 3:6

Today's Thought: *"Who is this that cometh out of the wilderness like pillars of smoke, perfumed with myrrh and frankincense, with all powders of the merchant?"*

When Jehovah God, in the time of Moses, wanted to talk to His people Israel, He first had to get their attention. What more dramatic way than to gather them around Mount Sinai with thunder, lightning, flames of fire, rumbling mountains, and a Voice. He had their attention.

So, just before the time to come out of the wilderness, the attention of the world was grabbed by the great Lisbon, Portugal earthquake of November 1, 1755. That earthquake was felt from the north to the south, the east to the west.

Then still to grab their attention, on May 19, 1780, the day that started out normally, suddenly grew dark. Cows came in to be milked, chickens took to their roosts, candles had to be lit at home and work in order to see. Applying more powder to the already smoking gun, that night the moon turned to the colour of blood.

Thirteen years later, and lasting three and-a-half years, from November 26, 1793 to June 17, 1797, the French Revolution broke out. This was quickly followed by Pope Pius being taken prisoner by the French General Berthier.

Then along comes November 13, 1833, when the whole of the heavens around the New England states seemed to fall down on Planet Earth with the great meteoritic shower. Like a fig tree being shaken by the mighty wind, stars flew irregularly in every direction.

The bride, as the Philadelphia Church, came out of the wilderness (1798-1844), in the awakening of the Great Advent Movement, *"perfumed with myrrh and frankincense, with all powders of the merchant."* Amid the signs and wonders of the heavens, the true bride was to come out of her 1,260 years in the wilderness.

Parting Gem: *With all of the "powder" being blown around in our day, the fires, floods, drought, wars, famines, corruption, bankrupts, fraud, wickedness in many places, can you hear the Beloved's voice? With another idea, is history going to be repeated, with earthquakes, a dark day, bloody moon, falling stars, etc.?*

MAY 7   Bed of Beds #2   Song 3:7

Today's Thought: *"Behold his bed, which is Solomon's."*

This starts Act 2, Scene 4, which took place from 1831 to 1844 in both the old and the new world.

This bed, according to the marginal reference, is a "litter," a transportable conveyance on which one could be carried. Once again, in verse 9 this "bed" is referred to as a chariot, and in the marginal reference to a "palanquin," which is a kind of sedan chair, carried on the shoulders of men. The Pope of Rome rides upon such a chair carried on the shoulders of his cardinals amid pomp and glory, demonstrating the kind of "bed" illustrated in this text.

Webster defines "palanquin" as a conveyance consisting of an enclosed litter, borne on the shoulders of men, by means of poles.

Christ, embodied in Present Truth, in a proclamation of prophetic Scripture, with its message of the coming of the Bridegroom anticipated in 1844, was carried forth to the world on the shoulders of men in a marching, living movement.

"Behold his bed." We are admonished to behold, to take notice, to consider this Great Advent Movement, this great army as it marched in formation towards the 1844 date to meet the Bridegroom. A bed surrounded by threescore valiant men, the valiant of all Israel, swords in their hands, every man in his place.

The prophecy of the 2,300 days had predicted accurately the first coming of the Messiah, and it appeared that by simple arithmetic, it had also foretold the time of the Second Coming. By application of the year-day principle—one prophetic day represents one literal year—the 2,300 days would end in 1844 AD, at which time the Bridegroom should return. This is the message this chariot carried to the world.

These Bible students presumed that the "sanctuary" referred to the earth, which the second coming of Christ would cleanse of sin. Although they were incorrect in their understanding of what the "sanctuary" represented, their arithmetic was correct. The date, 1844, was indeed an important point in time, which did reveal the position and work of the Bridegroom. Indeed, she had *"found Him."*

Parting Gem: *The song "Onward Christian Soldiers" comes to mind.*

MAY 8 — *Men of Men* — Song 3:7

Today's Thought: *"... threescore valiant men are about it, of the valiant of Israel."*

Now the curtain opens of Act 2, Scene 4.

These *"threescore valiant men... of the valiant of Israel"* were those students of Prophecy, using their "sword"—the Word of God, who by individual study simultaneously concluded that Jesus would come in 1844.

They are described in Ephesians as standing in their place wearing the whole armour of God, knowing that their fight was to be against principalities, powers, and the rulers of darkness.

L. E. Froom, in his volume *The Prophetic Faith of Our Fathers, Vol. IV*, states that there were threescore earnest students of prophecy who were from different denominations and languages who proclaimed that the 2,300-day prophecy would end around 1843-1844. This reached into India and Africa.

In the United States, William Miller was foremost and those who became involved were known as "Millerites." In South America, a priest known as Lucunza published a similar interpretation. He published under the pseudonym Rabbi Ben Ezra. Joseph Wolf traveled over much of Asia, Africa, and India, and in various places he found isolated tribes and barbarous people who knew of such prophecies and expected the Lord to come about 1844. Wolfe even spoke and gave his message to the United States Congress.

These threescore valiant prophetic expositors led out in the great movement as a marching army, called by the pioneers the "Captains of the Host" (*Captain of the Host,* Spalding). The inspired child preachers of Sweden quoted from the book of Joel 2:1-11

It was not the scholarly theologians of Christendom who had an understanding of the prophetic symbolism for their day. "Had these been faithful watchmen diligently and prayerfully searching the Scriptures, they would have known the time of the night" (GC 312).

Parting Gem: *Does this time in history call for the need of a "hero"? Choose today to stand up and be that hero, a man among men (or woman).*

MAY 9　　　　　　　　*Israelite of Israelites*　　　　　　　　Song 3:7

Today's Thought: *"Behold his bed, which is Solomon's; threescore valiant men are about it, of the valiant of Israel."*

"When the fulness of the time was come, God sent forth his Son... that we might receive the adoption of sons... and if a son, then an heir of God through Christ" (Galatians 4:4-5,7).

"For as many of you as have been baptized into Christ have put on Christ... And if ye be Christ's, then are ye Abraham's seed, and heirs according to the promise" (Galatians 3:27,29).

"For as many as are led by the Spirit of God, they are the sons of God... The Spirit itself beareth witness with our spirit, that we are the children of God: and if children, then heirs; heirs of God, and joint-heirs with Christ" (Romans 8:14,16-17).

"Now therefore ye are no more strangers and foreigners, but fellow citizens with the saints, and of the household of God" (Ephesians 2:19).

"For he is not a Jew, which is one outwardly; neither is that circumcision, which is outward in the flesh: But he is a Jew, which is one inwardly; and circumcision is that of the heart, in the spirit, and not in the letter; whose praise is not of men, but of God" (Romans 2:18-29).

"For they are not all Israel, which are of Israel: Neither, because they are the seed of Abraham, are they all children..." (Romans 9:6-7).

This can be understood in that Abraham had Ishmael, whom the Arabs claim as their ancestor. He was also the father of six other sons through a second wife who became ancestors of Arabia tribes.

What an awesome procedure. When we are adopted into the family of God through the acceptance of Jesus Christ into our lives, then we become sons and daughters of God, which makes us not only heirs of God, but joint-heirs with Christ. Yet who are the valiant of Israel?

Just in passing, as a child of the heavenly King, we now have royal blood within our veins.

Parting Gem: *"We know what we worship: for salvation is of the Jews"* (John 4:22). What a privilege to be an Israelite.

MAY 10   *Sword of Swords*   Song 3:8

Today's Thought: *"They all hold swords, being expert in war: every man hath his sword upon his thigh because of fear in the night."*

Remembering that Song of Songs is a prophetic, symbolic book, we take another look at these threescore valiant men, this time found in Ephesians 6:10-18, *"Finally, my brethren, be strong in the Lord, and in the power of his might. Put on the whole armour of God, that ye may be able to stand against the wiles of the devil. For we wrestle not against flesh and blood, but against principalities, against powers, against the rulers of the darkness of this world, against spiritual wickedness in high places. Wherefore take unto you the whole armour of God, that ye may be able to stand in the evil day, and having done all, to stand. Stand therefore, having your loins girt about with truth, having on the breastplate of righteousness; And your feet shod with the preparation of the gospel of peace; Above all, take the shield of faith, wherewith ye shall be able to quench all the fiery darts of the wicked. And take the helmet of salvation, and the sword of the Spirit which is the word of God: praying always with all prayer and supplication in the Spirit, and watching thereunto with all perseverance and supplication for all saints."*

Wow! What a picture. Can you visualize all those sixty valiant men (and women) as they stand shoulder to shoulder, united as one?

Because the sixty warriors, these men of men who have been handling the sword of the Spirit which is the Word of God, knew that Word, and were all instructed how to be an excellent swordsman by the same master Swordsman, they therefore all came, simultaneously, to the same conclusion, that Jesus Christ was to come to cleanse this earth in or around 1844. With great desire, they looked for the coming of the Bridegroom.

Parting Gem: *Catch the vision! Have your sword handy, by your side, and sharpened to a cutting edge, ready to stand like the brave with your face to the foe. This sword that you have handy, like strapped to your side, is sharpened to that cutting edge one needs by daily using it, getting practice wielding it, memorize the sweeps and the swipes of swordsmanship.*

MAY 11　　　　　　　　*Expert of Experts*　　　　　　　Song 3:8

Today's Thought: *"They all hold swords, being expert in war: every man hath his sword upon his thigh because of fear in the night."*

One example of experts in war occurred in 1838. Josiah Litch, an associate of William Miller, predicted that the power of the Ottoman Empire would be broken in August, 1840. He based his prediction on Revelation 9. Early in August, he predicted that it would be August 11, 1840. Based on historical precedent, he predicted that the Ottoman Empire would voluntarily give up power.

As the prophetic period of the sixth trumpet began by the voluntary surrender of power to the Turks, so we might conclude its termination would be marked by the same voluntary surrender of the power back into Christian hands.

In 1449 (note the date), the Greek emperor John Paleologus died, leaving no children to succeed him. Constantine Deacozes succeeded to the empire, but stated that he would only rule by permission of the Turkish sultan, a voluntary acknowledgement on his part.

In England, 1840, some 391 years later (note the date, and the number of years, 391), Russia, Austria, Prussia put together terms in the London Convention that determined how the Ottoman Empire would be voluntarily given up. Since this time of break-up, Turkey has been called, "The Sick Man of the East."

When Josiah Litch's prediction came as predicted, it caused quite some stir among the atheistic and sceptical community. Quite a number renounced their former opposition to such ideas as religion and the second coming, joined up with Miller and his movement, and began to preach it.

They say that to become an expert one must practice, yet not just practice, but practice the correct way. Practice doesn't necessarily make perfect, but it does make permanent. So, take your sword and start to yield it, asking God for heavenly wisdom and correct procedures.

Parting Gem: *Beloved, as our Commander-in-chief, help us prepare for the battles that are ahead of us today. Help us to have a sharp sword attached firmly to our side, and to be able to wield it with honour.*

MAY 12   *Calculation of Calculations*   Revelation 9:13

Today's Thought: *"And the sixth angel sounded, and I heard a voice from the four horns of the golden altar which is before God, saying to the sixth angel which had the trumpet, Loose the four angels which are bound in the great river Euphrates. And the four angels were loosed, which were prepared for an hour, and a day, and a month, and a year, for to slay the third part of men."*

Here is how Litch did his calculations. Remember the dates given to you yesterday. Calculated from the close of the fifth trumpet, July 25, 1499, which was 150 years from the first attack against the Ottoman Empire on July 25, 1299, and going 391 years to July 25, 1449, we have:

- One prophetic hour = 15 literal days.
- One prophetic day = 1 literal year.
- One prophetic month = 30 literal years.
- One prophetic year = 360 literal years.
  For a total of 391 years, 15 days.

From July 25, 1449, add 391 years. It comes to July 25, 1840,
    Add 15 days, and it brings you to August 11, 1840. It was on that date, August 11, 1840, that the Ottoman Empire voluntarily gave up their independence and supremacy.

This dead-on fulfillment of the prediction by Josiah Litch in 1838 brought tremendous impetus to the Millerite Movement, which was prophesying the second coming of Christ. It caused many inside the atheistic and infidel world to give up their beliefs and their fight; some even became preachers in the Millerite Movement, preaching the Second Coming of Christ.

This should bring to one a tremendous amount of confidence in his God and it builds his faith, brings his hope, and lets him know what is going to happen.

Parting Gem: *All Scripture is profitable for doctrine, reproof, correction, and instruction in righteousness. Yet this warrior, Josiah Litch, had a sharp sword of the Spirit and knew just how to wield it.*

MAY 13 — *Night of Nights* — Song 3:8

Today's Thought: *"They all hold swords, being expert in war: every man hath his sword upon his thigh because of fear in the night."*

In our drama, the first night we encountered was the night of the Dark Ages, those 1,260 years from AD 538 to AD 1798. In Song 2:11, this night is likened to the winter which is past, and spring is in the air by the beginning of the Reformation. In 2:17, we read about the daybreak and the shadows that flee away, indicative of the end of those dark days.

Yet, the darkest night of all nights broke out sometime in heaven when an angel, Lucifer, the covering cherub, broke rank and rebelled against God, the other angels, and theoretically against himself. Since that time this world has indeed been in a dark night.

It is this night that these warriors of warriors move out into. Their swords, the Word of the Living God, is upon their thighs, very handy in the event of a need, for they never know when a lion will burst out of nowhere to attack and consume.

Then also, they are aware of Ephesians 6:12. *"For we wrestle not against flesh and blood, but against principalities, against powers, against the rulers of the darkness of this world, against spiritual wickedness in high places."*

They are very much aware of 1 Peter 5:8, where it states, *"Be sober, be vigilant; because your adversary the devil, as a roaring lion, walketh about, seeking whom he may devour."*

However, like Song 2:17 states, we will experience a daybreak and the shadows will flee away. In Revelation 22:5, it says, *"And there shall be no night there; and they need no candle, neither light of the sun; for the Lord God giveth them light: and they shall reign for ever and forever."*

Just in passing, that's the way it was from creation to the flood; there was no night there. Only after the flood when the sun and moon were affected did night and darkness come into existence. See Appendix 6.

Parting Gem: *This long night that we are experiencing in our daily sojourn is dark or light according to our attitude. It's a self-fulfilling prophecy. If I think it is great, it is; should I think everyone is evil and after me, then they are. Today, think positively and keep your eyes on the Light of the World.*

MAY 14 — *Chariot of Chariots* — Song 3:7,9

Today's Thought: *"Behold his bed which is Solomon's… King Solomon made himself a chariot of the wood of Lebanon…"*

Notice the Hebrew structure. Should you miss the bed, then the chariot should draw your attention. Behold the bed, or chariot, the Great Second Advent Movement, who with the threescore valiant men from all parts of the world declared with a loud voice the first angels message of Revelation 14:7, *"The hour of His judgment is come."* Listen to this message echoing from thousands of pulpits all over the world, the Midnight Cry: *"Behold, the bridegroom cometh, go ye out to meet him"* (Matthew 25:6).

Behold His church which, like a comely and delicate woman, cometh out of the wilderness with all of the fanfare of lightnings, fire and pillars of smoke, perfumed with myrrh and frankincense, with all the *"powders of the merchant"* (Song 3:6). Behold her as she comes forth, attended with the signs and wonders in the heavens and on earth, emerging as the "remnant" people of God. The last of the seven women.

Behold Him, the Charioteer, as He is about to appear before the Ancient of Days, to receive the dominion, the glory, the kingdom. Behold Him as He comes into the Investigative Judgment, to the heavenly marriage to receive His kingdom.

Behold this chariot as it carries the first angel's message, *"Fear God, and give glory to him"* (Revelation 14:7). *"Let all the inhabitants of the land tremble: for the day of the Lord cometh, for it is nigh at hand"* (Joel 2:1). This *"day of the Lord"* is none other than the "Day of Atonement," "the cleansing of the sanctuary," and the time of the "marriage." I like to remember that after the wedding comes the party, the celebration; the Bible calls it the Marriage Supper of the Lamb.

Parting Gem: *Consider the Word of the Lord as supporting pillars, with a bottom of pure faith as the pure gold of Ophir, with ability to meet royalty in the coverings of purple, all paved with the love of Jehovah (Psalms 12:6, Revelation 3:8, 1 Corinthians 13).*

MAY 15 — Wood of Woods — Song 3:9

Today's Thought: *"King Solomon made himself a chariot of the wood of Lebanon."*

Do you remember who King Solomon is symbolizing? This is King Jesus, King of Spiritual Israel, King of the Universe just as Solomon was literal king of literal Israel. For we must remember that what we literally read is not what is literally meant, as this drama is in symbolic language. Therefore we must read that, *"King Jesus made Himself a chariot…"*

There are several definitions or synonyms of "made" (make) in Collins Essential Canadian English Dictionary and Thesaurus, such as "create," which means to assemble, build, construct, fashion, manufacture, produce, put together. So then, "King Jesus created, fashioned, put together for Himself a chariot."

He made "himself," or for Himself, not for any one else, this chariot. This is His chariot, His church, His establishment. This is the apple or the "pupil" of the eye. The eye reflects what it sees. As well, it is the one place in the body that is most in need of protection.

He made a chariot, or church, that comely and delicate thing which has often be described as the "enemies' worst nightmare." This is a conveyance carrying good news to all the world; that's what this chariot is.

To get the drama's picture of this chariot, read Song 3:6, *"Who is this that cometh out of the wilderness like pillars of smoke, perfumed with myrrh and frankincense, with all powders of the merchant?"* Or consider Song 6:4, *"Thou art beautiful, O my love… terrible as an army with banners."*

But the wood of Lebanon? In Lebanon were the world-famous cedars and fir, or cypresses. Beside these there were the pines, oaks, and a large selection of fruit and nut trees like olive, walnut, apricot, pear, pomegranate, mulberry, pistachio.

Today's Gem: *What a chariot! What a church! The selection, the variety, the choices are abundant. Take a look, take a good look, at that chariot, that church, then praise King Jesus for forging this chariot together.*

MAY 16 — *Support of Supports #1* — Song 3:10

Today's Thought: *"He made the pillars thereof of silver, the bottom thereof of gold, the covering of it of purple, the midst thereof being paved with love, for the daughters of Jerusalem."*

The Word of the Lord is seen as supporting pillars, with a bottom of pure faith like the golden wedge of Ophir, with the ability to meet royalty in the coverings of purple, all paved with the love of Jehovah (Psalms 12:6, Revelation 3:8, 1 Corinthians 13).

Should you see, coming down the road, some sixty armed warriors running beside this conveyance called a "bed," a chariot, a palanquin or an enclosed litter, being borne on the shoulders of some of these men by means of poles; what thinkest thou?

When high government officials like Prime Ministers and Presidents of countries move about the country, they have bodyguards around, between, beside and all over, just to protect. Here in this picture we have a Movement, the Great Second Advent Movement supported by scholars and warriors, with their Bibles always handy or swords by their thighs. They were carrying the First Angel's Message to all the world. It is a massive sight (Joel 2,7-9, Ephesians 6:14-17).

In other places, eight of them, the Bible, the Old Testament and the New Testament, are compared to grapes, to breasts, but here it is compared to pillars of silver. Psalm 12:6 says, *"The words of the Lord are pure words: as silver tried in the furnace of earth, purified seven times."* This movement, the Great Second Advent Movement, carried by warriors and evangelists, from 1833 to 1844, swept across the country. Mighty men of war like Miller, Himes, Litch, Fitch in North America, Lacunza in South America, Joseph Wolfe from Britain pushed the soon coming of the Bridegroom message until it was the talk of the town.

Yet this verse seems to say that the Word of the Living God is the support of this chariot (Movement) that Solomon (Christ) has made.

Parting Gem: *Should you feel that you would like to be one of the Adventist's warriors, the opportunities seem endless. Contact your local conference as to what is available, where the needs are or who to contact in order to serve. The rewards are staggering.*

MAY 17 *Gripping of Grippings* Revelation 10:9

Today's Thought: *"Take it [the book], and eat it up."*

A spiritual hunger for understanding gripped Miller; laying aside all preconceived ideas, using only his Bible and a concordance, he launched into a deep two-year Bible study from 1816 to 1818.

At the conclusion of his study in 1818, he found his thinking and conclusions very far distant from the popular theological teaching of his time. He concluded, among other doctrines, that the world was living at the end of the fulfillment of Daniel 2.

To Miller, as Adventists have found, Daniel 2 was the key to unlock prophecy. Daniel 8:14 gripped his attention, *"Unto two thousand and three-hundred days; then shall the sanctuary be cleansed."* His solemn conclusion in 1818 was "that in about 25 years, or near 1843, all affairs of our present world would be wound up."[8]

To Miller, the conclusions were clear-cut, sound, convincing, yet they were so very different from those generally held by people that he felt it his responsibility to restudy the complete matter. So for the next four years, 1818-1822, again in serious and deep study, he devoted as much time as he could to confirm or to retract his original conclusions.

At the conclusion of this four-year study, which was now 1822, his conclusions confirmed his previous convictions, yet they were wider and deeper in coverage. He again summarized his conclusions, and experienced a growing conviction come over him.

"Go, tell it to the world." He felt that urgent need to have everyone ready for the event due within twenty-five years.

It was gripping. According to Collins Thesaurus, gripping has meanings like fascinating, compelling, compulsive, engrossing, enthralling, entrancing, exciting, riveting, spellbinding, thrilling, and unputdownable.

Parting Gem: *I'm wondering if it could be possible for us to get this urgent need to GO tell it to the world, or at least our neighbours? No? Then could we get the urgent need to tell it to our children in such a way that they will grab that spiritual torch, hold it high, and run with it? Yes! Good.*

---

[8] Knight, George R. *Lest We Forget* (Washington, DC: Review & Herald), 2008, p. 6.

MAY 18 *Awakening of Awakenings* Song 3:6

Today's Thought: *"Who is this that cometh out of the wilderness like pillars of smoke, perfumed with myrrh and frankincense, with all powders of the merchant?"*

While Europe, Asia, and other countries were being stirred about the second coming of Christ, in America, a parallel and similar awakening was taking place.

William Miller, who lived most of his life in Low Hampton, New York, from February 15, 1782 to December 20, 1849, was a farmer. A man of honesty, truthfulness and clean living, he enjoyed the respect of his fellow townsmen. He was a deputy sheriff, a Justice of the Peace, a captain of the 30th infantry in the War of 1812 between Canada and the United States. He came out of that war much more serious than when he entered.

He attended the Low Hampton Baptist Church, although he was not a member. His uncle was the minister. If his uncle preached the sermon, he would attend; he would not attend, however, if some substitute reader took the service. Because it was so poorly read, Miller got nothing out of it. He hinted that he himself should read.

The church requested him to read on Sunday, September 15, 1816. While reading the sermon on Isaiah 53, Miller came under such strong conviction that he had to sit down, later to accept Jesus Christ as his Saviour.

A certain void in his heart, placed there by God, had been awakened and now filled; peace swept through him. The Bible became his delight, and in Jesus Christ he found a friend.

Yet that was not the end, maybe the beginning, for the best was yet to come. It was a scary time for William, although he didn't know it then. Read on in the days to come to see what happens when one commits himself to following God's leadings.

Parting Gem: *That's what happens when one spends time in the Word; he finds the Author of that Word, who then becomes his Friend, his constant Companion. That invitation is extended to you today.*

MAY 19　　　　　　　*Relief of Reliefs*　　　　　　　Jeremiah 20:9

Today's Thought: *"Then I said, I will not make mention of him, nor speak any more in his name. But his word was in mine heart as a burning fire shut up in my bones, and I was weary of forbearing, and I could not stay."*

Over the next nine years—1822 to 1831—Miller quietly, in private and through letters, told others of his expectations. As years passed, he struggled with a growing conviction to help warn the world. This struggle between his sense of conviction and his feelings of inadequacy reached a breaking point in mid-August, 1831.

August 13, 1831 was a Saturday. Miller was about to go to some task. He had had breakfast, and he had had his time of study. Suddenly, the conviction came, *"Go, tell it to the world!"* It came so vividly that Miller was forced to sit down and cry, "I can't go, Lord!"

As vividly, as forcefully as before, the reply came, *"Why not?"*

All kinds of reasons came tumbling out: "I am too old, nearly fifty years old, I am not trained, I am a farmer, not a preacher, I am slow of speech." Yet, all excuses seemed like patches of failure and were swept away with the overpowering conviction.

This distress became so sharp and so marked that Miller, in an effort to be relieved, promised the Lord that if He were to open the way very definitely, Miller would respond and perform his duty. The voice again, *"What do you mean by opening the way?"*

"I mean," replied Miller, "that should I have a personal invitation to speak publicly in any place, I will go and tell what I have found." Immediately relief and peace swept over him.

Move over, William, for here I come.

Parting Gem: *Another exciting and sweet portion of his study was Revelation 10, where he read of the little book experience and the sweetness of that message. The first portion of Revelation 10 truly is a sweet experience, the tremendous message of the soon-coming Bridegroom is enough to grip one's whole life. However, Brother Miller, please read a bit further to the stomach experience.*

MAY 20　　　　　*Encounter of Encounters*　　　　　Isaiah 65:24

Today's Thought: *"And it shall come to pass, that before they call, I will answer; and while they are yet speaking, I will hear."*

This is truly the experience that Miller had, for as this peace swept through him, his young nephew, Irving Guilford, was pushing his horse at top speed from nearby Dresden, where he lived, to Low Hampton, where Uncle William lived. He had a personal invitation for Miller to speak publicly at the Dresden Baptist Church explaining his views and convictions. The pastor was away, but Miller's sister and her husband proposed William be invited.

When the lad had delivered the invitation, Miller was thunderstruck, then he was angry—with himself for covenanting with God, then with God. He determined not to go.

Without a word, Miller stormed out of the house to the maple grove behind his house to pray. The longer he prayed, the stronger the conviction, *"GO, tell it to the world."*

Miller, being the kind of person he was, made his decision. "Lord, I will go." He went into that orchard a farmer; he came out of that same orchard a preacher.

The next day, Sunday, found him in the Guilford's home for his first sermon. He felt the church was too sacred for him to present his ideas. The house was well filled with surrounding neighbours eager to hear what he had to say. The excited neighbours, with the sweetness like honey of a message in their mouths, insisted he stay and continue his study through the week. He stayed and preached; they stayed and ate it up.

Parting Gem: *Should you really desire to work for the Lord, be careful what you ask for; it may just happen. I personally prayed for an opportunity to witness. That was on about Monday; on Friday our friends the Jehovah's Witnesses knocked on my door. The rest of that winter was spent comparing doctrines. They are fantastic people.*

MAY 21   *Venture of Ventures*   Song 3:7

Today's Thought: *"Behold his bed, which is Solomon's; threescore valiant men are about it, of the valiant of Israel."*

Arriving home the following Monday, an invitation to speak at Poultney, a few miles away, awaited Miller.

In quick succession, invitations followed Miller's first venture from Baptists, Methodists, Congregationalists, churches throughout New England, eastern Canada, then Ohio, south to Maryland. The Millerite Movement, as it was later known, was launched.

In 1834, he gave himself to preaching full-time. His sons did the farm work. In nine years, he preached four thousands sermons in about five hundred towns and cities. He never went uninvited. Due to his eating and sleeping habits, he was sick a fair bit of the time.

In 1838, Josiah Litch, a Methodist minister, joined forces with Miller. Josiah Litch brought on board Charles Fitch. Fitch was a former preacher with the Congregationalist Church of Boston and the Free Presbyterian Church of Newark, New Jersey. After reading and studying Miller's message deeply and finding everything he read Biblical, Fitch threw his life into preaching the soon-coming Bridegroom message.[9] Fitch became one of the most beloved and successful preachers in the Advent movement.

Fitch died October 14, 1844, some eight days before the expected Bridegroom's coming. He was in Buffalo, New York, where he baptized a group of believers in frigid Lake Erie. In wet clothes, he started back to his cabin to change only to meet a second group. He returned to baptize them. Then a third group requested baptism. Overexertion to the elements brought on illness and death (*Lest We Forget*).

As early as 1842, a prophecy in Habakkuk 2:1-4, *"Write the vision, and make it plain upon tables,"* suggested to Charles Fitch the preparation of prophetic charts to illustrate the visions of Daniel and Revelation (GC 392).

Parting Gem: *Father, give me that zeal and thirst for souls.*

---

[9] Ibid.

MAY 22 *Warrior of Warriors* Song 3:7-8

Today's Thought: *"Behold his bed, which is Solomon's; threescore valiant men are about it, of the valiant of Israel. They all hold swords, being expert in war: every man hath his sword upon his thigh because of fear in the night."*

Then in 1839, the preacher who likely contributed the most to the Millerite Movement, Joshua V. Himes, threw all his talents and energies into the task of proclaiming the Advent Message. Through Himes, Millerism took on a new thrust, a new dynamic, so much so that between 1840 and 1844 Millerism went into high gear until Millerism was a word everyone recognized.[10]

Please remember that by 1839 there were only five years left before 1843, the year pegged by Miller for the cleansing of the sanctuary.

It was Joshua V. Himes who was responsible for drawing Miller out of the smaller cities and towns and into the larger cities.

It was Himes who organized and managed camp meetings which brought out tens of thousands. In 130 camp-meetings in 1843 and 1844, an estimated one million came. The United States' population was only seven million.

It was Himes who started daily newspapers to publicize the advent teachings. His first paper was started March 20, 1840, and called "Signs of the Times." When its time and usefulness was over, it ceased to be published.

Years later, James White started a different paper also known today as "Signs of the Times," but not the same paper.

George K. Knight, in his book *Lest We Forget,* mentions how Himes was described as "an unprecedented media blitz... an unprecedented communication avalanche."[11]

Another describes him as the "Napoleon of the press."

Combining Miller with Himes, and a whole lot of less visible people, a dynamic movement surged ahead.

Parting Gem: *You are cordially invited, yea, urged to join this dynamic movement as it continues to surge forward.*

---

[10] Ibid., p. 23.
[11] Ibid.

MAY 23   *Messenger of Messengers #1*   Song 3:10

Today's Thought: *"He made the pillars thereof of silver, the bottom thereof of gold, the covering of it of purple, the midst thereof being paved with love, for the daughters of Jerusalem."*

Within a few weeks of the disappointment, on a December day in 1844, while five ladies were praying, one of them, seventeen-year-old Ellen Gould Harmon, had the power of God come upon her. Over the next seventy-one years, the Lord used her as His Messenger, giving His people infallible advice, thus giving God's people the assurance that He has been with us every step of the way, and of meeting one of the prerequisites for claiming to be God's chosen church, the apple of His eye, His spouse, the Holy Bride that He is coming to claim.

It is the woman that keeps the commandments of God and that has the testimony of Jesus Christ that the dragon was wroth with. This testimony of Jesus Christ is declared to be the Spirit of Prophecy (Revelation 12:17 and 19:10). It is also this gift of prophecy that is listed by Paul in Ephesians 4, that after Christ ascended He gave gifts unto men. He gave this gift along with others for the purpose of perfecting the saints in their work of the ministry as they edify the body of Christ until we all come into that unity and knowledge of Christ that He prayed for, not to mention it as an identifying characteristic of the Remnant bride-church, the last church.

Over the next five days, we will look at some nine tests of a true prophet and leave you to apply them to the prophet of our girl of all girls, even our messenger of all messengers.

The nominal Adventists rejected this distinctive truth as well. Looking back over the history of those who have rejected this precious gift reveals the consequences of doing just that. It is not a pretty picture.

Parting Gem: *As one contemplates what literal Israel of old would have been like had God not continually sent prophets, what would this movement, out of the 1800 Religious Awakening, have become without the guiding hand of our Almighty God through the years?*

MAY 24 — *Espousal of Espousals* — Song 3:11

Today's Thought: *"Go forth, O ye daughters of Zion, and behold king Solomon with the crown wherewith his mother crowned him in the day of his espousals, and in the days of the gladness of his heart."*

You have just received an invitation to the marriage of your best friend. You are cordially invited to the espousal (marriage) of King Solomon (Christ). The coming of Christ as our High Priest to the most holy place, for the cleansing of the sanctuary... is also represented by the coming of the Bridegroom to the marriage (GC 426). There in the sanctuary, He began the work of the Investigative Judgment, and this judgment is likened to a marriage. (See Appendix 4.)

In the eastern countries where women have no legal status, they do not enter into any of the legal aspects of the marriage. The bridegroom arranges with the bride's father to pay the dowry, and it is only males who sign the legal documents. The bride herself does not attend the "marriage," which involves legal procedures. Then, when all legal papers are signed and the dowry is paid, the bridegroom with his attendants comes to get his bride and the banquet begins. That's why, to the western world, the parable of the ten virgins seems so strange. Pause right now to read Matthew 25:1-13, the parable of the ten virgins. This will be clearer after realizing the make-up of an eastern wedding.

Can you hear the presiding minister, the heavenly Father, say to the Bridegroom, "Do you take this person to be a legal and lawful member of your heavenly kingdom? Will he have all of the protection, privileges, rights of your kingdom so long as that kingdom shall last?"

Listen to the Bridegroom reply as expressed with exceeding joy, "I do, I do, I really, really do." Name by name, beginning with the first generation, down to our own day, through the legal process Christ makes up His kingdom.

Parting Gem: *According to Jude 24, Christ is not only able to keep us from falling, but to present us faultless before His glory. But the exciting part is that He does this with exceeding joy, enthusiasm, eagerness, happy anticipation of the days ahead.*

MAY 25   *Atonement of Atonements*   Song 3:11

Today's Thought: *Behold, take notice, be aware of King Solomon in that day when he shall be married, when his mother crowns him.*

The Day of Atonement: *"And this shall be a statute for ever unto you: that in the seventh month, on the tenth day of the month, ye shall afflict your souls… For on that day shall the priest make an atonement for you, to cleanse you, that ye may be clean from all your sins before the Lord… And he shall make an atonement for the holy sanctuary… for the tabernacle… for the altar… for the priests, and for all the people of the congregation"* (Leviticus 16:29-30,33).

The "Day of Atonement" in ancient Israel was a type of the final atonement which Christ makes for His people in the time of the Investigative Judgment, or cleansing of the sanctuary. The word "Atonement" means "at-one-ment," a process of bringing back into unity or complete harmony that which has been separated. It is sin that has separated man from God. Christ, by an application of His blood sacrifice in the Investigative Judgment, brings His people back into complete harmony with God. As the record of their sins is removed from heaven, as the sanctuary is cleansed, then there is nothing left to separate them from God and it is a day of "at-one-ment." It is a day when Christ brings us, His children, into a unity, a oneness, a bonding relationship with Him. Is that not an awesome thought? Don't you just love Him?

"The intercession of Christ in man's behalf in the sanctuary above is as essential to the plan of salvation as was His death upon the cross. By His death He began that work which after His resurrection He ascended to complete in heaven. We are now living in the great day of atonement… The judgment is now passing in the sanctuary above… soon it shall pass to the cases of the living…" (GC 489-490)

Parting Gem: *"Heavenly Father, help us to look at the Investigative Judgment with joy and rejoicing, for it is the time that you have set aside to put our names on your wedding list, because we are friends."*

MAY 26 — *Change of Changes* — Song 3:11

Today's Thought: *Let us behold King Solomon on his wedding day.*

The Cleansing of the Sanctuary: "… now once in the end of the world hath he appeared to put away sin," and "on that day shall the priest [a type of Christ] make an atonement for you, to cleanse you, that ye may be clean from all your sins before the Lord" (Leviticus 16:30). "And he shall make an atonement for the holy sanctuary… for all their sins" (Leviticus 33:34). This is the part that grabbed William Miller.

In heaven, the confessed sins of God's people who place their faith in Jesus have been accumulating through the centuries on the books of record in the heavenly sanctuary, which defiles the heavenly sanctuary. In the Investigative Judgment, when Jesus confesses each name before the Father and the angels and witnesses of the universe, those records of sin are blotted out—thus the cleansing of the sanctuary.

The Seal of God: "Zechariah's vision of Joshua and the Angel applies with peculiar force to the experience of God's people in the closing up of the great day of atonement" The encouraging words are spoken, "Behold, I have caused thine iniquity to pass from thee…! the spotless robe of Christ's righteousness is placed upon the tried, tempted, yet faithful children of God. . .holy angels, unseen, were passing to and fro, placing upon them the seal of the living God" (5T 472-5).

The Change of Raiment: "In holy vision the prophet beholds Joshua the high priest, 'clothed in filthy garments', which representing the sins of God's people, applies with peculiar force to the experience of God's people in the closing up of the great day of atonement.

"As the people of God afflict their souls before Him pleading for purity of heart, the command is given, 'Take away the filthy garments' from them, and the encouraging words were spoken, 'Behold I have caused thine iniquity to pass from thee, and I have clothed thee with a change of raiment. The spotless robe of Christ's righteousness is placed upon the children of God. The despised remnant are clothed in glorious apparel, nevermore to be defiled by the corruption of the world. Their names are retained in the Lamb's Book of Life, enrolled among the faithful of all ages (5T 468-475).

Parting Gem: *Just think, you can be cleansed, receive a seal and a robe.*

MAY 27　　　　*Investigation of Investigations #1*　　　　Daniel 7:10

Today's Thought: *"The judgment was set, and the books were opened."*

The Investigative Judgment: *"I saw the dead, small and great, stand before God; and the books were opened… and the dead were judged out of those things which were written in the books, according to their works"* (Revelation 20:12).

"…that thou shouldest give reward unto thy servants the prophets, and to the saints, and them that fear thy name, small and great" (Revelation 11:18).

Jesus promised, *"Whosoever shall confess me before men, him shall the Son of man also confess before the angels of God"* (Luke 12:8).

In heaven, the confessed sins of God's people who place their faith in Jesus have been accumulating through the centuries on the books of record in the heavenly sanctuary which defiles the heavenly sanctuary. In the Investigative Judgment, when Jesus confesses each name before the Father and the angels and witnesses of the universe, those records of sin are blotted out—thus the cleansing of the sanctuary.

The Blotting out of Sin; *"And Aaron [a type of Christ] shall bring the goat upon which the Lord's lot has fell, and offer him for a sin offering… and bring his blood within the vail… and sprinkle it upon the mercy seat"* (Leviticus 16:9,15).

"Repent ye therefore, and be converted, that your sins may be blotted out, when the times of refreshing shall come from the presence of the Lord" (Acts 3:19).

"At the time appointed for the judgment at the close of the 2,300 days in 1844 began the work of investigation and the blotting out of sin" (GC 486). It was to begin with the Book of Life, and all those who at one time or another had accepted Jesus as Saviour and Lord and had their names recorded in that Book, were judged. Should they still have remained faithful to that Friend, then their name remains in that Book; whereas had they rejected in some way that Name, then their name would have been removed. The starting point would be with our first parents, Adam, Eve, then Abel, then on down through the ages.

Parting Gem: *After investigating your individual "Book," have you made sure that your Lawyer/Judge will blot out your sins? Just to be sure, pause to request that of Him right now. Have a great day.*

MAY 28 — Marriage of Marriages — Song 3:11

Today's Thought: *Let us consider, "Behold, king Solomon with the crown wherewith his mother crowned him in the day of his espousals."*

The Marriage—The Reception of His Kingdom: "The coming of Christ as our high priest to the most holy place for the cleansing of the sanctuary... is also represented by the coming of the bridegroom to the marriage" (GC 426).

"The proclamation, 'Behold the Bridegroom cometh,' in the summer of 1844, led thousands to expect the immediate advent of the Lord. At the appointed time the Bridegroom came, not to the earth, as the people expected, but to the Ancient of Days in heaven, to the marriage, the reception of His kingdom" (GC 427).

"And they shall be mine, saith the Lord of hosts, in that day when I make up my jewels; and I will spare them, as a man spareth his own son that serveth him" (Malachi 3:17). Christ is "making up His jewels" in this Day of Atonement, when He goes through the Book of Life making up His wedding guest list. His jewels are you and me.

Let's review, again, the eastern marriage arrangements. It is quite different from the western mode and by understanding the eastern marriage, we can understand the parable of the ten virgins, as well as our "delay" in the Bridegroom coming the second time.

Because women had no legal rights, they did not attend the wedding, per se; that was only for the men. The bridegroom would sit down with the bride's father and negotiate a dowry and sign all necessary legal papers. When all this was properly and legally arranged, then the bridegroom, with his attendants, would "cometh" to claim the bride. The bride and the bridesmaid were waiting for him. When the groom came and claimed his bride, then he would take her to his house which he had prepared. The wedding banquet would follow.

So Christ is at the "wedding" to join Himself with His bride-church. He has already paid the dowry at the cross. When all "legal" papers are completed, then He will come for us, His "bride-church."

Parting Gem: *Instead of considering the end-time experience as a time of judgment, which is usually scary, scary, scary, consider it an occasion of a wedding, joyous, joyous, joyous, even more joyful.*

MAY 29   *Mood of Moods*   Song 3:11

Today's Thought: *What a day of rejoicing that will be.*

As Christ claims His people for the kingdom in this Investigative Judgment, His mood and the mood of the entire Song of Songs, is the mood of a wedding celebration, a mood of the *"gladness of his heart,"* a mood of great joy.

Thus, the mood of God's people as they see that they will soon enter into this Investigative Judgment should be one of great joy, with "gladness of heart," the mood of a wedding, which is usually one of great excitement and joy, not to mention partying.

We are urged to *"go forth… [to] behold [our] king… with the crown wherewith his mother crowned him."* When Jesus can claim an individual as a member of His kingdom, it gives Him a gladness of heart. He is exuberant, glad, joyful when He can claim you as His own, as joyful as a bridegroom who rejoices over his bride on his wedding day. The Investigative Judgment, this blotting out of sin, this day of atonement, this change of raiment, this cleansing of the sanctuary should be joyfully looked upon as a celebration of marriage.

Put this mood of a marriage celebration into focus with Malachi 3:17, *"And they shall be mine, saith the Lord of hosts, in that day when I make up my jewels; and I will spare them, as a man spareth his own son that serveth him."* Don't you just love the Bridegroom?

When people get excited and involved in something that thrills them and makes them "feel" like they are someone and that they are doing something worthwhile, it almost seems as though that is the only thing they can talk about. Could that be why our pioneers and present day evangelists and missionaries get so excited and push their program forward?

My mood is rocketing heavenward; join me today. Please.

Parting Gem: *Importantly as well, when God's people see just who they are, their history, their status, offshoots will disappear. When they see the power, the victories that are theirs, they will have a testimony to bear to the world, their neighbourhood, their children.*

MAY 30 — Crowning of Crownings — Song 3:11

Today's Thought: *"Behold king Solomon with the crown wherewith his mother crowned him in the day of his espousals, and in the day of the gladness of his heart."*

There are three texts that we should keep in mind when things happen that we find difficult to understand. Then with these three texts, we'll look at David's two crownings and their implications.

Deuteronomy 29:29 says, *"Secret things belong unto the Lord our God: but those things which are revealed belong unto us and to our children..."*

1 Corinthians 10:11 says, *"Now all these things happened unto them for ensamples: and they are written for our admonition, upon whom the ends of the world are come."*

Romans 15:4 says, *"For whatsoever things were written aforetime were written for our learning, that we through patience and comfort of the scriptures might have hope."*

Now for David's crownings. Looking at David's experience, see 2 Samuel 2:3-4,11, which says, *"...and they dwelt in the cities of Hebron. And the men of Judah came, and there they anointed David king over the house of Judah... And the time that David was king in Hebron over the house of Judah was seven years and six months."*

2 Samuel 5:1,3-5 says, *"Then came all the tribes of Israel to David unto Hebron... So all the elders... anointed David king over Israel... and he reigned forty years. In Hebron he reigned over Judah seven years and six months: and in Jerusalem he reigned thirty and three years over all Israel and Judah."*

Remembering the three mentioned texts, the question is, what admonition, what learning, what example is given to us through the two crownings of David that is for us today?

Parting Gem: *As you go about your daily duties today, please consider this: could it be, just could it be, that Christ has already been crowned the first time as "King of the Unfallen Universe," figurative of Judah, and that after the 1,000 years He will be crowned the second time as King of the earth, figurative of Israel, so that then He will reign as total King of Israel, or literally "King of all heaven and earth?" Two crownings for David, versus two crownings for Christ. Consider.*

MAY 31 — Summary — Song 3:6-11

This past month, May, we watched as the bride-church, the woman, came out of the wilderness where she had been hiding from AD 538 to AD 1798 from the papal authorities We also reviewed the reasons why she was in the wilderness in the first place.

We noticed that she came out with a flash, a flare, an exuberance, an excitement that hit the world around her and woke them up. Coming out of the wilderness in 1798 was the Philadelphia Church. (See Appendix 2.)

Valiant men came upon the stage to push the sweetness of the little open book forward, not only in America where our emphasis was placed on the Millerites, but also worldwide.

We encountered some of the life of William Miller, his encounter with Christ in the pulpit as he was reading Isaiah, and his subsequent study to find Christ. Two years first, 1916-1918, and then another four years, 1918-1922, we learned of his encounter with his inner convictions to "Go, tell." He had a bit of a discussion, argument, dialogue with Christ before surrendering to God's procedures.

We saw his jaw drop when his nephew invited him to "preach" some of his views and findings in the Dresdon Church. Another encounter with Christ ensued, yet he did go tell his church his convictions. He stayed a week; his church stayed with him.

We were sparingly introduced to some of *"the valiant men of Israel,"* men like William Miller, Joshua V. Himes, Josiah Litch, Charles Fitch, all from different religious persuasions.

We received an invitation to the marriage of our Beloved to His bride. Hopefully we understood this marriage to be one of the many different names for the Investigative Judgment, the cleansing of the sanctuary, the Seal of God, the Change of Raiment, and the Blotting out of Sins.

We closed with a happy mood—the mood of this wedding—and we are urged to remember that after the wedding comes the reception. This one is called "The Marriage Supper of the Lamb." Everything has been prepared for this grand adventure. The robes needed to be worn at this occasion and as a part of one's everyday apparel are plentiful. The invitations needed to be accepted have been sent out. Have you accepted yours?

A Tree of Life

A Tree of Life before you stands,
    Awaiting now your outstretched hands.
Thy words were found and I did eat,
    This Tree of Life has many treats.

Thy Word I hid within my heart.
    Each morn and night you can impart.
    This Tree of Life, this Living Word
Is God's own voice that's to be heard.

No flaming sword is there to bar
    Your entrance to God's throne afar.
No angel stands before the gate,
    And waves his flaming sword to wait

The Table's set, the Food's laid out.
    The Bread of Life is all about.
    The Living water quenches thirst
There's lots about, but be there first.

Eternal life is there for you.
    Creator God can make life new.
The strength is there, the grace is too,
    Just act, decide His will to do.

June

June's Introduction and Aim

During this month of June, we will take our second look at the bride-church and the description of her in Act 2, Scene 5. This description is of the Philadelphia Church on the American stage from AD 1798 to AD 1844. It is a description of the church in the Great Second Advent Movement, often called the Great Religious Awakening of the 1800s.

This church is pictured in Revelation 3:7-12. Along with the Smyrna Church from AD 100 to AD 323, in Revelation 2:8-11, the Philadelphia Church receives no condemnation from He that was *"dead, and is alive"* (Revelation 2:8). Of the seven churches in Revelation 2-3, these two churches lasted in worshipping status until driven out in 1922 by the Moslems. The other churches were driven out long before that.

Philadelphia was a stronghold with a great deal of moral strength to withstand the onslaught of the barbarian nations that constantly overran Asia Minor. In AD 1306, they successfully withstood a siege from the Seljuks Turks, forcing them to withdraw. A second attack in AD 1324 brought similar victories for Philadelphia. In AD 1402, the Timur (Tamerlanc) lead a force of Mongolians, taking the city.

This catastrophe did not destroy the church's will nor quench their determination to remain faithful so that no man take their crown as admonished in Revelation 3:11. They took the counsel seriously. Even after the whole of Asia Minor was taken over by the Turks and Christianity in Asia Minor suffered a slow, lingering, but certain death, Philadelphia, as well as Smyrna, remained a Christian city.

In Philadelphia, at the end of WWI, the majority of the inhabitants were still Christians. Again, however, the Turks drove out the Christians and in AD 1923 the Moslems ravaged the city.

It is powerfully remarkable that these two cities, Smyrna and Philadelphia, which in John's time were so pure and so blameless that they received no rebuke, were the same two cities that retained their Christian character and their Christian population longer than any of the other five cities.

Your assignment for this month of June is to read Song of Songs 4:1 to 5:1. Please be sure to read it several times if necessary.

JUNE

Day 1	Behold of Beholds	Song 4:1	185
Day 2	Eye of Eyes #1	Song 4:1	186
Day 3	Hair of Hairs #1	Song 4:1	187
Day 4	Teeth of Teeth	Song 4:2	188
Day 5	Revenue of Revenues	Song 4:1	189
Day 6	Lips of Lips #1	Song 4:1	190
Day 7	Speech of Speeches	Song 4:3	191
Day 8	Temple of Temples	Song 4:3	192
Day 9	Neck of Necks #2	Song 4:4	193
Day 10	Tower of Towers	Song 4:4	194
Day 11	Armoury of Armouries	Song 4:4, 7:4	195
Day 12	Buckler of Bucklers	Song 4:4	196
Day 13	Shield of Shields	Song 4:4	197
Day 14	Breast of Breasts #2	Song 4:5	198
Day 15	Lily of Lilies #2	Song 4:5	199
Day 16	Daybreak of Daybreaks	Song 4:6	200
Day 17	Mount of Mounts	Song 4:6	201
Day 18	Fairest of Fair #4	Song 4:1	202
Day 19	Spouse of Spouses	Song 4:8	203
Day 20	Look of Looks #1	Song 4:8	204
Day 21	Den of Dens	Song 4:8	205
Day 22	Ravished Heart of Ravished Hearts	Song 4:9	206
Day 23	Chain of Chains	Song 4:9	207
Day 24	Smell of Smells #1	Song 4:10	208
Day 25	Tongue of Tongues	Song 4:11	209
Day 26	Robe of Robes	Song 4:11	210
Day 27	Garden of Gardens	Song 4:12	211
Day 28	Spices of Spices	Song 4:14	212
Day 29	Well of Wells	Song 4:15	213
Day 30	Summary	Song 4:1-11	214

Poems of the Month: "Anthems of Glory" — 215
"The Gospel in Work Boots" — 216

JUNE 1   *Behold of Beholds*   Song 4:1

Today's Thought: *"Behold, thou art fair, my love…"*

Song 4 is a description of the "bride" during the Great Advent Movement, as this is her chronological historical setting. Two prophetic symbols representing two *universal* systems of religion are portrayed, Jerusalem and Babylon.

Both are represented in prophetic symbols as a woman; there is the good woman in Revelation 12 versus a bad woman in Revelation 17-18.

Both of them are represented as a mother; one *"the mother of us all"* (Galatians 4:26), who gave birth to the man-child, and whom the serpent went after to destroy the *"remnant of her seed"* (Revelation 12:17), and then there is the *"mother of harlots"* (Revelation 17:5). That means that both women have daughters; one the daughters of Jerusalem, the other the harlot daughters of Babylon.

Both have names; one the name of *"Jerusalem… which is the mother of us all"* (Galatians 4:26), and the other's name, *"Babylon… that great city"* (Revelation 14:8).

Both have executive positions; one has *"upon her head a crown of twelve stars"* (Revelation 12:1), while the other simply states, *"I sit a queen"* (Revelation 18:7). Both have a support system; the one is supported by the *"moon under her feet"* (Revelation 21:1), while the other sits upon many waters, peoples, and a scarlet beast.

Both are clothed as well as adorned; one prepared and dressed as a bride adorned for her husband, clothed with the sun, while the other is arrayed in purple and scarlet, adorned in gold and precious stones.

During the 1,260 year period, both women were around. One *"fled into the wilderness… [to that] place prepared of God"* (Revelation 12:6), while the other drank and was drunken with the blood of martyrs during the same period.

Both women are merchants and deal with merchandise. One counsels us to buy of her wine and milk, without money, without price; while the other has the merchants of the earth weep and mourn over her. This one also deals in the *"slaves, and souls of men"* (Revelation 18:13).

Both invite all to eat and drink. Jerusalem says to eat bread, drink wine which she has mingled. Babylon forces all men to drink of her wine.

Both have firm priesthoods. Jerusalem consecrates with anointing oils of all principal spices. Babylon uses spices plus souls of men.[12]

Parting Gem: *Behold, Behold, and again I say, Behold!*

---

[12] Berry, Marion G. *The Prophetic Song of Songs, Resource Book* (Albia, IA: The Prophetic Song of Songs, Inc.), 1969, pp. 88-89.

| JUNE 2 | Eye of Eyes #1 | Song 4:1 |

Today's Thought: *"… thou hast doves' eyes within thy locks…"*

There are six references in our Song that mention "dove." One refers to the Beloved. Five refer to the bride, of which three of them are names of endearment, while the other two are descriptive of the bride. In 4:1, it is part of the description of the bride and one of her characteristics.

This reference of "dove" in our passage is after the bride has come out of the wilderness. She came out in Song 3:6. The Great Second Advent Movement has been born, and this description is of that massive movement. This appeal to "Behold" comes after Song 3:11, which is our invitation to the wedding of the Beloved Bridegroom to the bride. Picture in your mind's eye a bride on her wedding day, decked with all of the trimmings brides wear. Listen to the "oohs," and "ahhs" as she walks down the aisle.

According to our talk on 3:6, this movement came out with exciting good news, a sweet message, a committed worldwide global mission. It came out under the guidance and direction and moving of the Holy Spirit. That is one of her characteristics; the power of the Holy Spirit is with her, therefore she is spoken of as a dove.

Reading John as he wrote in John 1:32, *"And John bare record, saying, I saw the Spirit descending from heaven like a dove, and it abode upon him."* The symbol of a dove is generally associated with the Holy Spirit.

But our emphasis is on the eyes of a dove. Eyes are organs of sight; without them, a person is blind. Here is our invitation to behold this great Advent Movement with the sight, perception, as well as the guidance of the Holy Spirit.

Reading from Paul in 1 Corinthians 11:15. *"But if a woman have long hair, it is a glory to her: for her hair is given to her for a covering."* This symbol of hair is to show glory and honour.

Putting these three symbols together, we have a picture of a church, my fair, my love, with the ability to see as the dove of the Holy Spirit sees, and to do so with honour, power, and glory depicted by locks.

Parting Gem: *"And again I say, Rejoice." (Philippians 4:4)*

JUNE 3 — Hair of Hairs #1 — Song 4:1

Today's Thought: *"… thou hast doves' eye within thy locks: thy hair is as a flock of goats, that appear from mount Gilead."*

"If a woman have long hair, it is a glory to her, for her hair is given to her for a covering" (1 Corinthians 11:15).

The Biblical goat had many uses to the people of Israel. The meat of the young he-goat was very popular. Both Gideon and Manoah prepared a young goat for the angel of the Lord. The milk of the goat was used as a drink. The skin was used as a container either for water or for fresh wine, while the black hair was woven into tent cloth, some of which was used as a protective covering in the construction of the Tabernacle. Goat hair was also used by warriors for various articles. Many he-goats were regularly used as sacrifices. So the goat had many uses and our drama draws on the many facets of the goat in its description of the bride-church.

Mount Gilead is a tableland east of the Jordan River. Jeremiah 8:22 indicates that there were balms and physicians in Gilead. The name Gilead means "rocky" or "strong," or "a strong rock," referring to Christ. She gets her beauty from Christ.

The hair of the goat was generally black, and goat's hair could be confused with human hair. In Genesis 27, the story of Rebekah, telling her favourite son Jacob to deceive his father by covering his arms and neck with goat hair so that he could get the firstborn blessing, could now make more sense.

Within the locks of this bride are *"doves' eyes."* She has the discernment of the Holy Spirit in her many facets of operation.

When the pope was taken captive in 1798, and when the French Revolution—from November 26, 1793 to June 17, 1797, some three and a half years according to Revelation 11:1-13—ended, the Christian world woke up. They realized there was work to do and souls to save, and there followed a tremendous religious awakening across America. It was time for things to happen, and they did.

Parting Gem: *Should one be awake, one can see in mind and heart Jehovah waving the banners, saying, "Hold the fort, for I am coming."*

JUNE 4   *Teeth of Teeth*   Song 4:2

Today's Thought: *"Thy teeth are like a flock of sheep that are even shorn, which come up from the washing; whereof every one bear twins, and none is barren among them."*

This drama has got to be in symbolic language. What man would say this statement to his love? If he did, he had better have his car running and be ready for a fast exit out the door.

The Lord, through Solomon, is really giving His bride-church a thorough description. He's covered the eyes, hair, now the teeth. Later He'll describe the lips, speech, neck, breasts, and then a closing passionate burst of His love for her. No man would talk like this to his lover.

The teeth are organs for chewing, for masticating food. They are located in the mouth where the food first starts its process of digestion. No food in the mouth means no digestion, which means no strength, no life. Thus, we partake of the Word.

As Jeremiah states in 15:16, *"Thy words were found, and I did eat them; and thy word was unto me the joy and rejoicing of mine heart."*

In Revelation 10, which we will look at next month in July, teeth will be necessary to take a little book and eat it up. It will take teeth, strong and even, to chew, to masticate, to grind the difficult and meaty portions of God's Word, the prophecies not yet understood by William Miller. It will take some heavy chewing to understand "fully" the 2,300 days, the mark of the beast, the signs of Christ's second coming. It will take teeth, to chew, chew, chew. It's not enough to live on milk and cookies; one needs the meaty portions of doctrine.

There are no lost wandering in this chewing of God's Word. He will lead us into truth. We need to be sure, as in the literal, physical eating of food, that we not gulp it down whole. We need to "chew, chew, chew our food, gently through the meal. The more we eat, the more we chew, the better we will feel" (sung to the tune of "Row, Row, Row Your Boat"). Remember that song?

Parting Gem: *Have you taken the time today to chew your daily portion of God's Word, without gulping it down? This could be where that thoughtful hour each day contemplating the life of Christ would come in. They say that to read and read and not understand is worse than reading in the first place.*

JUNE 5 — *Revenue of Revenues* — Song 4:1

Today's Thought: *"Behold, thou art fair my love, behold thou art fair."*

"The Lord Jesus is making experiments on human hearts through the exhibition of His mercy and abundant grace. He is affecting transformation so amazing that Satan, with all his triumphant boasting, with all his confederacy of evil united against God and the laws of His government, stands viewing them as a fortress impregnable to his sophistries and delusions, they are to him an incomprehensible mystery. The angels of God, seraphim and cherubim, the powers commissioned to co-operate with human agencies, look on with astonishment and joy, that fallen man, once children of wrath, are through the training of Christ developing characters after the divine similitude, to be sons and daughters of God, to act an important part in the occupation and pleasures of heavens.

"To His church, Christ has given ample facilities, that He may receive a large revenue of glory from his redeemed, purchased possession. The church, being endowed with the righteousness of Christ, is His depository, in which the wealth of His mercy, His love, His grace, is to appear in full and final display. The declaration of His intercessory prayer, that the Father's love is ass great toward us s toward Himself, the only begotton Son, and that we shall be with Him where He is, forever one with Christ and the Father, is a marvel to the heavenly host, and it is their great joy. The gift of His Holy Spirit, rich, full, and abundant, is to be to His church as an encompassing wall of fire, which the powers of hell shall not prevail against. In their untainted purity and spotless perfection, Christ looks upon His people ass the reward of all Hiss suffering, His humiliation, and His love, and the supplement of His glory--Christ, the great centre from which radiates all glory. "Blessed are they which are called unto the marriage supper of the Lamb" (TM 18)

Parting Gem: *Should the title of today's reading have been "Reward of Rewards," or "Astonishment of Astonishments," or maybe even "Endowment of Endowment"? What an awesome, awesome, awesome God we have the privilege of knowing, serving, loving.*

| JUNE 6 | Lips of Lips #1 | Song 4:1 |

Today's Thought: *"Thy lips are like a thread of scarlet, and thy speech is comely."*

Lips are the organs used for speech. Although we met the lips back in 1:1, where the bride requests that her Beloved kiss her with the kisses of His mouth, which is one of the purposes of lips, these lips are like a thread of scarlet. Scarlet is quite often associated with royalty, a mark of distinction, a status of wealth and value.

Isaiah 57:19 says, *"I create the fruit of thy lips."*

Proverbs gives this advice in 10:13. *"In the lips of him that hath understanding wisdom is found."* While in 15:7, it says, *"The lips of the wise disperse knowledge,"* and one certainly knows that for a lack of knowledge God's people are destroyed (Hosea 4:6).

Hebrews 13:15 says, *"By him therefore let us offer the sacrifice of praise to God continually, that is, the fruit of our lips giving thanks to his name."*

In the lips being like a scarlet thread running, through, did you notice the second characteristic element of Hebrew poetry in this verse? The second approach is that her speech is comely. Various ideas can be had in verses like these and that's why Hebrew poetry gives two descriptions. Should you miss the meaning in your first pass, hopefully you grab it on your second pass. Our second pass is that her speech is comely. Tomorrow we find out how.

Our first pass was that the lips are like threads of scarlet, the speech of royalty, that mark of distinction and status of wealth and value. This bride-church brings life-giving words to those that hear her, words of wisdom, encouragement, elevating the status and the standing of the hearer who hears and follows.

Parting Gem: *To leave you this day with a provocative idea, let it be asked, do the words that you speak to whomever you speak bring power, comfort, encouragement to those who hear? Are our words like royal threads of scarlet, a status symbol of higher learning? May our lips, today, be used and dedicated to the use and advancement of God's kingdom and other's salvation.*

JUNE 7   *Speech of Speeches*   Song 4:3

Today's Thought: *"Thy lips are like a thread of scarlet, and thy speech is comely."*

Reviewing the meaning of comely, we find it is, (1) good-looking, attractive, beautiful, blooming, bonny, buxom, cute, graceful, handsome (for men), lovely, pleasing, pretty, wholesome, as well as (2) proper, decent, fitting, seemly, suitable.

So, using the proper, decent fitting definition, we have a picture here of the bride-church's speech being proper, fitting, suitable.

We will certainly aim not to be hit with the "Peter Syndrome," where someone asks us if we are a Christian because our speech has betrayed us. Maybe we should remember also what Jesus said in Matthew 12:36, *"But I say unto you, That every idle word that men shall speak, they shall give account thereof in the day of judgment. For by they words thou shalt be justified, and by thy words thou shalt be condemned."*

Here is a picture of our bride-church whose speech, her words, are uplifting, beneficial, life-saving. O, that we shall remember that by our words we shall save and encourage some or discourage and lose others.

As this bride-church speaks, she gives forth the life-saving words of life, those "beautiful words, wonderful words, wonderful words of life." Those are words from the song, "Wonderful Words of Life."

Yesterday's reading was on the "Lips of Lips," with the thought that the lips, which are the organs of speech, have been dedicated to God for His service.

In a bit of research on "jesting," it was found that the Christian should studiously avoid such speech, for it grieves the angel, let alone God, and it is language belonging to the world. The favour of God is lost, for it denies Him and it is a clear sign that the soul needs to be cleansed. Should you not believe this, check "Jesting" in the *Index to the Writings of E. G. White*.

Parting Gem: *"Let your speech be always with grace, seasoned with salt, that ye may know how ye ought to answer every man" (Colossians 4:6).* Then what happens if the salt has lost its flavour?

| JUNE 8 | *Temple of Temples* | Song 4:3 |

Today's Thought: *"Thy lips are like a thread of scarlet, and thy speech is comely: thy temples are like a piece of pomegranate within thy locks."*

We've already read about the lips, those organs of speech, being like threads of scarlet, the speech of royalty, dedicated to the service of God; then yesterday we looked at the life-giving, beneficial, uplifting, wonderful words of life that this church presents.

Today we are looking at the temples and the pieces of pomegranates within her hair's locks. This idea is repeated in 6:7, *"As a piece of a pomegranate are thy temples within thy locks."* The locks are symbols of beauty and a covering for a lady (1 Corinthians 11:15). The temples are on either side of the head

The SDA Dictionary, in talking about temples, mentions the physical structures of four well-known ancient temples, but does state that "a temple was considered a dwelling place of the deity, and only secondary as a place of worship."

In Revelation 7, it mentions the sealing of God's people, specifically in verse 3: *"Saying, Hurt not the earth, neither the sea, nor the trees, till we have sealed the servants of our God in their foreheads."* This indicates, as does Song 4:3 and 6:7, that the servants of God have firmly embedded within their minds the truths of God's Word, and are sealed so as not to have this truth and knowledge polluted.

In Jamison, Faucet & Brown Commentary, pomegranates are a symbol of knowledge (Berry, Song of Songs Textbook, P.91). Thus, God's knowledge, found in the Scriptures, is embedded within the minds of God's people, between the temples, and this knowledge has a beauty about it that draws the second and third look of people who first see the beauty of the gospel.

Parting Gem: *My teachers, mentors, preachers tell me that in order to have these pomegranates, this Scriptural knowledge, embedded in the mind, then I have to spend time with the Word, memorize Scripture, know what I believe, why I believe it, and be able to give to every man a reason for the faith I have within me. That would be an excellent thought to take with you today (1 Peter 3:15).*

JUNE 9 — Neck of Necks #2 — Song 4:4

Today's Thought: *"Thy neck is like the tower of David..."*

There are two symbols for today and tomorrow that are close together, both saying the same thing, a characteristic of Hebrew poetry. One is the symbol of the neck. In Isaiah 48:4, *"Because I knew that thou art obstinate, and thy neck is an iron sinew, and thy brow brass,"* we get a picture of a neck being the symbol of strength or power.

Jeremiah 17:23 says, *"But they obeyed not, neither inclined their ear, but made their neck stiff, that they might not hear, nor receive instruction."* Again, a picture of strength and power, this time to resistance.

Jeremiah 19:15 says, *"Thus saith the Lord... they have hardened their necks, that they might not hear my words."* Again, strong resistance.

Jeremiah 27:2 says, *"Thus saith the Lord to me; Make thee bonds and yokes, and put them upon thy neck."* The neck is closely connected to the shoulders in animals as well as man. It is the neck that carries the burden of the yokes as it pulls its load.

Job 41:22 says, *"In his neck remaineth strength..."*

Israel was noted for being "stiff-necked" and refusing to accept God's leadership. Exodus 32:9 says, *"And the Lord said unto Moses, I have seen this people, and, behold, it is a stiffnecked people."*

A symbol of strength for the neck is also very self-evident in animals. Should a bull have a strong, meaty, muscular neck, one knows that it is a strong bull. On the other hand, should it have a weak-looking neck, it is because it is weak.

One needs to constantly remember who we are talking about. We have here a portion of the description of the church shortly after it came out of the wilderness. Remember in Song 3:6, where it was discussed who this is that came out of the wilderness like pillars of smoke, perfumed with myrrh and frankincense, with all powers of the merchants. Now it describes her strength, similar to the smoke, perfume and powders by describing her neck.

Parting Gem: *The church was a powerhouse of strength. It was a place of protection, activity, and warfare. It had the strength to do what it was to do, and I might mention what it should be doing today.*

JUNE 10 — Tower of Towers — Song 4:4

Today's Thought: *"Thy neck is like the tower of David builded for an armoury, whereon there hang a thousand bucklers, all shields of mighty men."*

Continuing the symbolism of the neck, it is compared to a tower of David which has been built as an armoury to house the thousands of war shields for the mighty soldiers of the cross. A tower is a structure built for height, generally considerably higher than its width or diameter. Towers in ancient times were built as watchtowers and served defensive purposes. They usually formed part of everyday fortification, standing at intervals in the walls. They served not only as lookouts, but as vantage points to hurl missiles from, as places of refuge.

Even the word "tower" itself talks of strength. According to the concordance, this tower of David is part of the castle in Zion. Micah 4:8 gives us that same sense of strength and protection: *"And thou, O Tower of the flock, the strong hold of the daughter of Zion…"* Again, as above, it is a part of the castle in Zion where God's people can flee to in time of joy or trouble.

David had much to do with war and he states in Psalms 144:2, *"My goodness, and my fortress; my high tower, and my deliverer; my shield, and he in whom I trust; who subdueth my people under me."* Here is a description of the bride-church depicting strength.

2 Samuel 22:2-3 says, *"The Lord is my rock, and my fortress, and my deliverer; the God of my rock; in him will I trust: he is my shield, and the horn of my salvation, my high tower, and my refuge, my saviour; thou savest me from violence."* Here is picture of the Lord and what he is to His people: a rock, a deliverer, a shield, a horn of salvation, a high tower, a refuge—all symbols of strength. The symbolism of a tower is here applied to the bride-church, who has just come out of the wilderness.

Parting Gem: *Would it be possible to apply this tower to the church today, the church being you and me? Let us be a watchtower, a lookout for perishing souls, a place of refuge for hurting sinners, a defence for the family which is under constant attack.*

JUNE 11 — Armoury of Armouries — Song 4:4, 7:4

Today's Thought: *"Thy neck is like the tower of David builded for an armoury… Thy neck is as a tower of ivory."*

We have already looked at several aspects of this verse. The bride-church depicted in these verses is strong as said by the neck; she is beautiful, comely, richly appealing as said by the ivory; she is a place to flee to for safety as said by the tower; she is also looking out and over the countryside for those in danger and in need of protection, also as said by the tower.

Both the words "armoury" and "tower" are words that depict a well-built structure. In literal terms, one built with brick and mortar with thick, tall, massive walls. A structure that when it catches the eye, sets the looker back a pace to admire it.

So, this bride-church we are describing is a well-structured organization, a structure of beauty, efficiency and admiration as seen by the ones looking on. It is even cause for envy by the other organizations in the religious community.

From the grassroots, the local congregation, to the local conference, onward to the local union, then to the local division, and finally to the general conference, this structure of organization is unsurpassed in the religious community. This depiction of an armoury is apt when one understands the structure and make-up of an armoury.

The envious portion comes when the other ladies look at the support of the ministers and workers of this bride-church. Her ministers are not paid by the whim and fancy, nor the wealth of the local congregation, but all are remunerated from the local conference. Ministers in a large church are treated similarly as that of ministers in a small church.

Those who have gone through the educational system of this church, even for a few years, end up having friends and acquaintances no matter where they go in the world. This Sabbath truth has the tendency to glue us all together as one. As you hear the stories of such events, one's mind is boggled and finds it difficult to wrap itself around this blessing, for it surely is a blessing.

Parting Gem: *Are your shields and bucklers hanging in this armoury?*

JUNE 12　　　　　　*Buckler of Bucklers*　　　　　　Song 4:4

Today's Thought: *"Thy neck is like the tower of David builded for an armoury, whereon there hang a thousand bucklers, all shields of mighty men."*

According to the SDA Bible Dictionary, a buckler has been rendered several ways in different places. It could be a small shield, a large shield, bulwark, or spear. Yet one could easily catch the idea that a buckler is an instrument of war. The war implied here in our drama is the war against sin, evil, unrighteousness, the devil, falsehood, error, and whatever other similar synonym you wish to use.

Get the picture? Out there somewhere in enemy territory is a tower, a fortress, a place of refuge, reinforcement, reserve, and in this tower are shields of the mighty men who have fought the good fight of faith. They may have passed on to their resting place, laid down their shields, swords, and all their armour, but this tower still contains their weapons of defence. These weapons of defence and offence never wear out or need replacing. What an awesome thought.

The challenge to us today is found in Ephesians 6:10-18, where it mentions such instruments of protection and defence as shields of faith, helmets of salvation, breastplates, and the sword of the Spirit.

One thing I gleamed from the Bible story of David and Goliath was that David was familiar with the slingshot, the stones, running and shooting simultaneously because that was one thing he did while looking after *"those few sheep"* (1 Samuel 17:28). He knew the size and shape as well as the number of stones he needed to pick up from the brook as he made his way to meet Goliath. He was familiar with his equipment.

Today, while it is still day, while it is still safe and acceptable to practice your faith, take the time to become familiar with your equipment of prayer, Scriptures, commitment and sincerity. Practice in using these.

Parting Gem: *My favourite Bible passage fits nicely here. "According as his divine power hath given unto us all things that pertain unto life and godliness… Whereby are given unto us exceeding great and precious promises: that by these ye might be partakers of the divine nature" (2 Peter 3-4).*

| JUNE 13 | *Shield of Shields* | Song 4:4 |

Today's Thought: *"Thy neck is like the tower of David builded for an armoury, whereon there hang a thousand bucklers, all shields of mighty men."*

In Paul's book to the Ephesians, it says, *"Finally, my brethren, be strong in the Lord, and in the power of his might. Put on the whole armour of God, that ye may be able to stand against the wiles of the devil... Wherefore, take unto you the whole armour of God, that ye may be able to stand in the evil day, and having done all, to stand"* (Ephesians 6:10-11,13).

In verse 16, he emphasizes, above all, more than anything else, to make sure you take the shield of faith, for it is by this shield of faith that you will be able to quench, squash, obliterate all the darts of the wicked. Talk about a powerful shield.

Psalms 91:4 says, *"He shall cover thee with his feathers, and under his wings shalt thou trust: his truth shall be thy shield and buckler."*

Psalms 119:114 says, *"Thou art my hiding place and my shield: I hope in thy word."*

Shields are what a soldier hides behind for protection. So, behind the shield of faith, the shield of trust, the shield of our High Tower, Jesus Christ, we are overcomers of the enemy. In this tower spoken of above there hangs a thousand bucklers, bulwarks, spears, defences, all of which are shields to defeat the darts and arrows of the enemy.

Yes, we could even say in understandable language that there hangs a thousand promises to defeat the enemy. 2 Peter 1:3, 4, *"According as his divine power hath given unto us all things that pertain unto life and godliness, through the knowledge of him that hath called us to glory and virtue; Whereby are given unto us exceeding great and precious promises: that by these ye might be partakers of the divine nature, having escaped the corruption that is in the world through lust."*

Let's paraphrase this. The church's strength is in the Tower of her strength, Jesus Christ, where His Word has a thousand promises that guarantee victory.

Parting Gem: *As young David practiced using his slingshot so well that he could bring down Goliath, let us fortify our minds with the truths and promises of the Bible to allow us to stand in the latter days.*

JUNE 14   *Breast of Breasts #2*   Song 4:5

Today's Thought: *"Behold, thou art fair, my love…"*

Again we come to the breasts. This drama is endeavouring to get us to understand that this is speaking symbolically when she mentions the breasts. The drama wants us to understand that it is talking about the Word of God, regardless of the symbols used. They may use the symbol of clusters of grapes, fawns, roes and hinds, nursing at the breasts, not having any breasts, even lying all night between the breasts, but each symbol is pushing the idea that these breasts, regardless of symbol used, represent the Word of God. This Word of God can be the sincere milk of the Word, the meat of the Word, the heavy doctrines, the prophecies, Daniel and Revelation. The Old Testament and the New Testament.

As there are two breasts, so there are two Testaments, the Old and the New. As they are twins, say even identical twins, the Old Testament is a complement to the New Testament; Daniel is a book sealed, while Revelation is a book revealed. Notice that many times these two young animals are feeding among the lilies. That, too, is an important concept this drama wishes to convey. Are these two breasts up front and very noticeable?

Again it will be repeated so that the readers can grasp this "embarrassing" symbol, that the two breasts are up front, they are noticeable on every woman, they are uniform and twins; they catch the eyes of most men immediately. So, this bride-church should catch the attention of all who investigate her. Does she have the Word of God up front, noticeably present, is it the foundation of her doctrine based on a *"Thus saith the Lord,"* based on *"It Is Written"*? Or does it have even some of its doctrines and beliefs based on tradition or human philosophy?

Parting Gem: *This symbol of breasts on a woman helps make sense of Jeremiah 6:2, "I have likened the daughter of Zion to a comely and delicate woman." Have you been lying all night between her breasts, between the Old and the New Testament, giving them serious consideration? Maybe we should spend a thoughtful hour with them.*

JUNE 15 — *Lily of Lilies #2* — Song 4:5

Today's Thought: *"Thy two breasts are like two young roes that are twins, which feed among the lilies."*

Do you remember back in February where we looked at the rose of Sharon and the lily of the valleys, and presented the idea that both the rose and the lily are symbols of the church? Here now, is a picture of young roes, or deer, who are feeding among the lilies, or the churches.

The two breasts, or better understood, the Old Testament and the New Testament, Daniel and Revelation, the milk of the Word, the meat of the Word, even prophecies, are feeding and nourishing the young churches in the wilderness.

It is not really known how many small companies of believing Christians there were in the recesses of the wilderness, how close together they were, and how often they got together for fellowship and encouragement, yet it can be assured that they had the Word, in part or in whole. The Waldenses were the first to get the Bible. They copied it and distributed it to whomever they felt hungered for it. It can be assured that these two young roes were at each of these company of believers to instruct and feed the members.

Read Revelation 1:12-13,20, which says, *"And I turned to see the voice that spoke with me. And being turned, I saw seven golden candlesticks; And in the midst of the seven candlesticks one like unto the Son of man, clothed with a garment down to the feet… and the seven candlesticks which thou sawest are the seven churches."* Here is a picture of Jesus Christ and a description of Him, and He is standing in the midst of the seven churches. He is there in the middle, close by to each one.

In our drama, we have the very same picture, only in different words, of Jesus Christ feeding the lilies, the churches, while they were just coming out of the wilderness. He is feeding them, not only the simple fundamental milk of the Word (breasts) adapted for newborn babes, but he is now giving the members the heavier meat of the Word (the meat of the young roes).

Parting Gem: *It is amazing the "pains" the Lord will go to just to reach a people so they could be ready for the Bridegroom when He comes.*

JUNE 16 — *Daybreak of Daybreaks* — Song 4:6

Today's Thought: *"Until the day break, and the shadows flee away, I will get me to the mountain of myrrh, and to the hill of frankincense."*

In our Church Hymnal, is a song, #212, called *'Tis Almost Time for the Lord to Come.* The chorus starts off with, "O it must be the breaking of the day. The night is almost gone, the day is coming on, O it must be the breaking of the day." It's a song emphasizing the coming of the Bridegroom, at the breaking of the day.

In our drama, verse 6, it is also emphasizing the coming of the Bridegroom, when the day breaks, but until then, the bride will flee to the mountain of myrrh and to the hill of frankincense. She has a job to do. She must go to the Most Holy Place for the work of investigation. She must get herself to the mount (Exodus 30:22-26,30,34,36).

While I am in the Most Holy Place, I want you to take all of the shadows away, the shadows of unbelief, fear, unhappiness, and finish the work of taking the gospel to all the world. When the gospel has gone to all the world, then the day of deliverance will break. I will come. But, until then, I must go to the mount of myrrh and frankincense, the spices of anointing.

When this gospel of the kingdom shall be preached to all the world for a witness unto all nations, then shall the end come. We need first to hear about what Daniel said, *"But tidings out of the east and out of the north shall trouble him [papal powers]: therefore he shall go forth with great fury to destroy, and utterly to make away many"* (Daniel 11:44). This is a prediction of that time of trouble such as has never been seen before.

Then again, as the three angels' message goes forth with lightning, power and smoke, they get help from the other angel, the fourth angel of Revelation 18, to get added strength and impetus to do the work. Revelation is nearly fulfilled. We see and hear of ministers and lay-people going over to Asia, Europe, India, Africa, Russia carrying the message of the soon coming Bridegroom. When success is received, then Christ will break forth as the morning and the daybreak of all daybreaks will be a reality and not just a hope.

Parting Gem: *Yes, Friend, the daybreak is soon to break. Are you ready?*

JUNE 17 — Mount of Mounts — Song 4:6

Today's Thought: *"...I will get me to the mountain of myrrh, and to the hill of frankincense."*

A mountain and a hill are basically the same. The hill is small and not as high, whereas the mountain is high. That's basically the only difference. So we are talking here about the hills or mountains of myrrh and frankincense.

According to Exodus 30:22-36, the spices used in the Holy and the Most Holy Places are described. There are many of them, but our drama mentions only myrrh and frankincense. They were mixed in exact proportions and used for a specific purpose within the rituals of the sanctuary services. Should someone mix these spices for personal or selfish uses, then there would be dire consequences (Exodus 30:37-38).

Mountains were used figuratively as symbols of permanence (Deuteronomy 3315, Habakkuk 3:6), stability (Isaiah 54:10), great calamities (Jeremiah 13:16), and insurmountable obstacles (Zechariah 4:7) (SDA Dict. Mountains). What the Bridegroom is saying is, "I have some obstacles or work to do in the judgment hall. I need to go over My 'school register' to find out who is present, who is still in My bloodstained camp. I need to know who will make up My jewels so that I may spare them (Malachi 3:17). When I have done that and some other obstacles are overcome, then I will return for you, My bride, and take you to the home I have prepared for you."

Every one of His children can help hasten His coming. One of the best ways I heard of was to simply plant the seeds of truth and His soon coming, then pray for the rain of the Spirit to water that seed and leave the "converting" to the One who is responsible for it, and that is the Holy Spirit.

Parting Gem: *The second coming of Jesus Christ as King of kings and Lord of lords is the flagship of this bride-church. She has one strong passionate longing and that is to meet here Lover face to face. She is aware that the message of His soon coming, of His power and eagerness to forgive, is needed in the world as the only real cure for its troubles, so she waits for this breaking of the day.*

JUNE 18 — Fairest of Fair #4 — Song 4:1

Today's Thought: *"Thou art all fair, my love; there is no spot in thee."*

As this drama was eager to get across the idea of the breasts and what they stand for, so this drama wishes to emphasize the position of love, specialness, the idea of just who this bride-church is and how she is looked at in the eyes of her Beloved. This drama pushes the idea, if you can see it, this bride-church is the "First Lady of the Universe." She is comely, bonny, lovely, beautiful, uniquely special.

As stated in the Introduction, this Philadelphia Church from AD 1798, when the woman came out of the wilderness, to the end of the 2,300 day prophecy of Daniel 8:14 in AD 1844, along with the Smyrna Church of AD 100 to AD 323, were the same two cities that in John's time and letter were so pure and so blameless that they received no rebuke, that retained their Christian character and influence, and population longer than any other city.

This drama backs up the purity of this Philadelphia Church by stating above, *"There is no spot in thee."* Five of the seven churches in Revelation had a rebuke attached to them, *"I have somewhat against thee,"* but this church and the Smyrna Church received no rebuke. The Thyatira Church, from AD 538 to AD 1563, had the commendation that *"the last [is] to be more than the first"* (Revelation 2:19), indicating there was a growth in membership, but she had a rebuke against her regarding Jezebel.

Both churches lasted as Christian communities until after WWI; in the early 1920s, they were finally driven out by the Turks.

Notice that as each of the seven churches take their place on the Christian stage of history, each one is the fairest of the fair at that time. Each generation's description of the bride gets more replete as the scrolls unroll. The best one is yet to come.

Parting Gem: *When one thinks of the church and how most of the churches in Revelation had a rebuke against them, it is still the apple of God's eye, still the one object upon earth in which He spreads His special regards. Like Noah's ark, it may be cramped, smelly, noisy, unsettled, but then, what are the alternatives? Consider Rahab's apartment on the wall. Where would you have chosen to be as the Israeli army marched around Jericho? Consider the alternative.*

JUNE 19   *Spouse of Spouses*   Song 4:8

Today's Thought: *"Come with me from Lebanon, my spouse, with me from Lebanon: look from the top of Amana, from the top of Shenir and Hermon, from the lions' den, from the mountains of the leopards."*

Let's start today by stating that the spouse of Jesus Christ, our Bridegroom in our drama, is none other that the First Lady of the Multiverse, the church, even the New Jerusalem.

It is she that is the "apple of God's eye." It is she who is the jewel box wherein Christ keeps His most precious jewels, you and me. It is she who He is coming for in the powerfully near-future.

Paul told us he was jealous over us with godly jealousy. 2 Corinthians 11:2 says, *"For I am jealous over you with godly jealousy: for I have espoused you to one husband, that I may present you as a chaste virgin to Christ."*

According to the plan wherewith God planned, a husband should have one wife, one spouse. So, if God follows His own plan and has only one spouse, and according to this drama, the Song of Songs, this spouse is the church down through the ages until we arrive in the here and the now, that means that God has ordained Jesus Christ, the Beloved Bridegroom, to come for just one church. Is that what He meant when He stated in John 10:16, *"Other sheep I have, which are not of this fold: them also I must bring, and they shall hear my voice; and there shall be one fold, and one shepherd."*

Notice that the Bridegroom calls the bride His spouse after their marriage in 3:11. Before that, He calls her *"O my love"* and *"O thou fairest of all women,"* but now, after their wedding, she is called His spouse. Sounds like proper order. One can almost get the idea that He likes to call His bride "spouse," for He calls her His spouse in verses 8, 9, 10, 11, 12, whereas in those same verses he calls her "sister" only in 9, 10, 12.

Parting Gem: *In a kind and loving way, detour the talk of people who tear down this First Lady, who belittle her and refuse to accept the undeniable fact that she is the one the Beloved says she is, the apple of His eye, His jewel box, His tower of strength and truth in this revolting world. Do it with love in the voice, tears in your eyes.*

JUNE 20 — Look of Looks #1 — Song 4:8

Today's Thought: *"Come with me from Lebanon, my spouse, with me from Lebanon: look from the top of Amana, from the top of Shenir and Hermon, from the lions' den, from the mountains of the leopards."*

Looking at these main words and places in the SDA Bible Dictionary, one pulls together that Lebanon means "white mountain," because it is partially covered with snow the major portion of the year. Mount Hermon likewise is covered with snow the major portion of the year.

Lebanon is frequently mentioned as the northwestern boundary of the Promised Land, as well as for its abundance of cedars. Poets and prophets mention Lebanon for its snow wild beasts, such as leopards and lions. Greek authors called the western range Lebanon and the eastern range Anti-Lebanon. The mountains of the western range are most picturesque and the elevations of their highest mountains range from 8,000 to 10,000 feet above sea level with passes of 5,000 feet between them.

Hermon is the southern portion of the Anti-Lebanon Mountains. The names Hermon, Shenir, and Sirion have the same location depending on the language used. The greatest height of the eastern range is Mount Hermon, which rises 9,232 feet above sea level

Apparently the Bridegroom is saying to His bride, "Come with Me, My spouse. Come take a good look from the tall stately mountains and get a full view of the total surrounding area, like Moses did before the Camp of Israel entered into the Promised Land. Take a look from the area and homeland of the roaming lions and from the mountains where leopards have the range. Go right up to the top so that your view is unobstructed and you get the total picture of your calling. Come. Look down onto the world field where you will be taking the gospel to all the world. This is your work; however, remember that you are to come with Me. I will be with you all the way. I will never leave you, nor forsake you. As I was with Daniel in his lion's den, so I'll be with you if you get into a lion's den."

Parting Gem: *I understand that there is honour, glory, prestige at the top of mountain; you will not always be there. In the valley, well…*

JUNE 21   *Den of Dens*   Song 4:8

Today's Thought: *"Come with me from Lebanon, my spouse, with me from Lebanon: look from the top of Amana, from the top of Shenir and Hermon, from the lions' den, from the mountains of the leopards."*

In this eastern range of mountains, or in the valley between, there is Hermon, called by the Amorites *Shenir* or *Senir* in the southern range. Amana is applied to the adjacent mountains. The western range of mountains is called Lebanon, while the eastern range is called Anti-Lebanon, names that are still applied today.

This majestic mountain range is about fifteen miles long and rises over 9,000 feet above sea level, is snow-capped most of the year, and can be seen from many points in Palestine. Its summit affords a marvellous view of Lebanon, Galilee, the Jordan Valley with its two northern lakes, and the area around Damascus. On the slopes of Mount Hermon lie the sources of the various streams that form the rive Jordan (SDA Bible Dictionary).

Poets and prophets mention Lebanon for its snow, its wild beasts such as leopards, lions, and for its stately trees.

Our Beloved mentions Lebanon, Amana, Shenir, Hermon, the lion's den, and the mountain of the leopards as a viewing point to look out over the field of labour and survey the prospects. "Come My love, My spouse. Get a worldwide view of your task that is before you. As I rescued Daniel from his den, so I will be with you and support you in your den, in your Lebanon, in your mountains of the leopards."

The period this conversation takes place in is after the church has come out of the wilderness, is that one that looks like the breaking of a new morning, beautiful and fair as the moon, even a full moon, clear and warm as the sun, terrible, frightening, dreadful as an army as she raises her banners of the second angel's message. The enemy is in flight as our bride-church sees her mission. She is willing, eager to go even into the lion's den to take such a message.

Parting Gem: *Catch the vision; the best is yet to come. Join us.*

JUNE 22 — *Ravished Heart of Ravished Hearts* — Song 4:9

Today's Thought: *"Thou hast ravished my heart, my sister, my spouse; thou hast ravished my heart with one of thine eyes, with one chain of thy neck."*

It has often been stated by God's people, and it is also stated here in our drama, that the bride's greatest desire, her hungering longing, is for her Beloved to come and claim her. The Advent people have a similar hungering and longing to finish the work so that we can go home. We don't belong here.

Yet, did you get the picture portrayed here? This is the Beloved talking. He is hungry. He is longing. He is homesick for His people. His greatest, passionate, burning desire is to be with His people in a personal, visible, literal way. Did you get that picture here? It's there.

It was storied that Gabriel and Michael were strolling through the Holy City in the cool of one evening, when Gabriel asked about the beauty of the mansions, flowers, streets, and all the mansions that God had gone to prepare for His people.

"They are all finished, are they not, Master?" Gabriel asked.

"Yes," was His only reply. There followed a long pause as they strolled.

"As I watch our people down on Planet Earth, Master, I seem to notice a complacency with them. Other angels come back up from Earth saying the same thing. They seem so satisfied there. They go on long cruises, buy luxury homes and vehicles, sometimes more than one. Even on the Sabbath Day, they seem to forget who they really are, as well as Whose they are."

A long uncomfortable silence ensued as the two of them continued to meander through the empty mansions, neatly trimmed and manicured. A sadness rested upon Gabriel's countenance when he turned to speak once more to Michael, but halted at the look on Michael's face.

It was Michael who broke the silence, "Gabriel, don't they want to come home? My heart is ravished for them, Gabriel, ravished."

Parting Gem: *An assignment for today is for you to peruse these 117 verses finding out how passionate the Bridegroom is to come and claim you as one of His citizens in His heavenly domain. How many times does He have this hungering homesick feeling for you?*

| JUNE 23 | *Chain of Chains* | Song 4:9 |

Today's Thought: *"Thou hast ravished my heart, my sister, my spouse; thou hast ravished my heart with one of thine eyes, with one chain of thy neck."*

I'm assuming we all know that a person has two eyes and that a chain has more than one link. This Beloved is declaring to His bride that He is ravished, with a longing, hungering desire, for she has only one eye, and a one-link chain.

God created mankind with two eyes, for it takes two eyes to give depth and three-dimensional sight. Yet the Bridegroom is still ravished with her. That's the way our God is. We may not be perfect in many senses of the word, but we still are not only loved but wanted and needed.

Just coming out of the wilderness period, when the papal powers took every gem of truth from God's word and twisted it, adulterated it, or eliminated it, this bride really does not know what was what back there in the early church. She did not see all of God's truth, as it was locked in the Scripture, and the Scriptures had to some extent been controlled by the papacy. The Lord recognized that fact but loved her regardless, not to mention the third dimension of missions.

David's request in Psalms 119:18 reads, *"Open thou mine eyes, that I may behold wondrous things out of thy law."*

This bride only had part of the true doctrines of the Bible, portrayed by the expression *"ravished my heart with one of thine eyes."* As the scroll of Scripture, prophecy and history unrolled, this was to change.

The second part of our verse was about *"one chain of thy neck."* Still speaking symbolically, we look at Proverbs 1:8-9, where it states, *"My son, hear the instruction of thy father, and forsake not the law of thy mother: for they shall be an ornament of grace upon thy head, and chains about thy neck."*

Churches in the early movement of the Great Second Advent kept most of the Ten Commandments, especially nine of them. They did not know about nor keep the fourth commandment on the seventh-day Sabbath. So one chain upon the neck of this church just out of the wilderness symbolized knowing and keeping only part of the law.

Parting Gem: *By precept upon precept, line upon line, things changed.*

JUNE 24 — Smell of Smells #1 — Song 4:10

Today's Thought: *"How fair is thy love, my sister, my spouse! how much better is thy love than wine! and the smell of thy ointment than all spices!"*

Should we go back to the reading for February 2, "Love of Loves," we would find similar expressions: *"... thy love is better than wine"* (Song 1:2).

Down in the next verse, verse 11, it mentions that *"the smell of thy garments is like the smell of Lebanon."*

Should you have missed the *"smell of thy ointment"* in the first pass, it is repeated in the *"smell of thy garments"* in the second pass. That's that neat characteristic of Hebrew poetry displayed well in our drama.

The good Samaritan had the necessary ointments to bind up the wounds of the waylaid traveler on his way to Jericho. He not only had them, but he used them. So, in our drama, our bride-church has the necessary ointments that the world is desperately in need of. She has access to the milk of the Word, the Water of Life, the Bread of life, the wine of doctrine, and the honey of prophecy, even to the Great Physician.

Yet, the people need love. Do we have that to give to the rich, to the powerful of society, to the young and the restless, as well as to the down-and-out prostitute, the wino, the derelict, maybe even to those in our own household?

Spices, you will remember, were used in the sanctuary services. We are talking "church" here. All of the church-going one does is not as important, nor impressive as the love lived out in the life. This seems to cast a breath of heavenly-fresh air about the true Christian, or as our Thought for Today states—*"the smell of thy ointments,"* even the smell of thy garments, is better *"than all spices."* This is noticed by the common passerby, even though we notice it not. That's where the Robe of Righteousness comes in, given to us by the Great Physician to heal our own personal ailments, to cover our nakedness, to remove our shame and embarrassment. The ointments we need, like eye salve for one.

Parting Gem: *Your request for today, an assignment no less, is to speak oft with your Lord, requesting Him to give to you the eye salve and the healing ointments needed for today's joys.*

JUNE 25 — Tongue of Tongues — Song 4:11

Today's Thought: *"Thy lips, O my spouse, drop as the honeycomb: honey and milk are under thy tongue; and the smell of thy garments is like the smell of Lebanon."*

Honey is a symbol of prophecy, as we find out in Revelation 10. The honey here implied is that of the great, soon coming of Jesus Christ on October 22, 1844. How wonderfully sweet was that thought. Can you picture in your imagination honey dripping from the mouth, the tongue licking the lips to get all of it in, the satisfied look upon the face of those eating this honey?

Milk represents the basic fundamental concepts of salvation (1 Peter 2:2). This message of a soon-coming Saviour, soon like on October 22, 1844, was abundantly mixed with those concepts of salvation.

Lips are the organs of speech, while the tongue is needed in speaking. The tongue is also needed within the mouth to help mix the food with the saliva to begin the process of digestion. This process is further carried on within the stomach, where you will remember this once sweetness became bitter.

This bride-church, when she speaks or preaches, brings the basics of salvation, as well as the meat and potatoes of more solid truths and prophecies needed for full strong spiritual growth.

In Revelation, a "little book" is to be "sweet as honey." In our drama, the bride has taken a liberal serving! *"Thy lips, O my spouse, drop as the honeycomb: honey and milk are under thy tongue"*

Pictured here is the sweet honey taste in the mouth of the "little book" of Daniel, which she is eating. The sick stomach experience is yet to come. Our drama here only deals with the last part of Revelation 10:9, *"it shall be in thy mouth,"* and does not deal with the first part, *"it shall make thy belly bitter."*

Parting Gem *When one considers that honey and milk are under thy tongue, and that a wholesome tongue is a tree of life, let us, just for today, remember that life and death are in the power of our tongues. Let us speak with the honey and the milk (Proverbs 15:4, 18:21).*

JUNE 26 — Robe of Robes — Song 4:11

Today's Thought: *"Thy lips, O my spouse, drop as the honeycomb: honey and milk are under thy tongue; and the smell of thy garments is like the smell of Lebanon."*

What garment wisheth thou to wear? How about the Robe of Righteousness! This robe is supplied by the Bridegroom so that all of His guests at His wedding supper may be properly dressed for this auspicious occasion. Should you not have this necessary robe, then you would be barred from the reception. The wedding is taking place now.

Take the case in point found in Matthew 22:11, *"And when the king came in to see the guest, he saw there a man who had not on a wedding garment."* He had no answer to the king's question as to how he got into the ceremony; he was speechless. Yet the king supplied all necessary garments, so why not get one?

Was it not the Robe of Christ's righteousness that both Adam and Eve lost when they partook of the forbidden tree? Is that not why they found themselves nude, naked, without excuse?

Is this not what John means when he wrote in Revelation 3:18? *"I counsel thee to buy of me gold… and white raiment, that thou mayest be clothed, and that the shame of thy nakedness does not appear."*

Is this not the Robe that we should wear as part of our daily life? As I once heard at camp-meeting, this robe can be adjusted to the colour, the style, the fit we wish for the occasion we seek. Awesome thought.

Yet our Thought mentions the smell of thy garments is like the smell of Lebanon. Smell has the ability to stop one in his tracks, get attention, even comments. So it is with this Robe, this garment we chose to have our Creator God give to us. When we wear this garment, or have our ways please the Lord, it can even cause our enemies to think well of us and to be at peace with us (Proverbs 16:7).

Parting Gem: *Our bride has on this garment, the Robe of Christ's righteousness, which brings with it the many facets of the Bridegroom. Lebanon is that snow-covered mountain bringing fresh water to thirsty mouths. Feel free to accept Christ's Robe in your life.*

JUNE 27 *Garden of Gardens* Song 4:12

Today's Thought: *"A garden inclosed is my sister, my spouse; a spring shut up, a fountain sealed."*

Today we look at the bride-church, which is likened to a garden enclosed, to a spring shut up, to a fountain sealed. This is during the Great Second Advent Movement, between the coming out of the wilderness in 1798 and the close of the 2,300 day prophecy of Daniel 8:14.

Now, in practical purposes, of what value is a garden should it be closed up, or a spring should it not be allowed to flow, or even a fountain should it also be sealed? Of what value are they to anyone?

Here once more is that Hebrew poetic characteristic which states many of its concepts twice or even more, to reinforce correct interpretation. Our thought today has three, *"garden inclosed," "spring shut up," "fountain sealed."*

Before 1844, the Great Advent Movement was a garden enclosed, it was a spring shut up, it was a fountain sealed. It was just there, nothing organized, no one in charge, no aim, no long range mission program.

In a garden are found food, spices, fruits; actually, verse 13 and 14 call it an orchard. Verse 15 calls it a fountain of gardens, a well of living waters, streams from Lebanon.

You should remember Lebanon, that white snow-capped mountain area that feeds several main rivers which in turn feeds many peoples.

The Advent people, who came out of the Great Advent Movement of the 1800s, were destined to serve all the world, to bring a distinct, separating message to lead people away from the broken cisterns that contain no water to the unfailing Fountain of the Water of Life. She is likened to a "fountain," "a well," "streams" to bring to the world the Waters of Life.

Not until the exciting but disappointing experience of 1844 would she be ready to open those springs, those fountains, those wells.

Parting Gem: *Notice here that from 4:12 to 4:15 is one of those "capsules" spoken of in January.*

JUNE 28 — *Spice of Spices* — Song 4:14

Today's Thought: *"Spikenard and saffron; calamus and cinnamon, with all trees of frankincense; myrrh and aloes, with all the chief spices."*

The above mentioned *"chief spices"* were used to make an anointing oil by which certain individuals, like priests of Israel, were ordained and therefore consecrated and dedicated to a special ministry.

"Take thou also unto thee principal spices, of pure myrrh… of sweet cinnamon… of sweet calamus… And thou shalt make it an oil of holy ointment… And thou shalt anoint Aaron and his sons, and consecrate them, that they may minister unto me in the priest's office… This shall be an holy anointing unto me throughout your generations" (Exodus 30:23,25,30-31).

The Advent Movement was destined to serve as a great priesthood (1 Peter 2:9). Through a deep study of the Scriptures and the trial and shaking of a great disappointment soon to come in 1844, they were to be consecrated to a ministry to serve the world. This is stated in a different language and in a different book, *"Thou must prophesy again before many peoples, and nations, and tongues, and kings"* (Revelation 10:11).

1 Peter 2:9 tells us, *"But ye are a chosen generation, a royal priesthood, an holy nation, a peculiar people; that ye should shew forth the praises of him who hath called you out of darkness into his marvellous light."*

This is that other way of saying that this church-bride is anointed, dedicated, consecrated to carry the third angel's message before many peoples, nations, tongues, and kings. Let's put it in yet one other way. You and I are that chosen generation, that holy nation, that royal priesthood, that holy nation, that peculiar person special in the plan and purposes of God, so that we can show to others the greatness and the majesty of our coming Bridegroom. We have been anointed with these spices.

Parting Gem: *As you go about today's ups and downs, consider your position as a royal one, a chosen one, an holy one, a special one to do a powerfully special work for a powerful and wonderful God. He never leads you where He Himself can't go with you.*

June 29 — *Well of Wells* — Song 4:15

Today's Thought: *"A fountain of gardens, a well of living waters, and streams from Lebanon."*

Remember that this portion of our drama is describing the church just after she has come out of the wilderness and embarked on the Great Religious Awakening of the early 1800s. It was the Philadelphia Church, which according to Song 4:7, *"Thou art all fair, my love; there is no spot in thee."*

There are several names given to our Beloved, too many to list. The one I wish to list is "He is the Living Waters," which is recorded in John 4:10, *"Jesus answered and said unto her, If thou knewest the gift of God, and who it is that saith to thee, Give me to drink; thou wouldest have asked of him, and he would have given thee living waters."*

Then to explain what He meant, Jesus said in verse 14, *"But whosoever drinketh of the water that I shall give him shall never thirst; but the water that I shall give him shall be in him a well of water springing up into everlasting life."*

Do you get the picture of this garden, symbolic of the Christian Church? This garden-church is full of flowers and fruit. A lot of people reside in that garden; they have membership in it, they belong in it, the garden, the church.

In this church-garden is the living waters that those who drink of will enter everlasting life. It will spring up into him or her, a well-spring internal, bubbling up and over continually.

John 7:38 states it this way, *"He that believeth on me, as the scripture hath said, out of his belly shall flow rivers of living water."*

If we could slip ahead into the New Earth experience, we read in Revelation 7:17, *"For the Lamb which is in the midst of the throne shall feed them, and shall lead them unto living fountains of waters: and God shall wipe away all tears from their eyes."*

Thus is a small picture of this church. It has the necessary waters to feed the thirsty soul; the many flowers in that garden testify that they are alive and well because they get water from this well.

Parting Gem: *Most people are aware that water is one of the daily necessities of life, so drink, drink abundantly. O beloved, drink.*

| JUNE 30 | *Summary* | Song 4:1-11 |

The 1831 to 1844 Great Advent Movement was guided by the Holy Spirit with its honour, glory, and power coming directly from God. She was to "eat" the little book of Daniel as outlined in Revelation 10 with "teeth," ensuring mastication and digestion. Her doctrines are pure and productive. With her "lips," she brought forth a message with power, understanding, and reason. Her "mighty men" were the "threescore valiant men" armed as soldiers of a fortress.

Remember and understand that this church depicted here, the Church of Philadelphia, has just recently come out of the wilderness. It is a church that does not receive any rebuke from Him who is holy, true, and has the keys of David. This is told to us by Song 4:7, *"There is no spot in thee."*

Her neck conveys a massive assortment of symbolic gems as it is compared to a tower, an armoury, even a "Hall of Fame," as implied by the hanging of shields of these mighty men.

She is taken to the mountain top to view her destiny in verse 8. She sees the world field yet to be taken and that lies before her.

The Bridegroom says in verse 9, *"Thou hast ravished my heart with <u>one</u> of thine eyes, and with <u>one</u> chain of thy neck"* (emphasis added). Before 1844, she had but "half-sight" or "one eye" regarding the doctrines, even vision, and but "one chain" of the law, not yet comprehending the holy Sabbath of the Lord. Yet her affection is pure and true.

She is skilful with prophecy, with the "little book"—the Word of God. She wears the righteousness of Christ and her garments are perfumed with spices. She, the true church—the bride—is ready for the Bridegroom—ready in heart, but not in her experience. There is yet a work to do. The world field is before her as she looks from the mountain top.

May I suggest that you re-read our drama through today, 4:1-11, then ask yourself if this is really Solomon talking literally to his girlfriend, bride? I know of no lady who would nor could accept these "compliments" in the literal sense. Yet, in the spiritual sense, when everything has been properly decoded, it is a most beautiful picture of my church, maybe yours also, as a Seventh-day Adventist. Think on these things.

Anthems of Glory

The hills were green with the late season grass;
    Some sheep were grazing on these hills en mass.
The night skies that were empty showed an awesome sight.
    The stars were a blazing to lighten the night.

Some shepherds were standing round their fire aglow,
    Warming themselves as they mused how to know,
This Christ Child, the Messiah, they knew soon to come.
    For prophecy stated the long time was done.

Some angels returning from a mission in vain,
    Saw this bright glow on the lone pasture plains.
These shepherds were ready and seeking for aid,
    When these angels returning said, "Be not afraid."

"Behold 'or the hills in a manger of hay.
    The Messiah, the Christ-Child, arrived just today.
His mother has swaddled him deep in her love.
    This message we bring you is straight from above."

Soon all those night skies were drenched in glory,
    As angels sang with joy, redemption's story.
The shepherds made haste to the manger foretold.
    They knelt and adored this Gift from of old.

Then back to the sheep on the pasture they went,
    Telling all others of this blessed event.
The rest of that night was a time of pure praise,
    For anthems of glory they just had to raise.

The Gospel in Work Boots

In the beginning, at its very roots,
The gospel was given a pair of work boots,
Then told to go out to the field in work clothes,
To cure the world's ailments, its troubles, its woes.

When Mary was caught in that vicious scandal,
She felt not the stones, but say the Man's sandals.
As Naaman gazed down at his body of spots,
His maid wore an apron, at the back, tied with knots.

"Here is your sack lunch," a young mother said.
In the hands of Christ many people were fed.
Madmen at the grave yard were naked and bare;
Now clothed in their right minds for Christ had been there.

Whether the work boots are heavy or light,
Whether the collars are coloured or white,
The Lord has a place for you in His field,
And will eagerly use you as you daily yield.

July

July's Introduction and Aim

It was stated back on January 3, "Puzzle of Puzzles," that there is a parallelism between Daniel, Revelation, *The Great Controversy*, and our devotional Song of Songs, all well-supported and backed up by history.

During July, we will look at a portion of this parallelism of Revelation found in Revelation 10:1-11, remembering, *"I have told you before it come to pass, that, when it come to pass, ye might believe"* (John 14:29). The same is stated in Song 5:2-8, Revelation 10 reiterates it in different language, and history backs them up.

No other establishment but the Seventh-day Adventist Church can understand and correctly interpret Revelation 10, because it was that experience that led to the organization of that church. It was the commission of verse 11 that was obeyed, pushing this church into the far-flung regions of the globe. It was truly a "global mission" adventure. It is a similar commission to that found in Matthew 28:19-20.

We will launch out into Revelation 10 using Song 5:2-8 as a springboard. After you have completed this daily devotional, it is the prayer of the author that you will realize that, like Revelation 10, this Song of Songs drama can be understood and applied to only the Seventh-day Adventist community, for like Revelation, it is the experience of God's true church down through ages, culminating in that church.

Try to understand that the 1798 experience of Pope Pius being taken prisoner by the French General Berthier shortly after the French Revolution (Revelation 11), which ran for three and a half years from November 26, 1793 until June 17, 1797, woke the global world to their spiritual bankruptcy and their desperate need as well as their responsibility to the unchristian peoples of the world. This in turn opened up the Great Religious Awakening of the early 1800s, thus leading to the

Great Second Advent Movement of the 1830s and 1840s, culminating in the Millerite Movement to form the community of the Seventh-day Adventist Church.

The next pope was Barnabus Chiaromonti, who took the title Pope Pius VII. He was elected pope some 197 days after Pope Pius VI died. This new pope, Pius VII, was also taken prisoner, imprisoned in 1812 at Fontainbleau, just south of Paris, France. He was released, however, when he agreed to renounce control over the Papal States. These Papal States comprised much of what is now the country of Italy.

Once again, please be aware of the two references often given to you, TM 409-410 and Acts 17:11, and your duty.

During July, we will be introduced to a comparison between Revelation, our Song of Songs drama, and history to back things up. For an assignment for this month, please read Revelation 10:1-11, as well as Song of Songs 5:2-8. We will cover Act 2, Scenes 6-8, which corresponds to *The Great Controversy*, Chapters 19-23.

I have chosen, after some prayer and some contemplation, not to go through Revelation 10 and then come through with Song 5:2-8, but to weave these two passages together as the experience unfolds. I surely hope and pray that you will be able to follow and that it does make sense.

Marion G. Berry wrote this next portion of the introduction:

We are spectators, sitting in the theatre of our universe, watching a drama! This drama began 2,000 years ago, is still going on, and extends even into the future. From age to age, the spectator, get up out of their seats, go upon stage, and act the part that was written for them.

Did you ever wish to be an actor or an actress. You may not get the roll of lead character, but there are lines for you to say and act out.

The script for this drama was written 3,000 years ago by King Solomon under the inspiration of the Holy Spirit. For three millennia the theatre doors were closed to spectators, and the script coded in embarrassing language to save it for the last days of earth's history when that generation would be most tempted and tried.

Now, in July, we spectators will watch an anti-climax in the drama that occurred in the 1843-44 era. The actors then did not know they were part of this drama, but acted their parts faithfully, as had all those who took parts for 2,000 years.

Just sit back in your comfortable theatre seat and watch this strange incident unfold before your eyes! Enjoy.

July

Day 1	Angel of Angels	Revelation 10:1-2	221
Day 2	Little Book of Little Books	Revelation 10:2	222
Day 3	Thunder of Thunders	Revelation 10:3-4	223
Day 4	Lifted Hands of Lifted Hands	Revelation 10:5-6	224
Day 5	Start of Starts	Revelation 10:7	225
Day 6	Command of Commands	Revelation 10:7-8	226
Day 7	Cup of Cups	Song 5:1	227
Day 8	Acceptance of Acceptances	Revelation 10:9	228
Day 9	Slumber of Slumbers	Song 5:2	229
Day 10	Voice of Voices #2	Song 5:2	230
Day 11	Coat of Coats	Song 5:3	231
Day 12	Butterfly of Butterflies	Song 5:4-5	232
Day 13	Eat of Eats	Revelation 10:10	233
Day 14	Emphasis of Emphases	Song 5:5	234
Day 15	Presentation of Presentations	Song 5:2	235
Day 16	Weeping of Weepings	Song 5:6	236
Day 17	Withdrawal of Withdrawals	Song 5:6	237
Day 18	Request of Requests	Matthew 28:19-20	238
Day 19	Commission of Commissions	Revelation 10:11	239
Day 20	Reaction of Reactions	Song 5:7	240
Day 21	Separation of Separations	Mark 6:31	241
Day 22	Review of Reviews #1	Revelation 10:11	242
Day 23	Question of Questions #1	Song 5:8	243
Day 24	Band of Bands	Exodus 25:8	244
Day 25	Messenger of Messengers #2	Joel 2:28	245
Day 26	Acid Test of Acid Tests	Numbers 12:6	246
Day 27	Further Tests of Further Tests	1 Thessalonians 4:13	247
Day 28	Breast of Breasts #3	Exodus 20:8	248
Day 29	Conference of Conferences	Revelation 10:11	249
Day 30	Connecting Link of Connecting Links	Acts 9:15	250
Day 31	Summary	Isaiah 28:10,13	251

Poems of the Month: "Into the Very Presence of Christ"	252
"Jacob Gave the Victor's Shout"	252

JULY 1   *Angel of Angels*   Revelation 10:1-2

Today's Thought: *"And I saw another mighty angel come down from heaven, clothed with a cloud: a rainbow was upon his head, his face was as it were the sun, and his feet as pillars of fire: and he had in his hand a little book open."*

After the sixth trumpet of Revelation 9:13-21 has sounded, but before the seventh trumpet (Revelation 11:14) has sounded, a set of parentheses is inserted. Revelation 10 deals with the Adventist birth, while Revelation 11:1-14 deals with the French Revolution.

This mighty angel is distinct from the four angels which hold back the four winds (Revelation 7:1); different from the angels sounding the trumpets (Revelation 8:2); different from the angel of the altar (Revelation 8:3); but similar to the angel described in Revelation 1:10-16, which describes Christ, for this mighty angel is no less a person than Jesus Christ. His feet were likened to pillars of fire, likened unto fine brass as if they burned in a furnace (Revelation 1:15). A rainbow surrounds his throne (Revelation 4:3), and he is engulfed with a cloud, an association pertaining to Christ.

So our thought today depicts a *"little book,"* a miniature form of bibles, which is open. The Greek implies that the book has been opened, implying it was once closed. The only sealed *"little book"* mentioned is in Daniel 12:4, where Daniel has been instructed to *"shut up the words, and seal the book, even to the time of the end."* It therefore seems logical that the little book opened in the hands of the mighty angel is the book of Daniel, to be opened at the end of time.

In our present political environment, one can tell the importance the government places on a conference or gathering. The higher the government person sent, the higher the importance placed on the occasion. Many time riots break out because the highest personnel were not sent as the people expected. So the highest authoritative Person possible to send in this occasion indicates that this little open book is of tremendous importance. What higher Governmental Person could have been sent than the Son of the Most High God?

Parting Gem: *This message is from Jesus Christ, that angel, the highest authority possible.*

JULY 2   *Little Book of Little Books*   Revelation 10:2

Today's Thought: *"And he had in his hand a little book open."*

As a child, we had "big-little books." These books were about 3 inches by 5 inches and just under 2 inches thick. In the top-left corner of the left pages and the top-right corner of the right pages were small pictures. When these pages were flipped, one saw a movie as the pictures came alive.

So in our thought for today, we have depicted a "little scroll," a miniature form of bibles, "book," "scroll," which is open. The Greek implies that the book has been opened and still is open, which all in turn tell us that this little book was once closed.

The only sealed or closed "little book" is found in Daniel 12:4, where Daniel has been instructed to *"shut up the words, and seal the book, even to the time of the end."* It therefore seems logical that the little book opened in the hands of the mighty angel is the book of Daniel.

Notice that this little book, these sealed portions of Daniel's prophecy, were to open *"even to the time of the end,"* depicted in Daniel 12:6-7 as *"time, times, and an half."* This is speaking in symbolic language, which literally means 1,260 years.

At the close of the 2,300 day-year prophecy that ran from 457 BC to AD 1844, things happened, a lot of things. The peoples of the world jumped up and took notice when the French Revolution took place (from November 26, 1793 to June 17, 1797). Had they not been fully awake then, they woke when General Berthier went in and took Pope Pius VI captive on February 10, 1798. The next pope, Pope Pius VII, was also taken prisoner but released when he agreed to relinquish control of the papal states.

Is anyone looking at the events on the horizon indicating these event told to us in this little book?

(For a breakdown of this 2,300 day prophecy, see Appendix 2.)

Parting Gem: *This little book of Daniel, tucked away near the end of the Old Testament, will after 1844 be opened and understood. It will stand in its place in these latter days. The two books of Daniel and Revelation are one. One is a prophecy sealed; the other is a revelation revealed.*

JULY 3 — Thunder of Thunders — Revelation 10:3-4

Today's Thought: *"... and when he had cried, seven thunders uttered their voices. And when the seven thunders had uttered their voices, I was about to write: and I heard a voice from heaven saying unto me, Seal up those things which the seven thunders uttered, and write them not."*

These seven thunders are one of a set of fourteen sevens in the book of Revelation. The repeated use of the number seven using so many different types of symbols is an indication that they are to be used in the symbolic sense. Seven is understood to indicate completeness.

Daniel was commanded to *"shut up the words, and seal the book, even to the time of the end"* (Daniel 12:4), whereas John was commanded to seal up that which the seven thunders uttered and to write them not. He was not to seal up the entire book of Revelation as in the case of Daniel.

In Revelation 1:1, this is the revelation of Jesus Christ which God gave Him to show unto all His future servants the things which were to be shortly happening. This small and short portion of the trumpet section was to be sealed up, and only this thunderings section.

This special light given to John expressed in the seven thunders was a delineation of events which would transpire under the first and second angels' message. The message obviously was not a revelation for the people of John's day, but would be revealed at the end of time as the scroll unrolls.

Apparently John understood the voices of the seven thunders, and was prepared to record their message. This passage indicates that John recorded the visions of Revelation as they were presented to him.

The seven trumpets run from Revelation 8:6 to 11:19. There is an inserted chapter 10 experience of a bitter small book, plus the French Revolution. The seventh trumpet is getting ready, he's eager to sound. Trumpets 1-4 are against the Western Roman Empire. Yet, this little book is important, loaded with urgent messages for you and me.

Parting Gem: *It's amazing to me as to what methods God will use to get one's attention; if not the thunder of Sinai, then the still small voice.*

JULY 4 *Lifted Hands of Lifted Hands* Revelation 10:5-6

Today's Thought: *"And the angel which I saw stand upon the sea and upon the earth lifted up his hand to heaven, and sware by him that liveth for ever and ever… that there should be time no longer."*

In preparation for the utterance of an oath in ancient times, as well as in modern times, the raising of the hand, usually the right hand, takes place. In modern times, the left hand is usually placed on the Bible, the right raised from the elbow and close to the body to solemnly declare that one will tell "the truth, the whole truth, and nothing but the truth, so help me God."

In Genesis 14:22-23, it says, *"And Abram said to the king of Sodom, I have lift up mine hand unto the Lord, the most high God, the possessor of heaven and earth, that I will not take…"*

This angel with one foot in the sea, the other foot on dry land, is making a universal global oath, a very solemn and serious act. In Daniel 12:7, the angel lifts his hands to heaven that a vision is to last *"a time, times, and an half"* and His covenant will He not break, not alter the things that are gone out of His lips.

This angel is swearing by the highest possible authority that there will be time no longer, which is generally understood that there will be and are prophecies still to be fulfilled but none of them are based on time. A time-prophecy has a beginning date and works towards a closing date. There are still prophecies, such as the 1,335 days, the 1,290 days, and possibly even the 1,260 days of Daniel 12. Daniel 11 is nearly completed and yet we seem not to fully understand that chapter.

There is this nugget of understanding that when the Most High, His Son, and all of heaven lifts up both hands to heaven and swear, make a declaration, make a promise, then we mortals on Planet Earth would do well to sit up, stand up, and take notice. Things are serious when He lifts both hands to heaven.

Parting Gem: *When this mighty angel, Jesus Christ, lifted up His hands unto heaven, He is vowing by the God of heaven and earth, by the most high God, the possessor of heaven and earth, the highest possible authority that what He states will definitely come to pass.*

JULY 5   *Start of Starts*   Revelation 10:7

Today's Thought: *"But in the days of the voice of the seventh angel, when he shall begin to sound, the mystery of God should be finished, as he hath declared to his servants the prophets."*

Seven trumpets are mentioned in Revelation. Trumpets are a symbol of war. The first four trumpets are against Rome.

Trumpet #1 sounds in 8:7 and depicts the Visigoths under Alaric, and Western Rome's first fall in AD 410.

Trumpet #2 sounds in 8:8-9 and shows the Vandals under Genseric looting Western Rome in AD 455.

Trumpet #3 sounds in 8:10-11 where the Huns under Attila challenges Rome; Western Rome complies.

Trumpet #4 sounds in 8:12. Here, in the first part, the Heruli under Odoacer rules Rome from AD 476, when Western Rome fell until AD 493. Then, in the second part, the Ostrogoths under Theodoric ruled Rome from AD 493 until AD 538, Rome's final fall.

Trumpet #5 sounds in 9:1-12. This is the first woe and was the rise of Mohammed or Islam, whose followers are called Moslems. This started in AD 622 and continued until July 27, 1449.

Trumpet #6 in 9:13-21, the second woe, the period of the Moslems' hey-day and domination from July 27, 1449 until August 11, 1840. Thus Eastern Rome fell.

Between trumpet #6 and #7, the bitter, open little book experience, and the French Revolution—are recorded. Quickly after the second woe (Revelation 11:14), the third woe cometh.

Thus, we have the understanding of the trumpets of Revelation 8-11, by those who were part of the Great Advent Movement.

Read through from Revelation 11:15, when the seventh angel sounds, through to verse 19, and notice the events that take place: voices in heaven, thanks are given to the Most High by the four and twenty elders, nations are angry, the judgment of the dead takes place, the saints are rewarded, the temple of God is seen in the heavens. Contemplate these events.

Parting Gem: *So, quickly after August 11, 1840, comes October 22, 1844, ending the 2,300 day prophecy, the time for the mystery of God to be finished; this start of all starts.*

JULY 6 *Command of Commands* Revelation 10:7-8

Today's Thought: *"But in the days of the voice of the seventh angel, when he shall begin to sound, the mystery of God should be finished, as he hath declared to his servants the prophets. And the voice which I heard from heaven spake unto me again, and said, Go and take the little book which is open in the hand of the angel which standeth upon the sea and upon the earth."*

That mystery of God is that which He reveals to His children, His purpose for them, the Plan of Salvation. The ever-pressing burden of His servants the prophets is this declaration and the exposition of the mystery of God. When the seventh angel begins to sound, then this mystery should have been already taken to the world. Why, you ask? According to the above verse, *"the mystery of God should be finished."*

The same mighty angel, Jesus Christ, now speaks again. "Go, take the book which is opened in the hand of the angel."

One of the prophets of verse 7 has stated that God's people need to carefully and diligently study this little book, for it demands specific attention, and helps one to understand Revelation.

This little book, open, is the very book William Miller accepted from the angel's and he ate it up. Daniel 8:14 grabbed him seriously; *"Unto two thousand and three hundred days; then shall the sanctuary be cleansed."*

God's people today need to take that Book and eat it up. David mentions that God's words were found and he ate them and they were unto him the joy and the rejoicing of his heart. God's word was hid in his heart so that he might not sin against his God. That seems to be the way David found the Word; it cleansed him and his ways. It was a lamp to his feet, a light to his path (Psalms 119). In these last dark days of earth's history, we need to have the light of the Book to lighten our ways, not to mention our hearts.

Parting Gem: *This part of Revelation.10:8 corresponds to Song of Songs 5:2, "I sleep, but my heart waketh: it is the voice of my beloved that knocketh." Daniel 8:14 came knocking on William Miller's mind and heart, big time.*

| July 7 | *Cup of Cups* | Song 5:1 |

Today's Thought: *"I am come into my garden, my sister, my spouse: I have gathered my myrrh with my spice; I have eaten my honeycomb with my honey; I have drunk my wine with my milk: eat, O friends; drink, yea, drink abundantly, O beloved."*

What is the Beloved, Christ, telling His bride? He refers to His own experience. His reference to "myrrh" and "spice" bring into focus His own ministry: *"God anointed Jesus of Nazareth"* (Acts 10:38). "Honey," "wine," and "milk" are again the three symbols which refer to the Word of God. Before He entered the ministry, He was completely filled with "milk," which is the fundamentals of the plan of salvation, "wine," or doctrines, and "honey," or prophecy. He spent much time at His mother's knee, as well as in the quiet secluded place of His own personal sanctuary in nature. He has agonized in His garden, the Garden of Gethsemane, where He sweat great drops like blood, wrestling with the challenge and the cross which was just before Him.

Now He invites His bride-church to the same preparation for her ministry. He states to her, *"Eat, O friends; drink, yea, drink abundantly, O beloved."*

He is saying, "Eat, O friends. and I took the little book out of the angel's hand, and ate it up; and it was in my mouth sweet as honey: and as soon as I had eaten it, my belly was bitter."

"Drink, yea, drink abundantly, O beloved." So what is Christ asking the Advent people to drink?

Jesus said unto His disciples, "Can you drink of the cup that I drink of?" This cup is described in Gethsemane when Christ pleaded, *"Father, if this cup may not pass away from me, except I drink it, thy will be done"* (Matthew 26:42). Then He fell and prayed the third time, the same words.

Parting Gem: *Only by drinking this bitter cup could Christ enter upon His larger ministry. Before the disciples could fulfill their ministry to all the then-known world, they must drink the bitter cup of disappointment at the crucifixion. Before the Advent Movement should enter the ministry to all the world, they must be tested and tried by a bitter disappointment.*

JULY 8   *Acceptance of Acceptances*   Revelation 10:9

Today's Thought: *"And I went unto the angel, and said unto him, Give me the little book. And he said unto me, Take it, and eat it up; and it shall make thy belly bitter, but it shall be in thy mouth sweet as honey."*

During May, we looked at how William Miller accepted the "call" from God to go, tell the world. The void in Miller's heart, placed there by God, had to be filled to have needed peace.

His ideas of studying Scripture with nothing but the concordance and the Bible led him to a long detailed study, some six years in total. He figuratively took the Book and ate it up. He found in it, like others, the joy and the rejoicing of his heart, the lamp he needed in his daily sojourn.

His life and decisions in his life portrays an ideology that to read and study and come to no conclusion is worse than reading in the first place; that to come to a grasp of truth and do nothing with it was also worse than not grasping truth, or being introduced to it.

What was he to do when discussing or "arguing" with God didn't work? When the conviction came over him, one of his choices of rejecting the conviction was that he did have to live with himself. One choice he had, should he accept the conviction, was that he did not have to do it alone. He had God with him, and that was of more value and comfort than trying to go it alone.

Turn back to January 2 and read the Parting Gem—"To launch out into the deep, yet not to let down your net, is nothing but a drift in the sea of life." Now tell me, how many of us human beings on Planet Earth are actually adrift aimlessly on the sea of life?

My challenge to you this beautiful day is to take that same small book, open it, eat it up. It can be the thrill of a lifetime when you realize just what it is saying, to you and to me. As a teacher I am powerfully aware that one must go repeat, repeat, repeat a concept or idea many times before it becomes a part of your repertoire.

Parting Gem: *His acceptance of that conviction brought him the presence of God, gave him the important gospel that God loved him, desired him in His kingdom forever. This is the gospel, the story of salvation needed in people's lives.*

JULY 9 — Slumber of Slumbers — Song 5:2

Today's Thought: *"I sleep, but my heart waketh: it is the voice of my beloved that knocketh, saying, Open to me, my sister, my love... for my head is filled with dew, and my locks with the drops of the night."*

The parable of the ten virgins of Matthew 25 also illustrates the experience of the Adventist people. "Then shall the kingdom of heaven be likened unto ten virgins,...While the bridegroom tarried, they all slumbered and slept" (GC 397).

"By the tarrying of the bridegroom is represented the passing of the time when the Lord was expected... and the seeming delay" (GC 394). Some of the Advent believers had expected the coming of Jesus as early as the spring of 1844, even as early as March 21, 1843, but when the times passed they were involved in doubt and uncertainty (GC 391).

In Matthew 25, while the bridegroom tarried, they all slumbered and slept, and at midnight there was a cry made. In Song 5:2, *"It is the voice of my beloved."*

"At midnight there was a loud cry made... In the summer of 1844, half way between the time that it had been first thought that the 2,300 days would end, and the autumn of the same year... the message was proclaimed in the very words of Scripture, 'Behold the bridegroom cometh.' That which led to this movement was the discovery that the decree of Artaxerxes... which formed the starting point for the period of the 2,300 days, went into effect in the autumn of the year 457 BC and not at the beginning of the year, as had been formerly believed. Reckoning from the autumn of 457, the 2,300 years terminated in the autumn of 1844" (GC 398-399).

Notice that Matthew 25 states that all the virgins arose, whereas Song 5:5 states it this way, *"I rose up to open to my beloved."*

"...the midnight cry was heralded by thousands of believers. Like a tidal wave the movement swept over the land... until the waiting people of God were fully aroused" (GC 400).

Parting Gem: *It has been suggested by one that the decree signed by Artaxerxes was signed on that today we would call October 22, 457 BC.*

| JULY 10 | *Voice of Voices #2* | Song 5:2 |

Today's Thought: *"I sleep, but my heart waketh: it is the voice of my beloved that knocketh, saying, Open to me, my sister, my love, my dove, my undefiled: for my head is filled with dew, and my locks with the drops of the night."*

"Dew," "drops of the night," and moisture or "rain" represents the outpouring of the Holy Spirit (James 5:7, Joel 2:23, and Zechariah 10:1).

"It [the midnight cry] produced everywhere the most deep searching of heart and humiliation of soul before the God of high heaven…weaning of affections of the things of this world, a healing of controversies and animosities, a confession of wrongs, a breaking down before God, and penitent, heart-broken supplications to Him for pardon and acceptance. It caused self-abasement and prostration of soul, such as we never before witnessed… As God said by Zachariah, a spirit of grace and supplication was poured out upon His children" (GC 401).

"At that time there was faith that brought answers to prayers—faith that had respect to the recompense of reward. Like showers of rain upon the thirst earth, the Spirit of grace descended upon the earnest seekers. Those who expected soon to stand face to face with their Redeemer felt a solemn joy that was unutterable. The softening, subduing power of the Holy Spirit melted the heart, as His blessing was bestowed in rich measure upon faithful believing ones" (GC 402-403).

Three times, the Holy Spirit has been poured out with special power upon the Christian Church; each time is simultaneous with special movements in the sanctuary.

Earth	Heaven
1. Pentecost	Enthronement of Christ in the Holy Place.
2. 1844 Movement	Transition from Holy Place to the Most Holy Place.
3. Latter Rain-Loud Cry	The "Latter Rain" initiates or signals the completion of Christ's work and departure from the Most Holy Place.

Parting Gem: *As the work went to all their world when the Holy Spirit was poured at Pentecost, so expect the same in our coming days.*

| JULY 11 | *Coat of Coats* | Song 5:3 |

Today's Thought: *"I have put off my coat; how shall I put it on? I have washed my feet; how shall I defile them?"*

Pictured here is a bride all ready for her marriage. She has on whatever brides are supposed have on; ghe is ready, willing, and eager.

Our righteousness is as filthy rags (Isaiah 64:6). The Advent people could not come to the marriage nor expect to meet the Bridegroom in their filthy rags. In the parable of Matthew 22, concerning the marriage, *"the king came in to see the guests"* (Matthew 22:11) to see if they had put on the wedding garment—the robe of Christ's righteous, supplied by the host.

This picture here is one that shows the bride has on the Robe of Christ's righteousness, and has confessed all sins and is cleansed, as done in foot-washing ceremonies. She doesn't want to go back to her filthy rags or sinful life. "Must I put them off?" is her question.

Of all of the great religious movements since the days of the apostles, none have been more free from human imperfections, and the wiles of Satan, than was that of the autumn of 1844 (GC 401).

The bride states that she has washed her feet. This foot-washing ceremony which accompanies the Holy Communion is also a symbol of spiritual cleansing. John states that, *"Jesus saith to him, He that is washed needeth not save to wash his feet, but is clean every whit"* (John 13:10). Those of the Advent Movement, who sincerely expected the Bridegroom to come on October 22, 1844, made all things right with God and with their fellow man. With sins forgiven, conscience clear, they trusted in His righteousness and in His deliverance.

Could it be that our bride knew what she must be in order to be saved, what she must do to prepare herself? Could it be that she has done everything in her own power and diligent strength and was waiting?

Parting Gem: *This experience of our heroine is similar to the end of a camp-meeting. We have feasted on the mountain top that has been spread out with all the good news of the gospel. We have fellowship with our friends we haven't seen all year. Our minds have been taken up with all of the activities and blessings of camp-meeting, and now, we must pack up and head back down into the valley, back home to our everyday living complete with the temptations and trials.*

JULY 12 — *Butterfly of Butterflies* — Song 5:4-5

Today's Thought: *"My beloved put in his hand by the hole of the door, and my bowels were moved for him. I rose up to open to my beloved; and my hands dropped with myrrh, and my fingers with sweet smelling myrrh, upon the handles of the lock."*

Watch the bride as she anticipates the coming of her Beloved. She is excited to the point of having "butterflies" in her stomach. Nervous anticipation engulfs her. She is thrilled to the point of declaring, *"My bowels were moved for him."* She watches the door for it to open. She sees her Beloved's hand reach through to lift the latch. Can you catch the picture as to how certain and positive the bride knows that her Beloved will appear in 1844?

Remember the song, *"At the door, at the door, He is even at the door. He is coming, He is coming, He is even at the door."* This is how sure the Advent Movement was that He would appear in 1844! Our bride in our drama is so thrilled, she says, *"My bowels were moved for him."* Her heart thrilled within her. Today, one could describe it as a battle in her stomach between a Texas longhorn and a pit-bull, or a stomach full of butterflies. Excitement supreme. O, that God's people today would be that excited and sure about the Beloved Lord coming and coming soon.

In the very act of rising up, to "open the door," in going forth to meet the Bridegroom, with her hand upon the handles of the lock, she was anointed to a worldwide ministry! In the drama, the anointing oil ran down over her head, upon her hands, and dripped off her fingers! (Psalms 133:2). She had been anointed to a worldwide ministry! (Revelation 10:11). In going forth to meet the Bridegroom, she was identified as the *true bride!* She was destined to become the remnant of Revelation 12:17.

Parting Gem: *We have nothing to fear for the future, especially when one finds out that the Lord had His hands over this whole disappointment. It has been suggested that without the 1844 disappointment, the doctrine and truth of the sanctuary doctrine may not have come to light, so that God would have had to use a different experience to reveal this doctrine. (P.S. Fail not to remember TM 409-410.)*

JULY 13 — *Eat of Eats* — Revelation 10:10

Today's Thought: *"And I took the little book out of the angel's hand, and ate it up; and it was in my mouth sweet as honey: and as soon as I had eaten it, my belly was bitter."*

After Miller had spent some six years eating that little book in an in-depth study, and summarized his conclusions, he found that most of his convictions were diametrically opposite to those in the general churches of his day. One thing was clear in his mind, however: Jesus Christ would come in about twenty-five years, or about 1843. To him, it was sweet.

During 1840-1844, when William Miller preached on Daniel 8:14, those who heard experienced a beautiful sweetness like honey. This fabulous message of a soon-coming Saviour, coming soon, swept the nation.

Revelation 10:10 compares favourably, although in a very different way, with Song of Songs 5:5-6. *"I rose to open to my beloved; and my hands dropped with myrrh, and my fingers with sweet smelling myrrh [sweet as honey in the mouth], upon the handles of the lock. I opened to my beloved; but my beloved had withdrawn himself, and was gone: my soul failed when he spake [my belly was bitter]: I sought him, but I could not find him; I called him, but he gave me no answer [bitter disappointment]."*

Miller spent some six solid years eating his honeycomb with his honey and drinking his milk abundantly. His conclusion that Christ would return to earth around 1844 led thousands to expect the immediate advent of the Lord. At the appointed time, the Bridegroom came, but to the Ancient of Days to start the Investigative Judgment (Daniel 7:9-14).

Parting Gem: *Today, just for today, have you spent some significant time eating your needed spiritual food?*

JULY 14   *Emphasis of Emphases*   Song 5:5

Today's Thought: *"I rose up to open to my beloved; and my hands dropped with myrrh, and my fingers with sweet smelling myrrh, upon the handles of the lock."*

Miller himself never pinpointed the exact time for Christ to come, other than "about the year 1843." As the time approached, he was urged to define his year, "1843." His reply was in essence sometime between March 21, 1843 and March 21, 1844, all according to Jewish reckoning.

March 21, 1843 came and went; the disappointment was minor and only partial.

March 21, 1844 came and went; the disappointment was a little more intense, but still minor.

April 21, 1844 came and went; another date, another disappointment. Anxiety mounts.

Men continued to seriously study this whole question of time. The emphases on this 1843 time period resulted in many pastors and churches rejecting the message they had once eagerly listened to.

Doors closed to the Millerites; bans were put on Adventist teachings, members were disfellowshipped, ministers were relieved of credentials and discharged. Ridicule and mockery increased. Cartoons flourished.

By the summer of 1843, it was powerfully clear that a separation was taking place between Millerites and the churches of the day. Consequently, Adventist ministers began to call for those loyal to the Advent teachings and cause to separate themselves from their churches and to form Adventist congregations.

Miller himself did not advocate this breaking away from the other churches; he thought that it was going too far. The call grew to come out of her, my people. Martin Luther went through a similar case.

Parting Gem: *Our drama states this process of Revelation 10 by stating, "I am come into my garden, my sister, my spouse: I have gathered my myrrh with my spice; I have eaten my honeycomb with my honey; I have drunk my wine with my milk: eat, O friends, drink, yea, drink abundantly, O beloved" (Song 5:1). I have had my experience. Now it's your turn.*

JULY 15   *Presentation of Presentations*   Song 5:2

Today's Thought: *"I sleep, but my heart waketh: it is the voice of my beloved that knocketh, saying, Open to me, my sister, my love, my dove, my undefiled: for my head is filled with dew, and my locks with the drops of the night."*

Entering onto the stage came Samuel S. Snow, who, beginning in February 16, 1843 and progressively throughout 1844, emphasized and urged the Autumn Jewish Seventh-Month Theory as the true ending of the prophetic 2,300 day prophecy. Miller was using the spring month of March as his basis for determining the end of the 2,300 year prophecy; Snow was using the tenth-day of the seventh-month method.

Finally, on August 12, 1844, a camp-meeting in Exeter, New Hampshire was in progress. Joseph Bates was at the podium with nothing really new to say, but he was saying it anyway.

S. S. Snow entered, sat near the front where his sister was, and talked to her quietly for some time. She immediately stood up and announced, "Samuel has something powerfully important to say."

Here in this August 1844 camp-meeting, Snow expounded on his theory of a fall-month in a clear and logical manner. The next day, he repeated his presentation in more detail. Immediately, it became crystal clear that Snow had it correct, and the 2,300 day prophecy of Daniel 8:14 would end on October 22, 1844,* leaving some sixty-five days to complete the task of giving the warning to the world.

From that camp-meeting in the granite hills of New Hampshire, the stages and railway cars rolled away to the different states, cities, and towns with the rumbling cry, *"Behold, the bridegroom cometh; go ye out to meet him"* (Matthew 25:6).

See Appendix 2 for a breakdown of the 2,300 days.

Parting Gem: *Thus the message was launched, "Behold the bridegroom cometh," soon to be carried to the whole world. The "little book" took on new meaning. The earth was soon to be cleansed,*

JULY 16   *Weeping of Weepings*   Song 5:6

Today's Thought: *"I opened to my beloved; but my beloved had withdrawn himself, and was gone: my soul failed when he spake: I sought him, but I could not find him; I called him, but he gave me no answer."*

Like wildfire, that message flew on the wings of the wind. Men and women moved to the cardinal points of the compass, going with all the speed of locomotives, in steamboats and rail cars, freighted with bundles of books and papers wherever they went, distributing them like the leaves of autumn.

Property was sold and the money poured into the Advent cause. Bills were paid up, wrongs were made right, crops were neglected as not being needed, potatoes left in the ground. Goodbyes were said,

Then, the presses stopped and the Advent people waited expectantly for the dawn of October 22. Some fifty thousand to a hundred thousand expectant Millerites, believed in Christ's coming on October 22, 1844.

The long hours of the day, October 22, slowly passed, each hour increasing with excitement the expectancy of the waiting thousands. Darkness took over the fading hours of twilight, then the midnight hour struck, and disappointment was severe. It was exceedingly intense; it was sickeningly bitter.

Hiram Edson's expressed his feeling this way: "Our fondest hopes and expectations were blasted, and such a spirit of weeping came over us as I have never experienced before. It seemed that the loss of all earthly friends could have been no comparison. We wept and wept until the break of day."[13]

Parting Gem: *"I charge you, O ye daughters of Jerusalem… that ye stir not up, nor awaken my love, till he please" (Song 2:7), and then again, "Therefore be ye also ready: for in such an hour as ye think not the Son of man cometh" (Matthew 24:44). Take a few extra moments this morning before you rush off to do your daily business, to ponder whether you are ready or whether you are not ready for that climactic coming of the Bridegroom.*

---

[13] Knight, George R. *Lest We Forget* (Washington, DC: Review & Herald), 2008, p. 32.

JULY 17 — *Withdrawal of Withdrawals* — Song 5:6

Today's Thought: *"I opened to my beloved; but my beloved had withdrawn himself, and was gone: my soul failed when he spake: I sought him, but I could not find him; I called him, but he gave me no answer."*

Here is how our bride expresses her great disappointment when her Beloved Bridegroom did not come as expected in 1844. She states that, *"My soul failed."* The time of expectation passed, and their Saviour did not appear… they felt as did Mary, when coming to the Saviour's tomb and finding it empty, she exclaimed with weeping, *"They have taken away my Lord, and I know not where they have laid him"* (John 20:13).

Also, it was reported as *"a pang of disappointment… a parallel only in sorrow of the disciples after the crucifixion of their Lord… my feelings were almost uncontrollable. I left the place of meeting and wept like a child"* (The Advent Review, May 7, 1889, p.291). There was a testing time… The bride says, *"I sought him; but could not find him; I called him, but he gave me no answer."* During this time, the superficial and insincere fell away and denied the Great Advent Movement, but a handful of believers were faithful and returned to the Bible to seek the reason for the disappointment. It was these who were to become the founders of the Seventh-day Advent Church—the "remnant" of Revelation 12:17.

Prior to the disappointment, the nominal churches had disfellowshipped the Advent believers for their study of prophetic symbolism and their love for the coming of the Bridegroom. In the summer of 1844, fifty thousand Advent believers withdrew from their churches, declaring them to have the spirit of Babylon. The entire United States had only six million people at the time.

In many eastern or oriental countries, women do not hold legal rights. Therefore, all legal signatures and procedures for a marriage are performed only by males at the city hall or courthouse. The bride remains at home until all legal matters and signatures are cared for, then the bridegroom returns to pick up his new bride and take her to his house which is prepared for her. The marriage supper follows.

Parting Gem: *The Investigative Judgment is such a legal transaction. Jesus Christ had gone into the marriage ceremony (GC 476).*

JULY 18   *Request of Requests*   Matthew 28:19-20

Today's Thought: *"Go ye therefore, and teach all nations, baptizing them in the name of the Father, and of the Son, and of the Holy Ghost: Teaching them to observe all things whatsoever I have commanded you: and, lo, I am with you alway, even unto the end of the world. Amen."*

In this commission to His disciples, Christ not only outlined the work, but He gave them a message. Teach the people, He said, to observe all things whatsoever I have commanded you, not only in person but through all the prophets and teachers of the Old Testament. Human teachings are shut out. There is no place for tradition, for man's theories and conclusions, or for church legislations. No laws ordained by ecclesiastical authority are included in this commission. None of these are God's servants to teach. The Law and the prophets with the record of His own words and deeds are the treasures committed to the disciples to be given to the world. Christ's name is their watchword, their pledge of distinction, their bond of union, their authority for their course of action, and the source of their success. Nothing that does not bear His superscription is to be recognized in His kingdom.

It must follow Isaiah 8:20, *"To the law and the testimony: if they speak not according to this word, it is because there is no light in them."* As well, one should gather all the evidence from the various places in the Bible to put them together before one draws his conclusion, *"for precept must be upon precept, precept upon precept; line upon line, line on line; here a little, and there a little"* (Isaiah 28:10).

Two awesome promises are with this request to go to all the world. One is, *"All power is given unto me in heaven and in earth"* (Matthew 28:18). That power is ours. The second is found in verse 20, *"I am with you alway, even unto the end of the world. Amen."*

Parting Gem: *The gospel is to be presented not as a lifeless theory, but as a living force to change the life... Tell the people of Him who is the Chiefest of ten thousand, and the One altogether lovely.*

JULY 19   *Commission of Commissions*   Revelation 10:11

Today's Thought: *"And he said unto me, Thou must prophesy again before many peoples, and nations, and tongues, and kings."*

In all of the Protestant churches of that day, no one had any belief in the Second Advent doctrine. Christ admonished us to enter in through the Straight Gate which leads to life. Today's thought above is a reutterance of the great commission given by Christ in Matthew 28:19-20. *"Go ye therefore, and teach all nations, and, lo, I am with you alway, even unto the end of the world. Amen."*

Michael Belina Czechowski, an ex-Roman Catholic Polish priest, had converted to Sabbatarian Adventism in 1857, requested to go to his Polish people and give the good news. The church refused to send him, so under the auspices of a first-day Adventist group, he sailed. His departure date was May 14, 1864. He spent some fourteen years preaching in the Waldensian villages in the Italian Alps. When he had left, there were several baptized Adventists, as well as the first Sabbatarian Adventist company outside of North America.

Arriving later in Switzerland, he preached in public halls, visited door to door, printed and sold tracts, even to the point of starting a periodical called *L'Evangile Eternal* ("The Everlasting Gospel").

By the time of his death, he had laid a good foundation for J.N. Andrews to build upon. His work actually speeded up the "official" missionary being sent.[14]

Some ten years later, in September, 1874, John Neville Andrews, with his son and daughter, sailed for Switzerland, the first official Adventist missionary. When he got there, he found a solid foundation that had been laid by Czechowski. Also, he heard of congregations of believers in Prussia, and Russia and became convinced that there were Sabbathkeeping Christians in most of the countries in Europe. The church would prophesy again.

Parting Gem: *Song of Songs 5:6 puts it nicely. "I opened to my beloved; but my beloved had withdrawn himself, and was gone: my soul failed when he spake: I sought him, but I could not find him: I called him, but he gave me no answer."*

---

[14] Ibid., p. 198.

JULY 20   *Reaction of Reactions*   Song 5:7

Today's Thought: *"The watchmen that went about the city found me, they smote me, they wounded me; the keepers of the walls took away my veil from me."*

When Jesus did not come on October 22, 1844, the watchmen on the walls, the official clergy of nominal Christendom, reacted. *"A flood of scoffing, reviling and persecution burst forth, not from the infidel world so much, but from the professed friends of the Saviour…"* (*The Midnight Cry*. F.D. Nichol). The bride complains that they took her wedding veil from her—they denied that she was the true bride. She says, *"They smote me, they wounded me."* The spirit of persecution is the very characteristic of Babylon (Revelation 12:7).

The "veil" is the special attire of a bride. The message of the Great Advent Movement had been, *"Behold, the bridegroom cometh"* (Matthew 25:6), and thereby implied that they were the true bride going forth to meet Him. But after the 1844 Disappointment, the *"watchmen of the city"*—the scholarly theologians of the city of nominal Christianity—through ridicule and abuse, snatched away the "veil," declaring that the Advent people were not the true bride. Babylon declared herself to be the true bride, while the Advent people, to all outward appearances, seemed to be mistaken.

At this point, the Advent believers identified nominal Christianity as Babylon, who had not loved nor made ready for the coming of the Bridegroom and who persecuted the disappointed ones, and thereby gave the second angel's message! (Revelation 14:8) Babylon is fallen. They did not declare her final fall, but rather the beginning of her fall. This message has been declared faithfully by the remnant and will swell into the *"loud cry"* of Revelation 18:1-8, when there is a union of church and state to enforce laws contrary to the law of God and when in the spirit of persecution, Babylon (confused counterfeit religions) will seek to destroy the people of God.

This second angel's message against Babylon was first given just prior to 1844—reinforced after 1844—and has been given ever since and will swell into the Loud Cry at the time of the end.

Parting Gem: *What is your reaction at the nearness of the Bridegroom?*

JULY 21 — *Separation of Separations* — Mark 6:31

Today's Thought: *"And [Jesus] said unto them, Come ye yourselves apart into a desert place, and rest a while."*

Almost immediately after this very major disappointment—dubbed "The Great Disappointment"—by far the vast majority who had joined the Millerites Movement turned away from it. They gave it up, They felt the whole idea was based on faulty interpretation of Scripture. In the year 1844, the United States of America had a population of six-million: the Millerite Movement had a following of some fifty thousand.

There are still people today who also claim that October 22, 1844 is a non-important date, a non- significant experience, even within the Seventh-day Adventist community.

Beside those who gave it all up, there were those who still believed that the basic understanding of the prophecy was correct. They realized that some mistake had been made and fell into three groups:

Group 1: There were those who became extremists, repeatedly setting dates. They are still around today.

Group 2: There were those who continued in the Advent hope, differing but little from other Protestant Churches. These became known as "Advent Christians" or "First-day Adventist" and today have nearly the same membership as in 1844. This group is spoken of as "Nominal Adventists" in the writings of E.G. White. This group rejected any additional light.

Group 3: This third group regrouped, banded together, hunkered down into the Word of God to find the answers to their disappointment. Fewer than one hundred after the disappointment, they grew to be known as Seventh-day Adventists who, as of December, 2008, number over 15 million (NAD Adventist World Review, December, 2008). Speaking globally, this is one in every 425 persons. They cover the globe with schools from elementary to university; they operate many hospitals, printing presses, communications networks.

Parting gem: *We have nothing to fear for the future except as we shall forget how God has led us in our past history, through green pastures and still waters (LS 196).*

JULY 22   *Review of Reviews #1*   Revelation 10:11

Today's Thought: *"Thou must prophesy again [again, and yet again.]…"*

This group of disappointed Christians had only one safe course to follow, and that was to cherish the light which they had already received of God, hold fast to His promises, and continue to search the Scriptures, and patiently wait and watch to receive further light.

God had led His people in the Great Advent Movement. His power and glory had attended the work, and He would not permit it to end in darkness and disappointment.

With earnest prayers, they reviewed their position and studied the Scriptures to discover their mistake. As they could see no error in their reckoning of the prophetic periods, they were led to examine more closely the subject of the sanctuary.

The Scripture which above all others had been both the foundation and the central pillar of the Advent faith was the declaration in Daniel 8:14. In common with rest of the Christian world, Adventists then held that the earth, or some portion of it, was the sanctuary.

In their investigation, they learned that there was no Scripture evidence sustaining the popular view that the earth is the sanctuary; but they found in the Bible a full explanation of the subject of the sanctuary. They found that for eighteen centuries, this work of ministration continued in the first compartment of the sanctuary. The blood of Christ pleaded on behalf of penitent believers, secured their pardon and acceptance with the Father, yet their sins still remained upon the books of record. As in the typical service, there was a work of atonement at the close of the year, so before Christ's work for the redemption of men is completed, there is a work of atonement for the removal of sin from the sanctuary. This is the service which began when the 2,300 days ended. At that time, as foretold by Daniel the prophet, our High Priest entered the most holy, to perform the last division of His solemn work—to cleanse the sanctuary. So they saw that Christ went into the Most Holy compartment to cleanse the sins of His people (see GC Chapter 23).

Parting Gem: *Now in the Holy of Holies they again beheld Him, their compassionate High Priest, soon to appear as their king and deliverer.*

| JULY 23 | Question of Questions #1 | Song 5:8 |

Today's Thought: *"I charge you, O daughters of Jerusalem, if ye find my beloved, that ye tell him, that I am sick of love."*

After the Great Disappointment of October 22, 1844, the small group of believers who returned to the Bible to seek for the reason of their grief did not know at first why Jesus did not come as they expected. They knew that their mathematical calculations and dates for the 2,300 day-year prophecy were correct. But where was the Bridegroom that He had not come as anticipated?

Just after the 1844 disappointment, the bride makes a request in her charge to the daughters of Jerusalem. Her request is, *"If you find him… [let me know where you found him!]"* He had not come to earth as expected, so where did He go at the end of the 2,300 days-years? This lovesick bride left standing on the church steps is not feeling sorry for herself—but is still seeking Him. Where has He gone? What is He doing that He did not come for her?

This charge to the daughters of Jerusalem causes perplexity to those daughters. Who is this Beloved of yours that you give us such a challenge, such a charge, such a responsibility to tell him of your feelings? Who is He?

Why, though, is she lovesick? She is disappointed that her Lover did not come. She is disappointed, but still the apple of His eye. She is confident that He will come, but she wants Him to know that she is eagerly waiting for Him; yes, watching as well.

Parting Gem: *For those of you who are familiar with the film* Johnny Lingo, *the ladies of the village could and did say the same thing about this shy, backward bride of Johnny Lingo. In her culture, the bridegroom would pay a dowry of cows to the bride's father. The village had never seen such a high dowry given before; even the father did not expect but maybe one cow. This bride of Johnny Lingo could raise her head high, importantly, because Johnny had given her father seven cows as his dowry. This was never heard of before, so she could easily say, "I am the bride of Johnny Lingo."*

JULY 24 — Band of Bands — Exodus 25:8

Today's Thought: *"Let them make me a sanctuary."*

Besides the blessed hope of Christ's second coming, there were three other major, distinctive teachings that banded this group together, and at the same time set them apart from all other churches. The nominal Adventists rejected all three doctrines. They all start with "S" (the Second Coming, the Sanctuary, and the Spirit of Prophecy).

God began immediately to lead His people onward. The morning of October 23, after crying all night, Hiram Edson and O.R.L. Grossier chose to visit and encourage other disappointed Millerites. They cut across a corn field. While passing through that large field of corn, Hiram stopped about halfway. Grossier went on unawares. Heaven seemed to open to Hiram's view and he clearly saw that the High Priest was not coming out of the Most Holy Compartment of the heavenly sanctuary to come to earth, but was going into it for the first time, and that He had a work to do there before coming back the second time.

When in their study, they found the Day of Atonement idea set out in Leviticus: it all made perfect sense; it all had meaning. It gave them a clear picture of events up to the close of the thousand-year millennium.

The doctrine pertaining to "the Sanctuary" has given Adventists a profound advantage in understanding the ministry of Jesus Christ. Just what is Jesus doing now, is fully understood only by Seventh-day Adventists. The nominal Adventist rejected this first gift.

After all, how long does it take for Him to go and prepare a place for us? How long does it take to build all those mansions in the Holy City, especially in the light of Him creating the sun, moon, and the earth, the sea and fountains of waters and all that is in them is, in six days?

Parting Gem: *The doctrine of the **second coming** binds hearts together, making a family of believers different from just a church. The doctrine of the **sanctuary** allows one to understand the big picture of Christ's Bethlehem experience followed by the death and resurrection experiences. In order for Him to act as our High Priest, did He not have to come and die for us?*

JULY 25 — Messenger of Messengers #2 — Joel 2:28

Today's Thought: *"And it shall come to pass afterward, that I will pour out my spirit upon flesh; and your sons and your daughters shall prophesy, your old men shall dream dreams, your young men shall see visions."*

On a December day in 1844, just a few months after the bitter disappointment, a young seventeen-year-old girl was kneeling in prayer with four other ladies when the power of God came over her as she had never felt before. Ellen Gould Harmon was a sickly girl, possibly what one would call the weakest of the weak.

She was shown the Advent people and the pathway to the city. A light behind them brightened the way. This light was the "midnight cry" (Matthew 25:6).

In her second vision, about one week later, she saw something of the trials that she would experience. She was instructed to tell others that which had been made known to her.

Over Ellen's eighty-plus years, the Lord used her as "His messenger," giving her counsel to give to His church. Books, magazines articles, counsel, reproofs, plus her Godly example and much more has been her legacy to God's last day church.

The Advent people have found this gift, usually listed in second place whenever gifts are listed in Scripture, to be one of the identifying characteristics of the Remnant Church. *"And the dragon was wroth with the woman, and went to make war with the remnant of her seed, which keep the commandments of God, and have the testimony of Jesus Christ"* (Revelation 19:17). *"The testimony of Jesus is the spirit of prophecy"* (Revelation 19:10).

This second special gift from God given to the people of God living upon Earth in the last days was rejected by the nominal Adventists

Parting Gem: *"All these truths are immortalized in my writings. The Lord never denies His Word. Men will come up with scheme after scheme, and the enemy will seek to seduce souls from the truth, but all who believe that the Lord has spoken through Sister White and has given her a message will be safe from the many delusions that will come in these last days" (YSRP:238:4; Man. 760., pp. 22-23).*

JULY 26   *Acid Test of Acid Tests*   Numbers 12:6

Today's Thought: *"And he said, Hear now my words: If there be a prophet among you, I the Lord will make myself known unto him in a vision, and will speak unto him in a dream."*

Shortly after the disappointment of October 22, 1844, the Lord in His mercy gave to His people the gift of "the Spirit of Prophecy" through visions and testimonies of Ellen G. (Harmon) White. This special gift helps identify this bride of our drama as the remnant bride, the last church. The remnant church actually needed to have this gift of Prophecy in order to fulfill 1 Corinthians 1:5-7, where it says, *"That in every thing ye are enriched by him… even as the testimony of Christ was confirmed in you: so that ye come behind in no gift."* And also Revelation 12:17, where it says, *"And the dragon was wrath with the woman, and went to make war with the remnant of her seed, which keep the commandments of God, and have the testimony of Jesus Christ."* Revelation 19:10 identifies the testimony of Jesus as the spirit of prophecy.

There are four "acid tests" for this gift:

Acid Test #1: *"To the law and to the testimony: if they speak not according to this word, it is because there is no light in them"* (Isaiah 8:20).

Acid Test #2: *"Wherefore by their fruits ye shall know them"* (Matthew 7:20).

Acid Test #3: *"When the word of the prophet shall come to pass, then shall the prophet be known, that the Lord hath truly sent him"* (Jeremiah 28:9). (His Prophetic Prediction Quota, PPQ, must be 100%.)

Acid Test #4: *"Every spirit that confesseth that Jesus Christ is come in the flesh is of God"* (1 John 4:2). This would include Christ's incarnation, His sinless life, His crucifixion, His resurrection, His ascension, His mediation, and His second coming. These are sometimes called the "seven wonders of salvation," or "the seven wonders of the universe" (A Prophet Among You, Chapter 6).

Parting Gem *These tests, along with five further tests, must be applied consistently and insistently to any person claiming or whom others claim as a prophet. This PPQ must remain 100% or that prophet is false. Take into consideration conditionality of prophecy, but a prophet missing on one prediction is "out."*

JULY 27   *Further Test of Further Tests*   1 Thessalonians 4:13

Today's Thought: *"I would not have you to be ignorant."*

The four "acid tests" of yesterday are sufficient in and of themselves to enable one to determine who is a true prophet and who is false. In addition, however, there are five other factors that give added proof that the true prophet's messages are from the Lord.

A look at these additional evidences or tests, pertaining to this special gift of prophecy, when taken with the other acid tests, form convincing added testimony. These five additional tests are:

Test #5—Physical manifestations: In Daniel's case, a glorious being appeared to him. He lost his strength and fell into a deep sleep, yet heard the voice of the angelic being. He arose to his hands and knees and then stood to his feet, being at first dumb but later speaking, not breathing, then strength was given to him.

Test #6—Timeliness: Not all messages were given years or even centuries before fulfillment. The fascinating story of Elisha and the King of Syria recorded in 2 Kings 6:8-23 is a case in point. It is a part of God's plan to make available to His people, in any age, well-timed guidance to meet their needs. Many other more modern stories are available.

Test #7—The Certainty, the Fearlessness: The certainty and fearlessness of the prophets adds weight to their claim to have God's messages. Nathan boldly said before King David, *"Thou art the man"* (2 Samuel 12:7). Elijah proclaimed fearlessly to King Ahab, *"I have not troubled Israel; but thou, and thy father's house…"* (1 Kings 18:18).

Test #8—High Spiritual Plane: The messages given by God's servants are given in a dignified and fitting manner. The spiritual principles laid down are the most lofty known to the human mind. Both the theme of the Bible and the mode of expression are worthy of, and command, the respect of the most learned as well as the most humble.

Test #9—Practical Nature: Not weird fantasies, nor pointless ramblings, but practical, useful messages are given by God through His messengers, the prophets, for all Scripture is profitable, such as how to plant a tree, and the buying of property in Australia to build a college (T. Housel Jemison. *A Prophet Among You,* Chapter 6).

Parting Gem: *God promised that if there was a prophet among us, He would make Himself known unto him, or her.*

JULY 28 — Breast of Breasts #3 — Exodus 20:8

Today's Thought: *"Remember the sabbath day, to keep it holy.*

A chain of events was in motion to reveal the seventh-day Sabbath to the Advent believers. Mrs Rachael Oakes Preston, T.M. Preble, Joseph Bates were all used to draw the attention of the Sabbath to the Adventists.

Further, as the Advent people looked into the Most Holy Place of the heavenly sanctuary, they saw the Bridegroom standing before the ark of God, in which was the immutable law, the Ten Commandments.

"The temple of God was opened in heaven, and there was seen in His temple the Ark of His Testament within the holy of holies in the sanctuary in heaven, the divine law is sacredly enshrined" (GS 433, 434).

Their attention was drawn to the fourth commandment, enjoining upon all men the seventh-day Sabbath, which happened to have a glow about it. This gift, Sabbath, was also rejected by nominal Adventists.

"In the very bosom of the Decalogue, Ten Laws, is the fourth commandment... Remember the Sabbath day... the seventh day is the Sabbath of the Lord thy God..." (GC 434)

They accepted the seventh day as a sign, and a seal. *"Verily my sabbaths ye shall keep: for it is a sign between me and you throughout your generations"* (Exodus 31:13). The Sabbath commandment *contains* a seal as it designates the three identifying marks of a seal:

--name (Exodus 20:10, Sabbath of the LORD THY GOD), and

--the office (Exodus 20:11, the Creators of the Universe, the Lord made), and

--the territory (Exodus 20:11, the heavens and the earth and all that in them is).

They investigated the origin of Sunday worship, which by historical records and various sources confirmed the fact that Sunday worship was a symbol of allegiance to the sun-god of Babylon, accepted by apostate Christianity, enforced by Papal authority, and a mark of its power. At this point, the Advent people began to give *the third angel's message* of Revelation 14 in warning against the false Sunday sabbath and the "beast" power promoting its observance.

Parting Gem: *A seal is generally located in the lower left corner of a legal document. The Sabbath of the Lord our God is thus located in the Decalogue. As well, in the word "Sabbath" is the name of the Father, "Abba." It appears that God leaves nothing to chance.*

JULY 29   *Conference of Conferences*   Revelation 10:11

Today's Thought: *"Thou must prophesy again before many peoples, many nations, and tongues, even kings."* Should the bride go before all these nations, peoples, tongues, neighbourhoods, and yes, even kings, and prophesy to them, just what would she have to say to them?

Joseph Bates, the Whites, and Hiram Edson took the lead in promoting the new Bible truths after the disappointment. Dozens of other Adventists throughout New England and western New York were also convinced of one or more of the same doctrines. By 1848, these scattered believers felt a great need to draw together in small conferences, as they had done in their Millerites days. In such meetings, they could confirm each other in the faith, hammer out more details of last-day prophecies, and correct errors in their beliefs.

E.L.H. Chamberlain, of Middletown, Connecticut took the lead in calling the first of what would later be called "Sabbath Conferences." The first conference met from April 20-24, 1848, at Albert Belden's home in Rocky Hill, Connecticut. About fifty persons attended, with Bates and James White giving the principal addresses. Long hours were spent in prayer and earnest Bible study. So profitable was this meeting that plans were soon underway for some of the Eastern believers to accept an invitation to join in a similar conference in New York.

With no central organization to finance such meetings, the participants were thrown upon their own resources. James White mowed hay for five weeks so that he and Ellen could travel to Volney and Port Gibson, New York, where the second and third conferences were held in August. Attendance at the second conference was somewhat smaller than the first, yet a wider diversity of opinions were represented; each participant seemed to hold firmly to some pet interpretation. This discord oppressed Ellen White so greatly that she fainted. Some feared she was dying. As prayers were offered for her, she revived and was soon in vision. Many of the errors being promoted were shown her, and she was instructed to appeal to all to lay aside minor matters and unite with the basic truths making up the three angels' messages. Her appeals were heeded, and the meeting "closed triumphantly."

Parting Gem: *Think today of holding conferences, called small groups.*

JULY 30   *Connecting Link of Connecting Links*   Acts 9:15

Today's Thought: *"He is a chosen vessel unto me, [an example to you.]"*

Then came the connecting link between the Millerites and the Seventh-day Adventists, a retired financially secure sea captain, Joseph Bates.

When Bates joined, he had only one thought in his thinking: Jesus Christ is soon to come. He invested all he had into the project of spreading the Advent message. His stash of cash allowed him to retire.

It was Bates who found a tract written by T.M. Preble of Nashua, New Hampshire on the Sabbath. He read it and accepted the Sabbath truth, but that came in 1845. He, in turn, wrote and published a tract in 1846 called "The Seventh-day Sabbath, a Perpetual Sign." A copy of this tract fell into the hands of James White and Ellen Gould Harmon during the month of their wedding— August 30, 1846. They, too, accepted and began to observe the seventh-day Sabbath.

Bates was very health-conscious. As captain of his own ships, he had some unheard of requirements for his crew: no tobacco, no alcohol (including the daily grog to fight off illnesses), no swearing, and one day per week for rest and church. As strange as these "foolish" requirements seemed, sailors flocked to be crew members on his ships.

Most of the Millerites and early Adventists were relatively young, whereas Bates was older, a fatherly person. He died at a ripe old age of 80 years, whereas Miller, who was sick throughout his life due to his eating habits and lifestyle, died at the early age of 67.

Bates was the senior statesman and one of the founders of the Seventh-day Adventist Church. He was an active participant in the Sabbath Conferences held to "hammer out" the specific Bible doctrines that are foundational stones of that community. His descendents can be found alive and well within that same community today.

Parting Gem: *Bates' lifestyle is a tremendous testimony for healthful living and influence today. His faith and trust in God seemed to propel him forward in his witnessing and his longing for the Bridegroom's return.*

JULY 31   Summary   Isaiah 28:10,13

This month of July we have attempted to connect Revelation 10 with Song of Songs 5:1-9, and then with history. As previously stated, only the Seventh-day Adventist community has any idea what Revelation 10 is about. It has been preached many times. Song of Songs 5:1-9 may well be a bit different in that there is still this enigma, confusion, even embarrassment surrounding our fabulous drama.

Both Revelation and our drama portray an experience of bitter disappointment. It's called "The Great Disappointment." Yet, it is backed up and confirmed with history. This fascinating vision given to John is talking about the early Millerites as they studied and preached the sealed, but now open book of Daniel. William Miller was enthralled with Daniel 8:14, *"Unto two thousand and three hundred days; then shall the sanctuary be cleansed."*

One needs to remember that the 1798 experience of Pope Pius being taken prisoner by General Berthier, and the French Revolution, some three and a half years from November 26, 1793 to June 6, 1797, had a tendency to wake the world up to their spiritual bankruptcy and their desperate need, as well as their responsibility to all of the unchristian peoples of the world. This, in turn, opened up the Great Religious Awakening of the early 1800s, expanding into the Great Second Advent Movement of the Seventh-day Adventist Church.

Song of Songs 5:1-8 portrays the "same story or experience" that John had, only in Solomon's language. It portrays the Philadelphia Church of 1798 to 1844 as being without a rebuke, so stated in Song 5:3, *"I have put off my coat; how shall I put it on? I have washed my feet; how shall I defile them?"*

When you consider how much value you have, how much value is placed upon God's church down through the ages, and then have it culminate in Revelation 10 and Song of Songs 5:1-8, along with the sobering thought that no other community has any clue as to what these portions mean, does it not humble you and cause you to praise the Lord for His goodness, mercy, love, and all other gifts?

Into the Very Presence of Christ
8T 45:1

There is the inspiration; there the vision.
Catch it; hold it; dwell intently upon it.
Dwell upon the picture, clear and precise.
Lift the incense of praise; let thanksgiving ascend,
Upward, to the throne, from hearts purified, sanctified, glorified,
Into and by the very presence of Christ.

Jacob Gave the Victor's Shout

Jacob stood unarmed, defenceless, against his mightiest foe.
    The rushing weight of self-reproach for his sins had brought him woe.
His only hope of getting through was the mercy of the Lord.
    His one defence, and only one, was in the power of his prayer.

Yet, on his part, he leaves undone not one thing sweet or sour,
    And clung securely to his God to trust His awesome power.
Jacob gripped and fought all night refusing to lose out.
    As morning dawned, and he hung on, he gave the victor's shout.

August

August's Introduction and Aim

During this month, August, we see the curtain rise on Act 2, Scene 8, in the Most Holy Place of the heavenly sanctuary. It is October 22, and onward. We will endeavour to do justice to the drama's presentation of our Hero, Jesus Christ, the Bridegroom. The description of Him is given in Song 5:9-16. One continually needs to keep in mind that this drama is in symbolic language so that what is literally said is not what is literally meant. Back this reading up by reading *The Great Controversy*, Chapter 35.

As well, as well, as well, keep in mind that this commentary on the description of the Beloved is by no means complete, so this is an awesome undertaking as *"eye hath not seen, nor ear heard"* (1 Corinthians 2:9) all of the things pertaining to our Beloved. Throughout eternity, we will in all actuality be trying to uncover and bring to light the character, love, and operations of our Beloved. So, in one month of readings one just does not even try to fully uncover the magnitude of the Beloved.

We have been given some advice that, should we accept it and follow through with action, it would change our lives. We are encouraged to take one hour each day to study the life of Jesus Christ, who just so happens to be the Beloved in our drama (DA 83).

One way of doing this is to read the Gospels—Matthew, Mark, Luke, John—through each and every month. Use a different version each month. Even use two versions to compare the verses as you read.

Your assignment during August is to read our portion of the drama as many times as is practical. Have a beautiful, happy month.

AUGUST

Day 1	Comparison of Comparisons #2	Song 5:9-16	256
Day 2	Contrast of Contrasts	Song 5:9	257
Day 3	Cursed of Cursed	Galatians 1:6-9	258
Day 4	Righteousness of Righteousness	Song 5:9	259
Day 5	Location of Locations	Song 5:9	260
Day 6	Charge of Charges #6	Song 5:9	261
Day 7	High Priest of High Priests	Song 5:9,16	262
Day 8	Deliverer of Deliverers	Psalms 74:19	263
Day 9	Branch of Branches	Song 5:9	264
Day 10	Counterfeit of Counterfeits	Song 5:9	265
Day 11	Fabricator of Fabricators	Song 5:9	266
Day 12	Usurper of Usurpers	Song 5:16	267
Day 13	Head of Heads #1	Song 5:11	268
Day 14	Title of Titles #2	John 19:19-22	269
Day 15	Nazarite of Nazarites	Song 5:10-11	270
Day 16	Mission of Missions	Song 5:10,16	271
Day 17	Eye of Eyes #2	Song 5:12	272
Day 18	Cheek of Cheeks #2	Song 5:13	273
Day 19	Lips of Lips #2	Song 5:13	274
Day 20	Hand of Hands	Song 5:14	275
Day 21	Ring of Rings	Song 5:14	276
Day 22	Belly of Bellies #1	Song 5:14	277
Day 23	Leg of Legs	Song 5:15	278
Day 24	Countenance of Countenances	Song 5:15	279
Day 25	Mouth of Mouths	Song 5:16	280
Day 26	Most Sweet of Most Sweets	Song 5:16	281
Day 27	Altogether of Altogethers	Song 5:16	282
Day 28	Beloved of Beloved #2	Song 5:16	283
Day 29	Friend of Friends	Song 5:9,16	284
Day 30	Daughter of Daughters	Song 5:16	285
Day 31	Summary for August	Song 5:9-16	286

Poems of the Month: "I AM"   287
                     "In a Moment, Just a Moment"   288

AUGUST 1   *Comparison of Comparisons #2*   Song 5:9-16

Today's Thought: *"What is thy beloved more than another beloved...?"*

There are two symbols representing two universal systems of religion. There is *"Jerusalem... the mother of us all"* (Galatians 4:26), and there is *"Babylon... the mother of harlots"* (Revelation 17:5). From creation to the end of time, these two symbols portray the true church and the false, or counterfeit, church.

Both are represented as women, even mothers, the good woman of Revelation 12, *"the mother of us all,"* who gave birth to the man-child and who the serpent went after to destroy the *"remnant of her seed"* (Revelation 12:17). Then there is the evil woman of Revelation 18, the *"mother of harlots."*

Both have names given to them; one has the name "Jerusalem," the other "Babylon." Both have executive positions; one has a *"crown of twelve stars upon her head"* (Revelation 12:1), while the other simply states, *"I sit a queen"* (Revelation 18:7).

Both women have a support system. Jerusalem is supported by *"the moon under her feet"* (Revelation 12:1), while Babylon *"sitteth upon many waters, upon a scarlet beast, upon peoples, nations, multitudes."*

They are both clothed and adorned well. One is prepared and dressed as a *"bride adorned for her husband,"* while the other is *"arrayed in purple and scarlet colour... upon a scarlet coloured beast... decked with gold and precious stones..."* (Revelation 17:1-4)

Both are called *"that great city."* One is that great city the New Jerusalem, while the other is that great city Babylon. During the 1,260 year prophecy, both women were around. One woman fled into the wilderness to that place that was prepared for her of God, while the other drank and was drunk with the blood of martyrs.

Both women are merchants and deal with merchandise. One counsels us to buy of her wine and milk, without money, without price. The other has the merchants of the earth weep and mourn over her. This one also deals in the *"slaves, and souls of men"* (Revelation 18:13).

Both invite us to eat and drink of their wares. Jerusalem invites, *"Ho, every one that thirstest, come ye"* (Isaiah 55:1) to *"eat of my bread, and drink of the wine which I have mingled"* (Proverbs 9:5). The other forces all men to drink of the wine of her fornication.

Both have established priesthoods.

Parting Gem: *Both are out there; the choice is yours, choose well. And for your consideration today, those are the only two choices.*

AUGUST 2 — Contrast of Contrasts — Song 5:9

Today's Thought: *"What is thy beloved more than another beloved, O thou fairest among women? what is thy beloved more than another beloved, that thou dost so charge us?"*

The Third Angel's Message is both a positive and a negative proclamation. It is a positive presentation of Christ in His various offices connected with the salvation of His people. It is a negative warning as it contrasts Christ with anti-Christ, or "beast," even another beloved, which according to Paul is not really another beloved. It only thinks so. Galatians 1:6-7 says, *"I marvel that ye are so soon removed from him that called you into the grace of Christ unto another gospel: which is not another [gospel]..."*

It also identifies those who keep the commandments or true Sabbath, receiving the seal of God, against the *"mark of the beast"* (Revelation 16:2) or false sabbath perpetuated by another beloved (Song 5:10-16).

The nature and purpose of the Third Angel's Message is presented in this drama. This section of the book is the most challenging, yet at the same time, the most rewarding in spiritual depth, for it is a presentation of the matchless charms of Christ. These verses of inspired Scripture, like rings of keys, open to view various facets of Christ's office, in which He is presented as the Creator, Covenant-Maker, Priest-King, Judge, Deliverer. He is also revealed in His human ministry in the suffering Jesus of Nazareth and in His heavenly ministry as CHRIST OUR RIGHTEOUSNESS.

In this description of my Beloved, the other beloved which is not a beloved is also depicted. By looking at the original, one can discern the false, or put another way, when the false is put into the light of the original and true, then the false is seen for what it is—false.

The Bible states that principle, *"To the law and to the testimony: if they speak not according to this word, it is because there is no light in them"* (Isaiah 8:20).

Parting Gem: *In reply to the question, "What is thy beloved more than another beloved?" these same prophetic texts describe the anti-Christ, who is "another beloved" and presents a startling contrast between the true Christ and the anti-Christ.*

AUGUST 3   *Cursed of Cursed*   Galatians 1:6-9

Today's Thought: *"I marvel that ye are so soon removed from him that called you into the grace of Christ unto another gospel: which is not another; but there be some that trouble you, and would pervert the gospel of Christ. But though we, or an angel from heaven, preach any other gospel unto you than that which we have preached unto you, let him be accursed."*

Paul must be serious in this matter, for he follows a procedure found mightily in this drama of the Song, by repeating in verse 9, *"As we said before, so say I now again, If any man preach any other gospel unto you than that ye have received, let him be accursed."* This is Paul's New Testament definition of *"another beloved."*

These daughters of Jerusalem are amazed with *"thou fairest among women"* that they have been seriously charged and challenged to find the Beloved and give to Him His bride's message.

This *"another beloved"* has perverted, violated, raped the gospel of Christ, making it another gospel, which in reality is not another gospel. One needs to remember that by calling a person a liar does not in itself make him a liar. So, to call this *"another gospel,"* Paul testifies that it is not necessarily the gospel.

It is powerfully smart, as well as important, to put *"precept upon precept; line upon line, line upon line; here a little, and there a little"* (Isaiah 28:10), taking a principle or a concept from one book, adding to that principle another and corresponding principle and concept from another book to gather together all of the pieces of the puzzle before one can see the full and complete picture. Isaiah 28:10 triumphs this idea.

Have you considered the sickness the bride is experiencing in losing her Beloved?

Parting Gem: *The verse says that those who preach this "other gospel" are to be cursed. Does that mean that those who do not preach that "other gospel," but do preach the everlasting good news of salvation and Christ's second coming, will be blessed? What a fantastic, glorious thought.*

AUGUST 4 — *Righteousness of Righteousness* — Song 5:9

Today's Thought: *"What is thy beloved more than another beloved, O thou fairest among women? what is thy beloved more than another beloved, that thou dost so charge us?"*

While it is extremely true that, in our own human state, our personal righteousness is as filthy rags, what we need to do is to exchange our rags for the riches of Christ's Robe of Righteousness. From our rags to Christ's righteousness. Now, once Christ has given to us His Robe of Righteousness, is it not ours? Ours in Christ, of course, but still ours?

Check your concordance, look up "righteous, righteousness"; you may be surprised by what you find. In Psalms alone, there are fifty references to "righteous," most refer to God's people, many to that characteristic in Christ.

In Proverbs, there are over fifty. Yet in Revelation 22:11, one gets the picture that when probation closes, those who are righteous will remain righteous. So, Friend of mine, is it possible, even necessary, to be righteous?

How? Simply accepting this free Robe of Christ's Righteousness, which is required to attend the Banquet of the Wedding Feast, will keep us righteous and allow us to go the feast. Remember that one must not only accept the Robe, but put it on and wear it 24/7. When one gets a gift neatly wrapped and addressed, say at Christmas time, to accept the gift is of no value unless one opens that gift, and claim it as his own.

Jesus Christ of Nazareth, the Nazarene, antitype of the Nazarite, or BRANCH, places His righteousness upon the record and character of His people in the work of atonement, in the Investigative Judgment. This is the only way of salvation for the people of God. He places His own name and character upon His people in this Investigative Judgment. As in a typical marriage, the bride takes her new husband's name.

Parting Gem: *This is my beloved, this is my best Friend, this is the One altogether lovely. Don't you just love Him? If you have not accepted, put on, and are wearing the pure Robe of Christ's Righteousness, do not hesitate; accept it now and wear it for today.*

AUGUST 5 — *Location of Locations* — Song 5:9

Today's Thought: *"What is thy beloved more than another beloved, O thou fairest among women? what is thy beloved more than another beloved, that thou dost so charge us?"*

The sequence of verses in our drama of the Song of Songs places the Third Angel's Message (Song 5:10-16) directly after the Great Disappointment of 1844 (Song 5:1-9). This is historically the correct order of events as they occurred. When the Bridegroom did not return to earth on October 22, 1844, the Advent believers who searched the Scriptures to find the reason for the disappointment discovered that He had "withdrawn Himself" and had gone into the Most Holy Place of the heavenly sanctuary, and was standing before the ark of the Ten Commandments with its holy seventh-day Sabbath. They beheld Him as their Creator-Redeemer and in the many offices pertaining to their salvation. As they identified the true Christ and His true Sabbath, they were able to identify the false christ or "beast" of Revelation 14, and his "mark" or false sabbath.

As soon as the Advent people discovered Christ to be in the Most Holy Place of the heavenly sanctuary, they saw Him as the High Priest, Judge of the Investigative Judgment. *"For the Father judgeth no man, but hath committed all judgment unto the Son"* (John 5:22). They also knew that as soon as the judgment was to be completed that He would come to this earth as the Deliverer and King of kings.

One of the many benefits of knowing about the sanctuary and the Investigative Judgment doctrine, is that one now knows what has been going on for some two thousand-plus years, ever since Christ ascended from the Mount of Olives. In light of the creation week, where the Creator created everything creatable in six literal days, how long does it take to prepare a few mansions, streets, gardens, and all that is involved with heaven and the New Jerusalem?

Parting Gem: *Have you discovered Jesus Christ to be your High Priest, applying His blood on your behalf in the sanctuary above? Have you taken the time today to present to your Lawyer and Advocate your situation, your sins, and your life? Today would be an excellent day to either do so or to renew your commitment to Him. God bless you.*

AUGUST 6   *Charge of Charges #6*   Song 5:9

Today's Thought: *"What is thy beloved more than another beloved, O thou fairest among women? what is thy beloved more than another beloved, that thou dost so charge us?"*

The bride describes her Beloved in verses 9-16. This immediately calls forth one more question from the daughters of Jerusalem. In 6:1, the question is asked, *"Whither is thy beloved gone, O thou fairest among women? whither is thy beloved turned aside? that we may seek him with thee."*

Notice that the question is asked twice and is addressed to *"O thou fairest among women."* After all, who knows better than the bride? But the question is, "What or Who is your Beloved that you make such a request, such a challenge, such a charge to us? Who is He?"

There are three answers to that question, all of them the very same: *"My beloved is mine, and I am his"* (Song 2:16), *"I am my beloved's, and my beloved is mine"* (Song 6:3), and *"I am my beloved's, and his desire is towards me"* (Song 7:10). Putting it forcefully, the bride states, "He's mine; I'm his." End of discussion, period. The bride is saying, "His burning passion is for Him and me to be together where we belong. He can hardly wait to come get me and take me home, but it's not yet time. I'll be patient."

There are three other charges given, all of which are nearly the same: *"I charge you, O ye daughters of Jerusalem, by the roes, and by the hinds of the field, that ye stir not up, nor awake my love, till he please"* (Song 2:7,3:5,8:4).

The one in question is, *"If ye find my beloved… tell him, that I am sick of love"* (Song 5:8). Song 5:2-7 is the great disappointment experience. She has suffered the withdrawal of her lover. She has drunken the sweet honey-filled cup, only to have it turn bitter in her stomach. She is sick, disappointed, terribly disappointed; she is sick of waiting for Him to come. How would you feel if the greatest expectation of your life turned in vapour? She simply would like to have her Beloved know how she feels. Maybe He could do something about it!

Parting Gem: *How do you feel this day? Are you disappointed in your walk with the Beloved, disappointed in your self, your life, your success or failures? The strange and wonderful thing is, your Beloved is aware.*

AUGUST 7 — High Priest of High Priests — Song 5:9,16

Today's Thought: *"What is thy beloved more than another beloved… This is my beloved, and this is my friend."*

The words "Nazar-ite," "Nazar-eth," "Nazar-ene" have different endings; all come from the Hebrew root, *Nazar*, meaning "separated," "devoted," and "to dedicate" for religious or ceremonial use.

Aaron, the high priest in the sanctuary, was a type of Christ. He wore a crown in his work in the earthly sanctuary, which was a type of the heavenly sanctuary. On his crown was fastened a golden plate on which was the inscription, *"HOLINESS TO THE LORD"* (Exodus 28:36). This crown and inscription could also be quoted as saying, "THE LORD OUR RIGHTEOUSNESS." Christ as our High Priest in the Most Holy Place, serving in the works of justification and sanctification and final glorification, is indeed "THE LORD OUR RIGHTEOUSNESS."

Exodus 28:38 informs us that this Nazar was to *"be upon Aaron's forehead"* so that he may bear the sins and *"iniquity of the holy things… and it shall be always upon his forehead, that they may be accepted before the Lord."*

Aaron could not bear the records of the people's sins into the Most Holy Place except he wore the "Nazar" crown. In other words, this "Nazar" gave Aaron the needed authority and permission to act as Israel's High Priest in the work of the Day of Atonement in the Most Holy Place of the sanctuary (Exodus 28:36-38). Without it, if he went about that specific work, he would be struck down dead (Exodus 28:35).

Our trilogy of time Scriptures—Deuteronomy 29:29, 1 Corinthians 10:11, and Romans 15:4— tell us that all this mentioned above was for our learning and admonition, that we may find peace and assurance. Therefore, what gave Jesus Christ the authority and the permission to act as our High Priest in the courts above? As strange as it may seem, it was this "Nazar" written in three languages—Hebrew, Greek, and Latin—that was over His cross and which said, *"THIS IS JESUS THE KING OF THE JEWS"* (Matthew 27:37).

Parting Gem: *My Friend, this is my Beloved, my Friend, He whom we have waited for and He who will save us. What an awesome God we serve.*

AUGUST 8 — *Deliverer of Deliverers* — Psalms 74:19

Today's Thought: *"O deliver not the soul of thy turtledove unto the multitude of the wicked: forget not the congregation of thy poor for ever."*

In Numbers 6:2-4, we read, *"And the Lord spake unto Moses, saying, Speak unto the children of Israel, and say unto them, When either man or woman separate themselves to vow a vow of a Nazarite, to separate themselves unto the Lord: he shall separate himself from wine and strong drink, and shall drink no vinegar of wine, or vinegar of strong drink, neither shall he drink any liquor of grapes, or eat moist grapes, or dried. All the days of his separation shall he eat nothing that is made of the vine tree, from the kernels even to the husk."*

This Nazarite vow, as part of the ceremonial law, pointed forward to Christ. At the Lord's Supper or Communion, Jesus of Nazareth took a vow as an anti-type of the Nazarite vow, which dedicated Him and consecrated Him to His ministry to *deliver* His people. Thus He is the DELIVERER.

Jesus took the Nazarite vow at the Last Supper. Matthew 26:26-29, *"And as they were eating, Jesus took bread, and blessed it, and brake it, and gave it to the disciples, and said, Take, eat; this is my body. And he took the cup, and gave thanks, and gave it to them saying, Drink ye all of it; For this is my body of the new testament, which is shed for many for the remission of sins. But I say unto you, I will not drink henceforth of this fruit of the vine, until that day when I drink it new with you in my Father's kingdom."*

John 3:16 states, *"For God so loved the world, that he gave his only begotten Son, that whosoever believeth in him should not perish, but have everlasting life."*

Parting Gem: *He is an amazing God to love us that much, so much so that He gave everything He had just to save you, and me. As Matthew 13 states, "[He] went and sold all that he had" (Matthew 13:46). Should you apply this parable to Christ seeking us, then all of heaven was up for grabs in the great controversy. "This is my beloved, and this is my friend, O daughters of Jerusalem" (Song 5:16). He will not let the soul of His turtledove be overcome by the multitude of the wicked.*

AUGUST 9 — Branch of Branches — Song 5:9

Today's Thought: *"What is thy beloved more than another beloved, O thou fairest among women? what is thy beloved more than another beloved, that thou dost charge us?"*

The Hebrew words, with *Nazar* as a root, could refer to a "BRANCH," as did the name "NAZARETH." Although there is no direct statement in the Old Testament, Matthew declared that Jesus *"dwelt in a city called Nazareth: that it might be fulfilled which was spoken by the prophets, He shall be called a Nazarene"* (Matthew 2:23). Not by literal statement but by prophetic symbolism, it was understood that the Messiah must be a *Nazar*, or *"Branch."* The prophet Zechariah prophesies of Him in this manner.

Jeremiah 23:5-6 says, *"Behold, the days come, saith the Lord, that I will raise unto David a righteous Branch, and a King shall reign and prosper, and shall execute judgment and justice in the earth. In his days Judah shall be saved, and Israel shall dwell safely: and this is his name whereby he shall be called, THE LORD OUR RIGHTEOUSNESS."* See also Jeremiah 33:15.

Zechariah 6:12-13 says, *"And speak unto him, saying, Thus speaketh the Lord of hosts, saying, Behold the man whose name is The BRANCH; and he shall grow up out of his place, and he shall build the temple of the Lord… and he shall bear the glory, and shall sit and rule upon his throne; and he shall be a priest upon his throne: and the counsel of peace shall be between them both."*

The Advent people see Christ in the Most Holy Place of the heavenly sanctuary, engaged in the Investigative Judgment, building His temple, stone by stone, name by name, jewel by jewel. He is THE BUILDER OF THE TEMPLE. He is THE ALPHA AND THE OMEGA. His hands shall also finish it.

Parting Gem: *Catch a glimpse of the many, many facets of the ministry and character of my Beloved. Have you met Him today? Stop in your reading and simply say, "My Beloved, may I be yours, may You be mine?"*

AUGUST 10 — Counterfeit of Counterfeits — Song 5:9

Today's Thought: *"What is thy beloved more than another beloved... what is thy beloved more than another beloved, that thou dost so charge us?"*

Again, a repetition so that you understand that *"the thing is established by God, and God will shortly bring it to pass"* (Genesis 41:32).

It is powerfully important to study the original so that when a counterfeit is presented and compared to the original, the counterfeit will be revealed for what it is, a counterfeit.

Paul brings to light this counterfeit, and warns against it in 2 Thessalonians 2:3-4, *"Let no man deceive you by any means: for that day shall not come, except there come a falling away first, and that man of sin be revealed, the son of perdition; who opposeth and exalteth himself above all that is called God, or that is worshipped: so that he as God sitteth in the temple of God, shewing himself that he is God."*

This *"shewing himself that he is God"* is done by claiming such names as "The Holy Father," "The Holy Seer," "The Highest Priest and Pontiff," as well as "The Lord God the Pope," "The Vicar of Christ on Earth." The Pope of Rome wears the symbol of the Mosaic cross, which has a dove in its center, symbolic of his office as "Vicar of Christ."

This other beloved has thrown out a challenge through Cardinal Gibbons, in the Catholic Mirror, December 23, 1893. "Reason and sense demand the acceptance of one or the other of these alternatives: either Protestantism and the keeping holy of Saturday or Catholicity and the keeping holy of Sunday. Compromise is impossible."

"The doctrine that God has committed to the church the right to control the conscience, and to define and punish heresy is one of the most deeply rooted of papal errors" (GC 293).

They say, "The Pope is of so great dignity and so exalted that he is not a mere man, but as it were God, and the Vicar of God... Hence the Pope is crowned with a triple crown, as King of heaven and of earth and the lower regions" (Ferraris' Eccl. Dictionary [Catholic] Article, POPE).

Parting Gem: *Thus look at the original, the True One, to discover the counterfeit. If we keep our eyes on the Beloved, the original, we are safe. Have you got your eyes on the Beloved, my friend?*

AUGUST 11   *Fabricator of Fabricators*   Song 5:9

Today's Thought: *"What is thy beloved more than another beloved… more than another beloved…?"*

Two pillars, forty feet tall, stood before Solomon's Temple. One was called "Jachin" (meaning, "in his strength"), and the other was called "Boaz" (meaning, "He shall establish His kingdom"). Inside these hollow pillars the genealogy of God's people was kept.

In the Investigative Judgment, Christ makes up the true Israel, name by name, until Christ's gem-box is full (Malachi 3).

Again, this *"another beloved,"* the antichrist, attempts to establish his kingdom upon the two pillars or documents of two "decretals," or decrees. These documents, forged, provide the basis for the establishment of antichrist upon his throne (Berry, Text. P.158).

The boldness of Rome's growing claims had their bases in the false decretals, or the decretals of the pseudo Isodore.

"Before the end of the eighth century, some apostolically scribe, perhaps the notorious Isidore, composed the decretals, and the Donation of Constantine, the two major pillars of the spiritual and temporal monarchy of the popes.

"Upon these spurious decretals was built the great fabric of papal supremacy over the different national churches a fabric which has stood after its foundation crumbles beneath it: for no one has pretended to deny, for the last two centuries, that the impostors is too palpable for any but the most ignorant to credit..

"These purported prescripts or decrees, contain everything necessary for the establishing of full spiritual supremacy of the popes… The decretals supplied the popes with the means of establishing the superior jurisdiction of Rome and her authority over the faith and practices of Christendom… and the Decretals Epistle were declared by this pope to be on an equality with Scriptures" (The Prophetic Faith of Our Fathers, Froom, L.E. Vol. 1, p. 537-539; Berry, Text. p. 158).

Parting Gem: *Consider, just for today, the best two pillars to base one's faith and bases for belief on—the Old and the New Testament, or put one other way, "to the law and to the testimony" (Isaiah 8:20).*

AUGUST 12 — *Usurper of Usurpers* — Song 5:16

Today's Thought: *"He is altogether lovely. This is my beloved, and this is my friend."*

I don't want to spend too much time talking of the usurper, for this has the tendency to glorify him and give him the attention he craves, yet I need to do so enough for you to realize the enemy in the great controversy. It's nice to always be positive, yet in the great controversy, a look at the enemy and his tactics helps to arm the saints. To be forewarned is to be forearmed.

We have our Beloved and then there is that other beloved. Jesus Christ is the Head of the church and the Chief Cornerstone, yet the fact that the Pope of Rome claims to be the "head" of all churches is common knowledge. Thus we have the Beloved versus the other beloved.

Hebrews 8:12 tells us that we have a great High Priest who is set on the right hand of the throne of Majesty in the heavens; yet the Pope of Rome claims to be the "Highest Priest and Pontiff" and has set up his own priesthood. Again, we have the Beloved versus the other beloved.

In John 14 and 16, we read that Christ must leave so that the Holy Spirit can come and teach them all things. This Holy Spirit is the "Vicar of Christ," which Christ promised when He said, *"But the Comforter, which is the Holy Ghost, whom the Father will send in my name…"* (John 14:26). Now it just so happens that the Pope of Rome claims that title for himself, as the "Vicar of Christ." As well, he claims the titles "The Holy Father," "The Holy Seer," "Lord God the Pope."

The Pope of Rome certainly fulfills 2 Thessalonians 2:3-4, where it says, *"Let no man deceive you by any means: for that day shall not come, except there come a falling away first, and that man of sin be revealed, the son of perdition; who opposeth and exalteth himself above all that is called God, or that is worshipped; so that he as God sitteth in the temple of God, shewing himself that he is God."* Analyze that verse with the life and antics of the Pope of Rome and you can understand some of the usurping of the usurper.

Parting Gem: *Try to understand and remember that just because a person calls you stupid, that does not make you stupid. Just because the pope claims to be the Vicar of Christ doesn't make him the Vicar of Christ.*

AUGUST 13 — Head of Heads #1 — Song 5:11

Today's Thought: *"His head is as the most fine gold, his locks are bushy, and black as a raven."*

The Hebrew word for "head" implies leadership. "Rosh" (head) means: captain, chief, chief man, head, height, ruler, sum, top, excellent, first, principal.[15]

Although the Pope of Rome claims this title of position, it is simply another beloved trying to bring in another gospel which is not really another gospel, but a counterfeit, a perversion, a violation, a rape of the true gospel of Christ. It is only one of the many sips of the Wine of Babylon.

There is but one true church with Jesus Christ as the head of that church. This "other beloved" is simply a usurper, or the antichrist. Christ is the true cornerstone of the church. *"Whereby also it is contained in the scripture, Behold, I lay in Sion a chief corner stone, elect, precious: and he that believeth on him shall not be confounded. Unto you therefore which believe he is precious: but unto them which be disobedient, the stone which the builders disallowed, the same is made the head of the corner"* (1 Peter 2:6-7).

Through the Book of Leviticus, white hair is connected with the disease of leprosy. The converse or opposite would also be true, that hair black like a raven's denotes health, even strength.

Looking at Samson, who also was a type of Christ, his looks were a sign of his Nazarite vow. When he broke that vow by having his locks shaved off, he lost his massive strength. Our Beloved has massive, bushy, black hair indicating omnipotence. So, not only is our Beloved the head of the church but He shows strength in His leadership.

Parting Gem: *It's neat to understand and to follow the advice that by beholding the original, one can easily discern and uncover the counterfeit. That's one excellent reason why we should spend more time with the Word to discover the Beloved in the Word. Should you not taken the time so far today, stop and ponder, seek His help to carry you through whatever is ahead of you today. He's just waiting to send His angels and Spirit down to your aid.*

---

[15] Berry, Marion G. *The Prophetic Song of Songs, Resource Book* (Albia, IA: The Prophetic Song of Songs, Inc.), 1969, p. 142.

AUGUST 14 — Title of Titles #2 — John 19:19-22

Today's Thought: *"And Pilate wrote a title, and put it on the cross, And the writing was, JESUS OF NAZARETH THE KING OF THE JEWS. This title then read many of the Jews: for the place where Jesus was crucified was nigh to the city: and it was written in Hebrew, and Greek, and Latin. Then said the chief priests of the Jews to Pilate, Write not, The King of the Jews; but that he said, I am King of the Jews. Pilate answered, What I have written I have written."*

So to answer the question of Song 5:9, *"What is thy beloved more than another beloved, O thou fairest among women? what is thy beloved more than another beloved, that thou dost so charge us?"* The title prepared by Pilate, and written in three languages, placed on the cross of Jesus and in the providence of God, declared Him to be "Jesus, Jehovah's salvation, the BRANCH, the HIGH PRIEST, the JUDGE, the SAVIOUR, the SIN-BEARER, the BUILDER AND FINISHER OF THE TEMPLE, the KING OF KINGS, KING OF ISRAEL."

In mockery of the Saviour, the religious leaders in their blindness did not see that they were fulfilling prophecy. Yet this mockery, these words, led men to search the Scriptures as they had never done before. There were those who never rested until, by comparing Scripture with Scripture, they saw the meaning of Christ's mission. Never before was there seen such a general knowledge of Jesus as when He hung upon the cross (DA 749).

Usually, but not always, we consider Isaiah 9:6, where it says, *"For unto us a child is born, unto us a son is given: and the government shall be upon his shoulder: and his name shall be called Wonderful, Counsellor, The mighty God, The everlasting Father, The Prince of Peace."* Do we really understand what this is saying?

Parting Gem: *"This is my beloved, and this is my friend, O daughters of Jerusalem"* (Song 5:16). As you go about your day, consider these titles of the Beloved. The one that really baffles me is "The Everlasting Father."

AUGUST 15   *Nararite of Nazarites*   Song 5:10-11

Today's Thought: *"Her Nazarites were purer than snow, they were whiter than milk, they were more ruddy in body than rubies, their polishing was of sapphire." (Lamentations 4:7)*

In our drama, Song 5:9, the question is asked, *"What is thy beloved... what is thy beloved?"* It is asked twice for emphasis. The answer is given in Song 10-16, given in prophetic symbolism. The answer begins by saying, *"My beloved is white and ruddy..."* (Song 5:10). The phrase *"white and ruddy"* leads to a description of the Nazarite.

Yet, a second prophetic symbolism is given in verse 11, where there also is a reference to the Nazarite by the statement that *"his locks are bushy,"* such as hair is when uncut or untrimmed. One requirement in the vow of the Nazarite was that the hair not be cut.

In Judges 13:5, speaking to Manoah, Samson's mother said, *"For, lo, thou shalt conceive, and bear a son; and no razor shall come on his head: for the child shall be a Nazarite unto God from the womb: and he shall begin to deliver Israel out of the hands of the Philistines."*

What is a Nazarite? The SDA Bible Dictionary, for the term Nazarite, states that it means "separated," "devoted." It comes from a verb meaning "to separate," "to consecrate," "to dedicate," for religious or ceremonial use. The one taking the vow continued to live a normal life in society, except that (1) he abstained from all grape products (Numbers 6:3-4), (2) he left his hair uncut (Numbers 6:5), and (3) he refrained from approaching any dead body, to avoid ritual contamination (Numbers 6:6), and if he accidentally came in contact with a dead body he was to offer special sacrifices and begin again the whole process of his vow (Numbers 6:9-12).

A Nazarite was "holy unto the Lord" all the days of his separation (Numbers 6:8). At the close of his specified period, he was to appear before the priest with certain prescribed offerings, and to shave his hair and burn it (Numbers 6:13-21).

Parting Gem: *The Nazarite was a type of Christ and had several vow requirements; no razor coming on his head was only one of them.*

AUGUST 16   *Mission of Missions*   Song 5:10,16

Today's Thought: *"My beloved is white and ruddy, the chiefest among ten thousand… he is altogether lovely."*

As two points of tongs grasp an entire block of ice, Ellen G. White grasped the entire unit of the Song 5:10-16 in major significance by quoting from the beginning and the ending phrases. She said, "He is the chiefest of ten thousand… yea, he is altogether lovely" to describe Christ's mission which was to magnify the law of God (MB 49). Using the same quotations, she describes His commission to His disciples, outlining their work and their message (Berry, Text, p129).

"The gospel is… a living force to change the life… reflect in the character… holiness, meekness, mercy, and truth manifested to the world" (DA 826-27).

His message was to show the spiritual nature of the law, to present its far-reaching principles, and to make plain its eternal obligation. The divine beauty of the character of Christ of whom the noblest and most gentle among men, are but a faint reflection: of whom Solomon by the Spirit of inspiration wrote, He is *'the chiefest among ten thousand… he is altogether lovely.'* Jesus, the express image of the Father's person, the effulgence (radiance) of His glory; the self-denying Redeemer, throughout His pilgrimage of love on earth was a living representation of the character of the law of God. In His life it made manifest that heaven-born love, Christ-like principles, underlie the laws of eternal rectitude (MB 49).

It's sometimes difficult to witness to the neighbours, relatives, and co-workers in a Bible study-type way. Yet nothing can deny the Christ-like life, the selfless acts, the noble and high moral character of one of God's chosen. As Christ came to magnify the law of God, set yourself on record that you also will magnify God's law, the Law of Love, as well as the Moral Law, by the way we carry out our lifestyle.

Your assignment for today is found in Job, where he states he will set no unclean thing before his eyes. We could add ears, nose, and mouth.

Parting Gem: *Could it be that our mission in life is to magnify the law of God, maybe even by considering the laws of the land?*

AUGUST 17 — *Eye of Eyes #2* — Song 5:12

Today's Thought: *"His eyes are as the eyes of doves by the rivers of waters, washed with milk, and fitly set."*

Attempts to comprehend the descriptive verses of the Song of Songs 5:10-16 in literal language without decoding borders on the ludicrous. This is true in this passage as well as those which describe the bride in other chapters. (It would be like trying to understand the love and thinking of God throughout eternity. Will we ever get to a full understanding?) Yet, when correctly decoded by Biblical references, they are filled with meaning. In Song 5:12, there are three Biblical symbols that are used: "eyes," "doves," and "rivers of waters," all of which refer to the Holy Spirit. Notice these references:

Revelation 5:6 says, *"And I beheld, and, lo, in the midst of the throne and of the four beasts, and in the midst of the elders, stood a Lamb as it had been slain, having seven horns and seven eyes, which are the seven Spirits of God sent forth into all the earth."*

John 1:32 says, *"And John bare record, saying, I saw the Spirit descending from heaven like a dove, and it abode upon him."*

John 7:38-39 says, *"He that believeth on me, as the scripture hath said, out of his belly shall flow rivers of living waters. (But this spake he of the Spirit, which they that believe on him should receive: for the Holy Ghost was not yet given: because that Jesus was not yet glorified."*

Putting Revelation 12:17 and 19:10 together, the Advent-Remnant people were promised the gift of prophecy, called the Spirit of Prophecy. Shortly after the disappointment of 1844, this gift of "the Spirit of Prophecy" was given to the Advent people. According to Song of Songs 5:12, this gift was *"washed with milk, and fitly set."* "Milk" is a common symbol of the Word of God in its simplest elementary form, used especially for newborn babes. The writings of Ellen White were in harmony with the Word and magnified it in every way. "Fitly set" refers to the "eyes," or vision, a 20/20 vision in things spiritually continually aligned with the Word. They were "fitly set" and perfectly focused just as the two eyes of the literal human body are perfectly or fitly set just where they are supposed to be.

Parting Gem: *Stop today, get a glimpse of my Beloved, my Friend.*

AUGUST 18 — Cheek of Cheeks #2 — Song 5:13

Today's Thought: *"His cheeks are as a bed of spices, as sweet flowers: his lips are like lilies, dropping sweet smelling myrrh."*

In our verse for today, there are six biblical symbols used: cheeks, spices, flowers, lips, lilies, myrrh. Several of these simple symbols reinforce or verify the intended meaning. Should you miss one, the others help explain it. This is a very common characteristic in Hebrew poetry.

Spices, flowers, and myrrh were all used in the holy anointing oil, which brings to mind the idea of Christ having been anointed or consecrated to His ministry, both on earth and in heaven.

Cheeks consistently refer throughout Scripture to sufferings. Remember that the bride-church in the wilderness had cheeks smitten (Song 1:10).

Matthew 5:39 says, *"But I say unto you, That ye resist not evil: but whosoever shall smite thee on thy right cheek, turn to him the other also."*

Matthew 26:67 says, *"Then did they spit in his face, and buffeted him; and others smote him with the palms of their hands."* It is "assumed" that this smoting was on the cheeks, when you consider Lamentations.

Lamentations 3:30 says, *"He giveth his cheek to him that smiteth him: he is filled full with reproach."*

Listen to the action in Isaiah 53, which helps prepare Christ to become the *"author of eternal salvation"* (Hebrews 5:9) and to serve as the High Priest in the heavenly sanctuary, which our drama summarizes with cheeks:

"For he shall grow up… he hath no form nor comeliness… there is no beauty [in] him… he is despised and rejected… a man of sorrows, and acquainted with grief… he was despised… he hath borne our griefs, and carried our sorrows… he was wounded… he was bruised… He was oppressed, and he was afflicted… he is brought as a lamb to the slaughter… He was taken from prison and from judgment… he was cut off… for the transgression of my people was he stricken. And he made his grave… [yet] he had done no violence, neither was any deceit in his mouth… he shall see his seed, he shall prolong his days… He shall see of the travail… and shall be satisfied… he shall bear their iniquities… he shall divide the spoil… he hath poured out his soul… he was numbered with the transgressors… he bare the sin of many… he made intercession for the transgressors" (Isaiah 53:2-5,7-12).

Parting Gem: *This is my Beloved, and what He did, He did for us.*

AUGUST 19 — Lips of Lips #2 — Song 5:13

Today's Thought: *"... his lips are like lilies, dropping sweet smelling myrrh."*

Proverbs 15:7 says, *"The lips of the wise disperse knowledge…"*

Proverbs 16:13 says, *"Righteous lips are the delight of kings; and they love him that speaketh right."*

Proverbs 20:15 says, *"There is gold, and a multitude of rubies: but the lips of knowledge are a precious jewel."*

Psalms 89:34-35 says, *"My covenant will I not break, nor alter the thing that is gone out of my lips. Once have I sworn by my holiness that I will not lie unto David."*

Deuteronomy 7:9 says, *"Know therefore that the Lord thy God, he is God, the faithful God, which keepeth covenant and mercy with them that love him and keep his commandments to a thousand generations."*

These texts bring the idea that "I will not alter the things I have spoken with my lips; I will not alter the things that have gone out of my mouth. My words will I not alter."

Yet, our verse states that these lips speak sweet-smelling myrrh. Myrrh, remember, is a sweet-smelling substance. Eastern people regarded it highly as a perfuming agent and likewise as a medicine. Such is implied in John 7:46 when the ones sent to arrest Jesus gave their reason for not bringing Him in as, *"Never man spake like this man."*

Matthew records in 7:28-29 that these people who listened to Jesus speak were astonished at His doctrines, for He taught them as one having authority and not as the scribes.

Consider the parents, the centurion, the leper when Jesus was asked to heal them or their loved ones, *"I will; be thou clean"* (Matthew 8:3), *"Go thy way; and as thou hast believed, so be it done unto thee"* (Matthew 8:13), and *"I say unto thee, Child, arise, and the child opened her eyes and arose"* (Luke 8:49-55, paraphrased). Sounds sweet.

Parting Gem: *Should God answer our prayers "as thou hast believed," how many would be answered? Could this be why we get so few prayers answered? "This is my beloved, and this is my friend" (Song 5:16). Take the time today to reacquaint yourself with this Friend.*

AUGUST 20 — Hand of Hands — Song 5:14

Today's Thought: *"His hands are as gold rings set with the beryl: his belly is as bright ivory overlaid with sapphires."*

Again, here, as in all aspects of this drama, one becomes aware that what he reads literally is not what is meant literally… This is a symbolic drama and not a literal one.

Christ's hands are likened to *"gold rings."* Those who have given study to this verse in the original language indicate that these *"gold rings"* are as a seal. This impression is furthered by cross-reference in which He says, *"Behold, I have graven thee upon the palms of My hands"* (Isaiah 49:16). He raises His nail-pierced hands in the Investigative Judgment, and His people are safe and secure in His ministry for them.

Hebrews 1:10 says, *"And, Thou, Lord, in the beginning hast laid the foundation of the earth; and the heavens are the works of thine hands."*

Psalms 102:25 says, *"Of old hast thou laid the foundation of the earth: and the heavens are the works of thy hands."*

Psalms 95:5 says, *"The sea is his, and he made it: and his hands formed the dry land."*

The office of Creator is referred to here in the above three passages.

Psalms 111:7 says, *"The works of his hands are verity and judgment; all his commandments are sure."*

Deuteronomy 33:2 says, *"And he said… and he came with ten thousands of saints: from his right hand went a fiery law for them."*

These two references portray Christ as Judge, while three more are symbols of Jesus as Reaper (Hebrews 10:30-31, Luke 3:17, Revelation 14:14).

A favourite one is in Zechariah 13:6, which says,, *"And one shall say unto him, What are these wounds in thine hands? Then he shall answer, Those with which I was wounded in the house of my friends."*

Parting Gem: *You are invited to crawl up onto the lap of your Beloved where you are powerfully safe, for your name is graved into the palms of His hands, even into the brow of His head, or the side where the spear went in or even the soles of His feet, and the back where He was lashed. These are the seven places where your name are engraved, and nothing can remove them out of His hands, so His lap is safe for you.*

AUGUST 21 — *Ring of Rings* — Song 5:14

Today's Thought: *"His hands are as gold rings set with the beryl…"*

As stated yesterday, those who have studied this verse in the original language indicate that these *"gold rings"* are as a seal.

At canning time up in Canada, fruit and vegetables are canned in such a way as to preserve them and keep them from spoiling. Well-canned fruit can last for years, through the freezing cold of winter and the simmering heat of summer. When one opens a sealed jar of fruit after many years, it is delectable, edible, nourishing, and a whole lot more. These words are the "voice of experience," for it did happen to our family.

A ring in ancient times was used to "seal" a document, and such a sealed document had the voice of authority. Consider Esther 3:12, where Haman had the king's ring, giving him the power and authority to write in the king's name and to do what he did. In 8:8, again, *"… seal it with the king's ring: for the writing which is written in the king's name… may no man reverse."*

A ring is also a sign of "social status," as James states in 2:2-3. *"For if there come into your assembly a man with a gold ring, in goodly apparel… and ye have respect to him,"* you become partial.

In the case of the prodigal son coming home, as in Luke 15, a gold ring put on his hand implied his heirship was still in tact.

Joseph the son of Jacob was given the royal nod in Genesis 41:42-43. *"And Pharaoh took off his ring from his hand, and put it upon Joseph's hand, and arrayed him in vestures of fine linen, and put a gold chain about his neck… and he made him ruler over al the land of Egypt."*

Beryl was the first precious stone in the fourth row of the high priest's breastplate; it is the precious gem in the eighth foundation of the New Jerusalem. It carries weight, beauty, and awe.

Parting Gem: *Conclude that my Beloved's hands create, judge, reap, etc., as stated yesterday, but now they, like rings, designate power, authority, and a seal, for that which the Lord states and does cannot be reversed.*

AUGUST 22   *Belly of Bellies #1*   Song 5:14

Today's Thought: *"His hands are as gold rings set with beryl: his belly is as bright ivory overlaid with sapphires."*

Sapphire stones appear in the second row of the high priest's breastplate, and as the second foundation in the New Jerusalem. Prophets, who describe the throne of God when in vision, select the rich colour of the sapphire to describe the scene. It is described in its use as both beautiful and valuable. Ivory and sapphires are spoken of in Scripture in connection with a king's throne—particularly in God's throne.

According to Job 40:16, God tells Job that the hippopotamus' strength is in his loins or his belly, and his force is in the navel of his belly.

Jesus states in John 7:38-39, *"He that believeth on me, as the scripture hath said, out of his belly shall flow rivers of living water. (But this spake he of the Spirit, which they that believe on him should receive.)"*

He had previously told the Samaritan woman, *"Whosoever drinketh of the water that I shall give him shall never thirst; but the water that I shall give him shall be in him [his belly] a well of water springing up into everlasting life"* (John 4:14).

Revelation 22 talks of a pure river of water of life flowing out of the throne of God and of the Lamb. Because those who believe in Christ will have rivers of living waters flowing out of the belly, and because this well of water springs up into everlasting life, then the Belly of all bellies certainly is the source of this living water, for Christ is Life, Eternal Life, the Source of Eternal Life.

Parting Gem: *As I type this day's reading, I am struck with the thought that to speak in symbolic terms, as in our Song of Songs, brings no meaning to those who are not connected to this "spiritual community." How can you explain to a total unbeliever about blood cleansing one from sin, when they might not know what sin is? Looking at this description of our Beloved, Jesus Christ, in the literal sense makes this whole description a bigger puzzle than the whole of the drama. So, I repeat for the umpteenth dozen time that what you read literally is not to be taken literally, for what you really read is not what is really meant.*

AUGUST 23 — *Leg of Legs* — Song 5:15

Today's Thought: *"His legs are as pillars of marble, set upon sockets of fine gold…"*

In this verse, his two legs are likened to two pillars. There were two pillars, which stood in the front of Solomon's temple in Jerusalem. They were named "Jachin" (meaning "The Lord shall establish") and the other pillar, "Boaz" (meaning "In God is my strength") (1 Kings 7:15-31). Each pillar was thirty-three feet high and twenty-two feet around. Two bronze crowns four-and-a-half feet high were placed on top of the pillars.

These pillars were hollow, and within these pillars were kept the written genealogies of Israel—the names of His people, the people of God. This brings to view Christ in the Most Holy Place engaged in the Investigative Judgment, going over the names of all of God's people establishing His kingdom, to make up His jewels (Berry, Quarterly p. 62; Text p. 158).

It is in the Investigative Judgment, "in His strength," that "He shall establish" His kingdom by making up these true genealogies of Israel, name by name, until it is fully established. The entire history of God's people is reviewed in these judgment scenes.

In contrast, *"another beloved,"* the antichrist, has attempted to establish his kingdom upon two "pillars" or documents of two "decretals." These forged documents provide the basis for the establishment of antichrist upon his throne (Berry, Text. P.158).

Ecumenism is a character distinct in the life of the church, especially in our time. The goal to be achieved is the total inclusion of all Christians in one single organization with the head or leader designated as the Pope. This thought comes from *The Ecumenical Mirage,* Lowell, C. Stanley, p. 193, 194, as stated in Marion Berry's *The Prophetic Song of Songs*—Handbook. P.159.

Parting Gem: *The third angel's message is an identification of the Papacy as that beast, the great one of Revelation, as well as the great "antichrist" and usurper of the great offices and position of God's leadership of His people (Ibid).*

AUGUST 24 — *Countenance of Countenances* — Song 5:15

Today's Thought: *"His legs are as pillars of marble, set upon sockets of fine gold: his countenance is as Lebanon, excellent as the cedars."*

This outward appearance or facial expression, considered an expression of mental attitude and emotions, is compared to Lebanon which is noted for its cedars.

We've mentioned Lebanon several times and for various reasons. Here, our Beloved Bridegroom's countenance, His face or appearance, draws attention to His beloved. His expressive features attract, His magnetism draws. That's what He said, *"If I be lifted up… [I] will draw all men unto me"* (John 12:32).

Solomon obtained cedars from Lebanon for the erection of his temple. Along came Zerubbabel and did the same thing, getting cedars from Lebanon for the rebuilding of the temple. Poets and prophets mention the Lebanon for its snow (Jeremiah 18:14); for its wild beasts, such as leopards and lions (2 Kings. 14:9); for its stately cedars plus other trees (2 Kings 19:23); as well as the place where the Phoenicians obtained masts and timber for their ships. Does one get the picture of One who can supply all of our needs and who is the topic under most discussions?

At the time of Christ's resurrection, Matthew 28:3 records, *"His countenance was like lightning, and his raiment white as snow."*

When John recorded Revelation 1:16, speaking of who he saw after he turned to see the voice speaking to him, he stated *"… his countenance was as the sun shineth in his strength."*

In contrast, Daniel 8:23 states, *"And in the latter time of their kingdom, when the transgressors are come to the full, a king of fierce countenance, and understanding dark sentences, shall stand up."* Again we met *"another beloved"* trying to usurp the throne of God

Two pictures were once displayed in a city. One showed Jesus with worn clothing humbly riding on a mule, while the other pictured the pope in all of his splendour (Witnesses for Jesus, PPPA. Mountain View, California; p. 183).

Parting Gem: *It's powerfully difficult to give only the positive when there is so much negative around. We need to be aware of this roaring lion who is sneaking around searching out those he can devour. He who is aware and prepared has a lot of the battle conquered.*

AUGUST 25 — Mouth of Mouths — Song 5:16

Today's Thought: *"His mouth is most sweet: yea, he is altogether lovely."*

Song 5:10-16 is a set of "keys," which by cross-referencing also open to view a prophetic contrast between Christ and antichrist.

Back in early February, we dealt with the kisses of His mouth and how the virgins love Him. It dealt with reconciliation and the paying of the dowry, and how His love is greater than any doctrine. It is through the lips, a framework around the mouth that kisses are exchanged. The ears of the sick were often kisses with the words of the mouth of Jesus when they were healed by Christ speaking words.

The mouth is part of the organ of speech. Through the mouth, the Creator, Saviour, Lord heals by saying, *"I will; be thou clean"* (Matthew 8:3).

The book *Desire of Ages* speaks of how Jesus would be heard singing sweet melodies around the town. All seemed to have heard Him and it brought great joy to the residences of the town of Nazareth.

It has been said that out of the mouth can come both blessings and cursings, which ought not to be. Out of the mouth of Jesus came rich blessings, words that were as sweet as honey, without any bitterness in the stomach.

David stated that the words of Christ were found and he ate them and they were to him sweet like honey.

When Christ was being tried shortly before crucifixion, Isaiah 53 states that He opened not His mouth. He was like a sheep just before being slaughtered. There was no guile found within that mouth.

Matthew 5:2 states that when Jesus opened His mouth, He taught them. The residences of Nazareth were amazed, for Luke writes in 4:22, *"And all bare him witness, and wondered at the gracious words which proceeded out of his mouth. And they said, Is not this Joseph's son?"*

Should Jesus be your Mentor, He has just raised the bar for you today.

Parting Gem: *From this point onward, our drama is a description of, and a message to, the Seventh-day Adventist Church, for this church holds a unique position in the world upholding God's law, presenting Jesus as the Creator-Redeemer with the Sabbath as a sign of His authority.*

AUGUST 26 — *Most Sweet of Most Sweets* — Song 5:16

Today's Thought: *"His mouth is most sweet: yea, he is altogether lovely. This is my beloved, and this is my friend, O daughters of Jerusalem."*

Song #253 in the *Adventist Church Hymnal* reads,

> "There's no other name like Jesus, 'Tis the sweetest name we know,
> 'Tis the angel's joy in heaven, 'Tis the Christian's joy below.
> There's no other name like Jesus when the heart with grief is sad,
> There's no other name like Jesus when the heart is free and glad.
> Sweet name, dear name; there's no other name like Jesus."

Acts 4:12 mentions that *"there is none other name given… among men, whereby we must be saved."*

Have you ever wondered why His mouth is most sweet? Remember, the mouth is one of the organs of speech. Let's start with Song 1:2, where he exchanges the kiss of reconciliation. We could also spend a lot of time in His expressions of love to His bride, and His affirmation that *"My beloved is mine, and I am his"* (Song 2:16).

But, if you are like me, you want to hear Him say to you, "Your sins are forgiven, go in peace," then, "Come unto Me all you who are weak, heavy laden, discouraged, poor, and what have you." Those are neat words.

Others would want to hear Him say, "Yes, I can make you whole. Rise, take up your bed and walk," or "Go wash in the river," only to find that when you do you can now see. Mary and Martha were ecstatic over hearing Jesus say, *"I am the resurrection, and the life"* (John 11:25).

There might be others who live on John 3:16, *"For God so loved the world [me], that he gave his only begotten Son, that whosoever believeth in him should not perish, but have everlasting life."* Now that's something to feast on.

Parting Gem: *As was mentioned elsewhere, the real words I wish to hear, and they will be the sweetest words that ever filled my ears, are the words, "Well done, thou good and faithful servant, enter into the joy of thy Lord. Welcome home." Contemplate those words as you go about your excitements today.*

AUGUST 27   *Altogether of Altogethers*   Song 5:16

Today's Thought: *"His mouth is most sweet: yea, he is altogether lovely. This is my beloved, and this is my friend, O daughters of Jerusalem."*

As we look at today's thought, we just might need to remember the closing verse of John: *"And there are also many other things which Jesus did, the which, if they should be written every one, I suppose that even the world itself could not contain the books that should be written. Amen"* (John 21:25).

We might well be in line should we add, "Amen, Amen, and Amen." When one puts it all together, then one has the life of Christ, His words, teachings, lifestyle, miracles, sermons, compassion, charisma, all of Him. He is lovely, and Friend of mine, He is my Friend and He is my Beloved. Make Him yours today.

What would it have been like to be healed of deafness, and the first words you heard were the words of our Friend? Or to see the face of Jesus after being healed of blindness? Consider being able to walk, jump, do cartwheels after being healed from being crippled for forty or more years.

Consider the man carried by four of his friends and let down through the roof (Mark 2:4), then hearing this Altogether Lovely say, *"Thy sins be forgiven thee… rise up and walk"* (Luke 5:23). How would you react?

Howe about when you are fishing all night, catch nothing, then hear a voice say to you to throw your net over onto the other side, obeying, and not being able to draw the net full of fish in? How would you feel?

Let's finish today's reading by going down the road to Emmaus, being joined by a Stranger, and having your hearts burn within you as this Stranger starts at Moses, goes through all of the prophets, explaining their relationship to this newly crucified, raised Friend of yours. Tell me, how would you feel, think, act, respond? Thus Solomon could only say, *"This is my beloved, and this is my friend, O daughters of Jerusalem."*

Parting Gem: *I want your heart to burn within you as you go about your excitement today considering this Altogether Lovely, Desirable Person.*

AUGUST 28 — *Beloved of Beloved #2* — Song 5:16

Today's Thought: *"His mouth is most sweet: yea, he is altogether lovely. This is my beloved, and this is my friend, O daughters of Jerusalem."*

As one becomes acquainted with the history of the Redeemer, he discovers in himself serious defects; his unlikeness to Christ is so great that he sees the necessity of radical changes in his life. Still he studies with a desire to become like his great Exemplar. He catches the looks, the spirit of his beloved Master. By beholding, by looking unto Jesus, *"the author and finisher of our faith"* (Hebrews 12:2), he becomes changed into the same image. This is our Beloved.

It is not by looking away from Him that we imitate the life of Jesus, but by talking of Him, by dwelling upon His perfections, by seeking to refine the taste and elevate the character, by trying—through faith and love, and by earnest, persevering effort—to approach the perfect Pattern. His words, His habits, and His lessons of instruction—we borrow the virtues of the character we have much admired. Jesus becomes to us, *"the chiefest among ten thousand"* (Song 5:10), the one *"altogether lovely"* (6BC 1099, RH March 15, 1887). This is our Beloved.

On all occasions, Christ should be set forth as *"the chiefest among ten thousand,"* the One *"altogether lovely."* He should be presented as the Source of all true pleasure and satisfaction, the Giver of every good and perfect gift, the Author of every blessing, the One in whom all our hopes of eternal life are centered (6T 175). This is our Beloved.

Faith familiarizes the soul with the existence and presence of God, and, living with an eye single to the glory of God (Matthew 6:23, Luke 11:24), more and more we discern the beauty of His character, the excellence of His grace. Our souls become strong in spiritual power, for we are breathing the atmosphere of heaven, and realizing that God is at our right hand, that we shall not be moved. We are rising above the world, beholding Him who is the chief among ten thousand, the one altogether lovely, and by beholding we are to become changed (1SM 335). This is our Beloved.

Parting Gem: *I don't often recommend a rereading of a day's reading, but I think it would be well if we were to contemplate this thought today, either as we go about our joys or rereading it now.*

AUGUST 29 — *Friend of Friends* — Song 5:9,16

Today's Thought: *"What is thy beloved… This is my beloved,, and this is my friend."*

Jesus has roots in Greek, Aramaic, Hebrew, for "Joshua" means "Yahweh is Salvation." Christ comes from Hebrew and means "anointed" or "anointed one."

In New Testament times, "Jesus" was a common given name for Jewish boys. It expressed the parent's faith in God and in His promise of One who would bring salvation to Israel. In Spanish, it is still popular today.

"Christ" was not a personal name by which people knew Him while on earth, but was a title used to identify Him as the One in whom the messianic promises and prophecies of the Old Testament met their fulfillment. To those who believed in Him as "Sent of God," He was the Christ, the Messiah, the One anointed by God to be the Saviour.

The two names together constitute a confession of faith that Jesus of Nazareth, the son of Mary, is indeed the Christ, the Messiah. He was also to be known by the title Emmanuel, "God with us," in recognition of His Deity and virgin birth.

Christ's usual designation for Himself was "the Son of man," an expression never used by others when speaking of or to Him. Jesus seldom used the title "Son of God," which expresses Deity, of Himself.

However, His Father called Him His Son. John the Baptist and His disciples called Him the "Son of God." Jesus was fully aware and later admitted that He was the Son of God.

Paul declared that Jesus' resurrection from the dead designated Him "Son of God" in power. His disciples frequently addressed Him as "Master," then later as "Lord." The term "Son of David," a popular Messianic designation used by rulers as well as people, was an expression of hope for deliverance from political oppression.

Isaiah 9:6 declares Him to be called *"Wonderful, Counsellor, The mighty God, The everlasting Father, The Prince of Peace."*

Parting Gem: *Have you met my Beloved, my Friend? If not, meet Him right now; if so, reacquaint yourself with Him. Simply breathe a prayer of surrender and acceptance of His life, power, and presence.*

AUGUST 30 — *Daughter of Daughters* — Song 5:16

Today's Thought: *"His mouth is most sweet: yea, he is altogether lovely. This is my beloved, and this is my friend, O daughters of Jerusalem."*

We first met these daughters of Jerusalem back in January, in Song 1:5, where our bride-church exclaims that she is black but comely. Today, she exclaims to these daughters that her Beloved is altogether lovely, that He is her Friend.

In January, we found that these daughters are the spiritual virgins, undefiled by false doctrines and the wine of other churches. They represent the individual church members, some who have oil in their burning lamps and others who have no extra oil in the event of a long delay, as portrayed in the parable of the ten virgins. They are members in good and regular standing within the church; they are not hypocrites.

So, how do you stay a daughter of Jerusalem, or is it once a daughter always a daughter? Should we look at the seven churches, we would get some good advice. From Ephesus, remember from whence we are fallen. From Smyrna, fear not. From Pergamos, cast no stumbling block before your brother, keep pure in body and mind. From Thyatira, similarly as with Pergamos, stay pure, have no unchristian beliefs or practices. From Sardis, be watchful and strengthen the brethren. From Philadelphia, continue to keep My name and not to deny Me nor My name. From Laodicean, buy faith, hope, charity, put on the Robe of Christ's righteousness, open your eyes to see the truth of God, seek the Holy Spirit to guide you in your seeing. Always, on a daily bases, repent and seek the Lord.

Sound like works? Not really. It sounds more like good common Christian sense. It sounds like putting your belief in Jesus Christ into one's daily lifestyle. It sounds like really living.

Parting Gem: *2 Corinthians 6:17-18 says, "Wherefore come out from among them, and be ye separate, saith the Lord, and touch not the unclean thing: and I will receive you, and will be a Father unto you, and ye shall be my sons and daughters, saith the Lord Almighty" Now bear in mind Song 2:16, which says, "My beloved is mine, and I am his." Sound familiar?)*

AUGUST 31　　　　　　　　*Summary*　　　　　　　　Song 5:9-16

Attempts to comprehend the descriptive verses of the Song of Songs 5:10-16 in literal language without proper decoding borders on the ludicrous! This is also true when describing the bride in other chapters. However, when properly and prayerfully decoded, they are filled with great meaning, not to mention undying encouragement.

We started this month's reading by having the daughters of Jerusalem ask a question: *"What is thy beloved more than another beloved, that thou dost so charge us?"* (Song 5:9) It is asked twice for emphasis and to tell us that it is just as it is stated. We know that this question can not really be satisfactorily answered on this planet. Even when we spend a lot of time in eternity, will we still be unable to fully and completely answer that question? It's like the question given to the disciples, *"Whom do men say that I the Son of man am?"* (Matthew 16:13) Can we really answer that question?

During this month, there has been a contrast and a comparison between the lowly Shepherd and the pompous pope. August 1, on "Comparison of Comparisons," covers some of them. You just may wish to review that day.

The three angels' messages were placed within this description. We tried to decode His head and locks, His eyes (presence of the Holy Spirit), His cheeks (sufferings), His lips (part of the organ of speech), His hand (the various creative activities), His belly (streams of living waters), His legs, and His countenance. All these were briefly looked at.

We found that He is our Friend and that He is altogether lovely. One will definitely find that out as one gets acquainted with this Beloved.

In answer to the question, *"What is thy beloved... ?"* Song of Songs 5:10-16 provides an answer, that the Bridegroom for whom the church has been waiting over the centuries, and for whom we have waited, is resplendent in all His offices as He serves as our Advocate-Mediator-High Priest in the Most Holy Place of the heavenly sanctuary. The Advent people may say with surety: *"This is my beloved, and this is my friend, O daughters of Jerusalem"* (Berry Quarterly, p. 62; Song 5:16).

That could be one excellent reason why we should spent some time each day feasting on the life, death, resurrection, ascension, intercession, and soon return of Jesus Christ. These make up the seven wonders of salvation.

I AM

The father of Lies, he boldly states;
    I will ascend into heaven,
    I will exalt my throne,
    I will sit upon the Mount of the congregation, in the sides of the north,
    I will ascend above the heights of the clouds,
    I will be like the Most High God,

    Yet, it is powerfully comforting to know that

The Prince of Heaven triumphantly states, not I will, but;
    I AM the Almighty God,
    Before Abraham was, **I AM,**
    I AM THAT I AM,
    I AM the God of Abraham, Isaac, and Jacob,
    I AM the Creator of heaven, earth. and all that in them is,
        I AM the Bread of life,
        I AM the living Bread,
        I AM the Living Water of life,
        I AM the Door of the sheepfold,
        I AM the Good Shepherd,
            I AM the True Vine,
            I AM the Alpha and the Omega,
            I AM the Beginning and the End,
            I AM the First and the Last,
            I AM the Way, the Truth, and the Life,
    I AM the true Light,
    I AM the Living Way,
    I AM the Resurrection and the Life,
    I AM He who was dead, and is alive for evermore,
    I AM Love.
    I AM the Lord your God.

In a Moment, Just a Moment

In a moment of contemplation, Eve decided she was strong.
    In a moment of disobedience, she opened all the Gates Of Wrong.
In a moment, just a moment, that's all it took in time.
    Yet, back of that, before her act, Eve ignored the many chimes.

In a moment of decision, Mischak held his ground.
    In a moment just standing tall, with his colleagues all around.
In a moment, yes, every moment he decided all for God.
    Yet, long years ago he let God know he would always crave God's nod.

In a moment of frustration, Moses struck with rocky might.
    In a moment of boiling rage, he screamed and lost the fight.
In a moment, just a moment that's all it took to act.
    Yet, back before this act he bore, it was faith he really lacked.

In a moment of destruction, Harlot Rahab acted fast.
    In a moment of quick action, she laid aside her past.
In a moment, just a moment, that's all her thinking took.
    Yet, before the crash, her token stashed, her former gods forsook.

September

September's Introduction and Aim

As a new day opens a new month, we analyze Song of Songs 6:1-13. Take time, several times, to read Song 6 during September, always remembering you are reading symbolic language and what is literally read in not literally meant what it says.

This chapter opens Act 2, Scene 9, covering from 1844 and onward. It is a symbolic description of the Seventh-day Adventist Church, and continues into Song 7, which is taken up in October. This will correspond to *The Great Controversy*, Chapters 26-37, but specifically Chapter 26 ("A Work of Reform"), Chapter 32 ("Snares of Satan"), Chapter 37 ("The Scriptures a Safeguard").

In Act 2, Scene 8, last month, a symbolic picture of our Beloved, Jesus Christ, Son of the Most High God in contrast to another beloved was given.

There are areas within Song of Songs where no explanation is given. This is simply because no explanation has yet come to light. More study, prayer, research needs to be done. That will come, but it was felt that this devotional should be put out as soon as possible.

SEPTEMBER

Day 1	Gone of Gones	Song 6:1	292
Day 2	Field of Fields	Song 6:1	293
Day 3	Chorus of Choruses	Song 6:1	294
Day 4	Reply of Replies	Song 6:2	295
Day 5	Relationship of Relationships	Song 6:2-3	296
Day 6	Turn of Turns #2	Song 6:2	297
Day 7	Audit of Audits	Song 6:2	298
Day 8	Gathering of Lilies of Gatherings of Lilies	Song 6:2	299
Day 9	Confidence of Confidences #2	Song 6:3	300
Day 10	Conviction of Convictions	Song 6:4	301
Day 11	Overcomer of Overcomers	Song 6:5	302
Day 12	Flock of Flocks #2	Song 6:5-6	303
Day 13	Queen of Queens	Song 6:8	304
Day 14	Virgin of Virgins #2	Song 6:8	305
Day 15	Undefiled of Undefiled	Song 6:9	306
Day 16	Fairest of Fair #5	Song 6:9	307
Day 17	Fairest of Fair #6	Song 6:9	308
Day 18	Fairest of Fair #7	Song 6:9	309
Day 19	Look of Looks #2	Song 6:10	310
Day 20	Valley Fruit of Valley Fruits	Song 6:11	311
Day 21	Inspection of Inspections	Song 6:11	312
Day 22	Church of Churches #1	Song 6:11	313
Day 23	Church of Churches #2	Song 6:11	314
Day 24	Church of Churches #3	Song 6:11	315
Day 25	Consideration of Considerations	Song 6:11	316
Day 26	Shulamite of Shulamites	Song 6:13	317
Day 27	Dance of Dances	Song 6:13	318
Day 28	Amminadib of Amminadibs	Song 6:12	319
Day 29	Plea of Pleas	Song 6:13	320
Day 30	Summary	Song 6:1-13	321

Poems of the Month: "Unsinkable, Unburnable, Non-Destructable"	322
"Psalm 96"	323
"Through My Life My Scrolls They Read"	324

SEPTEMBER 1 — *Gone of Gones* — Song 6:1

Today's Thought: *"Whither is thy beloved gone, O thou fairest among women? whither is thy beloved turned aside? that we may seek him with thee."*

In Revelation 10, the prophet takes the little book, eats it up, and it is so sweet in his mouth, yet so bitter in his stomach. Now they wonder, ponder, analyze just where he has gone that caused such bitterness.

The progressive drama of this drama, Song of Songs, moves forward. Song 6-7 are one descriptive unit of the true bride-church from 1844 to our own day. The drama's sixth chapter begins with the theological question: *"Whither (where) is thy beloved gone… whither is thy beloved turned aside?"*

This question is addressed to "The Fairest Among Women" and none but the true bride, this fairest among women, can answer that question. In 1844, the beloved Jesus did not come to this earth as expected, but He turned aside and *"came with the clouds [angels] of heaven… to the Ancient of days"* (Daniel 7:13) into the Most Holy Place of the heavenly sanctuary to begin the work of the Investigative Judgment. Those who participated in the Great Advent Movement experienced the 1844 disappointment, searched the Scriptures afterward to find where He had *"turned aside."* They studied the prophetic symbolisms of Scripture, and particularly that of the sanctuary. They answered the question. Those who can answer that question today are God's true bride-church, "The Fairest Among Women," unique on earth today, known as the Seventh-day Adventist Church.

With confidence the bride-church answers the question, *"Whither is thy beloved gone, O thou fairest among women? whither is thy beloved turned aside? that we may seek him with thee."*

Parting Gem: *Our Beloved is in the church, the Mother Church, in heaven in the New Jerusalem, going over the clerk's records to "make up His Jewels," "to gather His lilies," "to identify His people." Notice the symbolism to tell us, among other things, that each one of us are precious as jewels, as beautiful as lilies, as sons and daughters of God, King of the Universe.*

September 2   *Field of Fields*   Song 6:1

Today's Thought: *"Whither is thy beloved gone, O thou fairest among women? whither is thy beloved turned aside? that we may seek him with thee."*

In 1874, the Advent people sent their first official missionary abroad. The bride must fulfill her obligation to send out the wedding invitation to all the world to prepare them for the coming of the Bridegroom. He had not come to this world as expected in 1844, and she alone knew *"whither [he had] turned aside"* into the Most Holy Place and could tell the world where He had gone and invite them to the wedding.

That wedding invitation does like this: "Give glory to Him for the hour of His marriage (judgment) is come. You are cordially invited to leave the city of Babylon to attend the wedding, and to enjoy the reception wedding supper in the city of New Jerusalem. As you travel, beware of the beast, because he has recovered from his deadly wound. In fact, he is masquerading as the very Bridegroom, and you must not receive his mark! You will be identified at the door! For you must be wearing the wedding garment. (See Appendix 4.)

Song 6-7 of our drama describes the bride-church, which is described by Holy Scriptures as such:

"Here is the patience of the saints: here are they that keep the commandments of God, and the faith of Jesus" (Revelation 14:12). *"The remnant... which keep the commandments of God, and have the testimony of Jesus Christ"* (Revelation 12:17), which is *"the spirit of prophecy"* (Revelation 19:10).

It is the Seventh-day Adventists, who descended from the pioneers of the Great Advent Movement and particularly those who emerged from the Great Disappointment of 1844, who meet the qualifications and description of the bride by keeping the commandments of God—the entire Ten Commandments, including the fourth. Remember, the seventh day is the Sabbath of the Lord thy God (Exodus 20:8-10). Keep it.

Parting Gem: *Today, in your field, give someone the wedding invitation.*

SEPTEMBER 3 — *Chorus of Choruses* — Song 6:1

Today's Thought: *"Whither is thy beloved gone, O thou fairest among women? whither is thy beloved turned aside? that we may seek him with thee."*

It is the Seventh-day Adventist Church which has the testimony of Jesus, which is the spirit of prophecy in the prophetic gift (Revelation 12:17 and 19:10). It is the Seventh-day Adventist who—as the true bride—has taken the wedding invitation in the form of the three angels' messages to all the world for more than a century. It is they who are still proclaiming the coming of the Bridegroom, not in secret rapture, but in a literal, open manner to all the world according to the prophecies and descriptions of the Bible.

Chapter 6 of our drama begins with a worldwide chorus of voices of those in darkness in every land, calling out to the remnant people to show them the truths of the three angels' messages, which proclaim a Saviour. He did not come to earth as expected in 1844 and they enquire: *"Whither is thy beloved gone... whither is thy beloved turned aside?"* The Seventh-day Adventist Church was called, dedicated, ordained to take to all the world the message that He is indeed *"turned aside"* into the Most Holy Place in the Investigative Judgment, shortly to return for His bride.

Chapters 6 and 7 are one descriptive unit—a set of prophetic keys which describe the Seventh-day Adventist Church since 1844. They describe its growth and prosperity and identify it as God's last remnant and true church-bride.

Jesus said, *"And this gospel... shall be preached in all the world for a witness unto all nations; and then shall the end come"* (Matthew 24:14). The angel said of the people who suffered the great disappointment in 1844, *"Thou must prophesy again before many peoples, and nations, and tongues, and kings"* (Revelation 10:11). The prophet John saw the messengers (a great movement) *"fly in the midst of heaven, having the everlasting gospel to preach unto them that dwell on the earth, and to every nation, and kindred, and tongue, and people"* (Revelation 14:6).

Parting Gem: *As you go about your joys today, rejoice with your chorus, and let the world see Jesus in you.*

September 4   *Reply of Replies*   Song 6:2

Today's Thought: *"My beloved is gone down into his garden, to the beds of spices, to feed in the gardens, and to gather lilies."*

Scriptures tells that our confessed sins are cast into the sea (Micah 7:19), that they are as far away as the east is from the west (Psalms 103:12), that they are hidden behind God's back (Isaiah 38:17), that they are behind a thick, dark cloud (Isaiah 44:22). God states that He, even He, has blotted out our transgressions for His name sake and that He will remember them no more (Isaiah 43:25). And yes, Isaiah 1:18 informs us that though our sins be as scarlet, they shall be as white as snow, though they be red like crimson, they shall be as wool. So just where are they?

Looking back into ancient Israel, we can see the daily service of the sanctuary. The repentant sinner brought his offering to the door of the tabernacle, and placing his hands upon the victim's head confessed his sins, thus transferring them from himself to the innocent sacrifice. By his own hand the animal was then slain, and the blood was carried by the priest into the holy place and sprinkled before the veil, behind which was the ark containing the law that the sinner had transgressed. By this ceremony the sin was, through the blood, figuratively transferred to the sanctuary.

In some cases, the blood was not taken into the holy place, but the flesh was then to be eaten by the priest… Both services alike symbolized the transfer of the sin from the penitent to the sanctuary.

Such was the work that went on day by day throughout the year. The sins of Israel being thus transferred to the sanctuary, the holy place was defiled, and a special work became necessary for the removal of sins. God commanded that an atonement be made for each of the sacred apartments. as for the altar, to *"cleanse it, and hallow it from the uncleanness of the children of Israel"* (Leviticus 16:19). (PP 354:2 to 355:1)

On a special day, the seventh day of the tenth month of each year (October 22, in 1844), every man was to afflict his soul while the work of atonement was in progress. A special work of cleansing the sanctuary was to be done on that day, called "the Day of Atonement."

Parting Gem: *Malachi 3:17 calls this the day God makes up His jewels.*

September 5   *Relationship of Relationships*   Song 6:2-3

Today's Thought *"My beloved is gone down into his garden, to the beds of spices, to feed in the gardens, and to gather lilies. I am my beloved's, and my beloved is mine: he feedeth among the lilies."*

"Lo, I am with you alway, even unto the end of the world" (Matthew 28:20). In our drama, Song 6:2-3, the bride-church answers with confidence: *"My beloved is gone down into his garden."* In 4:12, the Bridegroom says, *"A garden... is... my spouse."* When she says that He is gone down into his "garden," she expresses her knowledge that He is close beside her through the ministry of His Holy Spirit.

She also knows what He is doing, for she says that He is *"gathering lilies."* In 2:1, the bride says, *"I am... the lily of the valleys."* The true bride of Song 6 and 7 knows that the beloved Bridegroom is in the Most Holy place *"gathering lilies"*—gathering the people of God from every age into His universal kingdom through the process of the Investigative Judgment.

The Seventh-day Adventist Church is related to the universal church of all ages. In Song 6:4, the Bridegroom says of His true bride, *"Thou art beautiful, O my love, as Tirzah [delightful], comely as Jerusalem."* Throughout the Scriptures, the prophetic symbol of "Jerusalem" or the "mother" represents the universal church of all ages. The true church today identifies in character, and in the truth she presents with the kingdom of God of all ages. In the same verse, the Bridegroom says that she is *"terrible as an army with banners."* A "banner" is a slogan or motto which waves plainly before the people.

Isaiah 58:11-12 states, *"And the Lord shall guide thee continually, and satisfy thy soul in drought, and make fat thy bones: and thou shalt be like a watered garden, and like a spring of water, whose waters fail not. And they that shall be of thee shall build the old waste places: thou shalt raise up the foundations of many generations; thou shalt be called, The repairer of the breach, The restorer of paths to dwell in."*

Parting Gem: *Can you see the "army of God" going into war, with her banners of "truth and righteousness," the doctrines found in the Word of God and centered in Jesus Christ, the Beloved?*

SEPTEMBER 6   *Turn of Turns #2*   Song 6:2

Today's Thought: *"My beloved is gone down into his garden, to the beds of spices, to feed in the gardens, and to gather lilies."*

This verse must be powerfully important, for if they repeat a point for emphasis, so that we do not miss what they are trying to say, how about it when they repeat it four times? That's what happens here: *"into his garden," "beds of spices," "feed in the gardens," "gather lilies."* Do you get their point? O that the early pioneers, those Millerites, couldn't get this point. However, as strange as it may seem, and God works in strange and mysterious ways, His hand was over their mistake, for in His plan this disappointment had to happen (GC 373/4).

The time of expectation passed, and Christ did not appear for the deliverance of His people. Those who with sincere faith and love had looked for their Saviour experienced a bitter disappointment. Yet the purpose of God was accomplished: He was testing the hearts of those who professed to be waiting for His appearing. There were among them many who had been actuated by no higher motive than fear. Their profession of faith had not affected their hearts or their lives. When the expected event failed to take place, these persons declared that they were not disappointed; they had never believed that Christ would come. They were among the first to ridicule the sorrow of the true believers (GC 373).

"And he said unto them, Unto you it is given to know the mystery of the kingdom of God: but unto them that are without, all these things are done in parables" (Mark 4:11). Apply this text to our drama.

Parting Gem: *For you to contemplate today as you go about your joy and eagerness is the thought that maybe God in His strange way of working had His hand over this major disappointment, for should He not have had His hand over it, the early Adventist pioneers may not have delved into the subject of the sanctuary to find the reason for their disappointment. God had to bring out the sanctuary doctrine and the work Christ is doing in the heavenly sanctuary, and the method He chose was the 1844 experience. Consider that today. (Remember as well our constant concern in TM 409/410 and Acts 17:11.)*

SEPTEMBER 7 — *Audit of Audits* — Song 6:2

Today's Thought: *"My beloved is gone down into his garden, to the beds of spices, to feed in the gardens, and to gather lilies."*

Awesome location. In our drama, 2:16, our bride states, *"My beloved is mine, and I am his: he feedeth among the lilies."* In 6:3, she says basically the same thing, except in reverse, *"I am my beloved's, and my beloved is mine: he feedeth among the lilies."* We found in 2:16, April 11, that these lilies are the churches during the wilderness experience. In 2:1, she states that she is the lily of the valleys. so these lilies that the Bridegroom, Christ, is down into are His churches. Now, just what is Christ doing down in His churches?

In each church within the Seventh-day Adventist Church, as is probably true of other churches, there is a church list with the names of all of the members of that particular church. These names can be transferred from one church to another through a prescribed procedure.

In accounting terms, we would use an audit. God is in the Most Holy Place of the heavenly sanctuary auditing the "Book of Life." In this Book of Life are recorded all of the names of people who have ever accepted Jesus Christ as Lord and Saviour. Of course, not every one has remained faithful, so this "audit" will remove the names of those who have rejected or gone back into a sinful, non-Christ-like life, giving these people the consequences of their choices.

But their sins? The sins of those individuals retained in the Book of Life are to be placed on the scapegoat, Lucifer, as he was the instigator of those sins. This will be done at the end of the thousand years when fire bursts forth from inside Lucifer (Ezekiel 28:18).

The sins of those who have returned from following Christ or who reentered their old ways, their names are removed from the "Book of Life" and entered into the "Book of Death." Their sins go with them and they are judged according to the things done in the body (2 Corinthians 5:10).

Parting Gem: *In the audit of your "individual book," make sure that you have sent them on to your Lawyer. Do that today.*

September 8   *Gathering of Lilies of Gathering of Lilies*   Song 6:2

Today's Thought: *"My beloved is gone down into his garden, to the beds of spices, to feed in the gardens, and to gather lilies."*

Just one more look at our Beloved gathering lilies. All four activities mentioned above pertain to the same experience, going down into the garden, going to the bed of spices to feed, to gather.

Look at Malachi 3:16-17, which says, *"Then they that feared the Lord spake often one to another: and the Lord hearkened, and heard it, and a book of remembrance was written before him for them that feared the Lord, and that thought upon his name. And they shall be mine, saith the Lord of hosts, in that day when I make up my jewels."*

Now look at Daniel 7:9-12,13-14, which says, *"I beheld till the thrones were cast down, and the Ancient of days did sit… thousand thousands ministered unto him, and ten thousand times ten thousand stood before him: the judgment was set, and the books were opened… I saw in the night visions, and, behold, one like the Son of man… came to the Ancient of days… And there was given him dominion, and glory, and a kingdom, that all people, nations, and languages, should serve him: his dominion is an everlasting dominion, which shall not pass away, and his kingdom that which will not be destroyed."*

Now in Revelation 22:12, which says, *"And, behold, I come quickly; and my reward is with me, to give to every man according as his work shall be."*

In order for Christ to reward us when He comes, He must first investigate the evidence of our particular situation. When He finds that we fear the Lord, encourage one another, then the Lord hears us and goes to the Book of Remembrance, writes our name in it, thus making us one of His precious jewels. To these jewels He will reward with eternal life. To the others it is a different reward.

As a school teacher, it was my responsibility to check the daily register to "take the roll call." Christ is using this Book of Remembrance and the Book of Life for His roll call.

Parting Gem: *These two books are witnesses that must agree to our readiness, that we are safe to save. 2 Corinthians 13:1 says, "In the mouth of two or three witnesses shall every word be established."*

SEPTEMBER 9 *Confidence of Confidences #2* Song 6:3

Today's Thought: *"I am my beloved's, and my beloved is mine."*

We have come across this confidence before, the positive and strong awareness that these two, the Beloved and the bride-church, belong together; they belong to each other. The bride gets more passionate in 7:10, where she states that her Beloved's passion is towards her, the bride-church. Jeremiah 30:22 says, *"And ye shall be my people, and I will be your God."*

We looked at the first burst of confidence in April, covered by 2:16, when she was in the wilderness experience, the foxes of Italy were persecuting her, yet her confidence in her Beloved remained strong and vibrant. The pastors are out among the lilies, the churches, doing what pastors do. The church is growing, her confidence is soaring.

That bride-church has joined the mother church and we now look at the bride at the time of the 1844 disappointment. However, her confidence is still strong and vibrant; she is aware of whose she is. Can you see her clutch her fists together, bends her elbows, and bring her arms down close to her, in excitement as she proclaims, "He is mine"?

She has that confidence, that awareness as to whose she is, just as the church today must have. Those who have forgotten her historical-spiritual background and prophetic destiny seem not to understand the essence of the three angels' message.

As my minister's wife is the "first lady of my specific individual church," so our bride-church in our drama is "The First Lady of the Universe." An awareness of this just might be basic to firm church membership, preventing apostasy, weakness, and off-shoots. Should we not know that the bride-church is the apple of God's eye, and the major object upon earth in which He takes personal, up-close care, then do we have the authority, the strength and power, the assurance, the intimate connection to go out into the community, meet our neighbors, and introduce them to the Bridegroom, our Beloved.

Parting Gem: *Go into your closet, My children. Meet with Me as often as you can. Get from Me your directions for the day, similarly as Enoch did in his day. Rest awhile in My presence. Let Me teach you, then GO out to witness of what I've done for you.*

SEPTEMBER 10 — Conviction of Convictions — Song 6:4

Today's Thought: *"Thou art beautiful, O my love, as Tirzah, comely as Jerusalem, terrible as an army with banners."*

Tirzah, according to the SDA Dictionary, means "pleasure." It was a city renowned for its beauty. Joshua captured it from the Canaanites (Joshua 12:24), but it did not come into prominence until the time of the Hebrew kings, when Jereboam made it his royal residence and capital of the northern kingdom. It kept this position until Omri build Samaria and moved the capital there.

Jerusalem is one of the most important cities of the world. It is the Holy City of three great religious faiths: Judaism, Christianity, Islam. Since this name was attested, in differing forms, at least from the nineteenth century BC, long before the Hebrews invaded the country, it is of Canaanite or Amorite origin, meaning probably, "city of (the god) Shalim," but in Hebrew it means, "city of peace."

To the Jew, Jerusalem was the site of the temple and the capital of the nation. To the Christians, it was the scene of the suffering, death, resurrection, ascension of Jesus Christ. To the Moslem, it is the traditional place of the ascension of Mohammed into heaven.

David's men took the city, then called Jebus, for it was the home of the Jebusites, and renamed it *"the city of David"* (2 Samuel 5:4-10).

A "banner" is a standard or ensign, which might be a flag, or some other symbol that plainly goes before the people. The banners of the Seventh-day Adventist Church are her doctrines, specifically the three angels' messages that go to *"all them that dwell on the face of the whole earth"* (Luke 21:35).

This bride-church is the enemy's worst nightmare, as this army with banners, the blood-stained banners of Prince Emmanuel, goes out onto the battleground conquering and to conquer. She has on the whole armour of God, facing the foe, advancing in the power and the might of her Beloved.

Parting Gem: *Today as you go about your business, consider what the Beloved thought of His lover, the bride-church. Think, ponder, contemplate, then ask yourself the question, "Do I have the same opinion and descriptive image in my mind as the Beloved has in His?"*

SEPTEMBER 11 — *Overcomer of Overcomers* — Song 6:5

Today's Thought: *"Turn away thine eyes from me, for they have overcome me: thy hair is as a flock of goats that appear from Gilead."*

On June 2, we looked at the "eyes" of our bride-church, as *"thou hast doves' eye within thy locks."* (Song 4:1) Here the eyes and the hairs (locks) are again associated together.

According to Collins Paperback Thesaurus, "overcome" could mean either conquer or affected. If affected then "at a loss for words," "bowled over," "overwhelmed," "speechless," and "swept off one's feet" are its synonyms.

Let's Compare Song 4:9, where the Beloved is ravished by only one of the bride's eyes, with today's thought that thine eyes, in the plural, have overcome the Beloved. They have "swept Him off His feet," "bowled Him over," even left Him "speechless" with the vision this bride now has.

Coming out of the wilderness in 4:9, she had only one of her eyes; she had only part of the knowledge of the Scriptures, for the papal powers had "wiped out" much of it. The Reformation started the restoration of the Scriptural knowledge. But now the bride's progress in spiritual understanding, including the Ten Commandments and the Sabbath doctrine, has "overcome" the Bridegroom.

As the historical and spiritual scrolls unroll, greater sight and insight will be achieved. Old doctrines will be uncovered from the errors or misunderstandings of days past. Daniel and Revelation will open up more and more as one studies, reads, and watches how God opens up the hearts and minds of His people in these two books.

The great thrust of Revelation 14:6-12 becomes clearer and clearer in meaning, giving power to carry this last warning to the world. As history and daily events occur, the pieces of the puzzle are fitting in smoothly and excitedly.

Parting Gem: *Today is one more day in your life. Take advantage of it by opening your eyes that you may see great and wonderful things that God has revealed from His law. Have a great day.*

SEPTEMBER 12 — *Flock of Flocks #2* — Song 6:5-6

Today's Thought: *"Turn away thine eyes from me, for they have overcome me: thy hair is as a flock of goats that appear from Gilead. Thy teeth are as a flock of sheep which go up from the washing, whereof every one beareth twins, and there is not one barren among them."*

Just in passing, it should be mentioned, as we have done before, that we are talking symbolically, and that which is literally said is not literally meant. Today's thought is a good example. What lover would say this to his love? What lover would accept this "compliment?" Yet, when looked at in the symbolic setting, the whole of our drama makes exciting sense. So, what is being said?

While in the wilderness (1:15) our bride-church had doves' eyes. Eyes are symbolic of the Holy Spirit, so in the wilderness the bride could see with the aid of the Holy Spirit and discern the days yet to be sojourning there.

One thing that shepherds have is flocks of sheep and goats, otherwise they are not shepherds. The more sheep and goats one has, the more "fabulous and glorious" is his herd to him. So, as hair to a woman is her pride and her glory (1 Corinthians 11:15), so to our Shepherd is His bride to Him. Besides, you'll remember that Matthew 10:30 tells us that every hair on our head is numbered; every member of His flock is numbered, identified, and well-known to Him.

Remember that John 10:14,16 states, *"I am the good shepherd, and know my sheep, and am known of mine… And other sheep I have, which are not of this fold: them also I must bring… and there shall be one fold, and one shepherd."*

How do we get all into one fold with one Shepherd? *"And after these things I saw another angel come down from heaven, having great power; and the earth was lightened with this glory. And he cried mightily with a strong voice, saying, Babylon the great is fallen, is fallen… Come out of her, my people"* (Revelation 18:1-2,4).

Parting Gem: *Remember, "I am His and He is mine. We belong together." You are also His, He is also yours.*

SEPTEMBER 13 — Queen of Queens — Song 6:8

Today's Thought: *"There are threescore queens, and fourscore concubines, and virgins without number."*

Looking at the SDA Bible Commentary, there are two types of queens. One type is a queen who rules a kingdom. The queen of Sheba and Candace, queen of Ethiopia, are two examples of legitimate female rulers. Today Britain's Queen Elizabeth II is a modern example.

Queen Vashti and Queen Esther were Persian queens of the consort type, or the queens who are in consort (spouses) of the ruling king. They are queens because their husbands are kings. Queen Elizabeth II's mother was called the queen mother because her husband, King George VII, was ruling king of England until his death.

A concubine is an inferior wife in the system of polygamy. They were sometimes taken from among slaves and could be divorced more easily than regular wives. Their sons were also deemed to be inferior to those born of the true wife. Case in point was Ishmael and Isaac.

The virgins we found were the regular members of the church family, the saints of the Most High God.

The household of Christ in our drama is likened to an eastern family where there are queens, concubines, virgin daughters. In this household, the queens are executive-administrators, the concubines do the work of the household and bear children for their master, while the virgin daughters are simply members of the household. The church has a similar organizational structure of executive administrators, workers who win souls, and members of the church which is "without number" (Berry, Quarterly, P. 76/77).

An assignment for you today is to chew on this reading of today. Wrestle it in your mind to set it in place. Have a great day.

Parting Gem: *"It is amazing that God would preserve prophetic Scripture to the very end of earth's history, for three thousand years, behind an appearance so camouflaged, that out of embarrassment and complexity, it would be left to the time of its fulfillment, to make ready a people for the coming of the Bridegroom"* (Berry, Textbook, p. 170).

September 14   *Virgin of Virgins #2*   Song 6:8

Today's Thought: *"There are threescore queens, and fourscore concubines, and virgins without number."*

Is this another spot where the embarrassment comes when this song is read? According to the Collins Essential Canadian English Dictionary and Thesaurus, among other definitions, a virgin is one undefiled, chaste, immaculate, uncorrupted, not exploited nor explored.

In Matthew 25:1-13 is the well-known parable of the ten virgins—five wise, five foolish. These virgins generally refer to the church members who are waiting for the Beloved Bridegroom to return from the wedding to gather His bride and go into the marriage feast.

2 Corinthians 11:2 says, *"For I am jealous over you with godly jealousy: for I have espoused you to one husband, that I may present you as a chaste virgin in Christ."* Paul is concerned and desirous over his flock. He longs that they be in a meaningful, vibrant, saving relationship with Jesus Christ, and longs to present them as pure, undefiled, and uncorrupted in that relationship.

In Revelation 14:4, the 144,000 are mentioned as being virgins, undefiled with other churches and their Babylonian wines.

At the giving of the dowry in Calvary, the bride says, *"Let him kiss me with the kisses of his mouth: for thy love is better than wine. Because of the savour of thy good ointments thy name is as ointment poured forth, therefore do the virgins love thee"* (Song 1:2-3).

As discussed earlier, on January 18, a virgin is one who does not get involved with other *"beloveds."* They are the church members who claim to be waiting for the Bridegroom to return from the wedding so that He can claim His bride. In non-political terms, that's you and me. We are the virgins who are waiting for our Beloved to return and take us to the home He has prepared for us. We are the ones who will trim our lamps. We are the ones who love Him because of the balm He supplies, the sins He forgives, the victories He allows us to have, the life that is more abundant because He came to give life.

Parting Gem: *Today is an excellent day, as is every day, to stop and contemplate your relationship, as a virgin, with the Beloved.*

SEPTEMBER 15 — *Undefiled of Undefiled* — Song 6:9

The true remnant church is led by the Holy Spirit *("my dove")*, *"my undefiled"* (a daughter of Jerusalem—not Babylon), *"BUT ONE"* (unique), *"THE ONLY ONE"* (there is but one true church at the end of time), and *"THE CHOICE ONE."* In recent times, there have been many who have been in an identity crisis within the Seventh-day Adventist Church, seeming to forget just who they are! In ancient Israel, some desired to identify with nations around them by choosing a king, rather than being classified as a peculiar nation of God's people. Today there are some who have an inferiority complex, desiring to be a part of a "brotherhood of churches" and seeking to merge with the "mainstream" of nominal Christendom. Those who have forgotten or never understood the historical theological background of Adventism and its prophetic destiny do not understand the essence of the three angels' message. If we lose our identity as *"BUT ONE… THE ONLY ONE… THE CHOICE ONE,"* then we have lost our prophetic moorings and our message to the world; we no longer have a purpose to exist.

At that point, evangelism ceases. If we desire to be part of Babylon, there is no longer any need to call any out of Babylon nor to proclaim any warning to the world. Only as we see ourselves as a fulfillment of prophecy do we have the courage to warn the world (see Revelation 10, 14, 12:17, Song of Songs 6-7) (Berry - Quarterly, p.75).

Today we need the message in our drama that this remnant church, this very Seventh-day Adventist Church, is "The Fairest Among Women" and "The One and Only" to give us the self-image needed to complete God's work in the final crises. Understanding our prophetic platform and historical background and the nature and the purpose of this church is basic to firm church membership, preventing apostasy and weakness.

Parting Gem: *Did you get and grasp that statement above where it states that "basic to strong church membership, preventing apostasy and weakness, is an understanding of our prophetic platform?"*

SEPTEMBER 16 — *Fairest of Fair #5* — Song 6:9

Today's Thought: *"My dove, my undefiled is but one; she is the only one of her mother, she is the choice one of her that bare her. The daughters saw her, and blessed her; yea, the queens and the concubines, and they praised her."*

Is this a statement of arrogance, presumption, pompousness, or is it a statement of fact? There are hundreds of religions in the world today, and among Protestants there are hundreds of denominations, all of which claim to be God's true church. The Roman Catholic Church, until recently, has claimed itself alone, by virtue of apostolic succession, dominance and survival, to be the one and only true church. Are all other churches just different roads leading to the same destination—heaven? Who is God's true church or are there many? Is there *"but one"* true church which keeps the commandments of God and have the faith of Jesus? Where is the *"Thus saith the Lord?"* or the *"It is written"*? Just look at our thought for today.

"My dove, undefiled... BUT ONE... ONLY ONE... CHOICE ONE of her that bare her." Does that sound somewhat clear to you?

Look at John 10:16. *"And other sheep I have, which are not of this fold: them also I must bring, and they shall hear my voice; and there shall be one fold, and one shepherd."*

Again, look at Isaiah 56:8. *"The Lord God which gathereth the outcasts of Israel saith, Yet will I gather others to him, besides those that are gathered unto him."*

If God's people are to give the last great message, that of Revelation 14-18, to call God's people out of Babylon, they must know for themselves their own identity in direct contrast to all of apostate Christendom—Babylon.

They must know by experience that *"I am His and He is mine,"* or, the other way around, *"He is mine and I am His."*

Parting Gem: *Today, ponder in your heart and in your mind this fabulous statement that "I am His, He is mine," as well as this thought for today: "My dove, My church, My chosen people, the apple of My eye, the one and only object upon earth I claim as Mine."*

SEPTEMBER 17   *Fairest of Fair #6*   Song 6:9

Today's Thought: *"My love, My love, My love, You are My undefiled one, You are the only one, the choice one of your mother that bare you. You are My chosen body of believers." (paraphrased)*

The ecumenical movement is drawing all the religions of the world into one body, under one head, and the head they want is the Pope of Rome.

Revelation 13:3,7-8 says, "… and all the world wondered after the beast… and power was given him over all kindreds, and tongues, and nations. And all that dwell upon the earth shall worship him, whose names are not written in the book of life of the Lamb slain from the foundation of the world."

As history draws to its climax, there will be only two parties: one true church and one counterfeit "beast" power. It is imperative that God's people recognize from prophetic Scripture to which party they belong. It is only the prophetic Scriptures and true Bible doctrines which identify the true church beyond question. She must never forget that she is the "ONLY ONE, THE CHOICE ONE, THE ONE AND ONLY" true bride waiting for the Bridegroom to complete the arrangements for the marriage, to return from the wedding to receive her unto Himself.

It is she who gives the third angel's message in the power of the "Loud Cry" and the "Latter Rain" of the Holy Spirit.

"If any man [or woman] worship the beast and his image, and receive his mark in his forehead, or in his hand, the same shall drink of the wine of the wrath of God…" (Revelation 14:9-10)

Parting Gem: *What does this really mean to you and to me? If I worship the papal power and accept his authority, will I partake of the seven last plagues? Can I worship this power by believing in my mind or by working with my hand to enforce his dogmas? In this series of Sunday laws soon to be presented, the last one will force us to stop working on Sunday, and go to church, as well as start working on Saturday, or be killed. This will all be for the good and security of the nation. Does this mean anything to us, to you or me? Would it not be safer to accept the authority of King Jesus?*

September 18   *Fairest of Fair #7*   Song 6:9

Today's Thought: *"My dove, my undefiled is but one; she is the only one of her mother, she is the choice one of her that bare her."*

What a burst of emotion, what an explosion of affirmation, what a positive awareness of the high esteem the Bridegroom sees in His bride. It would do us well if we would contemplate not only who we are as a people, but also how heaven looks upon us.

Down through the ages, through the seven churches of Revelation 2-4, God's love and estimation of His church has repeatedly been expressed throughout the song. From 1:9-16 through to 6:9, it continually addresses her as "My dove, My spouse, My fair, My love," but now, in the final stages of this drama, as the final church—the Laodicean—bursts upon the stage, His description is more pointed and specific.

She is not only *"My dove,"* but *"My undefiled"*—chaste, pure, glorious, a terrible and horrible threat to Satan, the archenemy, as an army with banners sweeping across the globe with this everlasting gospel crying with a loud voice the messages of Revelation and Daniel.

Have you noticed, and if you haven't please start to take notice, that this declaration of the Beloved regarding His bride-church has been swelling in adjectives and grandeur since it was first introduced in 1:9? As previously mentioned, she is the apple of His eye, the one object upon earth on which He bestows His most supreme regard.

Could it be that when it states that she is but one, the only one, the choice one, that the Bridegroom is getting excited with the prospect of claiming His bride? Each one of the other six churches in Revelation 2 and 3 took their place in history; but it is the last church, the Laodicean Church, the Remnant Church, that is alive and well upon Planet Earth when the Bridegroom comes to claim her.

Should we let this mind be in us that is in Christ Jesus, then we should have the same reverence and regard for His bride, the same love and devotion, the same respect for her as does our Beloved.

Parting Gem: *Seeing as we as a people believe that Christ is organized, knows the end from the beginning, thinks so highly of His bride-church, should we not elevate the First Lady of the Multiverse?*

SEPTEMBER 19 *Look of Looks #2* Song 6:10

Today's Thought: *"Who is she that looketh forth as the morning, fair as the moon, clear as the sun, and terrible as an army with banners?"*

According to Peak's Commentary, the Song of Songs 6:10 verse has been misplaced. It does not belong here in Chapter 6. It belongs around Song 8:8-12. Commentators understand from context that it has been inserted or misplaced, but they do not where it should be. E.G. White has given its correct historical setting! She says, "While the investigative judgment is going forward in heaven, while the sins of penitent believers are being removed from the sanctuary, there is a special work of purification, of putting away of sin, among God's people upon earth... When this work shall been accomplished, the followers of Christ will be ready for His appearing... Then she will look forth "as the morning star, fair as the moon, clear as the sun, and terrible as an army with banners" (GC 425) (Berry, Quarterly, p.108).

Do you remember when and how the bride went into the wilderness in AD 538, and how she stayed there for 1,260 years, until AD 1798? Do you recall how she went in on eagle's wings, flying low, as the expression is? She knew that she had a place prepared for her in the wilderness; she also knew that the earth would open up and she would be able to flee to the New World where there was freedom of religion and freedom of speech, where there was a church without a pope and a country without a king.

Now, as she went into the wilderness quietly, secretly, slipping away at night, it is now with pomp, ceremony, fanfare, jubilation that she comes out of that wilderness. She is coming forth with an awareness that the world must know that the Beloved is soon to come. She is aware that all of the signs pointing to that return have basically been fulfilled, the sun, the moon, the stars, the earthquake. Left only are the gospel to all the world and a bride that is ready and willing.

She comes out looking like the morning, fair as the moon, clear as the sun, terrible as an army with banners, ready for battle, the enemies' worst nightmare.

Parting Gem: *Contemplate today just where you fit into this picture.*

SEPTEMBER 20 — *Valley Fruit of Valley Fruits* — Song 6:11

Today's Thought: *"I went down into the garden of nuts to see the fruits of the valley, and to see whether the vines flourished, and the pomegranate budded."*

Here we have three flags waving, hoping you will see them and understand just what is going on. The three flags are the garden of nuts, the fruits of the valley, the pomegranate budded.

Let's go back to Song 4:12. *"A garden inclosed is my sister, my spouse; a spring shut up, a fountain sealed."* Today, we go down into that garden of nuts, into that church which is symbolized by a garden, for that is my sister. We go down to see the fruits that are in that valley. The church is the rose of Sharon and the lily of the valleys. So, down there in that valley are the churches, those enclosed gardens, and we want to know if there is growth within those churches.

Jesus informs us that He is the vine, we are the branches. Therefore, going down into that valley of churches we wish to find whether or not Christ is growing among the inhabitants. Is He the heartthrob of the members within the church, or are there "foxes" around like there was during the Reformation period that are spoiling the vines?

We are going down into that valley to see if the pomegranate is budded. The pomegranate, when carefully peeled, appeared like the convolutions of the brain and from ancient times has been regarded as a symbol of knowledge. Knowledge is progressive and the question is whether the pomegranates have budded (not flowered as yet, nor borne fruit as yet). Present truth for each age is progressive. The great question is: Has the true church been open to receive Present Truth as prophecy is fulfilled day by day? Is it now ready to receive?

If the Bridegroom, our Beloved, is going to go down into the garden, then that means He is very near to His people, His chosen bride, His dove. And that is exactly what Scripture states. *"I will not fail thee, nor forsake thee"* (Joshua 1:5). *"Lo, I am with you alway, even unto the end of the world"* (Matthew 28:20).

Parting Gem: *Today, spend some time in your "closet" or in your "garden" so that the pomegranate can bud, so the vine can flourish.*

September 21 — *Inspection of Inspections* — Song 6:11

Today's Thought: *"I went down into the garden of nuts to see… whether the vine flourished, and the pomegranates budded."*

Christ inspects His church—His garden. He looks at two things: 1) the "vine," and 2) the "pomegranates." He states: *"I am the true vine, and my Father is the husbandman. Every branch in me that beareth not fruit he taketh away: and every branch that beareth fruit, he purgeth it, that it may bring forth more fruit… Abide in me, and I in you. As the branch cannot bear fruit of itself, except it abide in the vine; no more can ye, except ye abide in me.*

"I am the vine, ye are the branches: He that abideth in me, and I in him, the same bringeth forth much fruit: for without me ye can do nothing… As the Father hath loved me, so have I loved you: continue ye in my love.

"If ye keep my commandments, ye shall abide in my love; even as I have kept my Father's commandments and abide in his love" (John 15:1-2,4-5,9-10).

One of the neat things about the Bible is that people read the Bible through every year, finding each time they read it something new. Somewhere in my journey through this Christian experience, I have found it advantageous to go back over all that I was taught to see if I still believe now what I believed then. My high school Bible textbook, *Principles of Life,* has been glued and repaired many times and I still have it as one of my main sources of belief.

One other neat recommendation is to read through each year the *Conflict of the Ages* series of books, taking one through the entire Bible and revealing things both old and new.

Parting Gem: *How has it been with you, my friend? Have your pomegranates been advancing? Has your knowledge of Scripture, God's power, goodness, love for you, been growing, advancing since first you believed? Are you different today in all aspects of your Christian life, your attitude, your diet, your dress, your time, your study of God's Word, even your preparation for the blazing skies soon to break? May God bless you and keep you and make His face to shine upon you, today, even as you step outside of your comfort zone.*

SEPTEMBER 22 — Church of Churches #1 — Song 6:11

Today's Thought: *"I went down into the garden of nuts to see… whether the vine flourished, and the pomegranates budded."*

Many of you readers have no doubt encountered people who claim that the only difference between the Seventh-day Adventist Church and their church is the Sabbath. Let's look at that over the next three days. We'll consider first the perfect number of seven—the Seven S's. It's interesting as well as important to remember that these S's dovetail, hand-in-glove, with each other.

SABBATH: Yes, they agree the seventh-day Sabbath is different from their beliefs, but is it really that important? Should they understand that the question is not over a day we keep, but over an "authority we obey"? By default, we give homage to Satan when we follow the Sunday policy, whereas we given honour, glory, and prominence to Jehovah God as our Creator when we follow His authority.

STATE OF THE DEAD: There are a few churches who believe as Adventists believe on the state of the dead, but the majority do not. Their belief is that one goes to heaven, hell, or purgatory upon death. We believe the dead simply sleep, rest, until Christ comes. This Biblical belief shows God as a loving, fair, compassionate Being. Biblically, we all receive our rewards, be they eternal life or eternal death at the same time. No one goes before the other. It would not be fair to have Judas burn in hell two thousand years ahead of the evil ones of today. It would not be kind to those saintly ones to go to heaven upon death so that they can look down here on to earth and see their loved ones suffering. Yet, the *"other beloved"* has been spreading this evil falsehood through his churches.

Consider Revelation 18:24, where it says, *"And in her was found the blood of prophets, and of saints, and of all that were slain upon the earth."* Had all of the world's suicide bombers who blow themselves up for their cause could understand that after death comes the judgment (Hebrews 9:27), not a harem full of teenage virgins, there would be a difference in world events.

Parting Gem: *Have you gone down lately into your garden of nuts to check your pomegranates?*

SEPTEMBER 23   *Church of Churches #2*   Song 6:11

Today's Thought: *"I went down into the garden of nuts to see the fruits of the valley, and to see whether the vine flourished, and the pomegranate budded."*

SANCTUARY: There are very few churches that believe in the sanctuary as do the Adventists. Should they believe it as Adventists do, they would be very different in other beliefs, such as the Sabbath.

One might wonder just why it was necessary for the Great Disappointment of 1844. This experience brought out the fact that most were afraid for their lives and wanted to be saved, so they jumped up onto the Millerite bandwagon. These were weeded out.

Another reason for the Great Disappointment is to wonder whether the Adventist Church would ever have had brought to light the doctrine of the sanctuary, the Day of Atonement, the intercessory ministry of Christ without it?

Yet, who besides Adventist take the sanctuary system seriously?

SECOND COMING: Although "most" churches may believe in this event, their understanding of it is that it is way down the stream of time, where seven years of a second chance is given to the sinners and then Christ comes after this seven-year period. This bride-church believes His coming is imminent, like loomingly near.

This *"other beloved"* character is doing everything he can to prevent people from getting in oneness with Jesus Christ, so that when Christ comes they can be saved. The other beloved does not want that to happen.

SALVATION: The Plan of Salvation, or what has been called "The Seven Wonders of the Multiverse," where seven events into the life of Jesus are involved, is missing from most churches. The incarnation, virgin birth, sinless life, vicarious death, resurrection, intercession, second coming, are all involved in this Plan of Salvation. These are major epochs in this Plan and should be preached much more often.

Parting Gem: *Without a knowledge of the sanctuary, one has difficulty understanding what Christ is presently doing. As you go about your joys today, lift a thankful heart to your Beloved for His wisdom.*

SEPTEMBER 24 — Church of Churches #3 — Song 6:11

Today's Thought: *"I went down into the garden of nuts to see the fruits of the valley, and to see whether the vines flourished, and the pomegranate budded."*

One more day on the wisdom of the Choice one, the Fairest of the fair.

SPIRIT OF PROPHECY: This gift given to the church brings one of Satan's major attacks. Should he be successful in getting God's people (that's you and me) to doubt, reject, lose faith in this gift, then he has us and Christ does not. Is that a bold statement? Join the Berea Club of Acts 17:10-11.

STEWARDSHIP: A major, major blessing to the Adventist Church is their understanding of stewardship. Return (do not pay) one-tenth of increase in tithe back to God who gave it, plus additional gifts as God has blessed you.

Many statements from the Messenger of the Lord can be found should one look into *The Index to the Writings of E. G. White* regarding the tithe. It actually goes back to the time of Adam (3T 393), for it did not originate with the Hebrews (PP 525). It is of divine origin ordained by God (DA 616; 3T 388).

Many a story has been told of how other churches wished they had a system to pay their ministers like that of Adventists. Their small church-membership pastor gets what the congregation gives him, whereas the larger membership church pays their minister substantially more. Within the Adventist community, all pastors are basically paid the same with minor adjustments. This system is the envy of other churches.

CREATION: One other major difference with other churches is the first angel's message: *"...worship Him that made heaven, and earth, and the sea, and the fountains of waters"* (Revelation 14:7). If you are keeping your eyes and ears open, you will have noticed the tremendous upsurge in creation topics and beliefs coming from the scientific community. A literal seven-day creation of our solar system, as in Genesis, is biblical.

Parting Gem: *As we open the pomegranates and see the brain-like structure, we can understand its symbolism and find all this wisdom of the everlasting gospel covered up by the other beloved.*

SEPTEMBER 25   *Consideration of Considerations*   Song 6:11

Today's Thought: *"I went down into the garden of nuts to see the fruits of the valley, and to see whether the vines flourished, and the pomegranate budded."*

Today is a day of provocation. I wish to stir up your pure minds and ask you to think, to think deep, and to consider. Consider these possibilities.

The world knows that in 1798 a deadly wound was inflicted when Pope Pius VI was taken prisoner, and later died in prison. The next pope, Pope Pius VII, was also taken prisoner in 1812, but was released when he agreed to relinquish papal control over the Papal States. These states were then incorporated into the country of Italy.

Could it be, for your consideration, that in order for this deadly wound to be completely healed, these Papal States will have to be returned to papal control?

Could it also be that those who drink of the wine of Babylon now need to realize that the wine of Babylon includes such sips as the immortality of the soul, the mass, the Eucharist, the infallibility of the pope, the pope as the Vicar of Christ, confessional, purgatory, not to mention the Sunday sacredness in place of the seventh-day Sabbath?

Could it be that the counsel in Revelation to *"Come out of her, my people"* (18:4), means just that, to come out, all the way out, not just to the doorway, or to the city gates, but completely and wholly out of Babylon?

Could it be that God's people (that's you and me) have had our eyes and minds so glued on the Sabbath that we really fail to realize that the real question is not necessarily the Sabbath, as important as that is, but which authority we accept, the authority of the pope and his Sunday-sabbath or the authority of our Beloved Jesus and His authority of the seven-day Sabbath? Without the Author of the Sabbath, Jesus, the Sabbath is a tinkling cymbal, a sounding brass.

Parting Gem: *Going about your duties and responsibilities today, remember Acts 17:11 and TM 409/410. Has your mind been provoked to the point that you actually stop to consider your pomegranate?*

SEPTEMBER 26 — *Shulamite of Shulamites* — Song 6:13

Today's Thought: *"Return, return, O Shulamite; return, return, that we may look upon thee. What will ye see in the Shulamite? As it were as the company of two armies."*

A world-chorus of voices of the honest-hearted call out to the bride-church, *"Return, return, O Shulamite; return, return, that we may look upon thee."* She is so far advanced in spiritual comprehension and lifestyle that she is far out and ahead of all the rest. They cry out to her to come back to them to their station in life, to their primitive and fallen conditions, that they may look upon her—her doctrines, her advanced knowledge, her lifestyle—that they may join her, that they may all prepare to meet the Bridegroom together.

Then the question is put to us: *"What will ye see in the Shulamite?"* The answer is given: *"As it were the company of two armies."*

The bride-church is called the "Shulamite." In Scripture, the Shulamite was a kindly woman who provided lodging and comfort to the prophet Elisha, as he passed by in his missionary work. She was the HOSTESS who provided for the comforts of the missionary program.

In the church—as in a corporate body—the bride is the hostess to the missionary labourers, providing for them lodging and daily needs as they have accomplished their work for the Lord, all over the world.

The ark which Moses built, with its gold overlay and stone law, was heavy! It required strong men to bear the staves upon their shoulders over the rough ground. Thus the burden for carrying the truths pertinent in preparation for the returning Bridegroom have been heavy and the people have struggled to bear it to all the world. But in only one century, the message has extended far and wide. A groundwork-network has been laid so that in the final crisis, every person upon the earth will be warned of the coming Bridegroom.

Parting Gem: *"And it fell on a day, that Elisha passed to Shunem, where was a great woman; and she constrained him to eat bread. And so it was, that as oft as he passed by, he turned in thither to eat bread. And she said… Let us make a little chamber… and let us set for him there a bed, and a table, and a stool, and a candlestick."* (2 Kings 4:8-10)

SEPTEMBER 27 — *Dance of Dances* — Song 6:13

Today's Thought: *"What will ye see in the Shulamite? As it were a company of two armies."*

In the margin of Bibles, this company of two armies is also translated as "the dance of Mahanaim." The question is put to us, *"What will you see in the Shulamite?"* The answer is given: *"As it were the company of two armies,"* or "as the dance of Mahanaim" Mahanaim is the place where Jacob returned to meet Esau. Jacob left home with only his walking stick, but at Mahanaim he had so prospered that he divided his whole household into two "armies." In like manner, the Advent believers after 1844 were as a handful, some say half a handful, but today number into the millions.

It was at Mahanaim that Jacob gained spiritual victories and was named a "Prince of Israel." It was in that place that Jacob became "Israel." In the following verse, Song 7:1, the bride-church is called *"O prince's daughter."* This royal title recognizes the bride-church as triumphant and victorious in accomplishing the task given her in taking the gospel to all the world. If that verse in Song 6:13 is translates as "the dance of Mahanaim," it is simply one more way of describing the graceful activity in which the bride-church has "danced" her way to all the world.

Yet, let us look at this Shulamite woman; the story is found in 2 Kings 4:8-37. Read it as part of your devotions today. This Shulamite woman is hospitable, plain and simple. She and her husband went to some expense to provide a motel room for Elisha and Gehazi as the two traveled their rounds. She also knows just what to do in the case of emergencies, and that was to contact the prophet Elisha.

Parting Gem: *As God's children, let us determine to be hospitable. Who knows when some angel may need a meal or room for the night. As well, we know to whom we may flee in our time of need, for we know whom we have believed in, and are persuaded that He is able to keep that which we commit unto Him.*

SEPTEMBER 28 — *Amminadib of Amminadibs* — Song 6:12

Today's Thought: *"Or ever I was aware, my soul made me like the chariots of Amminadib."*

The bride-church suddenly exclaims, *"Or ever I was aware [before I knew or realized what was happening], my soul made me like the chariots of Amminadib."* Now, who was Amminadib?

Amminadib is found only once, and that is in Song 6:12. In the Hebrew language, it means "My generous and willing people," and this could apply to the generous contributions of tithes, offering, and personal service that has made the Seventh-day Adventist Church the church that it is.

However, Amminadab, spelt with a "dab," is the name of Aaron's father-in-law. Aaron married Elisheba about 1520 BC (Exodus 6:23). In about seven other Old Testament verses, Amminadab is mentioned as a prince in Judah and the father of Nahshon.

Amminadab is also mentioned as a Levite of the family of Kohath, who assisted in bringing up the ark from the home of Obed-edom, carrying it on their shoulders (1 Chronicles 6:22 and 15:10-12). Similar to Amminadab, the Seventh-day Adventist Church has been carrying upon its shoulders the "ark" of the Ten Commandments, complete with its seventh-day Sabbath, into the uttermost parts of the world.

So, our bride-church is saying, "Before I knew it, and without any planning or preparation for it, I found myself like a chariot, a great movement, responsible for carrying the Ark of the Covenant upon my shoulders. I'm taking it to all the globe. The big push of this movement is the seventh-day Sabbath, the fourth commandment in that Decalogue."

My soul made me like that chariot. My attitude, my spiritual make-up, my willingness and whatever else I had, made me a recipient of God's grace and commission to carry that responsibility to the whole globe.

Parting Gem: *Today, carry with you the gem of an idea that you are somewhat like Amminadib in that you too would like to carry that chariot.*

SEPTEMBER 29   *Plea of Pleas*   Song 6:13

Today's Thought: *"Return, return, O Shulamite; return, return, that we may look upon thee…"*

Carl George, an ordained Baptist minister, made the following insightful statement while serving as Director of the Fuller Institute of Evangelism and Church Growth. After having studied the Seventh-day Adventist Church for a decade, he had this to say:

"In a special sense the founders of your movement were people to who God spoke. He wanted to create a special witness so that the rest of His church could look at the faithfulness of your movement. He wanted the rest of the church to say, 'We could learn from them. We will be better people. We will be more obedient to our heavenly Father, and our Saviour, because we have watched the walk of the Adventists. We have watched the price they have paid. We have watched as they have been ostracized, as they have been misunderstood, as they have been slandered. But there will come a time when it's clear why they have had to go through these rather narrow channels and difficult pathways.' And God will say, 'Look. See these people? The rest of you take note.'"[16]

Could he have had any concept of what Song of Songs 6:13 said? Did he read that the Shulamite woman was so far ahead of the rest of the churches that she is being called to "slow down and wait for us. Come back here, return, don't go so far, so fast"?

The Shulamite woman, our bride-church, is so far advanced in spiritual comprehension, health tips, lifestyle, that she is being called to come back, return to them in their station of life, their doctrines, their lack of knowledge, their primitive and false condition, that they may look upon her, her doctrines, her health knowledge, her lifestyle, her extended life expectancy, and her advantages over the rest of them.

Parting Gem: *This bride-church in our drama is the only one that can understand and apply Revelation 10, Song of Songs, in specifics, let alone Daniel, Revelation, Genesis, and much more. Awesome thought.*

---

[16] George, Carl F. "Doctrines Evaluation—Seventh-day Adventist." *Columbian Union Conference of Seventh-day Adventists*, 1988.

SEPTEMBER 30　　　　　　*Summary*　　　　　　Song 6:1-13

September has thirty days, and this is the last day of that month. We found just where the Beloved had gone when He didn't come on October 22, 1844. This answered the important question as to where did your beloved go because he didn't come here. Where did He turn aside? Her Beloved was feeding among the many churches, going over the clerk's records to see just which ones would be invited to join Him at the Marriage Supper of the Lamb.

The bride again exuberantly exclaims that she was the Beloved's and that her Beloved was hers. Then her Beloved describes the bride in all of her glory. She has improved, grown, advanced in her knowledge of the Law and is now seeing all of it, thus has two eyes and not one like before. This is repeated the second round with the pomegranates within her locks. Verse 9 is replete with meaningful adjectives to describe this Remnant Church, in this Laodicean period.

Catch the excitement of the Beloved when He describes His last-day church. This is no ordinary church. This is His jewel case where you and I are velvety wrapped in His love. Of all of the churches, all seven of them, down through the centuries, this last church is the one that gets the most descriptive adjectives. The other six churches may have been great and wonderful, but then they were the one on the stage of action at that time. Now, in this last day period, the Laodicean Church takes center stage, and He gets excited about it because now He can come—as soon as they are ready.

A picture is painted of a coming out of a wilderness, fierce and terrible as an army of workers ready to attack the enemy. The enemy recognizes this as their worst nightmare. It's a coming out in a progressive movement, just as the sun breaks forth each morning and gets hotter and highest as the day wears on.

Before she knew what was happening, she had been given the task of raising the standards, the banners, the Law, high and lifted up. This privilege seemed to have been thrust upon her. This position has placed our bride-church so far ahead of the rest of other churches that they cry for her to slow down and wait for them. She is far ahead in education, schools, universities, health, missions outreach, volunteer services to third world countries, organization, and the list goes on.

Unsinkable, Unburnable, Non-Destructible

Man had such an awesome goal to build a massive ship,
    He filled that ship with noble souls to make that maiden trip.
He built that ship in such a way, unsinkable they said.
    Yet, hit a burg to all's dismay, and sank with many dead.

Jehovah God gave Noah prints to build his massive ship.
    On prairie sod, no sea around, few joined him on his trip.
The flood so fierce that Satan quaked, that ark cupped in God's hands.
    When all was 'or, upon that shore, Noah led his crew to land.

Man built two towers, massive, tall, to be his pride and glory.
    Both towers built to never fall, story after story.
Those towers marked New York's landscape with pride, with bulging hope.
    But found no safety anywhere when in the terrorist's scope.

Our mighty King has gone away to build for us some mansions.
    On city streets of solid gold with living green's expansions.
All walled within that Holy Place we call Jerusalem.
    Come rest beside that Living street, and simply listen to Him.

Psalm 96

Let us sing unto the Lord;
>Let us call upon His Name.
Let the earth be glad and full;
>Let the heavens all proclaim.
Let the heathen now declare,
>That the Lord be lifted up.
Let the fields be full of joy;
>Let these joys o'er flow her cup.

Let the glory of the Lord,
>Through the earth be all proclaimed;
Let us give unto the Lord,
>All the glory due His Name.
Let us bring into His courts,
>All our offerings, purse and heart.
Let all seas with gladness roar,
>For the Lord His judgement starts.

Let the judgement now begin;
>Let His righteous voice now ring.
Let the courts be filled with truth;
>Let all saints and angels sing.
Let that song be new with gladness;
>Let us all the Lord address,
Let all worship rich in beauty;
>Let us worship in His rest.

Let the gods of all the nations,
>Know that God has made the earth;
Let all know that they are idols,
>With no values, with no worth.
Let all know the God of heaven,
>Is Creator, Lord, and King;
Let the universe in chorus,
>All vibrate with joy and sing.

Through My Life My Scrolls They Read

'Twas
Every road,
    Every river,
        Every line of contact,
Flows through the Control Room of my soul.

Every touch,
    Every smell,
        Every taste,
Must be pure and under strict control.

Should they sneak within my borders,
    Reach the inner self and thought,
        Should they catch me unconnected,
I must pay some heavy tolls.

Once inside they always linger,
    Once inside they're there for life,
        Once inside they leave their message .
Then through my life all read the scrolls.

October

October's Introduction and Aim

During the month of October, our focus will be on Song of Songs 7:1-13. This is another description of the bride-church described as she was after the Great Disappointment of October, 1844. Should the drama have the "right" or the "wherewithal" to describe the bride-church three times in three different stages of her history, then we as the virgins, the comely ones, should have the privilege of reviewing just who this bride-church is. It just might be that we do not look at this drama and this bride often enough; similarly, we should spend more time confronting the Bridegroom in our daily walk. We should therefore spend some thoughtful time with Him each and every day in some manner, so that when He speaks we recognize His voice.

As a teacher of young students and being a student myself, I am aware that we should review, review, review. There is danger of passing too rapidly from point to point. We should allow a period of rest to occur before presenting another discourse. That's where these pages come in, one per day (6T 56). Greater attention should be given to our past church history as well as Bible history, for we have nothing to fear for this coming future except as we forget how we have been led by a pillar of fire by night and a pillar of cloud by day, both beside the still waters and in green pastures.

Should you read something one day that you remember reading some days previous, I would be powerfully pleased. I would then know that you have indeed pondered the counsel and admonitions as grown to a fuller knowledge of who you are spiritually, as well as who this bride-church is denominationally. After all, review, review, review. God bless you on a daily basis this month of October.

It is a law of the mind that what we spend our time thinking and dreaming about has a tremendous effect upon our daily living, attitude, reactions. There are three areas that I would like for you to ponder as time permits; understand the symbolic meanings of "breasts," "my Beloved." These will be dealt with more fully on December 29, "Review of Reviews." Understand the confidence expressed in "I am his, he is mine."

October

Day 1	Beauty of Beauties	Song 7:1	329
Day 2	Shoe of Shoes	Song 7:1	330
Day 3	Jewel of Jewels	Song 7:1	331
Day 4	Cunning Workman of Cunning Workmen	Song 7:1	332
Day 5	Navel of Navels	Song 7:2	333
Day 6	Belly of Bellies #2	Song 7:2	334
Day 7	Breast of Breast #4	Song 7:3,7	335
Day 8	Neck of Necks #3	Song 7:4	336
Day 9	Eye of Eyes #3	Song 7:4	337
Day 10	Nose of Noses	Song 7:4	338
Day 11	Head of Heads #2	Song 7:5	339
Day 12	Hair of Hairs #2	Song 7:5	340
Day 13	Gallery of Galleries	Song 7:5	341
Day 14	Delight of Delights	Song 7:6	342
Day 15	Palm Tree of Palm Trees	Song 7:7	343
Day 16	Going Up of Going Ups	Song 7:8	344
Day 17	Shaking of Shakings	Song 7:8	345
Day 18	Smell of Smells #2	Song 7:8	346
Day 19	Roof of Roofs	Song 7:9	347
Day 20	Lips of Lips #3	Song 7:9	348
Day 21	Confidence of Confidences #3	Song 7:10	349
Day 22	Confidence of Confidences #4	Song 7:10	350
Day 23	Desire of Desires	Song 7:10	351
Day 24	Confidence of Confidences #5	Song 7:10	352
Day 25	Vineyard of Vineyards #2	Song 7:11-12	353
Day 26	Look of Looks #3	Song 7:12	354
Day 27	Tender Grapes of Tenders Grapes	Song 7:12	355
Day 28	Mandrake of Mandrakes	Song 7:13	356
Day 29	Gate of Gates	Song 7:13	357
Day 30	Beloved of Beloved #3	Song 7:13	358
Day 31	Summary	Song 7:1-13	359

Poem of the Month: "I Have Some Goals"   360

October 1   *Beauty of Beauties*   Song 7:1

Today's Thought: *"How beautiful are thy feet with shoes, O prince's daughter! the joints of thy thighs are like jewels, the work of the hands of a cunning workman."*

The progressive drama of the Song of Songs moves forward. Chapter 6-7 are one description of the true bride-church from 1844 to our day. Song 6:1 begins with a theological question: *"Wither [where] is thy beloved gone… whither is thy beloved turned aside?"* This question is addressed to "The Fairest Among Women" and none but the true bride can answer that question. In 1844, the beloved Jesus did not come to this earth as expected, but he turned aside and *"came with the clouds of heaven… to the Ancient of Days"* (Daniel 7:13) into the Most Holy place of the heavenly sanctuary to begin the work of the Investigative Judgment. Those who participated in the Great Advent Movement experienced the 1844 disappointment, searched the Scriptures afterward to find where he had *"turned aside,"* studied the prophetic symbolism of Scripture and particularly that of the sanctuary, answered that question. Those who can answer that question today are God's true bride-church, "The Fairest Among Women," and they are unique on earth today, known as the Seventh-day Adventist Church. In Song 6:2-3, the bride-church answers with confidence: *"My beloved is gone down into his garden."* In 4:12, the Bridegroom said, *"A garden… is… my spouse."* When she states that he's gone down into his garden, she expresses her knowledge that He is close beside her through the ministry of His Holy Spirit. Prophecy gives double reference to insure correct interpretation.

Putting it into modern English, one would say, "He is in the church in heaven, the mother church, the New Jerusalem, going over the church's membership list in the clerk's records to make up His jewels, to gather His lilies, to identify His chosen people." Why is He doing this? He needs to do this before He comes so that He can be prepared to reward every man according to his works, to call His own from the grave and from the earth to take them home.

Parting Gem: *It is important to make sure you are one of His jewels.*

OCTOBER 2 — *Shoe of Shoes* — Song 7:1

Today's Thought *"How beautiful are thy feet with shoes, O prince's daughter!"*

A portion of the armour of God is pictured here. Ephesians 6:10-17 describes that armour. Verse 15 states, *"And your feet shod with the preparation of the gospel of peace."* So, Friend Reader, are these shoes in our thought for today the gospel of peace?

In Isaiah 52:7, it states, *"How beautiful upon the mountains are the feet of him that bringeth good tidings, that publisheth peace; that bringeth forth tidings of good, that publisheth salvation; that saith unto Zion, Thy God reigneth!"*

After the 1844 disappointment of Revelation 10:9-10, the bride-church was to *"prophesy again"* of the Bridegroom's Second Coming Advent. Adventists were to take the message *"before many peoples, and nations, and tongues, and kings"* (Revelation 10:11). Seventh-day Adventists were to prophesy again *"the everlasting gospel... unto them that dwell on the earth, and to every nation, and kindred, and tongue, and people"* (Revelation 14:6). They were to announce that *"the hour of his judgment is come"* (Revelation 14:7) and to call all men to worship him that made heaven and earth and the sea, and the fountains of waters. This was all in accordance with Revelation 14:6-12. To *"worship him"* was to keep the seventh-day Sabbath as a memorial of his creative works. They were to take a balanced message of the law and the everlasting gospel to all the world. Thus in our drama, Song 7:1, the bride-church is described: *"How beautiful are thy feet with shoes, O prince's daughter!"*

Looking at Paul's words in Romans 10:15,18, we read, *"And how shall they preach, except they be sent? as it is written, How beautiful are the feet of them that preach the gospel of peace, and bring glad tidings of good things!... Yes verily, their sound went into all the earth, and their words unto the ends of the world."*

Parting Gem: *Every morning when you put your shoes on is an opportunity to dedicate and consecrate yourself and your day to that cunning Workman you have been introduced to.*

October 31 — *Jewel of Jewels* — Song 7:1

Today's Thought: *"How beautiful are thy feet with shoes, O prince's daughter! the joints of thy thighs are like jewels, the work of the hands of a cunning workman."*

One of the joyful truths Christians, especially Seventh-day Adventist Christians, need to really realize is just how much God loves them. I know we will study throughout eternity His great love and never fully understand it; however, He has not left us in the dark about His passion, eagerness, homesickness for us.

Take the parable starting in Matthew 13:45-46, *"Again, the kingdom of heaven is like unto a merchant man, seeking goodly pearls: who when he had found one pearl of great price, went and sold all that he had, and bought it."* WOW! Did you realize that the merchant *"sold all that he had, and bought it"*? He sold all that he had.

The Merchant Man, God the Father, loved the world so much that He sold all that He had to redeem it. He loved the world so much that He gave His only begotten Son that whosoever believeth on Him should not perish but have everlasting life. He saw in this world created beings that They, God the Father, God the Son, and God the Holy Ghost, together created, Jesus Christ the Son being the Active Agent.

One better than that, He saw one pearl of great price, YOU, then went and sold all that He had. He emptied heaven for your salvation, yes and mine, too. He gathered all of the galaxies, the heavens, the suns, moon, stars, the Unfallen created world, and the entire multiverse which is made up of thousands of Universes, and put them up for collateral for the safe return of His one fallen planet, solar system, for you and me. What a jewel, of great price it is added, you and I are.

If Christ saw nothing in us, He would not have spent time with us. We insult Him when we claim we are worthless and He foolish (7T 21).

Parting Gem: *"The Lord is disappointed when His people place a low estimate upon themselves. He desires His chosen heritage to value themselves according to the price He has placed upon them. God wanted them, else He would not have sent His Son on such an expensive errand to redeem them"* (DA 668).

OCTOBER 4 — Cunning Workman of Cunning Workmen — Song 7:1

Today's Thought: *"How beautiful are thy feet with shoes, O prince's daughter! the joints of thy thighs are like jewels, the work of the hands of a cunning workman."*

You, my bride-church, are the works of a cunning workman. Within this bride-church are the virgins that love Him, and who are fearfully and wonderfully made.

In Collins Paperback Thesaurus, it states that cunning is (1) craft, and (2) skilful. Under skilful, it lists adroit, deft, dexterous, imaginative, ingenious.[17]

In the SDA BC, it states that the KJV uses cunning in the archaic sense of skilful. Thus Hiram in 1 Kings 7:14 and 2 Chronicles 2:7,13 was a skilful workman. The curtains were to be skilfully worked into the curtains and veil of the temple (Exodus 26:1,31).

In the beginning, Genesis, the Creator formed man out of the dust of the ground and then gave to him the necessary power to breathe on his own and man became a living soul. It would be difficult to explain all of the intricacies in the actual process of the creation of man.

Besides being fearfully and wonderfully made, according to Psalms 139:14, Psalms 40:5 states, *"Many, O Lord my God, are thy wonderful works which thou hast made, and thy thoughts which are to us-ward: they cannot be reckoned up in order unto thee: if I would declare and speak of them, they are more than can be numbered."*

That principle is found in the last verse of John that *"there are also many other things which Jesus did, the which, if they should be written every one, I suppose that even the world itself could not contain the books that should be written. Amen"* (John 21:25).

When one wonders at the intricacies of the eye, ear, nose, nervous system, at the value of the thumb and forefinger, the reproductive system, or whatever other aspect of our bodies you would consider, one simply has to admit that we are the works of a cunning Workman. The bride-church is no different; it, too, is the work and management of that same cunning Workman.

Parting Gem: *An analysis of the church sees a cunning Workman.*

---

[17] *Collins Essential Canadian English Dictionary & Thesaurus* (Toronto, ON: Harper Collins), 2006, p. 159.

October 5 — Navel of Navels — Song 7:2

Today's Thought: *"Thy navel is like a round goblet, which wanteth not liquor: thy belly is like an heap of wheat set about with lilies."*

In the book of Job 40:16, speaking of a hippopotamus, it states, *"Lo now, his strength is in his loins, and his force is in the navel of his belly."*

Proverbs 3:6-8 says, *"In all thy ways acknowledge him, and he shall direct thy paths. Be not wise in thine own eyes: fear the Lord, and depart from evil. It shall be health to thy navel, and marrow to thy bones."*

Combining these two texts, we can conclude that to depart from evil will give us health and force.

Thy strength and thy power is compared to a goblet, a drinking cup that has no handles, and this cup doesn't need, desire, nor crave liquor.

The navel is the one mark which identifies a child as having come from the mother. As the veil of the bride is the identifying mark of the true bride, so the navel, the commonly known "belly button" is the mark of a person born of a woman. The navel of this bride-church identifies it as having *been "born" from* the true mother, *"Jerusalem… the mother of us all"* (Galatians 4:26).

The connecting link between the mother and the unborn child is the umbilical cord. When the cord has been cut and tied, then that end of the cord is called the navel, and the child becomes an entity of its own. So the church is an entity of its own.

The goblet does not want liquor, but it does need a relationship. A relationship with mother. Back in Song 1:2, we discovered that *"love is better than wine,"* so the church needs a relationship, a love relationship, for should the church not have love, Corinthians tells us it is like a sounding brass and a tinkling symbol (1 Corinthians 13:1).

Parting Gem: *Keep that relationship with the Lord Jesus Christ, keep that love flowing out so others can see that relationship in action. You may have to wrestle with this symbolism during your day, but chew well and digest it with the help and power of the Holy Spirit.*

October 6 — Belly of Bellies #2 — Song 7:2

Today's Thought: *"Thy navel is like a round goblet, which wanteth not liquor: thy belly is like an heap of wheat set about with lilies."*

That's quite a compliment to give to your lover, if one has the gallantry to give such a compliment without fear of repercussions. So, what does it mean? Remember, what you read in the symbolic is not meant to be taken in the literal.

This is still part of the parcel of the symbolic description of the church in the Laodicean period.

John 7:38 states, *"He that believeth on me, as the scripture hath said, out of his belly shall flow rivers of living water."* Christ was speaking of the Holy Spirit that would fall on them that believe. This same principle or promise can be applied to the bride-church, the Laodicean Church. She has the living waters to give to every one who is thirsty. Somewhat of an awesome responsibility. From this church flows streams of living waters.

The woman at the well in John was told, *"But whosoever drinketh of the water that I shall give him shall never thirst; but the water that I shall give him shall be in him [in his belly] a well of water springing up into everlasting life"* (John 4:14). Again, apply this to the church, for the church does have that living water that she receives from Christ. She does give it out to the thirsty ones and to these it becomes a well of water that bubbles up into everlasting life.

But this verse states that the belly is like a heap of wheat set about with lilies. The belly of the Beloved in Song 5:14 is like bright ivory overlaid with sapphires.

Lilies, we have found out, are symbolic of churches; wheat is symbolic of precious souls in the kingdom. The navel was the connecting link between mother and child. From this belly will flow streams of living waters so there is no need for heavy doctrine nor prophecies, as important as these may be; these come with the umbilical connection.

Parting Gem: *Spend some time, much time, on your knees as you wrestle with these prophetic symbolic expressions. They don't come easily. Enjoy the day that the Lord has given you.*

OCTOBER 7 *Breast of Breasts #4* Song 7:3,7

Today's Thought: *"Thy two breasts are like two young roes that are twins… and thy breasts to clusters of grapes."*

Here, Scripture goes at it again. Why? Could it be that the Bible, the Old Testament and the New Testament, the prophecies of Daniel and Revelation, are twins, are important, are upfront with this bride-church? Could it be that this bride-church, via this Song, wants the world and God's people to know that the Bible and the Bible only is the foundation of its purity, its chastity, its truthfulness, its doctrines? Could it be that the first thing that should be noticed about this bride-church is that very fact, that it bases its every doctrine upon the Word of God? This is upfront, balanced, appealing. Later, one will learn of the thorns of the rose and the sweet fragrance of the plants and spices, the great commission given, but to start, let's focus on the Word of God, symbolized by breasts. Could we get that important point?

Did you notice that this symbolism of the breasts starts with the sincere milk of the Word (1:13), progresses to the heavier meat of the Word (4:5; 7:3), then passes on to the real heavy prophecies of Daniel and Revelation (7:7)? Our trilogy of texts—Corinthians, Deuteronomy, and Romans—might just tell us that in discussion of heavenly things, start with the simple basics of the gospel, then progress into the Word.

Could it be that Adventists, who used to be "people of the Book," need to return to that Word, that Book, that sincere milk of the Word, the fundamental doctrines and the *"whatsoever I have commanded you"* (Matthew 28:20) and even a deeper insight into Daniel and its companion book Revelation? This is one major push that the servant of the Lord has stressed throughout her writings, even saying that had God's people been people of the Book and followed those "whatsoever things," there would not have been a need for the Testimonies.

Parting Gem: *It is powerfully important that one remember that this Song we are looking at is written in symbolic language, so what it says literally is not really what it means literally. So, with that said, is it not time we as God's people take time to squeeze these clusters of grapes so that we extract every drop of truth from Daniel, from Revelation?*

OCTOBER 8 — Neck of Necks #3 — Song 7:4

Today's Thought: *"Thy neck is as a tower of ivory;"*

In this description of the bride-church, her neck is *"as a tower of ivory."* In the first description (1:10), the neck is *"comely... with chains of gold."* In Song 4:4, our second description, her neck is *"like the tower of David builded for an armoury, whereon there hang a thousand bucklers, all shields of mighty men."*

We know that the neck is a symbol of strength, and this strength is found in all three descriptions of the church. The church down through the ages has always been a tower of strength for its believers. It has been a tower of beauty, as depicted by the gold and ivory, and of protection for those who run into it to be safe.

Consider the awesomeness of this church and of its value in any community, that it is a tower or fortress of strength and beauty. As we meet from week to week, and as we drive into the parking lot of our church, look at the church building as a Tower where we can hide, regroup, get instructions and encouragement to meet the next week.

As we found in 4:4, the Tower of David was where the shields of the mighty men were kept. These towers were used not only for lookouts, but as a vantage point to hurl missiles down to the enemy. Here it seems to be descriptive of the Throne Room of God, the place of commanding and giving instructions and orders for the people of God.

Notice that should we compare these verses, the neck is like the tower of David which seems to be like a tower of ivory. Ivory is indicative of royal palaces and kingly thrones. Here from the kingly thrones lies the strength needed for our daily needs.

One powerful method of gaining strength is found in Hebrews 10:24-25. *"And let us consider one another to provoke unto love and to good works; not forsaking the assembling of ourselves together, as the manner of some is; but exhorting one another: and so much the more, as ye see the day approaching."*

Parting Gem: *Repeating the Gem for June 9, we say that, "The church is a powerhouse of strength. It is a place of protection, activity, and warfare. It has the strength to do what it has to do."*

OCTOBER 9   *Eyes of Eyes #3*   Song 7:4

Today's Thought: *"Thy neck is as a tower of ivory; thine eyes like the fishpools in Heshbon, by the gate of Bathrabbim..."*

You know that eyes are organs of sight; we see using our eyes. Without eyes, we would be in the dark, literally, dependent on something else to get around. We would miss all of the colourful beauty of nature.

In both the first and the second description of the bride (1:5 and 4:1), these eyes are as the eyes of a dove, representing the Holy Spirit's presence. Notice, though, that in 4:9 there is only one eye that ravishes the Beloved's heart, as with one chain about the bride's neck. This, you will remember, is representative of only a partial presence of the Spirit and only partial awareness of the law. The Sabbath was yet to come.

Now in this Laodicean Church period, when this bride has a powerful connection to the Holy Spirit, so strong and so firm that it overcomes her Beloved, passes over the stage with terror to her enemies, glorious as the morning to her virgins, with a message clear and bright as the sun, while at the same time fair as the moon. What an awesome bride-church she is.

King Solomon may have used the town of Heshbon, as that location was strategically located on two hills of a plateau which gave an extensive view of the lower Jordan Valley. Our bride-church has an extensive view, not only of the valley but of the entire global mission before her. She takes the great commission powerfully serious and reaches out with the three angels' messages, the gospel commission of the seven wonders of the multiverse, the wonders of the life of Jesus.

Bathrabbim is the name of a gate of Heshbon of which nothing is known.

Parting Gem: *As you go about your joys and triumphs today, remember that God has a place for you in His workforce, and that He can and will use your eyes to search out His people not of this fold, so that they can be invited to join.."*

OCTOBER 10   *Nose of Noses*   Song 7:4

Today's Thought: *"Thy nose is as the tower of Lebanon which looketh toward Damascus."*

Let me start by asking, would you say this to your lover, "Your nose is like the Tower of Lebanon"? The reason I say this is that we need to understand that this is not about Solomon and his favourite wife, but about Jesus Christ, the Bridegroom, and His church down through the ages, or church history to our day. The language given in symbolical tones is difficult, even sensuous, unless properly decoded by Biblical cross-referencing.

The nose is where the breath goes in and out, from the outside air to the lungs and back; it is the organ needed for breathing.

The Tower of Lebanon is unknown to have existed but, according the SDA dictionary, as a poetic simile, it is possibly an imaginary structure, whose name suggests beauty, loftiness, prominence.

Now, why looking toward Damascus? The region around Damascus is watered by the Albani River, which branches widely just before it gets to the city. These waters make the city and its surroundings a large, fertile oasis on the edge of the desert, a circumstance that accounts for its importance, making it to the desert what a good port is to the sea. Important roadways lead from Damascus in every direction. Its position at the crossroads of the nations makes Damascus "the head of Syria" (SDA Dict. Damascus).

In Song 7:8, *"the smell of thy nose [is] like apples,"* Try giving that compliment to your lover! The nose is the organ of scent. With keenness of scent, one can have quick perception of evil and of good. Once one has devoured the grapes or prophecies, and eaten and drunk of the milk of the Word, then this perception of correct doctrine or heresy is detected by the nose, this organ of perception of right and wrong. Could it be time to return to being "People of the Book"?

Parting Gem: *"The scent thereof shall be as the wine of Lebanon"* (Hosea 14:7).

October 11 — Head of Heads #2 — Song 7:5

Today's Thought: *"Thine head upon thee is like Carmel, and the hair of thine head like purple; the king is held in the galleries."*

Inside of each head is a brain. This brain is the organ that controls the rest of the body from the thought to the action, from the feeling to the speech. Everything, somehow, is connected to the brain. Should there be no brain, nothing would operate. So this head, containing the brain, upon our bride is like Carmel. Now what is Carmel?

According to the SDA Bible Dictionary, Carmel is a garden or an orchard. On Mount Carmel were dwarf oaks, wild olive trees, and junipers. Many cisterns and wine and oil presses show its ancient fertility. A barren and sterile Carmel was therefore the sign of its greatest want and destruction. According to the SDA Bible Dictionary, Carmel means "garden" or "fruitful."

Our bride in our drama, therefore, is like a garden or an orchard filled with the good things found in an orchard, from the oil of the olive trees (Holy Spirit) to the wine of doctrines from the wine presses, from the living water in cisterns to the fruit within.

The brains within that head operate the entire "bride" or church. At the head of every organization there must be some sort of leadership. In the early 1900s, there was need for a reorganization of the church so that smoother workings could be carried on. This was needed due to the growth of the world field. Decisions took too long to go all the way from the mission field to the headquarters and back, so divisions were installed within the organization.

Other than Jesus Christ being the head of the church, which is an agreeable statement, what is the highest position or organization in the world? We give the title "First Lady of the land" to the wife of the President or Prime Minister, and the title of the office of government as the highest in the land. Yet, consider that the church is the highest organization in the world, the General Conference as the highest office, and the office of the Chief Executive Officer as the highest in the world. Remember, though, that Christ is the CEO.

Parting Gem: *This certainly may be a new thought, but move outside the box for today and chew on this gem.*

October 12 — *Hair of Hairs #2* — Song 7:5

Today's Thought: *"Thine head upon thee is like Carmel, and the hair of thine head like purple; the king is held in the galleries."*

To start with today, let us look at "purple." Any colour within a vaguely defined range of shades from violet to a deep-blue red, even ancient crimson, can be classified as "purple."

According to the SDA Bible Dictionary, purple has been the royal colour of antiquity from the Neo-Babylonian period, through those of Media and Persia, and even the Median kings. The purple (or scarlet) robe put on Jesus by the Romans was in mockery of His claim that He was a king. Then mystical Babylon the great is described as being clothed in purple. So purple is a royal colour.

1 Corinthians 11:15 tells us, *"But if a woman have long hair, it is a glory to her: for her hair is given to her for a covering."* This bride-church is a "woman" and her "hair" is given to her for a covering. This covering is like purple, royalty, glory. Now, what does that mean?

Our Beloved is the King of the Multiverse; therefore our church-bride is the Queen of the Multiverse. (Are we way outside of our box and comfort zone again?) Because our King is royalty, then that makes His bride royalty as well. She is entitled to many privileges not allotted to a commoner, a non-royal person. Just in passing, should the Bridegroom and His bride both be royalty, then that makes His sons and daughters royalty as well.

Without raising the goosebumps of the readers, could it be that some of the privileges entitled to the Queen of the Multiverse is for the members to dress for the occasion when visiting her, speak reverently and quietly within the church, and to remember that she is who she is, the bride of our Beloved.

Previously we read of her hair in Song 4:1, on June 3. There it was compared to a flock of goats that appeared from Mount Gilead. You just might like to reread June 3, "Hair of Hairs #1."

Parting Gem: *As you take up your duties today, think often about this woman with hair like purple, her position and status in the multiverse, and determine to be part of that experience.*

October 13 — Gallery of Galleries — Song 7:5

Today's Thought: *"Thine head upon thee is like Carmel, and the hair of thine head like purple; the king is held in the galleries."*

A gallery is a room or building for displaying works of art, a balcony in a church or a theatre, a long narrow room for a specific purpose. Our beloved King is in that gallery. His throne is high and lifted up, approachable to all mankind.

There is a song about our King in His gallery;

"Love is a flag flying high from the castle of my heart;
From the castle of my heart; from the castle of my heart.
Love is a flag flying high from the castle of my heart,
 Where the King is in residence there."

Stanza two speaks of, "Joy is a flag," while the third stanza three says, "Peace is a flag."

"The Lord is exalted; for he dwelleth on high: he hath filled Zion with judgment and righteousness" (Isaiah 33:5).

Habakkuk 2:20 puts it nicely. *"But the Lord is in his holy temple: let all the earth keep silence before him."* Oh, how profitable it would be for us to keep silence in the temple of our God and contemplate just where we are and Who we are with.

Yet, I could not pass the opportunity to invite each of you readers and listeners to open the gates of your gallery and enthrone this King there so as to take up permanent residence. Your heart and mind is the throne room where Christ would love to set up His throne, within you, your heart, your mind, your everyday activities.

Isaiah saw this great King, for he wrote about it: *"In the year that king Uzziah died I saw also the Lord sitting upon a throne, high and lifted up, and his train filled the temple"* (Isaiah 6:1).

Let's climax today with Revelation 4:2-3. *"And immediately I was in the spirit: and, behold, a throne was set in heaven, and one sat on the throne. And he that sat was to look upon like a jasper and a sardine stone: and there was a rainbow round about the throne, in sight like unto an emerald."* Awesome, awesome, awesome.

Parting Gem: *Love, Joy, Peace are flags flying high in the sky where my King is in residence there, in His galleries, high and lifted up.*

October 14 — Delight of Delights — Song 7:6

Today's Thought: *"How fair and how pleasant art thou, O love, for delights!"*

You may have noticed already that there are several points this drama is trying desperately hard to bring across. Should you not have noticed, let me tell you of one point.

"Behold, thou art fair, my love; behold, thou art fair... Behold, thou art fair, my beloved, yea, pleasant" (Song 1:15-16).

"Behold, thou art fair, my love; Behold, thou art fair" (Song 4:1).

"Thou art all fair, my love; there is no spot in thee" (Song 4:7).

"How fair is my love, my sister, my spouse! How much better is thy love than wine!" (Song 4:10)

"My dove, my undefiled is but one; she is the only one of her mother, she is the choice one of her that bare her" (Song 6:9).

"How fair and how pleasant art thou, O love, for delights!" (Song 7:6)

Six times, as above, the bride is described by her Beloved as fair, pleasant, undefiled, the one and only choice one. These do not include the other shorter descriptions, for there are many, many of those.

Remember this is Jesus Christ, the Bridegroom, talking to and about His bride, the church. What a lesson or example for us on how to talk about and treat the "First Lady of the Multiverse," the church.

We have mentioned several times, and it is good to repeat it, that the church is the one object upon earth in which the Lord takes special delight in bestowing His richest blessings. Should we not do the same?

The church is the jewel case in which the Lord keeps His precious people. If I can rephrase this idea, the church is the case where God keeps His precious gems, you and me. Just pause a moment and think on that thought. You and I, gems of precious value, encased in His jewel box. What an awesome thought. He jewel case is on display throughout the universes.

Parting Gem: *Would it help you today, as you go about your duties, to consider the fact that the unfallen worlds can look down on God's jewel case and see some of His precious gems like you and me?*

OCTOBER 15   *Palm Tree of Palm Trees*   Song 7:7

Today's Thought: *"This thy stature is like to a palm tree, and thy breasts to clusters of grapes."*

Scholars generally agree that the palm of the Scriptures is almost always the date palm, an upright, branchless tree, which held an important part in the economy and daily life of the peoples of Palestine. Under proper cultivation, this tree grows to a height of about sixty to eighty feet, and may live and produce until it is two hundred years old. Generally it yields fruit beginning at about its sixth year, attains maturity at thirty, and reaches its peak of productivity at the end of its first century. Its long feathery leaves (called branches in the Bible) die and drop down to the ground around the trunk as new leaves grow out, giving the tree a parasol appearance. The dates themselves grow in clusters weighing from thirty to fifty pounds, and constitute a major part of the diet among some Arab tribes. The seeds are ground up for animal feed. The giant leaves of the date palm, from six to ten feet long, serve many functions in the Palestinian economy—thatch, fencing, matting material, and decorations. The Arabs have a saying that there are as many uses for the date palm as there are days in the year. The tree grows both in the dense groves and by themselves, alone. Much of the Jordan Valley, from the shores of the Gennesaret to the end of the Dead Sea, may once have contained date palm groves, but now there are few of these trees in Palestine except along the maritime plain of Philistia and in the region around Jericho. The near extinction in Palestine of these graceful and important trees has been attributed to a neglect of their cultivation, for they still grow abundantly in other regions of the Near East.

On their flight from Egypt, the Israelites came upon a grove of seventy palm trees at Elim, and they later were instructed to use palm leaves in erecting their booths for the Feast of Tabernacles. Because the tree was so familiar to the Israelites, it was natural that it be employed in architectural design in Solomon's Temple, and in the temple of Ezekiel's vision. Jericho was called the "city of palm trees." According to the SDA Bible Dictionary, Palm fronds were used for various celebrations.

Parting Gem: *Find the similarities between the palm and the church.*

OCTOBER 16 — *Going Up of Going Ups* — Song 7:8

Today's Thought: *"I said, I will go up to the palm tree, I will take hold of the boughs thereof: now also thy breasts shall be as clusters of the vine, and the smell of thy nose like apples."*

In the Song of Songs 7:7, the church is likened to a palm tree. The Bridegroom warns them, saying, *"I will go up to the palm tree, I will take hold of the boughs thereof."* When one takes hold of the boughs at harvest time, it is usually to shake them.

Now, you ask yourself, is there any evidence in the Seventh-day Adventist Church that there has been a shaking taking place since 1844 to our own day?

"We are in a shaking time, the time when everything that can be shaken will be shaken" (CM 12).

Ask yourself one other question: Under such shaking, what will preserve the true church? The answer comes loud and clear. "Now also (in the shaking time) the Old and the New Testament will yield doctrines and safety for God's people. The Bible is the source of Truth and a sure foundation."[18]

"God's Spirit has illuminated every page of Holy Writ… When the shaking comes, by the introduction of false theories, these surface readers, anchored nowhere, are like shifting sand… Let there be light, yes, light, in your dwelling. For this we need to pray. The Holy Spirit, shining upon the sacred page, will open to our understanding, that we may know the truth…" (TM 112)

Yet we need to expect Satan to work within this bride-church. *Testimonies to Ministers* (p. 409/410) states, "Many will stand in our pulpits with the torch of false prophecy in their hands, kindled from the hellish torch of Satan." Remember reading that before?

Parting Gem: *"The conflict is to wax fiercer and fiercer. Satan will take the field and impersonate Christ. He will misrepresent, misapply, and pervert everything he possibly can, to deceive, if possible, the very elect"* (TM 411). The best is yet to come. Have an exciting and profitable day.

---

[18] Berry, Marion G. *The Prophetic Song of Songs, Quarterly* (Albia, IA: The Prophetic Song of Songs, Inc.), 1969, p. 79.

OCTOBER 17 — *Shaking of Shakings #2* — Song 7:8

Today's Thought: *"I said, I will go up to the palm tree, I will take hold of the boughs thereof: now also thy breasts shall be as clusters of the vine, and the smell of thy nose like apples."*

Again we find another indication that this song is prophetic in nature. Yet, once again, we repeat that one of the many points our song is trying to triumphantly get across is that the Bible and the Bible only, or as it was mentioned during Luther's days, *sola Scriptura*, is the theme, the flagship of Protestants. The Bible and the Bible only is the religion of Protestants.

We have looked at the sincere milk of the Word, which will help prevent us from being shaken out of the figurative palm tree. This is necessarily useful for new babes in the Christian walk, as well as more mature Christians. One never leaves the simple themes of God's Word.

As one grows, both physically and spiritually, one moves from the milk to the meat and potatoes. This meat has been looked at several times in the symbolism of the roes, the hinds, the young hart. One needs to feast and fellowship not only on the milk but on the stronger meat of the Word. This solidifies our connection, preventing a shaking out.

A babe needs only to suck to get the necessary nourishment prepared for him. One older needs to chew the meat to get its nourishment. However, one needs to squeeze the grapes to extract its juice.

The wine used in Scripture could be fermented, as when talking about the wine of Babylon, (Revelation 14:8; 18:3) or it could be unfermented, the pure juice of the grape, symbolic of the truth of Christ and His Word (Matthew 26:27- 29; Song 1:3).

A daily partaking of this wine of God's Word would build our spiritual strength, our spiritual connection with our Saviour, our foundation, our soul's anchor to the Rock of our salvation. This all in turn would prevent one from being shaken out of God's palm tree.

Parting Gem: *Today would be a great day for us to drink abundantly of the wine of God's Word, to rededicate our being to Him, to prepare and look for the coming of the Bridegroom.*

October 18 — Smell of Smells #2 — Song 7:8

Today's Thought: *"I said, I will go up to the palm tree, I will take hold of the boughs thereof: now also thy breasts shall be as clusters of the vine, and the smell of thy nose like apples."*

In Song 1:12, we read, *"While the king sitteth at his table, my spikenard sendeth forth the smell thereof."* Ever wonder what the smell of spikenard is like? That's the spikenard Mary poured over Jesus' feet. It's a powerful perfume used only for special occasions or for the very rich. It is usually kept sealed in alabaster boxes until needed.

In Song 4:11, it states, *"… and the smell of thy garments is like the smell of Lebanon."* Ever wonder what the smell of Lebanon was like? Lebanon is a fertile country once well-known for its cedars. There were also firs, cypresses, pines, and oaks. A large variety of nuts and fruit trees like almonds, mulberry, fig, olive, walnut, apricot, pear, pomegranate, and pistachio also grew there. At blossoming time, the aroma must have been profound.

Now here in Song 7:8, it says *"… and the smell of thy nose like apples."* Is this saying that the smell of your breath, what your nose smells, is the rich delectable smell like the sweet smell of ripened apples?

Yet, do not forget that what you read is not literally what is meant. Back in March, we read of the "Apple of Apples" and the "Apple Tree of Apple Trees."

These three different "smells" are in three different periods of time. The powerful smell of the expensive spikenard wafts through and engulfs the king at his table during the Dark Ages, emblematic of the sheer delight and joy for the King, the Beloved, as He contemplates His people and their conditions.

It was the smell of the spikenard that Mary poured over the feet of Jesus that drew some strong rebuke, as well as, from Jesus, some tremendous commendations and a prophecy.

Parting Gem: *As your wear the Robe of Christ's Righteousness today, may it breathe a breath of heavenly spiritual fresh air to those you come into contact with. Have a great day.*

October 19 — *Roof of Roofs* — Song 7:9

Today's Thought: *"And the roof of thy mouth like the best wine for my beloved, that goeth down sweetly, causing the lips of those that are asleep to speak."*

Let us consider what Job 29:10 states. *"The nobles held their peace, and their tongue cleaved to the roof of their mouth."* Is this saying that when one does not speak, it is the same as having the tongue cleaved or stuck to the roof of the mouth? What an awesome thought.

Consider Psalm 137:6. *"If I do not remember thee, let my tongue cleave to the roof of my mouth."*

It is very plain in Ezekiel 3:26. *"And I will make thy tongue cleave to the roof of thy mouth, that thou shalt be dumb, and shalt not be unto them a reprover…"*

A similar idea is expressed in Mark 7:35. *"And straightway his ears were opened, and the string of his tongue was loosed, and he spake plain."*

So then when the tongue does not cleave to the roof of the mouth, then that person's tongue is loosed and he can speak.

Now this roof of the mouth of our bride is like the best wine, say like the wine of wines, which causes those dead in sin to repent and live. Another awesome thought.

What is the best of wines? Remembering this is symbolic, the roof of the mouth has the best prophecies possible to get. Could it be the prophecy that Jesus Christ, the Bridegroom of our drama, is soon to come and claim His bride? This whole drama is about the Bridegroom and His coming. It is about His bride, the church down through the years and her relationship to Him, coupled with her hungering passion for Him to come and claim her as His rightful bride, not to mention His hungering passion to be with His people.

She has stated that several times, "I am his and he is mine, his passion is for me," and we looked at the passion of the Bridegroom, His hungering, longing desire to be with His people so that *"where I am, there ye may be also"* (John 14:3).

Parting Gem: *Look for opportunities today, as you do your things, where the roof of your mouth may present some of this best of wines.*

OCTOBER 20 — Lips of Lips #3 — Song 7:9

Today's Thought: *"And the roof of thy mouth like the best wine for my beloved, that goeth down sweetly, causing the lips of those that are asleep to speak."*

The description of the churches down through the years has mentioned lips before. Song 1:1 implies the use of lips when the bride remembers the kisses of the mouth, depicting a reconciliation.

On June 6 and 25 (Song 4:3,11), we considered the lips as a thread of scarlet and a liberal portion of honey. This thread is woven into all of the words of the mouth. It has been said that if there is one doctrine that does not have this scarlet thread, of Christ-centeredness, then that doctrine should be discarded. Christ must be in every doctrine of this bride-church. This portion was a large portion, this 2,300 day-prophecy, that it is portrayed as dripping from the mouth. It was a sweet-smelling, or a sweet taste like honey in Revelation 10. The soon-coming of Jesus, the Bridegroom, on October 22, 1844, was the main topic or item on the menu, and the one and only topic worth discussing.

Can you picture the eater licking his lips of the honey to get all of it? So the people ate up this soon-coming Saviour idea.

On August 19 (Song 5:13), we considered the lips as lilies, or churches, dropping sweet-smelling myrrh, a message of the seven wonders of salvation, the Plan of Salvation, bringing hope, courage, salvation to those that hear and respond.

Now today, the wine of prophecy causes those who are asleep in sin, dead as it were, to awaken and speak praises to Jehovah-God. Usually, evangelists start with Daniel 2 to start their evangelistic programs. The reason is so that the people can see the accuracy of the Bible and of Bible prophecy, and thus have their faith and confidence strengthened.

Parting Gem: *May the words of our mouth and the meditations of our hearts be acceptable to our God in His sight and may He, today, add to us blessing unspeakable.*

OCTOBER 21   *Confidence of Confidences #3*   Song 7:10

Today's Thought: *"I am my beloved's, and his desire is toward me."*

One gem prominent within this drama is the assurance, the confidence, the awareness of just who this bride-church is and, more importantly, just who her Beloved is.

In teaching school, there have been times when a student will say that he or she must find themselves, find their identity, find out just who they are, why they are here and where they are going. Not so with this bride-church; she knows without any question just who she is and who her Beloved is. She knows.

Looking back, for sake of review, into the discouraging circumstances of the Roman counter-reformation and the realization of a long wait until the return of the Bridegroom, our bride-church's confidence is revealed in 2:16—*My beloved is mine, and I am his."*

A second flashback into the discouraging aftermath of the Great Disappointment, her confidence oozes gloriously—*"I am my beloved, and my beloved is mine"* (Song 6:3).

Now in 7:10, under the extended delay of the coming of the Bridegroom over the past one hundred sixty plus years, her confidence is still as strong as when in the wilderness, or maybe even more so—*"I am my beloved's, and his desire is toward me."*

Yet in each historical period over these last one hundred sixty plus years, the true bride has recognize her identity as THE ONE AND ONLY, THE CHOICE ONE, and she has done her work in an appropriate manner to make ready for His coming.

From the comforting words, *"Come unto me"* to the more active words, *"Go ye therefore into [all the world]"* (Matthew 22:9), you can realize that you are not only a child of the King as you have come to Him, but that you are an ambassador of heaven to Planet Earth as you go into all of your world.

Parting Gem: *After reading of the confidence and the assurance of our bride in our drama, can you say that your confidence is as strong or stronger than when you first believed? As you go about your joys and excitements today, consider your value in the eyes of your Beloved and His hungering desire to be with you. See you tomorrow.*

OCTOBER 22 — *Confidence of Confidences #4* — Song 7:10

Today's Thought: *"I am my beloved's, and his desire is toward me."*

Let us look at this idea again, for it is important, as well as exciting and confidence building. I am His; He is mine. Now, the Song of Songs is not the only place where this gem of confidence is put.

Look at Revelation 21:7. *"He that overcometh shall inherit all things; and I will be his God, and he shall be my son."* He shall be our God; we shall be His son or His daughter. What an awesome thought to grab your attention today. Remember it. That's what the New Testament states.

Look into the Old Testament, in Zechariah 8:8. *"And I shall bring them, and they shall dwell in the midst of Jerusalem: and they shall be my people, and I will be their God, in truth and in righteousness."*

Have you ever watched the sunrise, even on a cloudy day? It gradually breaks forth over the earth bringing in a new day, burning off that fog. It grows stronger and warmer, constantly increasing in light until we have the full glory of the day. This breaking forth of the morning is an excellent illustration of what God wants to do for us in the perfecting of our Christian character and experience.

Look at Jeremiah 31:1, where it says, *"At the same time, saith the Lord, will I be the God of all the families of Israel, and they shall be my people."*

Go down a few verses, *"But this shall be the covenant that I will make with the house of Israel; After those days, saith the Lord, I will put my law in their inward parts, and write it in their hearts; and will be their God, and they shall be my people"* (Jeremiah 31:33).

Don't forget John 14:1-3. *"Let not your heart be troubled; ye believe in God, believe also in me. In my Father's house are many mansions: if it were not so, I would have told you. I go to prepare a place for you. And if I go and prepare a place for you, I will come again and receive you unto myself; that where I am, there ye may be also."*

Parting Gem: *As you go about your exciting journey today, consider that God has a longing, a burning hunger, a strong passion, and that is expressed in these verses. He says, "I want to be with you, and I died so that you and I can be together throughout eternity."*

OCTOBER 23   *Desire of Desires*   Song 7:10

Today's Thought: *"I am my beloved's, and his desire is toward me."*

Once again, we repeat that what you read figuratively is not what you understand literally. For here is one of those sneaky areas that could be taken sensuously; His desire is towards me—His church, His bride. So what is His desire?

Exodus 25:8 sums it all up so nicely. *"And let them make me a sanctuary; that I may dwell among them."* There it is in thirteen simple words. His passion, His hunger, His longing, His craving, passionate desire, is to be with His people. Is that not what the Plan of Salvation is all about? Is that not the one reason why God gave His only Son to go through some thirty-three and a half years of torture, humiliation, rejection, abuse, then finally death by crucifixion, so that His people could be with Him, with Them?

Stop and pause for just a minute. Is there any other reason why the Trinity got involved in Planet Earth and the Plan of Salvation, than to work out Their plan so that They could be together with Their people?

Isaiah 53:11 says, *"He shall see of the travail of his soul, and shall be satisfied."* He shall be satisfied for several reasons that you might wish to enumerate. The one I like the most is that He shall have you and me with Him. He shall be satisfied because He has you there. Don't disappoint Him after He went through so much in those thirty-three and a half years just so that you could live eternally with all of the benefits of being His son or daughter.

God has a strong desire to be our God and that we be His people; yet is that strong desire of any substance if we are always apart?

You should have felt the same passion, hunger, desire, longing (call it what you wish) in the bride's constant remarks, "I am his and he is mine. My Beloved is mine and I am his."

Parting Gem: *There is nothing embarrassing, or even sensuous, about this book. It is simply my Beloved's deep and passionate desire to be with His people that He redeemed at such an exorbitant price. He wishes to inform you of His great love, and His homesickness for His people. He wants them, you and me, to come home.*

OCTOBER 24   *Confidence of Confidences #5*   Song 7:10

Today's Thought: *"I am my beloved's, and his desire is toward me."*

Permit me one more day on this topic, for it is important. His longing desire is to be with His people. In John 14:2-3, it says, *"I go to prepare a place for you. And if I go and prepare a place for you, I will come again, and receive you unto myself; that where I am, there ye may be also."* That's one of His desires, and it just may be His greatest desire, but there is more, much more. We don't have to wait for heaven.

In John 10:10, *"The thief cometh not, but for to steal, and to kill, and to destroy: I am come that they might have life, and that they might have it more abundantly."* This more abundant life is in the here and the now.

You have heard, I'm sure, that, "Higher than the highest human thought can reach is God's ideal for His people. Godliness—Godlikeness—is the goal to be reached" (Ed. 18/19; MYP 40). What a desire to have.

There is a long paragraph in *In Heavenly Places* that states, among many other things, "Everyone who believes on Christ, everyone who believes on the keeping power of a risen Saviour that has suffered the penalty pronounced upon the transgressor, everyone who resists temptation and in the midst of evil copies the pattern given in the Christ life, will through faith in the atoning sacrifice of Christ become a partaker of the divine nature, having escaped the corruption that is in the world through lust. Everyone who by faith obeys God's commandments will reach the condition of sinlessness in which Adam lived before his transgression" (IHP 146). Talk about desires and ideals.

There's one in *The Upward Look* (p. 303) for October 16, that reads, "Christ took humanity and bore the hatred of the world that He might show men and women that they could live without sin, that their words, their actions, their spirit, might be sanctified to God. We can be perfect Christians if we will manifest this power in our lives."

Parting Gem: *According to Matthew 22:29, we "err, not knowing the scriptures, nor the power of God." Could I add that we err not really knowing nor understanding the lies and deceptive accusation Lucifer made against our Beloved Jesus. Contemplate today the power and the victories Christ gave to you at the cross.*

OCTOBER 25 — *Vineyard of Vineyards #2* — Song 7:11-12

Today's Thought: *"Come, my beloved, let us go forth into the field; let us lodge in the villages. Let us get up early to the vineyards; let us see if the vine flourish, whether the tender grape appear, and the pomegranates bud forth: there will I give thee my loves."*

Early in our drama, this bride-church declared: *"My mother's children were angry with me; they made me the keeper of the vineyards; but mine own vineyard have I not kept"* (Song 1:6)

In Matthew 20 is Christ's parable of the one who went out to get help to work in his vineyard. So the vineyard represents the world field of where the harvest is. This bride says to her Lover, *"Let us get up early to the vineyards."* Let us take a tour of the world mission stations to see how the missionaries are succeeding or failing.

She wants to see how the work is progressing, for the work is progressing. She wants to check the vines as well as to see if there are grapes, tender grapes, new converts, new believers. Remember back in Song 2:13, when the tender grapes gave a good smell? That was in the wilderness experience. She wants to check out the pomegranates to see if knowledge is being improved and increased. She wishes to check on the advancement, not only of the church as a body but of individuals. Are the members growing in wisdom and understanding? More importantly, are they applying to their personal lives the information they have processed?

Yet, it is in the vineyard that the bride will give to her Beloved her love. What is her love? In John 15:9-10, it says, *"As the Father hath loved me, so have I loved you: continue ye in my love. If ye keep my commandments, ye shall abide in my love; even as I have kept my Father's commandments, and abide in his love."*

Parting Gem; *Is there anything else besides love that the Bridegroom wishes to receive from His people? If we give Him our love, like in 2 Corinthians 13, then He gets everything we have. As you journey through this day, stop now and again, like Enoch did, and lift your prayer to Him in thanksgiving, praise, intercession, requests, confession. Have another great day. The Lord has given you this day.*

October 26 — Look of Looks #3 — Song 7:12

Today's Thought: *"Let us get up early to the vineyards; let us see if the vines flourish, whether the tender grape appear, and the pomegranates bud forth: there will I give thee my loves."*

This is the fifth time we have met the pomegranates, there is one more time to come. As well, this is another place where the sensual could take over. Should one be looking for the sensual, they could grab onto the phrase, *"there will I give thee my loves."* So, what's the meaning?

You should remember 7:10, where *"his desire is toward me."* That was the great desire, longing of the Bridegroom to be with His people. Now the bride is saying to her Beloved, "I wish to give to You all the people that have accepted You through the great gospel commission. That will be my love-gift to You. As well, my love for You is what you wish for me to give to You, so I will willingly, eagerly, without reserve give to You my undying and unbroken love."

For those of you who have the 3ABN, LLBN, and Hope Channel networks, you see many times the work going forward. Maranatha Mission Outreach is full of exciting stories; the health programs, the cooking programs, the conversion interviews, the preaching of the Word which are powerful, dynamic, enlightening, are being broadcast around the globe and into every home and corner. Knowledge is being increased, running to and fro across the nations, a sure sign of the times in which we live.

It seems new programs, new ministries, new outreaches are coming on a regular and timely basis. Frontier Missions, as well as the regular mission, the English Language Schools are making their mark in the world mission program. Can you see, as you look across the church's landscape, the tremendous growth taking place?

Parting Gem: *Today, take a good look at your church, at its progress, outreach, and give of yourself to help the area where you live to become aware that soon the skies are going to burst into rapturous flames and thunderous trumpeting to announce a special event. Have another great day.*

OCTOBER 27 — *Tender Grapes of Tender Grapes* — Song 7:12

Today's Thought: *"Let us get up early to the vineyards; let us see if the vines flourish, whether the tender grape appear, and the pomegranates bud forth: there will I give thee my loves."*

We have met tender grapes before. The Reformation had begun by Song 2:13, and the vines with the tender grapes gave a pleasant smell. That was on April 6-9, when the saints were counselled to *"Rise up, my fair one, and come away"* (Song 2:10).

Then on April 8, we read where William Tyndale grieved that he no sooner got one flock settled than the foxes would destroy the one he had previously set up. *"Oh, what are we to do?"* was his cry (GC 246).

The vineyard is to produce grapes. The foxes of Rome tried, though unsuccessfully, to uproot and destroy the vines themselves so that the vines could not produce fruit, the grapes, meaning if they could destroy, kill, eradicate, do away with the Christians in one way or another, then these Christians deleted from active service could not win more souls for the kingdom. Make sense?

Consider Isaiah's words in Isaiah 27:2-3,6. *"In that day sing ye unto her, A vineyard of red wine. I the Lord do keep it; I will water it every moment: lest any hurt it, I will keep it night and day... Israel shall blossom and bud, and fill the face of the world with fruit."* Feel free to claim that promise today.

New converts to the Christian community, symbolized by tender grapes, are very vulnerable to Satan's attacks. It has been stated that a new convert must know a specific number of the church members, on a first name basis, within six months or that new grape is gone.

So, here the bride wants to go with her Beloved to see if the new converts are appearing.

Parting Gem: *We are all tender, subject to like passions, temptations, and maybe even failure, so it is good advice to talk positively and encourage fellow journeyers on the way to the kingdom. Try it today and see what happens.*

OCTOBER 28 — *Mandrake of Mandrakes* — Song 7:13

Today's Thought: *"The mandrakes give a smell, and at our gates are all manner of pleasant fruits, new and old, which I have laid up for thee, O my beloved."*

Mandrakes are an herb of the belladonna family, bearing an odoriferous apple-like or tomato-like fruit. Ancients believed the mandrake possessed qualities that would stimulate sensual desire and encourage fertility. It does produce a narcotic effect, and is known to have been used medicinally in former times. The supposed sexual, fertility value is implied in the Biblical usage (SDA BC Mandrake).

According to Genesis 30:14-16, Rachael, Jacob's favourite wife, gave up her night with Jacob so that Reuben's mandrakes could be given to her. She in turn was hoping these mandrakes, these love-apples or love-tomatoes, would fertilize her womb and she would conceive.

The smell of mandrakes, the smell of fertility, the smell of new growth, the smell of new converts and former members returning is in the air. Does that sound feasible?

One needs only to listen to the Hope Channel, Loma Linda Broadcasting Network (LLBN), to 3ABN, and listen to such programs as Adventist World Radio or Maranatha International to realize that in the air is this saturation of mission emphases, that this gospel is going to all the world, that the Spirit of the Living God is active in His work.

As we see the baptisms taking place, it would almost seem that people are banging on the door, or the gates, according to the next phrase, to get into this church, this Tower of strength and protection, this ark of Noah's or this apartment of Rahab. But then again, one needs to consider the alternatives.

When you hear the stories of a huge shining person coming into a village carrying a radio, then showing the chief how to tune into AWR, which is just next to CBS, then disappearing into "thin air", and hearing next that thousands of villages have met the same huge, shining man, then one realizes that the mandrakes are powerfully at work.

Parting Gem: *May God's blessing rest upon you and yours as you go about yours joys and perplexities this day. His strength is yours.*

OCTOBER 29 — *Gate of Gates* — Song 7:13

Today's Thought: *"The mandrakes give a smell, and at our gates are all manner of pleasant fruits, new and old, which I have laid up for thee, O my beloved."*

Remember reading about Jacob as he flees from his twin brother, Esau? He had a dream and when he awoke he declared in Genesis 28:17, *"And he was afraid and said, How dreadful is this place! this is none other than the house of God, and this is the gate of heaven."*

Look through a concordance of the Bible under "gates" and one certainly gets the idea that gates are places to enter through or into a place. So remembering that this book is prophetic and symbolic, at the gates of the church, in front of the church, at the door of the church, just waiting to be allowed in to the church, are all manner of pleasant fruit. There are all manner of nations, of kindreds, of tongues, of peoples at the church door, at the gate of heaven.

Notice the words "pleasant" and "all manner." One should look at all of these nations, peoples, tongues as being powerfully pleasant to the Lord, and they should be to us. It is exciting to hear of the progress that is being made in the black communities, as well as the East Indians, Chinese, Japanese, South Americans, Europeans from the different countries or nations. It is exciting. It just may be more exciting if more North Americans were involved.

This fruit at the church doors is both new and old. New converts, brand new ones, will enter those gates, as well as former church members who have slipped out of contact with the family of God. They, too, will be at the gate of heaven waiting to get in. So Mom, Dad, Sister, Brother, do not give up hope. Take this verse as a promise and lay it out before the Lord and "demand" an answer.

The bride, the church, will take great pleasure in presenting those precious gems or that delicious fruit to her Bridegroom, her Beloved.

Parting Gem: *What a thought! What a promise our text has given to us today. Fruit, both brand new converts as well as former members, reclaimed for the kingdom of God. As you go about your excitement today, present to your God the names of your significant others.*

October 30 — Beloved of Beloved #3 — Song 7:13

Today's Thought: *"The mandrakes give a smell, and at our gates are all manner of pleasant fruits, new and old, which I have laid up for thee, O my beloved."*

Permit me to end October with an emphasis on *"O my beloved."* This phrase brings to my attention a statement to the effect that we should spend a thoughtful hour each day contemplating the life of Christ, the *"O my Beloved"* in our lives. Spend time on the closing scenes. Consider just what He was willing to do to get you and me into the Kingdom of Heaven, into eternity (DA 83. 4T 374).

Read the Gospels to see just how magnetic Christ must have been. It seems that no matter where Christ went, or even when, a crowd was always following Him. He had such a magnetic character or personality that He drew men and women, especially children to Him. All I can say to that is, *"O my Beloved."*

John 12:32 tells us *"And I, if I be lifted up from the earth, will draw all men unto me."* That's also what Christ said to Nicodemus in the night interview: *"And as Moses lifted up the serpent in the wilderness, even so must the Son of man be lifted up, that whosoever believeth in him should not perish, but have eternal life"* (John 3:14-15).

I can see—I seem to be able to hear them as well—Adam and Eve on that special day when God presented Eve to Adam. There is Adam, just stunned to such an extent that all he could say was, "O my Lord, my Creator, my God, what have you given to me? Thank you."

The last verse of John implies that there many other things which Jesus did, that should all be written down, the sky would not be a big enough scroll, not the ocean ink enough to use. That is my Beloved.

Parting Gem: *There is verse in Isaiah 64:4, stating, "For since the beginning of the world men have not heard, nor perceived by the ear, neither hath the eye seen, O God, beside thee, what he hath prepared for him that waiteth for him." So, because this is true, I challenge you today to meditate, contemplate, even speculate on what your Beloved is like, what He has in store for you, and all of the good things He will restore in and for you.*

OCTOBER 31　　　　　　　*Summary*　　　　　　　Song 7:1-13

Did you get some ideas this month that the Beloved Bridegroom, Jesus Christ, has a hungering passion to be with His people? Did you get that idea? Cultivate that hungering passion in your own life today.

Also, did you notice that the description of this bride-church in this last day period has many more adjectives than the first church in the wilderness? Count the descriptive adjectives in the church in the wilderness and you'll find four: cheeks, neck, eyes, smell; but in this last-day church, there are over twenty. They may not all be definitively understood, but that will come as the scroll unrolls. That's a promise. The only one found in the wilderness church and no other church is that of the "cheeks," symbolic of the persecution they endured.

Song 6-7 together make up a description of the last-day church, the Seventh-day Adventist Church.

On two occasions, the poet forces his idea that this bride-church has the Bible and the Bible only as its flagship It stresses, as it does in the other two descriptions, that the neck, symbolic of strength, is as a tower. Remember that inside these towers are shields, swords, battering rams, all equipment needed to battle the enemy and smash down the false ideas the enemy has.

In my Grade 12 Bible book, *Principles of Life*, is a picture of a Bible, on end, solidified in Rock. The people on top of this Bible, labelled "The Remnant Church," are hurling rocks down on the infidels and forces of evil. These rocks are labelled, "'Thus saith the Lord,' It Is Written." That's the picture given in this month's readings.[19]

The confidence this bride-church has been strongly presented, just like before, although now she stresses that her Beloved has a hungering passion to be with His people, you and me. How is your passion for Him to come in the clouds, or do you have things to do, places to go, people to meet, before you wish Him to come? That's not the case with our bride or Beloved.

---

[19] *Principles of Life*. Department of Education, General Conference of Seventh-day Adventists. (Mountain View, CA: Pacific Press), p. 17.

I Have Some Goals

I have some goals that I must reach,
    I wish my Lord each day to seek.
To spend much time with Him in prayer,
    To go with Him just everywhere.

To walk and talk, to stop and plan,
    To go together hand in hand
If there be places He won't go,
    It's no big deal, He'll tell me so.

Then I can change my plans and be
    With Him through out eternity.
What an awesome, solemn, simple thought
    To know through life what God hath wrought.

November

November's Introduction and Aim

Here it is, November already. I trust your heart has been burning within you as you have walked with my Beloved. Before us this month, we look at Song of Songs 8:1-7 covering Act 3, Scenes 1-4. Your assignment for November is to read Song of Songs 8:1-7 several times throughout the month. As well, *The Great Controversy*, Chapters 36-40 are covered during November.

The year 1844 was an important date, because it was the beginning of the Investigative Judgment; but now more than a century later, this generation must focus on the ending or "closing up" of the Investigative Judgment, which involves the Investigative Judgment of the living.

To proclaim the closing up of the judgment prematurely is error. To wait too long is fatal! "Present Truth" must be given at the correct time. Man in his own wisdom cannot know the right time. How then can it be discerned? Correct timing is arranged by God Himself, through the opening up of prophetic Scripture which pertains to the subject at hand. The opening up of the Song of Songs is evidence that the time has come, because it traces the prophetic lines of church history in the past, brings us to the present at the very point in the chapter which deals with the closing up of the judgment and the sealing of God's people.

"Perhaps one of the most conspicuous lessons of all prophetic testimony through the years is contemporary recognition, or interpretation, of each major epoch or event in the prophetic outline at the very time of fulfillment—the announcement of contemporary fulfillment--repeats itself again and again. This is the clear testimony of the early centuries" (The Prophetic Faith of Our Fathers. Vo. 1. P.890).

The fact that our drama has remained an enigma for nearly three thousand years, yet has just opened to our understanding today—and the fact that the drama is about the coming of the Bridegroom, and the fact that we can trace the drama right up to Song 8:5—reveals the fact that we are on the verge of a turning point in history. We are coming powerfully close to the long expected advent of the Bridegroom and those events which immediately precede it.

P.S. Be sure to read the poem at the end of November.

November

Day 1	Lament of Laments	Song 8:1	365
Day 2	Breast of Breasts #5	Song 8:1	366
Day 3	Nakedness of Nakedness	Song 8:1	367
Day 4	Mother's House of Mothers' Houses	Song 8:2	368
Day 5	Spiced Wine of Spiced Wines	Song 8:2	369
Day 6	Pomegranate of Pomegranates	Song 8:2	370
Day 7	Instruction of Instructions	Song 8:2	371
Day 8	Support of Supports #2	Song 8:3	372
Day 9	Embrace of Embraces #3	Song 8:3	373
Day 10	Charge of Charges #7	Song 8:4	374
Day 11	Coming Out of Comings Outs	Song 8:5	375
Day 12	Leaning of Leanings	Song 8:5	376
Day 13	Rearing of Rearings	Song 8:5	377
Day 14	Order of Orders	Song 8:5	378
Day 15	Stage Setting of Stage Settings	Song 8:5	379
Day 16	Closure of Closures	Revelation 3:18	380
Day 17	Synopsis of Synopses	Song 8:5	381
Day 18	Refreshing of Refreshings	Song 8:6	382
Day 19	Test of Tests	Song 8:6	383
Day 20	Seal of Seals	Song 8:6	384
Day 21	Heart of Hearts	Song 8:6	385
Day 22	Arm of Arms	Song 8:6-7	386
Day 23	Amnesia of Amnesias	2 Timothy 5:24	387
Day 24	Terribleness of Terribleness	Song 8:6	388
Day 25	Blotting Out of Blotting Outs	Song 8:6	389
Day 26	Forehead of Foreheads	Song 8:6	390
Day 27	Wafting of Waftings	Song 8:6	391
Day 28	Flood of Floods	Song 8:7	392
Day 29	Condemned of Condemned	Song 8:7	393
Day 30	Summary	Song 8:1-7	394

Poem of the Month: "Have We Crossed the Bridge?"   395

NOVEMBER 1 — *Lament of Laments* — Song 8:1

Today's Thought: *"O that thou wert as my brother, that sucked the breasts of my mother! when I should find thee without, I would kiss thee; yea, I should not be despised."*

Our bride sees herself as despised by the Bridegroom. She expresses her grief and her distress over their relationship, crying out, *"O that thou wert as my brother, that sucked the breasts of my mother!"*

In the Laodicean message of Revelation 3, the true church is given a picture of herself as being despised.

Revelation 3:14-17 says, *"And unto the angel of the church of the Laodiceans write… I know thy works, that thou art neither cold nor hot: I would that thou wert cold or hot. So then because thou art lukewarm, and neither cold nor hot, I will spue thee out of my mouth. Because thou sayest, I am rich, and increased with goods, and have need of nothing; and knowest not that thou art wretched, and miserable [despised], and poor, and blind, and naked."*

So, what really is wrong with the bride? What troubles her? She is wretched, not able to go to the marriage. She is miserable, not knowing how to get ready for the marriage. She is poor, not able to get the wedding garment. She is blind, not able to see advancing light to get ready. She is naked, not wearing the necessary wedding garment.

It is this Song which heralds the closing up of the Investigative Judgment which began in 1844. This Song must be opened up to God's people just before the close of probation and it, together with other portions of prophecy, prepares them for the final test and judgment. The bride needs to take definite action.

Parting Gem: *Present Truth does not come from new sources. It is derived from expositions of the Word of God and from the Spirit of Prophecy, explanations of the closing up of the judgment which are not presently understood. The Holy Spirit is to reveal and bring to mind those things which have been studied and learned. Let us give Him something from which to draw so that in our time of need for His help, He can reach in and draw out.*

NOVEMBER 2 — *Breast of Breasts #5* — Song 8:1

Today's Thought: *"O that thou wert as my brother, that sucked the breasts of my mother!"*

Chapter 8 of this Song of Songs presents an outline to prepare the bride-church for the marriage, the Investigative Judgment of the living and the coming of the Bridegroom. It reveals how she may put on the wedding garment of *"THE LORD OUR RIGHTEOUSNESS"* (Jeremiah 23:6).

Remember, the bride represents the corporate church. Not only is there an enigma regarding the condition in which the individual Christian must prepare for the judgment of the living, but an even greater puzzle is how the corporate body will all be prepared at the same time.

The "mother" represents the universal church of all ages. Her house is the "House of Present Truth," advancing the light for each specific age. The bride declares that this mother would *"instruct me."*

For decades, the church has been grappling to clarify the exact meaning of justification, sanctification, the nature of man and of God, perfection and how it applies to those sealed—in their sinful nature or in a state of perfection?

What is the exact work to accomplish under the latter rain? How will God's people live through the seven last plagues without a Mediator? Will the saints ever get to live without sinning? What will the Investigative Judgment do for the living?

As the bride advances towards the marriage of the living, she is entering a new era in the history of the church. She must enter into the House of Present Truth to comprehend the message in this Song, which is the song about the marriage. It is this very Song which will prepare her for the marriage and the coming of the Bridegroom. It is this Song which will enable her to give the loud cry: *"Behold, the bridegroom cometh; go ye out to meet him"* (Matthew 25:6).

Parting Gem: *One has said that Sanctification is the work of a lifetime done on a day-by-day basis, whereas Justification is the work of a moment done moment by moment throughout the entire lifetime. Those are terrific definitions to remember.*

NOVEMBER 3 — *Nakedness of Nakedness* — Song 8:1

Today's Thought: *"I would kiss thee; yea, I should not be despised."*

"*I counsel thee to buy of me gold tried in the fire, that thou mayest be rich; and white raiment, that thou mayest be clothed, and that the shame of thy nakedness do not appear; and anoint thine eyes with eyesalve, that thou mayest see*" (Revelation 3:18).

Although the bride in our drama is lukewarm, lacking awareness, feeling and enthusiasm, she is not defiant, but rather desires reconciliation. How is this statement confirmed? How does the bride-Laodicea indicate that she desires reconciliation or atonement?

Let's go back to the kiss in Song 1:2, where she states, *"Let him kiss me with the kisses of his mouth,"* as she is requesting atonement as it was accomplished at the Calvary's cross. Now, again, she is requesting this statement, *"I would kiss thee,"* indicating that she is now requesting atonement, as it must be accomplished on the antitypical "Day of Atonement" or Investigative Judgment, which is the judgment of the living. She indicates that when she is prepared for the judgment, then *"I should not be despised."* Then she would not be naked.

Comparing Revelation 3 with Song 8, we find these gem-capsules.

3:15-16— *"Thou art neither cold nor hot… thou art lukewarm."*
  8:1—*"O that thou wert as my brother."*
3:17—*"Thou art wretched, and miserable, and poor, and blind, and naked."*
  8:1—*"Yea, I should not be [I do not want to be] despised."*
3:16—*"I will spue thee out of my mouth."*
  8:1—*"I would [wish to] kiss thee."*
3:20—*"I stand at the door, and knock."*
  8:1-2—*"I should find thee without… I would… bring thee [in]… "*
3:20—*"If any man hear my voice… I will come in."*
  8:2—*"I would lead thee, and bring thee into my mother's house, who would instruct me."*
3:20—*"I will come in… and will sup with him."*
  8:2—*"I would cause thee to drink of spiced wine… juice of my pomegranate."*

Parting Gem: *Line upon line, line upon line, here some, there some. What a neat and effective way to get dressed and not be naked.*

NOVEMBER 4 — *Mother's House of Mother's Houses* — Song 8:2

Today's Thought: *"I would lead thee, and bring thee into my mother's house, who would instruct me."*

A similar statement was made by the Advent Movement bride in Song 3:4, as they discovered the Daniel 8:14 prophecy which revealed the time for the beginning of the Investigative Judgment. By coming into the *"mother's house,"* they discovered the "Present Truth" of that day, which they were to proclaim to the world. In like manner, the Laodicea bride desires to come into the *"mother's house"* to discover the Present Truth for our day regarding the closing or ending of the judgment. This will be the "loud cry" message to be given again to all the world.

Our bride is declaring the words of Proverbs 4:13, *"Take fast hold of instruction; let her not go: keep her; for she is thy life."*

Are you remembering that the "mother" is the universal church down through the ages that have passed off of the stage; the bride is the church on the stage at any particular moment. They will be united as one when the Bridegroom comes.

Inside this *"mother's house"* which "Wisdom" has built over the years and has hewn out her seven pillars, is a place for understanding where the simple can come in and eat the Bread of Life, drink the wine of prophecy, eat the meat of the Word (Proverbs 9:1-5).

As the Advent people gathered at the conferences through the 1880s to dig into the Word of God and place His truth and doctrines on an understanding footing, they placed these "newfound" truths into the *"mother's house."* They went into the mother's house and swept it clean of all of the rubbish, garbage, tradition, and church council dictates that had been piled up inside by *"another beloved."* Each truth discovered revolved around *"Jesus Christ, and him crucified"* (1 Corinthians 2:2). As many have said, "If the Adventists have a doctrine that is not immersed in Jesus Christ and in which Jesus Christ cannot be found, then that doctrine is discarded into the dung-pile."

Parting Gem: *You are cordially invited to the mother's house for a daily "Open House" where you may tour to see its beauty and splendour.*

NOVEMBER 5 — *Spiced Wine of Spiced Wines* — Song 8:2

Today's Thought: *"I would cause thee to drink of spiced wine of the juice of my pomegranate."*

The bride requests that the Bridegroom come into the *"mother's house"* of Present Truth—advancing light and wisdom—and drink of the spiced wine of the juice of her pomegranate. This pomegranate represents knowledge. She is asking her Beloved to sup with her and He has promised in the Laodicean message to do just that. He counsels her to (from Revelation 3:18):

--*"buy… gold tried in the fire, that thou mayest be rich."*
--*"[buy] white raiment, that thou mayest be clothed, and that the same of thy nakedness do not appear."*
--*"anoint thine eyes with eyesalve, that thou mayest see."*

During the 1880s, the bride-church sat down with her Beloved in a serious of six "Sabbath Conferences" to sup with Him. He, in turn, brought forth the "seven pillars" of wisdom. Seven usually signifies completeness, so during these conferences the entire pomegranate was squeezed so that all or nearly all of the juice of wisdom could be formulated and brought into the *"mother's house."*

We are told that never again will God's people need to sit down to hammer out the doctrines of the church as did the early pioneers, doctrines like the state of the dead, the millennium, the Sabbath, Sanctuary, the Second coming, and a whole lot more.

As the bride advances towards the marriage—the judgment of the living—she is entering a new era in the history of the church. She must enter into the "House of Present Truth" to comprehend the message in the Song of Songs, which is the song about the marriage! It is this very song which will prepare her for the marriage and the coming of the Bridegroom. It is this song which will enable her to give the Loud Cry: *"Behold, the Bridegroom cometh; go ye out to meet him"* (Matthew 25:6).

It is this song which heralds the closing up of the Investigative Judgment which began in 1844. This Song of Songs must be opened up to God's people just before the close of probation and it, together with other portions of prophecy, prepares them for the final test and judgment.

Parting Gem: *This Song identifies just who you and the bride are.*

NOVEMBER 6 — *Pomegranate of Pomegranates* — Song 8:2

Today's Thought: *"I would cause thee to drink of spiced wine of the juice of my pomegranate."*

Advancing light and knowledge are acknowledged three times by the words "spiced wine," "juice," "pomegranate." The pomegranate is an ancient symbol for knowledge. "Juice" is a concentrate and the "spiced wine" is the ultimate in flavour. As Laodicea expresses her desire to enter into her mother's house of Present Truth to receive "instruction," she may expect to receive the culmination of truth—a distillate of all the ages in preparing her for the coming judgment-marriage. This advancing light and truth takes God's people one step further than they have been; our drama is one method of bringing God's people close to His coming.

The high priest of ancient Israel, who was a type of Christ, leaving the Most Holy apartment of the earthly sanctuary, wore a robe of special significance. Beneath the hem of his robe were *"pomegranates of blue, and of purple, and of scarlet, round about the hem thereof; and bells of gold between them round about"* (Exodus 28:33).

The people who gathered about the sanctuary on this typical Day of Atonement listened for the tinkling of these bells as the priest came from the Most Holy Place. These bells testified that he was still alive; the cleansing of the sanctuary, the blotting out of sins was indeed in progress. The pomegranates interspersed among the bells were a type of "knowledge"—specifically of the judgment and its meaning.

In this time setting of Song of Songs 8:3, Laodicea today, as she drinks the spiced wine of the pomegranate, signifies that she is aware of the antitypical Day of Atonement as it is being carried out by her High Priest, from 1844 to the present. She is also aware that she herself is about to enter the judgment of the living. The chiming of the bells proclaims the progress of the cleansing of the sanctuary and day of judgment. They testify that He is still alive and at work. The spiced wine of the pomegranate pertains only to those who understand and believe in the Investigative Judgment now going on in heaven and the awareness of the coming judgment of the living.

Parting Gem: *Can you hear the tinkling of our High Priest's bells?*

NOVEMBER 7 — *Instruction of Instructions* — Song 8:2

Today's Thought: *"I would lead thee, and bring thee into my mother's house, who would instruct me."*

Instruction is advancing knowledge or light. According to Collins Paperback Thesaurus on knowledge, it can be (1) learning, (2) understanding, (3) acquaintance. Breaking these down further, it can be education, instruction, intelligence, discernment, judgment, recognition, familiarity, and wisdom, so this is what is going to take place in the *"mother's house."*

The "instruction" given in the mother's "house of truth" is always from the Word of God. The advancing light of prophecy is found in the triad of Daniel, Revelation, Song of Songs. Their prophetic outlines of church history has been the torch which lit the path of God's people, giving them a sense of where they were in God's plan for them. The Song of Songs is a song about a marriage—an epithalamium—a wedding song, and it is mainly about the marriage-judgment, opened at this time of God's people to prepare this last generation to go into the judgment-marriage of the living.

Proverbs 9 is a psalm of wisdom, wisdom which has built her house. Inside that house is the wisdom of all wisdom, truth of all truth. It is called "Mother's House." It contains all of the accumulative knowledge and truth of all ages, even from eternity. Only truth, pure and unadulterated, is in that house. There are no falsehoods, heresies, church councils, edicts, or ultimatums. Any thing, any doctrine, any characteristic that enters that house is truth, as well as eternal.

Our bride-church implies and states that she would bring the Laodicean Church into this "house of truth," often called "Present Truth," for it is the truth for that particular time. Coming into that "House of Wisdom," "Mother's House," where all truth and wisdom is, the bride would have her mother instruct the Laodicean Church on just how to get ready for the judgment of the living.

Parting Gem: *As Noah preached "Present Truth" about the flood, putting his influence and power behind his belief, so should we, as we get ready to enter the judgment of the living. Think about that today.*

NOVEMBER 8 — *Support of Supports #2* — Song 8:3

Today's Thought: *"His left hand should be under my head, and his right hand should embrace me."*

The bride-church expresses her great need and desire for His support and tender love as she approaches the closing up of the judgment! She expresses her great desire that He shall come to the marriage. The theme of the church has been for over a century the nearness of the coming of Jesus and the leadership has urged the finishing of the work.

But can four, five, six or more generations preach the nearness of His coming for more than a century without embarrassment over the delay? Does the delay imply a lack of credibility of the message?

According to Revelation 14, is the corporate church ready for the Bridegroom to come, or are any of the virgins ready? What lies ahead? God's servant states, "We have nothing to fear for the future except as we shall forget the way the Lord has led us and His teachings in the past" (LS 196). The word is out that we have nothing to fear except fear itself.

This drama, the Song of Songs, has been given us with its reiteration of the history of the church, that we may not forget the way the Lord has led us and it also guides us into future events.

Let the Bridegroom tell us how the bride shall be made ready and how she shall enter the judgment of the living. He says, *"Who is this that cometh up from the wilderness, leaning upon her beloved? I raised thee up under the apple tree: there thy mother brought thee forth… that bare thee."* (8:5) He is saying that the bride-church in the wilderness was not raised up nor brought forth in her own strength but that she came forth out of the wilderness *"leaning upon her beloved,"* and that is exactly the same way that she will go into the judgment of the living, *"leaning upon her beloved."* He is stating that He raised her up under the apple tree, under His own protection, and that He fed her with the fruits of that tree which were His own righteousness.

Parting Today: *As you go about the excitement of your day, be sure that you lean upon your Beloved so that your support is solid and secure.*

NOVEMBER 9   *Embrace of Embraces #3*   Song 8:3

Today's Thought: *"His left hand should be under my head, and his right hand should embrace me."*

Should you happen to remember, this is the very same verse found in Song 2:6. It's another one of those capsules starting and ending with the same words or thought. Reread March 25, "Right Hand of Right Hands." Within this capsule is the thought that we really do not have anything to worry about as far as our journey with the Bridegroom is concerned. He has our head cradled in His right hand, while His left hand is encircling around us. We need to just snuggle up close to Him and accept His protection.

It would be profitable for us to remember that not only are our names engraved within the palms of His hands to handle our daily encounters, but they are also bedded deep within the skull, His mind, where the crown of thorns pierced His head, thus giving us a "kindred spirit," like the song that states, "When He was on the cross that day, we were on His mind."

Then there are the two feet which were spiked to that cross. Our names are also there. Those two organs of our bodies that take us wherever we wish to go, they are marked in Christ's body and we are His.

A passing thought as I type today's thought out: at communion services, in the service of humility, when you are washing your partner's feet, envision in your mind and vocalize with your voice to your partner that you are washing the dust of daily travel from your companion's feet so that you can see the scars and the nail-prints of your Master's love for you. Your name's on His back as well.

The seventh notation of God's love for you and me is embedded in His side. That tells us that we are ever close to Him, like sidekicks.

In Psalms 3:3 it states, *"But thou, O Lord, art a shield for me; my glory, and the lifter up of mine head."*

Parting Gem: *In both Song 1:2, "Let him kiss me," and in 8:1, "I would kiss thee," nothing is mentioned about the way a "kiss" is given. Usually with the kiss there is an embrace, so my Beloved will not only embrace us, but will kiss us with the kiss of reconciliation.*

NOVEMBER 10 — *Charge of Charges #7* — Song 8:4

Today's Thought: *"I charge you, O daughters of Jerusalem, that ye stir not up, nor awake my love, until he please."*

This is our third time dealing with this charge. We looked at it first in Song 2:7, during the 1,260 year wilderness experience, then again in Song 3:5, during the Millerite Movement. These two charges are identical. We also looked at a charge in Song 5:8, where the bride states that she is lovesick. This charge above lacks the *"by the roes, and by the hinds of the field"* found in the first two charges.

In Hebrew poetry, a repetition such as we have seen in our drama is put there for emphasis and to make sure that if you miss the first clue, you can pick up the second. In this case, the third. The roes and the hinds have been fulfilled. The time prophecies based on time, like those in Daniel and Revelation, are fulfilled. The prophecies yet to come are not time prophecies like the 2,300 days or the French Revolution of Revelation 11. God's people now wait for the fulfillment of Daniel 11-12, in Revelation, the 1,335 days, the 1,290 days. We wait for the bride to get ready to go into the judgment—the judgment of the living. We wait for the gospel to go to the world for a witness. Christ just may be waiting for us to carry that message to all the world so that He can come.

In Revelation 3:14-22 is the message to the Laodicean Church. The counsel is for that church to buy gold tried in the fire, to buy white raiment to cover our nakedness, to buy eye salve so that we may see.

Faith and love are the true riches, the pure gold which the True Witness counsels the lukewarm to buy. It makes the heart rich, for it has been purged until it is pure (4T 88).

The white raiment is purity of character, the spotless white robe of the righteousness of the Bridegroom imparted to the sinner. This is indeed a garment of heavenly texture, which can be bought only of Christ for a life of willing obedience (4T 88).

The eye salve is the wisdom and the grace which enables us to discern between evil and good, to detect sin under any guise. We are to anoint our eyes with wisdom so that we may see clearly.

Parting Gem: *Pause before you go to buy; buy without money or price.*

NOVEMBER 11 — *Coming Out of Coming Outs* — Song 8:5

Today's Thought: *"Who is this that cometh up from the wilderness…?"*

In Revelation 12, the story is told of how the church was a target of Satan since before He entered the manger. When Lucifer, now known as the devil, was cast out of heaven, you can read about his antics in persecuting the "church," or God's people from the Garden of Eden to the Garden of Gethsemane, from Christ's temptations in the wilderness, to the wilderness experience of 1,260 years where the church went into that wilderness on eagle's wings, and where that church came out gloriously arrayed as the morning, fair as the moon, clear as the sun, terrible as an army with banners, leaning upon her beloved, with His right hand supporting her head and His right arm encircling her in a loving embrace. What a picture of overcoming; what an experience to have come through.

Amos 3:7 mentions that God will do nothing without first telling His prophets, who in turn will tell His people. Somewhere there must be some sort of text that states that God will also prepare the way or set the stage for some great, worthy happening.

Do you remember the happenings at Noah's flood time? He gave those long-living people some 120 years, watching the ark being built. Some may even have had to help build that ark. Can you see him on the deck of that ark pleading with the people for nearly the last time? God was not going to fail doing His part, so He caused the animals to come into the ark, each animal led by an angel no less. They came in orderly, two by two, or seven by seven, unclean versus clean. "Amazing," you can hear those people say.

A major interruption came next as birds of all kinds, colour, dispositions thundered through the sky, making the ground shake yet making orderly landings going into the ark. Wasn't Somebody making a statement?

Parting Gem: *Many times, I get this thought that if God was going to do something, something important, He was going to do it with "gusto," with class, with all His might. Yes, with the Still Small Voice, but even then it is with gusto. "Stage setting" will give us some of this "gusto."*

NOVEMBER 12 — *Leaning of Leanings* — Song 8:5

Today's Thought: *"Who is this that cometh up from the wilderness, leaning upon her beloved?"*

As our bride-church was faced with the decision to surrender her faith or flee, she was informed that a place had been prepared for her. She was given two wings of a great eagle that she might quickly fly into the wilderness. She knew that she would be there 1,260 long years. She knew that she would be nourished for this time period (Revelation 12). As she went into the wilderness *"leaning upon her beloved,"* so she came out the same way, *"leaning upon her beloved."* She will go into the marriage-judgment of the living the very same way, leaning upon her beloved.

The early church which started with Christ and the early apostles, and which migrated to headquarter in Rome, fell in apostasy in what appeared to be a defeat and a failure of Christ's work on earth. Yet, He raised up in the wilderness, in the secluded mountains of Europe, later the newly discovered haven of the New World, His church of scattered peoples which existed through those hot and scorching seasons of great persecutions. He brought His church through the European Reformation, The Great 1800 Awakening, The Great Advent Movement, and will finish His work through the last generation and judgment of the living.

Looking back in hindsight, He states that He brought thee up under the apple tree. What is the Beloved really trying to say to us today? He declares that the bride-church in the wilderness was not raised up nor brought forth in her own strength, but that she came out of the wilderness LEANING UPON HER BELOVED, and that is exactly the same way that she will go into judgment of the living, *"leaning upon her beloved."* This should give us strength and courage. In our drama, Song 2:3, Christ is likened to an apple tree and He declares that He raised her up under the apple tree, under His own protection, and He fed her with the fruits of that tree which were His own righteousness.

Parting Gem: *Today as you go about your exciting experiences, lean upon your Beloved. Practice that neat art of doing so.*

NOVEMBER 13 — *Rearing of Rearings* — Song 8:5

Today's Thought: *"I raised thee up under the apple tree: there thy mother brought thee forth."*

Christ is not only the Author but also the Finisher of His works; He is not only the Cornerstone, but the Headstone of His temple-kingdom.
"Not by might, nor by power, but by my Spirit, saith the Lord of hosts" (Zechariah 4:6).
In every age, the true bride or true church is brought forth or identified as they give the "Present Truth," the truth meant for their day. In the days of Noah, it was to get ready for the flood. At the time of Christ, it was John the Baptist proclaiming, *"Behold the Lamb of God"* (John 1:29). At the time of the Reformation, it was the Bible and the Bible only, as well as justification by faith in God alone.
In 1844, it was the cleansing of the sanctuary, the Investigative Judgment, and the coming of the Bridegroom. Today, the true bride will be identified with the "Present Truth" concerning the judgment of the living, just before the second coming of the Bridegroom.
"As the book of record is opened in the judgment, the lives of all who have believed in Jesus come in review before God. Beginning with those who first lived upon earth, our Advocate presents the cases of each successive generation, and closes with the living" (GC 483).
The Mother's House is the house of Truth. Truth identifies the mother—the universal church of all ages. The bride is related to her only as she proclaims the Present Truth for her own day. The true church of the last generation must proclaim the truth of the closing up of the judgment, that of the living, or she cannot go into the wedding.
This truth must be noticeable from the very beginning, from the very first encounter with the bride. That's one very important reason why the breasts have been outlined and described some eight times in our drama. They must get that point across—the doctrines of the Seventh-day Adventist Church are based on Bible truth and Bible truth alone.

Parting Gem: *In every well-written drama, the action builds towards the grand climax. Song of Songs 8:6 begins that culmination towards that which all history has been ascending. It is the "coup de theatre."*

NOVEMBER 14 — *Order of Orders* — Song 8:5

Today's Thought: *"Who is this that cometh up from the wilderness, leaning upon her beloved?"*

In 1844, the "mother" went into the marriage. In 1844, the judgment began with the first generations which lived upon the earth. The mother, this universal church of all ages, beginning with those who first lived upon the earth, came into the judgment in 1844.

Now, at the end of time, the true bride, the living corporate church, must also follow, proclaiming the close of probation for the living and go into the judgment of the living.

In a formal wedding, the bride's mother is brought in by the ushers first, then the bride is brought in by her father. So, according to 1 Peter 4:17, judgment must begin at the house of God. Thus, starting with Adam, Eve, Seth, and all the dead down through the ages who had their names written in the Lamb's Book of Life, judgment begins. In proper order, the judgment must now switch to the bride herself, the "living." Thus, the bride, this last generation, goes into the judgment of the living.

Our drama presents a unit, from 3:6 to 8:5, which describes the remnant bride-church from her emergence in 1798 to our own day. Her identity is beyond question, for it is she who came forth from the wilderness (Song 3:6; Revelation 12), it is she who suffered the Great Disappointment of 1844 (Song 5:2-10), it is she who proclaims the three angels' messages (Song 5:11-16), it is she who has given out the wedding invitations in preparation for the literal coming of the Bridegroom to all the world (Song 6-8:5), and it is she who keeps the commandments of God and the faith of Jesus (Revelation 14:12; 12:17)

But, finally, the poetic structure of our drama, Song 8:5, brings this unit to an end. The church has come practically to the end of its sojourn and wanderings on earth as the Bridegroom has been dealing with the Investigative Judgment of the dead. The next verse swings to the living.

Parting Gem: *In the setting of 1844, the beginning of the Investigative Judgment, the "mother" is already present. She is the one who "crowns" him in the day of His espousal.*

NOVEMBER 15   *Stage Setting of Stage Settings*   Song 8:5

Today's Thought: *Who is coming and how is it announced?*

In Song 6:10 it states, *"Who is she that looketh forth as the morning, fair as the moon, clear as the sun, and terrible as an army with banners."*

This is how our bride-church came out of the wilderness. Let's look at the setting of the stage for her to come out.

On November 11, 1755, the great Lisbon, Portugal earthquake shook the world.

For three and a half years, from November 26, 1793 to June 17, 1797, the French Revolution shook Europe, according to Revelation 11.

On May 19, 1780, the Dark Day and blood-like moon experience came.

During the night of November 13, 1833, it seemed the sky fell in with its great meteoritic shower.

Many eyes were on the indignities heaped upon the priests of Rome, reaching the peak when Colonel General Louis Berthier established the Roman Republic in 1798 and took Pope Pius VI off to die in exile in France. A new interest was sparked in the prophecies of Daniel and Revelation, particularly the 1,260-day period, which many interpreters now believed had come to an end with the dramatic events of 1798. This rebirth of prophetic interest soon moved on to the closer look of the longest time prophecy—the 2,300 days of Daniel 8:14.

In Great Britain and the United States, a renaissance of Protestantism brought forth numerous congregations. Spiritualism flourished, as did a strong missionary movement. The Sunday School Movement took off to combat growing up in homes without Christ. The Industrial Revolution brought prosperity which in turn opened up revenues for mission expansions. A goodly number of reforms came onto the stage such as anti-slavery, temperance, education and understanding of the deaf and blind, more humane treatment of orphans, vagrants and the poor as well as the mentally handicapped... The public school system took on a more acceptable state.

It seems hardly coincidental that Britain and the United States, two pillars of the growing evangelical Protestant outreach, should also be the two countries most firmly committed to a democratic form of government.

Parting Gem: *The stage is set, the props are in place. Are you ready?*

NOVEMBER 16   *Closure of Closures*   Revelation 3:18

Today's Thought: *"I counsel thee to buy gold... white raiment... eyesalve."*

According to Revelation 13, fearful is the issue to which the world is to be brought. The powers of the earth, uniting to war against the commandments of God, will decree that all... shall conform to... the observance of the false Sabbath. The Sabbath will be the great test of loyalty... The third angel's message will produce an effect which it could not have had before... Thus the message of the third angel will be proclaimed... with greatest power. The power attending the message will only madden those who oppose it. As the movement for Sunday enforcement becomes more bold and decided, the law will be invoked against commandment keepers... The advent movement of 1840-44 was a glorious manifestation of the power of God... but these are to be exceeded by the mighty movements under the last warning of the third angel. The work will be similar to that of the Day of Pentecost. As the *"former rain"* was given, in the outpouring of the Holy Spirit at the opening of the gospel, to cause the up springing of the precious seed, so *"latter rain"* will be given at it close (GC 604-611).

The counsel given to the Laodicean Church, the bride-church that is presently on the stage, is to buy *"gold"* tried in the fire—a faith strong enough to carry one through the judgment of the living—to buy *"white raiment,"* to be clothed with Christ's Robe of Righteousness—a necessary garment in order to enter into the "Marriage Supper of the Lamb." This garment, by the way, is totally free for the asking. Then buy *"eye-salve,"* that she may see the present truth for our day.

Now, really, what more does one need? He's rich with this precious gold, he's richly clothed with this unique robe, he's got excellent eyesight so that he can see just where he is going or is supposed to go. All, may it be added, are free, just for the asking.

Parting Gem: *The next verse, Song 8:6, swings the drama into the future, into the judgment of the living. The great issues and final crises are right before us! As this drama opens up to our understanding at this time, the church is ready to step from verse 8:5 into 8:6—the judgment of the living before us.*

NOVEMBER 17 — *Synopsis of Synopses* — Song 8:5

Today's Thought: *"Who is this that cometh up from the wilderness, leaning upon her beloved? I raised thee up under the apple tree…"*

The synopsis of the literary-poetic structure of the Song of Songs concludes past history and identifies the present. Hebrew poetry is not identified by rhyme or meter, but rather by the structure, particularly that of parallel concepts or double expressions of one concept and by its meaningful units concerning sublime themes.

The Song of Songs' poetry provides insight into meaning by its very structure, in which certain sections are bounded—at the beginning and the end—by similar statements. In this way, those particular sections which deal with a particular event in history are set apart and thereby recognized as a unit. Examples follow:

Beginning the EUROPEAN REFORMATION UNIT, at 2:8-9—*"Behold, he cometh… leaping upon the mountains, skipping upon the hills."*—and ending with the unit in 2:17—*"… be thou like a roe or a young hart upon the mountains…"*

Beginning THE ADVENT MOVEMENT UNIT, at 4:1—*"Behold, thou art fair, my love; behold, thou art fair…"*—and ending with 4:7—*"Thou art all fair, my love; there is no spot in thee."*

Beginning THE THIRD ANGEL'S MESSAGE UNIT, at 5:9—*"What is thy beloved more than another beloved."*—and ending with 5:16—*"This is my beloved, and this is my friend."*

This same poetic structure marks the beginning and the end of the section which describes the remnant church from 1798 to the present time.

Beginning THE REMNANT PEOPLE UNIT from 1798 to the present with 3:6—*"Who is this that cometh out of the wilderness…?"*—and ending with 8:5—*"Who is this that cometh up from the wilderness?"*

Beginning THE INVESTIGATIVE JUDGMENT UNIT, at 3:4—*"I had brought him into my mother's house [those dead]."*—and ending with 8:2—*"… and bring thee into my mother's house [those living]."*

Parting Gem: *Feel free to go back to January's reading and check out some of the characteristics mentioned there. Specifically "Construction of Construction" on January 24. Have a happy day!*

NOVEMBER 18 — *Refreshing of Refreshings* — Song 8:6

Today's Thought: *"Set me as a seal upon thine heart, as a seal upon thine arm: for love is strong as death; jealousy is cruel as the grave."*

"Said the angel, 'List ye!' Soon I heard a voice like many musical instruments all sounding in perfect strains, sweet and harmonious. It surpassed any music I had ever heard, seeming to be full of mercy, compassion, and elevating holy joy. It thrilled through my whole being. Said the angel, 'Look ye!' My attention was then turned to the company I had seen who were mightily shaken. I was shown those whom I had before seen weeping and praying in agony of spirit. The company of guardian angels around them had been doubled, and they were clothed with an armour from their head to their feet. They moved in exact order, like a company of soldiers. Their countenance expressed the severe conflict which they had endured, the agonizing struggle they had passed through. Yet their features, marked with severe internal anguish, now shone with the light and glory of heaven. They had obtained the victory, and it called forth from them the deepest gratitude and holy, sacred joy.

"Evil angels still pressed around them, but could have no power over them. I heard those clothed with armour speak the truth with great power… I asked what made this great change. An angel answered, 'It is the latter rain, the refreshing from the presence of the Lord, the loud cry of the third angel'" (EW 270/271).

One refreshing thought for you today as you go about your joys and excitements is found in Acts 3:19. *"Repent ye therefore, and be converted, that your sins may be blotted out, when the times of refreshing shall come from the presence of the Lord."*

Parting Gem: *Determine this day to be like that young boy who, when asked if he could do the required work expected of him, replied, "I sleep powerfully well on stormy nights." When a stormy night did break open, the farmer could not wake that youngster, yet found when he went out that everything was fastened down, closed up, secured. As he went back to the warmth of his bed, he had a strange smile on his face as he whispered, "I sleep powerfully well on stormy nights."*

NOVEMBER 19 — *Test of Tests* — Song 8:6

Today's Thought: *"Set me as a seal upon thine heart, and as a seal upon thine arm."*

"The Lord has shown me clearly that the image of the beast will be formed before probation closes; for it is the great test for the people of God, by which their eternal destiny will be decided… This is the test that the people of God must have before they are sealed" (7 SDA BC 976).

This image of the beast will be formed when the United States in the New World withdraws Constitutional freedom and forms a union of church and state to enforce the false Sabbath-Sunday, which is the mark of the authority of the beast of the Old World—Papal Rome.

"As the siege of Jerusalem by the Roman armies was the signal for flight to the Judean Christians, so the assumption of power on the part of our nation is the decree enforcing the papal Sabbath will be a warning to us. It will then be time to leave the large cities, preparatory to leaving the smaller ones for retired homes in secluded places among the mountains" (5T 464/5).

Experience has found that when a "city dweller" decides to move out into the country, he has a different experience than one who was reared in the country. In the country, there are no shopping malls handy, no hospitals, no grocery stores or gas stations, no sidewalks to take an evening walk on, no church schools, without long driving distances, and sometimes no good roads. In the city they are paved, while in the country they are gravel roads. This can be a drastic change, even a "culture shook" for those venturing out there. Behold, now is the time to move out into the country, find a piece of land where you can grow your own vegetables, even fruit trees, without pesticides, get away from the evil and corrupting influences inundating these cities. The counsel from the Lord is to move out into the country

"While one class, by accepting the sign of submission to earthly power, receive the mark of the beast, the other, choosing the token of allegiance to divine authority receive the seal of God" (GC 605).

Parting Gem: *Is it a matter of a day that we keep, or is it a matter of whose authority we accept?*

NOVEMBER 20 — *Seal of Seals* — Song 8:6

Today's Thought: *"Set me as a seal upon thine heart."*

The voice of the bride, which exclaims, *"Set me as a seal upon thine heart,"* is not the voice of the dead; it is the voice of the living bride. It is the voice of the living, active church which comes to the time of the Investigative Judgment and requests that she, too, as well as the generations of the past, be set *"as a seal"* upon the bridegroom's heart.

"And Aaron shall bear the names of the children of Israel in the breastplate of judgment upon his heart, when he goeth in unto the holy place, for a memorial before the Lord continually" (Exodus 28:29).

As like Aaron, so is Christ, the Priest and Judge, who has entered the names of the saved into the "Lamb's Book of Life" as though they were engraved upon His very heart. While the dead rest in their graves, the irrevocable seal of the Investigative Judgment and final decision has been placed upon their record at their name in the Book of Life. Christ has pledged to save them for eternity in His own image.

The names of the twelve tribes of Israel were engraved upon twelve precious stones, inlaid work, in the breastplate. These names represent all of the people of God. Christ in the Investigative Judgment, as High Priest, seals the names of His people upon His heart.

Remember, it is the day of the gladness of His heart, and is likened to a marriage. Then they tell me that after the wedding comes the banquet and the celebrations.

Parting Gem: *The only aspect of the "seal of God" (Revelation 9:4) which is considered in this setting of our Song is that which has to do with the seal, as it shall be placed upon those who face the Investigative Judgment of the living—the close of probation, the seven last plagues without a Mediator, and translation.*

NOVEMBER 21 — *Heart of Hearts* — Song 8:6

Today's Thought: *"Set me as a seal upon thine heart."*

Here the bride-church is requesting that the Seal of God (Revelation 9:4) be allotted to her. She knows that this seal must be placed upon the last generation, which will live through the seven last plagues without having a mediator. She is aware that this last generation will be translated without seeing death and will meet the Bridegroom when He comes. The tone of verses 6-7 is that of great stress. Words and phrases such *as "death," "cruel as the grave," "a most vehement flame," "quench love," "floods drown it," and "utterly contemned"* make this point clear. In this setting of fear and pending disaster, the bride cries out for protection and deliverance in the seal of God.

The seal of God, as mentioned in Revelation 7:3, is found in the forehead. The forehead or mind is the decision section of the body. After the law of God is written indelibly and permanently in the hearts and minds of God's people and they receive the *"seal of God"* (Revelation 9:4), they are nevermore to be defiled, and they are "secure from the tempter's devices" (5T 472-476). An illustration of this is a jar of fruit; when it has been canned, it is safe from spoilage, even high temperature and freezing cold. Thus God's people are sealed and ready to go through the times just ahead before Christ comes.

When the last individual in the last generation has passed successfully through the judgment of the living and his name is retained in the Lamb's Book of Life, Christ will have received His total kingdom: that is "the reception of His kingdom," happening from 1844 to the close of the judgment and the Seal of God.

After this sealing in the heart and mind, God's people are delivered from sin.

Parting Gem: *Time marches on. We stand on the line between verses 5 and 6 of the drama of this Song of Songs. The bride-church watches this world spinning on towards self-destruction. Four angels hold back the winds of strife, but only until the saints of the Most High God have been sealed in their foreheads, their minds, their thinking processor. We stand very close and may very well be the last generation-bride which cries out, "Set me as a seal upon thine heart."*

NOVEMBER 22   *Arm of Arms*   Song 8:6-7

Today's Thought: *"Set me… as a seal upon thine arm."*

Yesterday we looked at the bride's request, *"Set me as a seal upon thine heart."* This is a plea for deliverance from sin and for heart unity. The bride's request today is, *"Set me as a seal upon thine arm."*

"The arm of the Lord" (Isaiah 53:1, John 12:38) is used in Scripture to describe the Lord in battle for His people. At the Red Sea, the children of Israel were delivered by *"the greatness of thine arm"* (Exodus 15:16). *"And the Lord brought us forth out of Egypt with a mighty hand, and with an outstretched arm, and with great terribleness, and with signs, and with wonders"* (Deuteronomy 26:8).

This drama of the Song of Songs is the story of the great controversy between good and evil. The action begins in AD 31 and intensifies to the final and complete deliverance of God's people. A well-written drama follows a pattern of action in which the intensity of the conflict reaches a crisis. Just as the suspense reaches its climax, there is an incident which occurs which is called the *"coup de theatre,"* in which the hero delivers the heroine from the villain, mysteries are solved, and the action quickly descends until the curtain closes on stage.

Our verses for today, Song 8:6-7, reveals the bride-church under great stress and crisis—extreme danger. The *"coup d'theatre"* is that act of the Bridegroom hero as He delivers His bride from her literal enemies. She has already been delivered from sin; it is now time to deliver her from the persecution, stress, and harassment of her enemies.

The remnant church will be brought into great trial and distress. Satan has gained control over the apostate churches, but there is a little company that is rejecting and resisting his supremacy. If he could but blot them from the face of the earth, his triumph would be complete. Yet, the remnant have only one hope, the mercy of God; they have but one defence, and that will be prayer.

Parting Gem: *God's people are fully aware of the sinfulness of their lives; they see their weaknesses and their unworthiness, and as they look upon themselves they are ready to despair. The flames of the furnace seem about to consume them, yet they come forth as gold.*

NOVEMBER 23 — *Amnesia of Amnesias* — 2 Timothy 5:24

Today's Thought: *"Some men's sins are open beforehand, going before to judgment; and some men they follow after."*

Eternity would not be an enjoyable experience if one was to be constantly tormented and harassed of his earthly sins, even though God has forgiven the person of those sins. Therefore, God blots them from our minds, our memory, our thoughts. Clean, gone and forgotten.

"But they have a deep sense of their unworthiness, they have no concealed wrongs to reveal. Their sins have gone beforehand to judgment and have been blotted out, and they cannot bring them to remembrance" (PP 202; GC 620).

"They cannot bring to mind any particular sins, but in their whole life they can see but little good. Their sins have gone beforehand to judgment, and pardon has been written. Their sins have been borne away "Into the Land of Forgetfulness" and they cannot bring them to remembrance" (3SG 135).

"As in the final atonement the sins of the truly repentant are to be blotted out from the records of heaven, no more to be remembered or come into mind, so in type they were borne away into the wilderness, forever separated from the congregation" (PP 358).

Let's look at a few texts and see if we can catch the spiritual, symbolic meaning of what is being said. First, Micah 7:19, where it says, *"And thou wilt cast all their sins into the depths of the sea."*

Psalms 103:12 says, *"As far as the east is from the west, so far hath he removed our transgressions from us."*

Isaiah 38:17 says, *"…for thou hast cast all my sins behind thy back."*

Isaiah 44:22 says, *"I have blotted out, as a thick cloud, thy transgressions."*

Isaiah 1:18 says, *"Come now, and let us reason together, saith the Lord: though your sins be as scarlet, they shall be as white as snow."*

Parting Gem: *A man knelt and prayed to God, acknowledging and pleading for God to forgive him of some horrendous sin that he had committed. There was no response. The next night, he once again begged God to forgive him of that despicable sin. This time there was a response. "What sin?" That's amnesia!*

NOVEMBER 24 — *Terribleness of Terribleness* — Song 8:6

Today's Thought: *"Set me… as a seal upon thine arm."*

Isaiah 59:16 records, *"And he saw that there was no man, and wondered that there was no intercessor: therefore his arm brought salvation unto him; and his righteousness, it sustained him."*

Isaiah, in vision, looked into the sanctuary in heaven, down at the end of the Investigative Judgment, when there would no longer be mediator, and wondered how Israel should be delivered. When there was *"no man… no intercessor,"* when the Investigative Judgment is finished, during the time of the plaques, how shall God's people be able to stand?

The arm of the Lord is a Scriptural expression for deliverance. *"Therefore his arm brought salvation unto him; and his righteousness, it sustained him."* What a text to put into our repertoire of verses.

Deuteronomy 26:8 reminds us today of a similar experience. *"And the Lord brought us forth out of Egypt with a mighty hand, and with an outstretched arm, and with great terribleness, and with signs, and with wonders."*

There are several neat stories that emphasize God's deliverance. There were at one time three Hebrew teenagers who were bound and thrown into a furnace that was heated as hot as it could get, just because they had chosen to obey God and not the king. I understand that they came out "smelling like a rose."

On another occasion, their fellow friend was cast into a den of lions for continuing his practice of praying to God from his open window. Apparently he had a warm and comfortable sleep, was awakened the next morning by the king, and then hauled out. His accusers were immediately then thrown in. They never reached the bottom before the lions had a hay-day with them. It's good to reread these stories.

Parting Gem: *Can you see here Christ as the Redeemer and Deliverer of His people? Think about that today.*

NOVEMBER 25 — *Blotting Out of Blotting Outs* — Song 8:6

Today's Thought: *"Set me as a seal upon thine heart, as a seal upon thine arm."*

The work of the Investigative Judgment and the blotting out of sins is to be accomplished before the advent of our Lord. The apostle Peter distinctly states that the sins of the believers will be blotted out "when the times of refreshing shall come from the presence of the Lord and He shall send Jesus Christ" (GC 485:2).

"Thus will be realized the complete fulfillment of the new covenant promise. "I will forgive their inequities, and I will remember their sins no more." In those days, and in that time, saith the Lord, the iniquity of Israel shall be sought for, and there shall be none; and the sins of Judah, and they shall not be found… he that is left in Zion… shall be called holy, even everyone that is written among the living in Jerusalem" (GC 485:1).

God's promises that *"Their sins… I will remember no more"* (Hebrews 8:12). And the sins of God's people are blotted out in the records of heaven. But there is more! The record of sin will be blotted out of the minds of God's people—as they are sealed in their "forehead," in their minds.

"Some men's sins are open beforehand, going before to judgment; and some men they follow after" (1 Timothy 5:24).

"While they have a deep sense of their unworthiness, they will have no concealed wrongs to reveal. Their sins will have been blotted out by the atoning blood of Christ, and they cannot bring them to remembrance" (PP 202/ GC 620).

"They cannot bring to mind any particular sin but in their whole life they can see but little good. Their sins have gone beforehand to judgment, and pardon has been written. Their sins have been born away into the land of forgetfulness, and they cannot bring them to remembrance" (3SG 135).

Parting Gem: *Eternity would not be an enjoyable experience if one was to constantly be tormented of his earthly sins even though they are blotted out. So God blots them out of our minds.*

NOVEMBER 26 — *Forehead of Foreheads* — Song 8:6

Today's Thought *"Set me as a seal upon thine heart, as a seal upon thine arm."*

"And I looked, and, lo, a lamb stood on the mount Sion, and with him an hundred forty and four thousand, having his Father's name written in their foreheads" (Revelation 14:1).

Two other texts go nicely with Revelation. One is Philippians 2:5, where it says, *"Let this mind be in you, which was also in Christ Jesus,"* and then John 13:15, which says, *"For I have given you an example, that ye should do as I have done to you."*

The saints are sealed with the Father's name in their foreheads, and they are sealed by their loyalty to His true Sabbath which contains *"the seal of God"* (Revelation 9:4).

Notice a connection between the Father's name and the true Sabbath. The name "Father" is in the very word *"Sabbath"*—*"abba,"* is in "S-abba-th." *"Abba, Father"*—two words meaning *"father,"* the first Aramaic which is the common speech of Palestine, and the second Greek. (Mark 14:36/, Romans 8:15. *Walking Through Your Bible with H.M.S. Richards,* Day 330.)

"And because ye are sons, God hath sent forth the Spirit of his Son into your hearts, crying Abba, Father" (Galatians 4:6).

In many languages, as their calendar agrees, the word *"Sabbath"* and *"seven"* are synonymous, and the concept of *"Abba"* is inherent in the word.

Job helps us to understand this sealing process. *"I made a covenant with mine eyes; why then should I think upon a maid?"* (Job 31:1) As well, in Psalms 119:89, *"For ever, O Lord, thy word is settled in heaven."* So in the mind of the sealed one, the Sabbath, as well as other *"whatsoever things,"* are settled in the heart, the mind, the thinking, the belief. Why then, should he think of other *"things?"*

Parting Gem: *This sealing is like a settling into the truth, a saving, active conviction in your mind, heart, and life of this truth. Thus our bride cries loud and clear, "Seal me, seal me, in Your heart, on Your arm, just seal me."*

NOVEMBER 27 — *Wafting of Waftings* — Song 8:6

Today's Thought: *"For love is strong as death; jealousy is cruel as the grave."*

"I saw some, with strong faith and agonizing cries, pleading with God. Their countenance was pale and marked with deep anxiety, expressive of the internal struggle. Firmness and great earnestness was expressed in their countenance, large drop of perspiration fell from their foreheads. Now and then their faces would light up with the marks of God's approbation, and again the same solemn, earnest, anxious look would settle upon them.

"Evil angels crowded around, pressing darkness upon them to shut out Jesus from their view that their eyes might be drawn to the darkness that surrounded them, and thus they be led to distrust God and murmur against Him. Their only safety was in keeping their eyes directed upward. Angels of God had charge over His people, and as the poisonous atmosphere of evil angels pressed around these anxious ones, the heavenly angels were continually wafting their wings over them to scatter the thick darkness" (EW 267).

"As the praying ones continued their earnest cries at times a ray of light from Jesus came to them, to encourage their hearts and light up their countenances. Some I saw, did not participate in their work of agonizing and pleading. They seemed indifferent and careless. They were not resisting the darkness around them, and it shut them in like a dark cloud. The angels of God left these and went to the aid of the earnest, praying ones. I saw angels of God hasten to the assistance of all who were struggling with their power to resist the evil angels and trying to help themselves by calling upon God with perseverance. But His angels left those who made no effort to help themselves, and I lost sight of them" (EW 269, 270).

Parting Gem: *One asked the meaning of the shaking, and was shown that it was caused by the straight testimony called forth by the counsel of the True Witness to the Laodiceans. It will have its effect upon the heart of the receiver, lead him to exalt the standard, and pour forth the straight truth. Some will not bear this straight testimony rising up against it, and this is what will cause a shaking among God's people.*

NOVEMBER 28 — *Flood of Floods* — Song 8:7

Today's Thought: *"Many waters cannot quench love, neither can the floods drown it."*

Waters and floods in prophetic symbolism represent not only peoples, nations, and tongues, as in Revelation 17:15, but also persecutions, as in Revelation 12:13,15. *"And when the dragon saw that he was cast unto the earth, he persecuted the woman... and the serpent cast out of his mouth water as a flood... that he might cause her to be carried away of the flood."*

So, what is this section in today's thought saying? In symbolic language, it tells us that persecution and falsehoods cannot squash, whip out, destroy, or squelch one's love for our Beloved, yet more importantly it cannot destroy the love God has for us.

Persecution over the centuries has been one of the fascinating aspects and reasons for a vast upsurge of growth within the Christian community. Notice Revelation 3:10 during the Thyatira church period, AD 538-1563, where the last is greater than the first. There was an increase in the Christian community even during the wilderness experience with its harassing persecutions.

After AD 1563, things "got better" in that the Reformation was launched. Near the close of this period, the Morning Star of the Reformation, John Wycliffe came onto the scene.

Satan sought to destroy the Christian Church by the inundation of false doctrines, as well as by persecution. However, true agape love, as described in Song 1:2, the love of the Beloved, cannot be quench.

Notice this thought: "As the movement for Sunday enforcement becomes more bold and decided, the law will invoke against commandment keepers. They will be threatened with fines and imprisonment" (GC 607).

"Some will be thrust into prison... exiled... treated as slaves... accused of bringing judgments upon the world..." (GC 608, 614)

"A decree will finally be issued against those who hallow the Sabbath... deserving the severest punishment... to put them to death... the Lord permits Satan to try them to the uttermost. Their faith must endure weariness, delay, and hunger" (GC 615-621).

Parting Gem: *Go today realizing that God's agape love sustains you.*

NOVEMBER 29 — *Condemned of Condemned* — Song 8:7

Today's Thought: *"Many waters cannot quench love, neither can the flood drown it: if a man would give all the substance of his house for love, it would utterly be contemned."*

In a thesaurus, the word "contemn" means to regard with contempt. Contempt means to scorn, derision, distain, disrespect, mockery, neglect, slight. The word contemptible means despicable cheap, detestable, shabby, shameful, vile, and so much more.

In verse 6, we just looked at the sealing of the saint, both in the heart as well as upon the arm. So, if any man, woman, or child thinks that he can be sealed on the arm or in the heart by selling everything he has and giving it for this sealing, it is utterly and purely despicable, disgusting, shameful, and all the other adjectives above.

In Acts 8 is the story of a man, Simon, who tried to buy the power of laying on hands to give the power of the Holy Spirit. Then he wanted to buy that power. Simon Peter was quick to call sin and evil just what it was by telling Simon, *"Thy money perish with thee, because thou hast thought that the gift of God may be purchased with money"* (Acts 8:20). So it goes with love. Love is earned, is given, is returned, but never bought, no matter how much one is willing to pay.

Love is a decision, as is hatred, envy, jealousy. The love chapter in Corinthians needs to be read daily, maybe even memorized and often repeated, then practised. Love gives continual attention, is adaptable, gives forgiveness instantly, is stubborn in its trust.

Love is one of the eternal characteristics of Christ. Should we happen to desire to emulate Christ, love will play a powerfully important part in this emulation. Somehow love carries with it an influence that is not noticed by the carrier, but is often easily recognised by the beholder, and draws people together. Thus Christ had this love that drew all men unto Him.

Parting Gem: *You read in John 3:16 that, "God so loved the world, that he gave his only begotten Son, that whosoever believes in him should not perish, but have everlasting life." God did not loan His Son to us for thirty-three years. He gave Him to the human race for eternity. That, my friend, is love—pure, unadulterated, unrelenting love.*

NOVEMBER 30 — *Summary* — Song 8:1-7

The prophetic drama of the Song of Songs, Chapters 1-7, traces the history of the true church from AD 31 through to the rise and progress of the Seventh-day Adventist Church. Chapter 8 brings the drama to our present day. This Christian bride-church of the Most High God was forced into the wilderness in AD 538. Nearly two centuries ago (AD 1798), the bride-church came out of the wilderness and The Great Advent Movement prepared the people for the beginning of the Investigative Judgment. But now, this generation must focus on the ending or "closing up" of the Investigative Judgment, which is the judgment of the living. "As the books of record are opened in the judgment, the lives of all who have believed on Jesus come in review before God" (GC 483). Beginning with the mother and those who first lived upon the earth, our Advocate presents the cases of each successive generation, and closes with the living, the present bride.

When the work of the Investigative Judgment closes, the destiny of all will have been decided for life or death. Probation is ended a short time before the appearing of the Lord in the clouds of heaven (GC 490).

We looked at the lament of the bride, the bride who is not ready to be given in marriage. We approached the judgment of the living, and we were counselled to buy gold, raiment, eye salve as we compared Revelation with our drama. We walked through Mother's House. We tasted a sip of spiced wine of the pomegranate, and received instruction in the house of truth. We saw the support system God outlined as we were embraced with His arms.

We were given our last charge not to expect our Beloved to come, not yet. We watched this bride-church, which went into the wilderness in AD 538, come out of that same wilderness with gusto, with class, with the mighty power of God, heaven, and the Spirit in AD 1798. We saw that as she went into the wilderness leaning upon the everlasting arms, so she came out the very same way. Did you notice the order spoken of on November 14, of how the wedding occurs?

We were intimately introduced to *"Abba, Father,"* which has a connection with the true Sabbath within the word itself. How about the utter foolishness, the derision, the mockery of trying to buy love, even to the point of selling everything one has? Have a great day.

Have We Crossed the Bridge?

This parable in poem is written to show,
    We are not far from home, just a short ways to go.
When I was a child, we all lived in the sticks,
    Out in the boon-docks like a bunch of hicks.

Any trip into town was some major event.
    It took a long time and the whole day was spent.
At the end of the day when we just staggered about,
    We went to Dad's truck, crawled in, sacked out.

We trusted our dad to deliver us home,
    To our bit of turf where we all loved to roam.
I remember those trips as in the truck we would creep,
    To curl up in bundles to catch up on some sleep.

Our eyes were so heavy, our bodies so worn,
    Like Job in the Bible, oh! why were we born?
But Dad was responsible for driving the truck,
    We just slept on in confidence, not trusting to luck.

On the way out of town ran the super hard top,
    As we headed for home, it would all be non-stop.
The sound of the engine would give us the clue,
    The road would soon narrow like each of us knew.

Then on down a space we continued our trip,
    Till the engine had told us Dad shifted the stick.
The brakes slowed us down, a sharp corner was next,
    The gravel that shook us said the black-top was nix.

After the corner, as Dad stepped on the gas.
    We could gauge where we were, we were entering the pass.
The further from town and the closer to home,
    The worse got the road yet, the sharper Dad's hone.

The gravel was taken because that was the road.
    The road up ahead had no gravel that showed.
Once more that old engine told us just where we were,
    As one by one we began all to stir.

More awake than asleep for dead up ahead,
    Came that old wooden bridge where we all had a dread.
Soon Dad shifted the gears to crawl over the boards,
    We were never near home until over this gorge.

We all felt the truck as it eased off the planks,
    And awaited Dad's sigh as he offered his thanks.
We kids came alive then for just up ahead.
    Was home and comfort, sweet milk and Mom's bread.

The movements were rapid after crossing those planks.
    We'd soon all be home; give Dad hearty thanks.
I still live in the boon-docks, I still live like a hick.
    I live on this planet where everything's sick.

The hard-top is history, the narrow strip's worse.
    Since Eve left her Adam we have sin as a curse.
The sound of the gravel as each newscast we hear,
    Definitely tells us our real home is near.

But, then that old bridge, what fear it evoked,
    Yet, one thing is certain, we kids sure awoke.
What fear , what danger, we saw in that wood.
    If any could cross it we knew our dad could.

On September 11, did we cross the bridge?
    Or are the front tires nosed up to the ridge?
Ready to take us the last lap of the way,
    For we're going home without any delay.

December

December's Introduction and Aim

This month, the last month of the year, December, only twenty-five days until Christmas, we enter the Epilogue, from Song of Songs 8:8-4. According to Webster, an "epilogue" is a speech, a short poem, or something like that, an address to the spectators or audience, spoken after the conclusion of the play or drama.

The opposite of an epilogue, which is at the end, is the foreword, preface, introduction, or prologue, which comes at the beginning.

The drama of this Song was concluded in Chapter 8, Verse 7, at the end of Act 2, Scene 5. Here the Bridegroom and His bride sing their duets, "The Song of Deliverance." The bride was first delivered from the record of her sins in the blotting out of sins both in the heavenly sanctuary and in her mind. This is recorded as *"a seal upon thine heart"* (Song 8:6).

Second, as the seven last plagues are poured out and the wicked seek to destroy the bride, she is delivered by the "Voice of God." This delivery is as a seal upon His arm.

Then when Jesus comes, their third deliverance is from *"the body of this death"* (Romans 7:24) through the putting on of immortality and the changing of this vile body. We will look at the little sister who has no breasts and the Trinity's plans to prepare her so that she will be ready for Him. "All who believe that the Lord has spoken through Sister White, and has given her a message shall be safe from the many delusions that will come in, in these last days" (YSRP 254/5).

December

Day 1	First Lady of First Ladies	Song 8:8	400
Day 2	Breast of Breasts #6	Song 8:8	401
Day 3	Question of Questions #2	Song 8:8	402
Day 4	Responsibility of Responsibilities	Song 8:8	403
Day 5	Understanding of Understanding	Song 8:8	404
Day 6	Investigation of Investigations #2	Song 8:8	405
Day 7	Day of Days	Song 8:8	406
Day 8	If of Ifs	Song 8:9	407
Day 9	Wall of Walls #2	Song 8:9	408
Day 10	Turret of Turrets	Song 8:9	409
Day 11	Solution of Solutions	Song 8:9	410
Day 12	Door of Doors	Song 8:9	411
Day 13	Knock of Knocks	Song 8:9	412
Day 14	Preparation of Preparations	Song 8:10	113
Day 15	Placement of Placements	Song 8:10	414
Day 16	Breast of Breasts #7	Psalms 119:105	415
Day 17	Awareness of Awarenesses	Song 8:10	416
Day 18	Task of Tasks	Song 8:11	417
Day 19	Acknowledgement of Acknowledgements	Song 8:12	418
Day 20	Sacrifice of Sacrifices	Song 8:12	419
Day 21	Loud Cry of Loud Cries	Song 8:13	420
Day 22	Harvest of Harvests	Song 8:13	421
Day 23	Urge of Urges	Song 8:13	422
Day 24	Double Take of Double Takes	Song 8:13	423
Day 25	Urgency of Urgencies	Song 8:14	424
Day 26	Haste of Hastes	Song 8:14	425
Day 27	Opening of Openings	Song 8:14	426
Day 28	Surge of Surges #2	Revelation 22:20	427
Day 29	Review of Reviews #2	2 Timothy 1:12	428
Day 30	Appeal of Appeals	Galatians 4:4	429
Day 31	Summary of Twelve Summaries	John 14:29	430

Poems of the Month: "The Saga of the Second Coming" 431
"The Polishing of a Stone" 433
"A Poem That Can His Love Display" 434

December 1   *First Lady of First Ladies*   Song 8:8

Today's Thought: *"We have a little sister, and she hath no breasts: what shall we do for our sister in the day when she shall be spoken for?"*

As the Trinity spoke in Genesis, *"Let us make man in our image, after our likeness"* (Genesis 1:26), so They again speak, *"We have a little sister."* In Song 4:10, it states, *"How fair is thy love, my sister, my spouse!"* Then in Song 8:1-3, the bride-church refers to the Bridegroom as her brother, so they agree with each other, that they are siblings. Because the Bridegroom is the man-child of the woman in Revelation, the bride has the same mother; this makes them siblings.

As Christ is the Son of God, we become sons and daughters of God, and joint heirs with the Son, making siblings of each of us.

The Trinity looks upon the bride—the church—as their little sister. They have a concern for the church right now, at this present time. Down through the centuries, they have had a similar concern, yet this concern is intensifying. The church, enfeebled and defective, needing to be reproved, warned, and counselled, is the only object upon earth upon which Christ bestows His supreme regard. He extends to all the world His invitation to come to Him and be saved. He commissions His angels to render divine help to every soul that cometh to Him in repentance and contrition, and He came personally by His Holy Spirit into the midst of His church (TM 15).

We need to take advantage of the Holy Spirit now, seeking perfection of the soul, and then when the Holy Spirit comes, the Trinity can do its perfect work as we, the last generation, pass through the judgment of the living (Berry, Quarterly, p. 108).

Consider that the church is the only safe place on earth. In Noah's time, the only safe place was the ark. To describe the condition within is another story. During the time of the taking of Jericho, the only safe place was in Rahab's apartment, and remember, Rahab was a harlot.

Parting Gem: *The little sister seems to be the theatre of His grace, in which she, the church, delights to reveal His power to transform hearts. She is the first lady of the Universe.*

December 2   *Breast of Breasts #6*   Song 8:8

Today's Thought: *"We have a little sister, and she hath no breasts: what shall we do for our sister in the day when she shall be spoken for?"*

Having no breast is a form of immaturity. It is not a form of deformity, nor illness. No young female child can speed up the time of her maturity. She must patiently wait, for in due time, according to the Creator's blueprint for her, she will mature. Each day she eats, plays, and works, doing the daily things young girls do. Yet no amount of worry will change her. As the normal child develops into adulthood in the process of normal growth, so the church is scheduled to mature according to the Creator's plan (Berry, Quarterly, p.106).

In this epilogue, the Trinity is discussing the current problem of the lack of readiness on the part of the church today, for the judgment of the living, for the final crises, for the final deliverance, for the loud cry of the third angel. They are discussing what the church must be in order to live in the sight of the Lord without a High Priest (1T 466). Should we dispute this, we need only to read the message to the Laodicean Church in Revelation 3:14-22.

Breasts are described in the drama symbolically as the Word of God, be it as the sincere milk of the gospel, the grape wine of doctrine, or the roes and hinds of prophecy. This has been one, and only one, of the main thrusts of this drama. This church represented by our bride-woman has the Bible and the Bible only as their standard of conduct, doctrine, lifestyle, dress, diet, and what-have-you. Anything other than the Bible needs to be judged according to the Bible. God's people, once known as "people of the Book," need to get back to the Book so that we are properly clothed with that white raiment.

Parting Gem: *We know that Christ is waiting for you and me to manifest Himself in our lives. When His character is perfectly reproduced in you and me, He will come to claim us as His very own. We also know that the Lord Jesus is conducting experiments on human lives through the exhibition of His mercy and abundant grace.*

DECEMBER 3   Question of Questions #2   Song 8:8

Today's Thought: *"What shall we do for our sister in the day when she shall be spoken for?"*

How shall the church reach a state in which the character of Christ shall be perfectly reproduced, or reflect the image of Jesus fully? How does one individual do it or the entire corporate body all reach this state at the same time? How shall God's people live without a Mediator through the seven last plagues or obtain the "victory" over every besetment, pride, selfishness, love of the world, and every other wrong word or action? How shall they meet the decree, *"He that is... let him be... still"* (Revelation 22: 11)?

Has that not always been the question throughout Scripture? *"What must I do to be saved?"* That's what the Philippian jailer asked Paul in Acts 16:30.

What did the men of Israel ask when Peter preached at Pentecost? *"Men and brethren, what shall we do?"* (Acts 2:37) Or the rich young ruler asked Christ? Even in our drama, the big question, although worded differently, is still the same: *"What is thy beloved more than another beloved?"* (Song 5:9) Now again, the Trinity is asking the question that They feel responsible to answer. *"What shall We do?"*

"Never should we begin the day without committing our ways to our heavenly Father. His angels are appointed to watch over us, and if we put ourselves under their guardianship, then in every time of danger they will be at our right hand. When unconsciously we are in danger of exerting a wrong influence, the angels will be by our side, prompting us to a better course, choosing our words for us, and influencing our actions. Thus our influence may be a silent, unconscious, but mighty power in drawing others to Christ and the heavenly world."[20]

Parting Gem: *Once one has answered the question of all questions, he knows whom he hath believed. Then he will realize that Jesus sees His true church on the earth, whose greatest ambition is to cooperate with Him in saving souls.*

---

[20] White, Ellen G. *Christ Object Lessons* (Washington, DC: Pacific Press Publishing Association), 1941, pp. 341-342.

December 4   *Responsibility of Responsibilities*   Song 8:8

Today's Thought: *"What shall we do… when she shall be spoken for?"*

Soon, like just around the corner, the day draws near when she *"shall be spoken for"* in marriage—in the judgment of the living, in the Investigative Judgment. Are we really not ready? Many do not realize what they must become in order to live in the sight of God without an Advocate in the high courts of heaven (EW 71).

It appears, in the question *"What shall we do?"*, that the responsibility lies with the Trinity, not with the little sister. The verse does not say, "What shall the little sister do?"

Ephesians 5:27 exposes the ultimate aim of Christ for His church. *"That he might present it to himself a glorious church, not having spot, or wrinkle, or any such thing; but that it should be holy and without blemish."*

It is not left to the church to prepare herself, although the church, like any small immature child, does have some responsibilities in the process of maturation. The church must understand two points; she cannot get ready on her own, but she does a part to play. Two points.

This idea also applies to us virgins. On our own, we cannot get ready, but we do have a major part to play in getting ready. Much counsel has been give to us as to "how to" get ready, to the point that we have no excuse for missing out. "All who consecrate body, soul and spirit to God's service will be constantly receiving a new endowment of physical, mental and spiritual power. The inexhaustible supplies of heaven are at their command. Christ gives them the breath of His own Spirit, the life of His own life. The Spirit puts forth its highest energies to work in heart and mind" (6T 306:1).

One secret to spiritual growth and development is to respond to the light given and render corresponding obedience, keeping our souls in the love of God, abiding in Christ (The Upward Look, Dec. 25).

Parting Gem: *"If my people, which are called by my name, shall humble themselves, and pray, and seek my face, and turn from their wicked ways; then will I hear from heaven, and will forgive their sin, and will heal their land"* (2 Chronicles 7:14).

December 5   *Understanding of Understandings*   Song 8:8

Today's Thought: *"We have a little sister, and she hath no breasts: what shall we do for our sister in the day when she shall be spoken for?"*

This is how Solomon expresses what 1T 486 states: "God's people are not prepared for the loud cry of the third angel. They have a work to do for themselves which they should not leave for God to do for them. He has left this work for them to do. It is an individual work: one cannot do it for another."

1T 466 says, "…nearly all who profess to believe the present truth are unprepared to understand the work of preparation for this time… They are wholly unfitted to receive the latter rain."

The first prophet among men, Enoch, gives, through his life, some answers as to how he walked with God, as well as how we today may walk with God as he did. Firstly, Enoch was aware that he had heavenly companions with him at all times and continually requested them. This we can do; we can be aware of the heavenly presence and talk to them throughout the day.

Secondly, every thought and action was first filtered through the Control Room of heaven by asking, "Is this the way of the Lord?" (6BC 1098) Or, "Is this what You want me to do?" This will take conscious effort until the habit is formed. It is not easy.

Thirdly, by continual, earnest prayer he would lift his heart to God, putting his prayer and conversation into the censor of Christ's righteousness (SC 98-99). Throughout the day, in his workplace, in his private study, in his association with friends and family, he would often lift his voice in prayer and praise.

Finally, Enoch knew just what he had to do in order to be saved, and he met those requirements. Speaking non-politically, this may be where many fail, fall down, never recover. Should we know the power that heaven has given us, we would walk a victorious, vibrant walk, for God's people are destroyed for lack of knowledge, according to Hosea 4:6. If we only realized what we can do in God's power.

Parting Gem: *Our prayer should be, "O Master. Let me walk with Thee as Enoch did."*

December 6   *Investigation of Investigations #2*   Song 8:8

Today's Thought: *"What shall we do for our sister in the day when she shall be spoken for?"*

The day draws near when *"she shall be spoken for"* in marriage—in the Investigative Judgment of the living. The Investigative Judgment for the dead, from our first parents, Adam and Eve, down to the last person who has had his name recorded in the Lamb's Book of Life, is closing. Probation has not yet closed. This investigation now passes on to the living. Remember, this bride-church represents the living church in any particular period.

Consider that I am (or you are) a part of the modern, current church, and that I am alive, when my name comes up in this investigation of the living. Am I prepared for my name to pass the powerfully close scrutiny of this court case, or marriage ceremony? Will my Beloved say with exceeding joy, "I do, I do, I do. I really, really do," when the officiating minister, the Father, asks His Son if He takes me as a legal citizen of His kingdom?

Now is the best time, now being every day, to accept the counsel of the Amen, the faithful and the true Witness, the beginning of the creation of God, to buy of Him gold tried in the fire, white raiment, and eye salve to anoint my eyes, without money, without price. Then I shall be rich, rich in faith. Then I shall be clothed with the whole armour of God, and the fruit of the Spirit, and Christ's robe of righteousness; as well, I shall see my need and my solution.

"When we learn the power of His Word, we shall not follow the suggestions of Satan in order to obtain food or to save our lives. Our question will be 'What is God's command, and what are His promises.' Knowing these we shall obey the one, and trust the other" (Ev. 242:0). Let us, today and every day, take time to investigate our spiritual standing, and take appropriate action.

Parting Gem: *If any man hear His voice, let him come.*

DECEMBER 7 *Day of Days* Song 8:8

Today's Thought *"What shall we do for our sister in the day when she shall be spoken for?"*

One exciting day in every girl's life is that of her marriage. Yet, here is depicted the day our bride-church is to be spoken for in the day of judgment, at the marriage of the Lamb.

It was in 1954. I was twenty years old, working in a British Columbia sawmill. My friend Glenn and I rode the carriage which carried the log back and forth in front of the double-head saws. We set the carriage so that the saws could cut the logs into lumber.

Suddenly, an overwhelming impression came over me. I was transported to the Most Holy compartment of the heavenly sanctuary. I stood before the Judge. My name had come up for review. The impression was so overwhelming that I just had to jump off the carriage onto the boardwalk, stretch both arms to heaven and scream as loud as I could, "My name just came up in the Judgment. My name just came up in Judgment!" Needless to say, work stopped until I returned to the carriage. That impression has never left me.

When your name comes up for review in the judgment of the living, and your Father asks your Beloved, "Do you take this person as a lawful, legal citizen of your New Jerusalem; do you promise to love him, protect him and treat him royally throughout eternity?" Will your Beloved declare, "I do, I do, I really, really do"?

Today the church is approaching *"the day when she shall be spoken for,"* the time of the sealing. But the church is immature, not prepared. "They do not realize what they must be" and are "wholly unfit to receive the latter rain" (EW 71). How shall the church become prepared? Where is the power of the message? What must be done?

Consider the answer in the verse, *"What shall we do?"* It is only for us to submit to the Trinity's plan, claim the many exceeding great and precious promises as those given to us personally. Open the Gift (2 Peter 1:4).

Parting Gem: *Remember Jude 24, "Now unto him that is able to keep you from falling, and to present you faultless before the presence of his glory, with exceeding joy."*

DECEMBER 8 — *If of Ifs* — Song 8:9

Today's Thought *"If she be a wall, we will build upon her a palace of silver: and if she be a door, we will inclose her with boards of cedar."*

"If" is a short word, only two letters, but horrendous, sobering in meaning. Some even claim that it is the longest and the strongest word in the English language. Many times it is accompanied by the word "only." If only I had done it differently. If only I had asked Alice instead of Joan. If only I had gone home instead of staying. If only I had said no instead of yes. If only; if only. Many lives would certainly have been different, some for the better, some for the worse.

Scriptures also uses "if" to show our part in helping the "we" of Song 8:8-9.

1 John 1:9 says, *"If we confess… he is faithful and just…"*

Matthew 16:24 says, *"If any man will come after me…"*

2 Chronicles 7:14 says, *"If my people, which are called…"*

John 16:7 says, *"If I go not away, the Comforter will not come…"*

Revelation 3:20 says, *"If any man hear my voice, and open…"*

One has said that every promise of God in the Bible is an "if" promise, conditional. Even His coming the second time is based on an if. *"If I go… I will come again"* (John 14:3).

So here a conditional promise is given to the bride-church. *"If she be a wall, we will… if she be a door, we will…"* If we do our part, God will do His part.

Come with me back to our Parting Gem from December 4, *"If my people, which are called by my name, shall humble themselves, and pray, and seek my face, and turn from their wicked ways; then will I hear from heaven, and will forgive their sin, and will heal their land"* (2 Chronicles 7:14).

My Reader Friend, are you up to the challenge given to us today? We need only do three things: humble ourselves, pray, seek God's face. The results are awesome. He will hear, forgive, heal. Try it.

Parting Gem: *"He which hath began a good work in you will perform it until the day of Jesus Christ"* (Philippians 1:6).

DECEMBER 9 — *Wall of Walls #2* — Song 8:9

Today's Thought: *"If she be a wall, we will build upon her a palace of silver: and if she be a door, we will inclose her with boards of cedar."*

Christ is waiting for His people to show forth His character in their lives. When this happens, when His character is shown in the lives and the life-style of His people, Christ has promised to come (COL 69).

In ancient times, a wall was built around cities as a means of protection, or fortress from invaders. In Solomon's time, gun-powder was unknown, so two ways to protect the cities were by a wall or a mote. So, if this young sister will become a wall, "We," the Holy Spirit, will build upon her a palace of silver, or a fortress.

We need to consider carefully the awesome thought that the Eternal One has a people, a chosen people in this sin-ridden and evil-stricken, revolted world (TM 16). We are His ambassadors, His light-bearers, His feet, His hands, His voice to all the world, to our family, our significant others.

In this fortress, there is to be no authority known, no laws acknowledged except His own. We find no evidence that this fortress is to be disorganized or broken up into individual pieces, one here and one there (2SM 68-9). We do, however, have plenty of evidence that this fortress seems about to fall and come apart at the seams, but it does not (2SM 380).

The author is the first to acknowledge that all information regarding our drama is not known. How will the Trinity build a palace of silver if I will be but a wall? How will They inclose me with boards of cedar if I am but a door? What is the full, full meaning of these words? I would love to dig deeper into the gold mine, the silver mine of God's storehouse to find the answers. The challenge can also be yours.

P.S. I would love for you to keep your eyes on these walls over the next week until we come to the Tower.

Parting Gem: *Enfeebled and defective as she may appear to be, this fortress is His case in which He keeps His jewels and is the only object upon earth in which He bestows His supreme regard (2SM 396).*

DECEMBER 10 — *Turret of Turrets* — Song 8:9

Today's Thought: *"If she be a wall, we will build upon her a palace of silver."*

In the margin of the Bible for the word "palace" is "turret." A turret is a tall, movable, rotatable structure, moved usually on wheels, carrying soldiers, engines, battering rams, heavily armoured, usually revolving, used for breaching or scaling enemy walls.

The great commission of Matthew 28 challenges us to this very activity of breaching and scaling the enemy's strongholds. A church that is alive and well is always a church that is at work. A church that is at work is a growing church, which comes back to the fact that a working church is a living church.

"The world will not be convinced by what the preacher in the pulpit teaches, but what the church lives daily" (6T 260).

There are two experiences in John 1 where his disciples left him to follow Jesus. They asked Jesus, *"Where do you live?"* Jesus did not argue, but simply said, *"Come and see"* (John 1:38-39).

When Philip found Christ and later told Nathaniel he had found Jesus of Nazareth, Nathaniel's question was, *"Can any good thing come out of Nazareth?"* Philip's reply was similar to Christ's: *"Come and see"* (John 1:46).

Can you imagine in your mind, this large silver turret rolling up to the walls of wickedness to scale and climb over in their attack of evil? Inside are all of the aforementioned warriors with their swords by their side. You may not be inside that turret, but you can help push that machine up to the walls, so that the warriors can attack.

Are you looking forward to being a palace of silver, or even one enclosed with cedar? Contemplate what this means to you.

Parting Gem: *This "turret" or palace of silver—built by the Trinity—represents the church militant, moving forward with the loud cry, "Come and see." Remember also, If "we," you and I, will be a wall, They, the Trinity, will build upon us a "palace of silver." Awesome thought?*

December 11 — *Solution of Solutions* — Song 8:9

Today's Thought: *"If she be a wall, we will build upon her a palace of silver: and if she be a door, we will inclose her with boards of cedar."*

As one listens to the happenings in the world, either by reading about them in the newspapers, listening to them on the TV or radio, or seeing them happen firsthand, one could be plagued by the question, "Is there no solution?" One might wonder, "Why?" Yet, the reason and the answers are easy to find. There is only one solution, the solution of all solutions.

As one experiences the tornadoes, hurricanes, tsunamis, floods, fires, earthquakes, and whatever else is not particularly pleasant to the eye or ear, one who reads the Word will be familiar with Matthew 24, but more excitedly with Luke 21:28—*"And when all these things begin to come to pass, then look up, and lift up your heads; for your redemption draweth nigh."* Lift up your head for the solution, in the singular please notice. The solution draweth nigh.

Is that not what Song of Songs is all about, the Bridegroom skipping across the prairies, calling His people together?

The bride's solution is echoed a few times throughout the Song: *"I am His and He is mine."* When He comes skipping and dancing across and over just to get His bride, I will lift up my heart, I will shout, I will rejoice for my Redeemer is here.

Did you catch the picture of the church giving the "Loud Cry" of the third angel's message found in Revelation 14, as well as the message of Revelation 18? "I was shown those whom I had before seen weeping and praying… their features… now shone with the light and glory of heaven… I asked what had made this great change. An angel answered, "It is the latter rain, the refreshing from the presence of the Lord, the loud cry of the third angel… I heard those clothed with armour speak forth the truth with great power" (E.W. P. 271).

Parting gem: *This solution of my Beloved Bridegroom coming for me is sweet in the mouth and will be even sweeter in the stomach. It is the only solution that will work—the coming of the Bridegroom.*

December 12 — *Door of Doors* — Song 8:9

Today's Thought: *"And if she be a door, we will inclose her with boards of cedar."*

In our previous text, *"If she be a wall… [or] if she be a door"* (Song 8:9), the Trinity has promised to bring her to maturity. The Trinity is saying here that it does not matter what she lacks by way of immaturity—what she lacks, whatever she needs, in whatever her present state. If she is willing, the Trinity guarantees that she shall be made ready for the day when she shall be spoken for—the judgment of the living.

Individually, when your name comes up in the judgment for the living, if you be willing and obedient, you shall eat from the Tree of Life. Then, suddenly, she finds that the work has been finished.

Jerusalem represents God's people. The church is likened to a house or a temple. Among the finishing touches of a house, the doors are hung by being encased with wooden door casings. As Solomon built and finished the temple in seven years, so Christ, the Prince of Peace, the antitype of earthly Solomon, shall build and complete His temple.

1 Kings 6:9 says, *"So he built the house, and finished it; and covered the house with beams and boards of cedar."*

Take some extra time this morning to read the Laodicean message in Revelation 3:14-22. It states there that the Amen is aware of our works, that we are neither cold nor hot, that we are miserable, wretched, poor, blind, that we believe we are rich and in need of nothing. However, He is also fully aware that we know it not. We know not that we are miserable, that we are poor, that we are blind, that our nakedness is repulsive. One of the first steps, if not the first, in rectifying our miserable unsaved condition is to admit that we are like we are. We have no concept of what we must become in order to be saved. We simply don't know our condition. What a pity; let's change.

Parting Gem: *Could it be that when God's people really realize that "I am His and He is mine"—or as Jeremiah states, "And ye shall be my people, and I will be your God" (Jeremiah 30:22) and "they shall be my people,e and I will be their God" (Jeremiah 32:28)— we will realize who and whose we are and do something about it?*

DECEMBER 13 — Knock of Knocks — Song 8:9

Today's Thought: *"And if she be a door, we will inclose her with boards of cedar."*

In the angel's message to us Laodiceans, Christ states, *"Behold, I stand at the door, and knock; if any man hear my voice, and open the door, I will come in to him, and will sup with him, and he with me"* (Revelation 3:20).

So in order for Christ, this bride-church, or us, to sup together, the bride must not only hear His voice, she must open to His knocking. If she be a door and opens unto us, then we will do our part. Again, the big "if." A gift, regardless of its size, weight or wrappings, is of no value unless and until it is not only accepted but opened.

Isaiah 1:19 says, *"If ye be willing and obedient, ye shall eat the good of the land."* And we wish to eat of the good of the land.

If, however, we refuse and rebel, we shall not only eat not of the good of the land, but be devoured with the sword (Isaiah 1:20).

All of us should be interested in finishing the work, first and foremost in our own hearts and lifestyle. That way, when it is finished in the world and Christ comes, we will eat the good of the land. Yet it is by the power of the Holy Spirit, the pouring out of this Spirit upon God's people, that will finish it in our hearts, and it will happen when we realize that Christ is waiting with a longing desire for His church to manifest Himself in their every day lives and actions. When we realize that His people must have Christ's character perfectly reproduced in their lives, this gives Christ an awareness that we are wanting Him to come and that we are ready. It tells Him that we are deadly serious. What then does all that mean?

So if we are a door, then let us open our lifestyle, our very being, to Him. Let us allow Him through His Holy Spirit to come in and take possession of our every thought and action, so that we may sup together.

Parting Gem: *In George R. Knight's book,* From 1888 to Apostasy *(page 135), after quoting COL, "when the character of Christ shall be perfectly reproduced in His people," he states that in essence it is having the Spirit of unselfish love, the Spirit of caring in every forgiven Christian.*

December 14 — *Preparation of Preparations* — Song 8:10

Today's Thought: *"Then was I in his eyes as one that found favour."*

Obedience to God's Word has in every age been a sign or a seal. In Abraham's day, it was circumcision. In Noah's day, it was the flood situation. In Luther's day, it was the Bible and the Bible only. In our age, it has been righteousness by faith.

Since 1844, the Word of Truth has been that of the three angels' message in Revelation 14. It has encompassed the Present Truth of the Investigative Judgment now in session, the identity of the Remnant People in their keeping of God's commandments and the faith of Jesus. The test of their obedience has been focused, since 1844, upon the Sabbath. The keeping of the fourth commandment has distinguished the remnant people of God, and by it they have been sealed.

"I then saw the third angel. Said my accompanying angel, 'Fearful is his work. Awful is his mission.' He is the angel that is to select the wheat from the tares, and seal or bind, the wheat for the heavenly garner. These things should engross the whole mind, the whole attention" (EW 118).

Yet, how does one find favour in God's sight? What must "I do" in order to stand before God? Try these:

In Jeremiah 9:23-24, it says, *"Let not the wise man glory in his wisdom, neither let the mighty man glory in his might… but let him that glorieth glory in this, that he understandeth and knoweth me… for in these things I delight, saith the Lord."*

"Come unto me all ye that labour and are heavy laden, and I will give you rest. Take my yoke upon you, and learn of me; for I am meek and lowly in heart: and ye shall find rest unto your souls. For my yoke is easy, and my burden is light" (Matthew 11:28-30).

Parting Gem: *The sealing of those who shall live without a Mediator is a unique experience and special preparation for that time is needed. In the judgment of the living, the sealing of God's people not only identifies them, but also prepares them to live without a Mediator. They live through the plagues, receive the Latter Rain, give the Loud Cry, and experience circumstances of no equal in past history.*

DECEMBER 15   *Placement of Placements*   Song 8:10

Today's Thought: *"... then was I in his eyes as one that found favour."*

In this epilogue, suddenly the bride takes centre stage. With arms stretched towards her Beloved, she exclaims abruptly, *"I am a wall, my breasts like towers: then was I in his eyes as one that found favour."*

The final movements will be rapid ones. The Latter Rain will bring the church to full maturity. Her understanding of the Word of God will be perfect. Her character perfect, her labours perfect.

According to Peak's Commentary, the Song of Songs 6:10 verse has been misplaced. It does not belong in Chapter 6. Commentators understand from the context that it has been inserted or misplaced, but they do not know where it should be. Ellen G. White has given the correct historical setting! She states, "While the investigative judgment is going forward in heaven, while the sins of the penitent believers are being removed from the sanctuary, there is to be a special work of purification, of putting away of sin, among God's people upon earth... when this work shall have been accomplished, the followers of Christ will be ready for His appearing. Then she *'will look forth as the morning, fair as the moon, clear as the sun, and terrible as an army with banners'* (Song 6:10)" (GC 425).

In the Marriage Encounter program, they kept saying, "The best is yet to come." That is exactly what we can say here, "The best is yet to come."

They also kept saying that love is a decision. Should we apply that to the rest of one's day, then hatred, happiness, temper are also decisions. The greatest decision, or at least one, is to put away sin from one's life. Send them on ahead to judgment, as so stated in 1 Timothy 5:24—*"Some men's sins are open beforehand, going before to judgment; and some men they follow after."*

At the present time, the church is the church militant; yet in a short while it will be the church triumphant. Hang in there, keep the faith.

Parting Gem: *This is "Onward Christian soldiers, marching as to war, with the cross of Jesus going on before," not just as a song, but as an activity.*

December 16   *Breast of Breasts #7*   Psalms 119:105

Today's Thought: *"Thy word is a lamp… and a light…"*

There are at least three very important emphases that are placed in this drama. The first emphasis which is very prominent is our Beloved, and His tremendous love for us. He is our Hero. The second is the heroine, the First Lady of the Universe, the church and the precious position this church has in the eyes of our Hero, the Bridegroom. The third emphasis is on the "breasts" of our bride.

Notice Song 8:10, *"I am a wall, and my breasts like towers."* Why such an emphasis on the bride's breasts? These are mentioned some eight times (1:13, 4:5, 7:3, 7:7, 7:8, 8:1, 8:8, and 8:10), representing the sincere milk of the Word, the Old and the New Testament, the meat of the Word, the wine of doctrine. I trust that this point is solidified in your minds.

The Bible and the Bible only must be our authority on which all doctrines are based. This upfront Bible should be noticeably present, well-balanced, full of milk, meat, wine. The Bible should be the first thing people notice when they meet the church-bride.

Here, now, in the epilogue we see the breasts representing towers, which represent Christ, His Word. In earlier days, walls were needed to protect cities; now this tower, God's Word, is needed to protect our bride-church with, "It Is Written," or a "Thus saith the Lord." Like the "Cities of Refuge," one needs to learn how to flee through the walls. Review the early warriors and you will see that they could handle their swords extremely well. Their tower of Strength was their Creator-God, their Beloved, the Bibles. They knew how to fly into it for protection, rest, even ammunition.

Remember that text, *"Thy word have I hid… that I might not sin…"* (Psalms 119:11).

Another one from the Tower, *"All scripture is given by inspiration of God, and is profitable for doctrine, for reproof, for correction, for instruction in righteousness: that the man of God may be perfect, throughly furnished unto all good works"* (2 Timothy 3:16-17).

Parting Gem: *There is no other Book so potent to elevate the thoughts, give vigour to the faculties, broaden the mind, nobilize the character, give a stability of purpose as the broad ennobling truths of the Bible, the Word, the breasts, the clusters of grapes.*

December 17 — *Awareness of Awarenesses* — Song 8:10

Today's Thought: *"I am a wall."*

This sudden exclamation is a statement of the finished work. Apparently the bride-church knows that she has been sealed! *"My breasts [are] like towers"* (Song 8:10). Her understanding of the Word of God and all its prophetic content is complete and her character perfected under the seal of the Living God. She has passed the final test successfully and she exclaims, *"I am a wall."* This knowledge that she has been sealed runs parallel to inspiration.

"Said the angel, 'List ye!' Soon I heard a voice like many musical instruments all sounding in perfect strains, sweet and harmonious. It surpassed any music I had ever heard, seeming to be full of mercy, compassion, and elevating holy joy. It thrilled through my whole being. Said the angel, 'Look ye!' My attention was then turned to the company I had seen who were mightily shaken. I was shown those whom I had seen before weeping and praying in agony of spirit. The company of guardian angels around them had been doubled, and they were clothed with an armour from their head to their feet. They moved in exact order, like a company of soldiers. Their countenance expressed the severe conflict which they had endured. Yet their features, marked with severe internal anguish, now shone with the light and glory of heaven. They had obtained the victory, and it called forth from them the deepest gratitude and holy, sacred joy" (EW 270, 271).

Once one understands the Song of Songs, what it is saying, what it means, who it refers to, and becomes aware of the whole drama with its implications and applications to us as Seventh-day Adventists today, then it is believed that offshoots will disappear from among us, apostasy will decrease, former members of God's flock will be reclaimed. As well, God's people will get serious about Whose they are and will then grab the message and spread it, especially to their significant others.

Parting Gem: *One of the methods of preparing for this expression of deepest gratitude mentioned is to practice now. Always, whenever an opportunity comes up to express gratitude, grab it and run.*

December 18   *Task of Tasks*   Song 8:11

Today's Thought: *"Solomon had a vineyard at Baalhamon; he let out the vineyard unto keepers…"*

According to the SDA Bible Dictionary, "Baal" means "lord, possessor, husband." "Haman" means "multitudes."

In Joel 3:13-15, it says, *"Put ye in the sickle, for the harvest is ripe: come, get you down; for the press is full, the fats overflow; for their wickedness is great. Multitudes, multitudes in the valley of decision: for the day of the Lord is near in the valley of decision. The sun and the moon shall be darkened, and the stars withdraw their shining."*

The task that the church sees before her today and the task to be finished is to put in the sickle and reap the harvest, for the harvest is ripe. The loud cry of the three angels broadcasting into this valley of decision will tip the scales to the side of the blood-stained banner of Prince Immanuel.

This vineyard of Solomon is in *"the valley of decision,"* for there are many on the verge of the kingdom waiting only to be gathered in. This vineyard is global wide, within our state or province, within our town or hamlet, close by within our neighbours' lives, even to our own family and loved ones.

When you come to December 22, it will be mentioned that your responsibility is to sow, sow, sow? The Holy Spirit's responsibility is to convert, convert, convert, and to take the blame or credit for both the failure and the success. Now another responsibility for us is to reap, reap, reap the harvest which is now white.

Parting Gem: *There are some who can't go to mission fields, preach, give out literature door to door. So, don't feel guilty. Our job is to sow seeds of truth and salvation to all, live that Christian life we profess, speak that word in due season, do the task that is currently at hand. Then when people are forced to make that decision of all decisions, they will remember our witness and respond.*

DECEMBER 19   *Acknowledgement of Acknowledgements*   Song 8:12

Today's Thought: *"My vineyard, which is mine, is before me…"*

This acknowledgement at the end of the drama is powerfully different from the one at the beginning of the drama, where she states in 1:6, *"… but mine own vineyard have I not kept."*

She's not going to make the same mistake again, even though she seems to have made it frequently through history. Now, endowed with the Holy Spirit and the power entailed, she is empowered. She sees, for now she has eye salve, the task before her, and under the power of the Holy Spirit she moves forward, onward, upward.

"Nearly all… are wholly unfitted to receive the latter rain" (1T 466). "God's people are not prepared for the loud cry of the third angel" (p 486). "I also saw that many do not realize what they must be in order to live in the sight of the Lord without a high priest in the sanctuary through the time of trouble. Those who receive the seal of the living God and are protected in the time of trouble, must reflect the image of Jesus fully… I saw that none could share the 'refreshing' unless they obtained the victory over every besetment, over pride, selfishness, love of the world, and over every wrong word and action. We should, therefore, be drawing nearer and nearer to the Lord and be earnestly seeking that preparation necessary to enable us to stand in the battle in the day of the Lord" (EW 71).

Catch a vision, a picture, an overview of your vineyard that is before you, for each one of us has a vineyard and it is always just before us. It's nice to go far away for mission service, but right in our own backyard, front yard too, is a large mission field just waiting to be enlightened. There's our neighbourhood in general, our neighbours in particular, but even closer in our backyard is our spouse and our heirs, our children, our own flesh and blood offspring which are needed to carry our hope to the next generation.

Parting Gem: *Christ is waiting with longing desire for the manifestation of Himself in His church. When His character shall be perfectly reproduced in His people, He'll come. Contemplate just what that means to you personally. It sounds scary and impossible, yet it has been stated that it is a very enjoyable, as well as an easy experience.*

December 20 — *Sacrifice of Sacrifices* — Song 8:12

Today's Thought: *"Thou, O Solomon, must have a thousand, and those that keep the fruit thereof two hundred."*

The bride acknowledges her task in the vineyard in the final harvest, for she states, *"My harvest is mine"* (Song 8:12, paraphrase). She knows what her work is to be: she must give the "Loud Cry" in the power of the "Latter Rain" of the Holy Spirit.

In the vineyard, each has his own responsibility, each person works and uses his own gifts. The glory of the redeemed is shared between Christ and the "keepers."

Revelation 3:21 says, *"To him that overcometh will I grant to sit with me in my throne, even as I also overcame, and am set down with my Father in his throne."*

A thousand pieces of silver is an exorbitant price. Those who finish the work will give all.

Nevertheless, the true bride says, *"My vineyard, which is mine, is before me"* (Song 8:12). She is going to finish the work regardless of the sacrifices required. Yet, she also knows that she will share in the glory of the kingdom for she states, *"… those that keep the fruit thereof [will have] two hundred."*

One is humbled tremendously when he considers the sacrifice the early pioneers made to spread the gospel truth they loved, that of the sacrifice that Jesus Christ, their Lord and soon-coming King made when He made the sacrifice of all sacrifices.

Looking at 1T 176, 239, 419, among others, is the ideas that the early pioneers sacrificed to the point of selling their homes to buy cheaper ones just for the sake of the work. They esteemed it a tremendous privilege to do such a deed. They spent many a weary hour hammering out the beliefs to take into "mother's house of present truth," to the point that these need not be hammered out again.

Those of us in our days need to be thankful for the sacrifices the early pioneers made, with the understanding that we really do not know what they did nor the cost they bore.

Parting Gem *Contemplate today as you venture out just what sacrifice you are willing to make so that the cause can be advanced.*

DECEMBER 21   *Loud Cry of Loud Cries*   Song 8:13

Today's Thought: *"Thou that dwellest in the gardens, the companions hearken to thy voice: cause me to hear it."*

This is the loud cry of Revelation 18:1. *"And after these things I saw another angel come down from heaven, having great power; and the earth was lightened with his glory."*

"The angel who unites in the proclamation of the third angel's message is to lighten the whole earth with his glory... The work will be similar to the Day of Pentecost. As the 'former rain' was given in the outpouring of the Holy Spirit at the opening of the gospel, to cause the up springing of the precious seed, so the 'latter rain' will be given at its close for the ripening of the harvest... Servants of God, with their faces lighted up and shining with holy consecration, will hasten from place to place to proclaim the message from heaven. By thousands of voices... truth is seen in its clearness... a large number take their stand upon the Lord's side" (GC 610-612).

"Precious light is to shine forth from the Word of God, and let no one presume what shall be and what shall not be brought before the people in the messages of enlightenment that He shall send, and so quench the Spirit of God" (CSSW 28).

There is an interesting verse in Daniel 11:44 which states, *"But tidings out of the east and out of the north shall trouble him: therefore he shall go forth with great fury to destroy, and utterly to make away many."*

For your consideration, could it be that the *"Edom, and Moab, and the chief of the children of Ammon"* (Daniel 11:41) that shall escape could refer to the Arabs who are descendents of Ishmael and children of Abraham, descendents of Cush? Because God knew that Abraham would command his household after him and Abraham believed in monotheism, did these descendents get a knowledge of only one God? Please consider.

Parting Gem: *"When a message comes in the name of the Lord to His people, no one may excuse himself from an investigation of its claims"* (CSSW 28).

DECEMBER 22 — Harvest of Harvests — Song 8:13

Today's Thought: *"Thou that dwellest in the gardens, the companions hearken to thy voice: cause me to hear it."*

Another way to say *"cause me to hear it,"* is *"speak louder,"* or to give the "Loud Cry," which is in connection with the final harvest.

Revelation 14:15,18 says, *"And another angel came out of the temple, crying with a loud voice to him that sat on the cloud, Thrust in thy sickle, and reap: for the time is come for thee to reap; for the harvest of the earth is ripe... And another angel came out from the altar, which had power over fire; and cried with a <u>loud cry</u> to him that had the sharp sickle, saying, Thrust in thy sharp sickle, and gather the clusters of the vine of the earth; for her grapes are fully ripe"* (emphasis added).

"When the storm of persecution really breaks upon us, then will the message of the third angel swell to a LOUD CRY, and the whole earth will be lightened with the glory of the Lord" (6T401).

When the Sunday law enforcement brings about the "storm of persecution," the bride will be mature and ready to give the final "Loud Cry," which finishes the work and final harvest.

In this verse, the Bridegroom is speaking. "You who have been anointed, baptized, joined God's family, raise your voice, give your testimony, cry aloud that Christ is coming. Angels will accompany you, and I, your Saviour, will hear you. Thus you will draw together , give to the enemy a united front, present the message of the third angel with a loud cry so that the whole earth will be enlightened with the glory of the Lord" (6T 401).

Yet, one thought for you. Your responsibility is not to "win souls." That is the responsibility of the Holy Spirit. You are simply to sow seeds, sow seeds, sow seeds. The Holy Spirit takes "credit or blame" for either the success or the failure.

Parting Gem: *Christ is waiting with longing desire for the bride to accomplish her task. As they draw together, they present to the enemy a united front. Could it be that this "united front" presented to the world would be one reason for the world to stand up and take notice of what the Loud Cry is all about? The Lord is waiting for the Spirit of Unselfish love, the perfection of His character, to manifest itself in His people.*

DECEMBER 23 *Urge of Urges* Song 8:13

Today's Thought: *"Thou that dwellest in the gardens, the companions hearken to thy voice: cause me to hear it."*

The weather is completely unpredictable and way out of control. Forecasting correctly is nigh unto impossible. Populations are mushrooming, wickedness is multiplying. Global wars are impending. Terrorism is flourishing. Starvation and pestilences are stalking the earth. Ecological disasters threaten. Global warming is exploding. World finance teeters on the verge of collapse. The very earth's crust is crumbling and earthquakes speak of the destruction of this planet. The stage is set and the drama escalates towards the final disaster.

Amid all this, the bride is pleading for the Bridegroom to come quickly—to make haste to deliver her from this self-destructing planet. He gives the promise in prophecy, by the roes and by the hinds. "Surely I come quickly." She implores Him, *"be thou like a roe or a young hart"* (Song 2:17). She implores, "According to your prophecies, make haste."

Acts 16:9 says, *"And a vision appeared to Paul in the night; there stood a man of Macedonia, and prayed him, saying, Come over into Macedonia and help us."*

Matthew 28:19 implies, *"Go ye therefore into all the world, teach…"* (paraphrase). Even if the world is your family, GO.

Putting these two texts together, the Bridegroom urges us to "Go," while the Macedonians urge us to "Come."

Too many times, we have been encouraged to do great and wonderful things for God. But what is a great and wonderful thing? We need not be a preacher preaching, a teacher teaching. How about being a truly honest mechanic? Those are desperately needed. What would you think of being a farmer, a construction worker, a baker, a real estate agent, a bus driver, a healthcare worker? God wants to use you wherever you choose to locate yourself. Even a stay-at-home mom or dad is powerfully effective when he or she connects with the Source of heaven, remembering that they are training the next generation to do great and wonderful things for God.

Parting Gem: *Not too often do we hear of bad news which is really good news: but these signs point to the nearness of Christ's soon coming.*

DECEMBER 24 *Double Take of Double Takes* Song 8:13

Today's Thought: *"Thou that dwellest in the gardens, the companions hearken to thy voice: cause me to hear it."*

The "Latter Rain" of the Holy Spirit accomplishes a double work:
(1) It ripens the grain, completes the work of God's grace in the soul, wherein the moral image of God is to be perfected in the character of those who receive the final seal of God.[21]
(2) It also gives them power to give the Loud Cry warning against the beast. Apparently, there is a simultaneous or interactive process, both going on at the same time.

"The latter rain falling near the close if the season ripens the grain and prepares it for the sickle... The ripening of the grain represents the completion of the work of God's grace in the soul... By the power of the Holy Spirit the moral image of God is to be perfected in the character. We are to be wholly transformed into the image of Christ" (TM 506).

"I heard those clothed with the armour speak forth truth with great power. It had effect... I asked what had made this great changer. An angel answered, 'It is the latter rain, the refreshing from the presence of the Lord'" (1SG 186).

"Servants of God, endowed with power from on high, with their faces lighted up, and shining with holy consecration, went forth... proclaiming the message from heaven" (1SG 196).

Who are those who dwell in the gardens? The church members who have been baptized with the Holy Spirit, have His power and grace, and who go forth into all the world, to give to that world the "Loud Cry." They are the ones who have eagerly received the counsel to buy gold tried in fire, to buy the white raiment to hide their lack of spiritual knowledge, and have had their eyes swabbed with eye salve so that they now understand spiritual truths that were clouded before.

Parting Gem: *"I counsel thee to buy of me gold tried in the fire" (Revelation 3:18). The gold spoken of is a special measure of faith to believe the Trinity will complete the work in us. Christ's prayer to lead us not into temptation is that temptation of not believing God's power and authority and accepting it.*

---

[21] Berry, Marion G. *The Prophetic Song of Songs, Quarterly* (Albia, IA: The Prophetic Song of Songs, Inc.), 1969, p. 108. Quoting from TM 506.

DECEMBER 25 — *Urgency of Urgencies* — Song 8:14

Today's Thought: *"Make haste, my beloved."*

Seventh-day Adventists have preached the nearness of the Bridegroom's coming, somewhat to their embarrassment, for over a century and a half. All that time, the church has been cautioned by the Song of Songs 2:7 and 3:5—*"I charge you, O ye daughters of Jerusalem, by the roes, and by the hinds of the field, that ye stir not up, nor awake my love, till he please."* As well, in 8:4— *"I charge you, O daughters of Jerusalem, that ye stir not up, nor awake my love, until he please."* Notice that this last charge does not include *"by the roes, and by the hinds,"* as the others have. All time prophecies have been finished, so there is time no longer. All that is left is for this gospel to go to all the world, and for Song of Songs to be used to help prepare God's people for God's day.

But today, according to Song 8:14, we enter into a new historical era—the final events and His coming. This has been and is the message of the Song of Songs. The Bridegroom has dedicated and consecrated Himself to this purpose.

This modern generation of Adventism is so far down the line from the pioneers of Adventism that they need special help as they come to the close of probation. God does not bring His people to the greatest climactic events of history without a prophetic message of warning, comfort, cheer.

Could it be that the Bridegroom is getting "impatient," if such a thing could be, that He is starting to take things into His own hands? Listen to the stories, incredible stories, of a tall shining being surrounded by brilliant light appearing in a "heathen" village with a black box, a radio. He then gives the chief instructions on how to use this black box to get Adventist World Radio. The entire village listens to the programs, are converted, and are ready for baptism. Baptism is a long, multiple-day walk to the nearest facility. Then it's reported that many other villages have been visited by this glowing angelic being with similar results.

Parting Gem: *Could it be, just could it be, that the bride is saying to you, to me, "My time has come because it was for this hour that I was born"?*

December 26 — *Haste of Hastes* — Song 8:14

Today's Thought: *"Make haste, my beloved, and be thou like to a roe or to a young hart upon the mountains of spices."*

"One of the most solemn and yet most glorious truths revealed in the Bible is that of Christ's second coming. To God's pilgrim people, so long left to sojourn in the 'region and shadow of death,' a precious joy-inspiring hope is given in the promise of His appearing, who is 'the resurrection and the life,' to 'bring home again the banished.' The doctrine of the Second Advent is the very key-note of the Sacred Scriptures. From the day when the first pair turned their sorrowing steps from Eden, the children of faith have waited the coming of the Promised One to break the destroyer's power and bring them, again to the lost paradise" (GC 299:1).

John the Revelator, closing his epoch on the Isle of Patmos in Revelation 22:20 states, *"Surely I come quickly. Amen. Even so, come, Lord Jesus"* (Revelation 22:20). These two messages of haste run parallel to each other, another similarity between these two prophetic books.

Our bride-church charges her Beloved by roes and hinds, by the Word of the Lord, by the prophecies of Daniel and Revelation, by the very Song of Songs itself, that the time has come for His return. This time, there will be neither more delay nor disappointment.

While we were in the Garden of Eden, we heard the Creator say to the serpent, *"And I will put enmity between thee and the woman, and between thy seed and her seed; it shall bruise thy head, and thou shalt bruise his heal"* (Genesis 3:15). Now that language, although easy to understand, was written in King James' language. What does it mean in our modern language? "I, Jesus Christ the Creator, will cause hostility and hatred to be between you, Satan, and My church; it will be between your followers and My followers. You, Satan, will have your head crushed in the final conflict after the a thousand years, but before that you will crush the heal of the Creator by crucifying Him."

It certainly didn't take long for our Creator to start laying out great and precious promises so that we might be victorious followers of Christ.

Parting Gem: *"The return of Christ to our world will not be long delayed. Let this be our keynote of every message"* (6T 406:1).

December 27 — *Opening of Openings* — Song 8:14

Today's Thought: *"Make haste, my beloved, and be thou like to a roe or to a young hart upon the mountains of spices."*

Prophecy is given to enable God's people to know where they stand in history. Prophetic exposition of the past has revealed that God has led Bible students to study prophecies which are about to be fulfilled. William Miller's preaching on the 2,300 day prophecy is one example. As prophetic Scripture is opened up, its fulfillment directly follows. As the Song of Songs is opened up to God's people, it brings them with historical and chronological sequence to those events connected with the close of probation, the end of the Investigative Judgment, the latter rain, the loud cry, the time of trouble or seven last plaques, the final deliverance, and the Second Coming.

This time, there will be no delay, no disappointment. The chronological sequence of this drama places these closing events directly before us.

God will not bring His people to the greatest event in history without first giving them the understanding of their exact location and position in the picture. The Lord will do nothing unless He first reveals it to His prophets (Amos 3:7). One other important characteristic of God is that if something magnanimous and stupendous is going to happen, something as dramatic as the flood, would He not tell us what is going to happen and even give us signs? He gave Noah's people tremendous signs, that of birds and animals coming into the ark in an orderly manner. Do you think He would not do something as spectacular in our day, getting ready for the morning of mornings?

This drama, the Song of Songs, is given and opened to God's remnant people today that they may confidently know where they stand in God's great timeline of events, and equally important, just who they really are. This points to the hour of the judgment of the living, and all closing events, as well as to give them a fresh and invigorating view of the beautiful Saviour and His righteousness.

Parting Gem: *This drama is a song in the night. One could even say that it is a light in the night.*

DECEMBER 28   *Surge of Surges #2*   Revelation 22:20

Today's Thought: *"Even so, come, Lord Jesus."*

That's John the Revelator adding his own personal testimony to the visions and dreams, the challenges and the warnings of his book, Revelation. He closes his prophecy depicting his plea, his passion, his hunger with "Amen, amen, amen. Even so, come, Lord Jesus; delay no longer. Come, come, come."

The apostle Paul needed to warn the Thessalonians and the Corinthians of the expected second coming of Christ and just what to expect. Similarly, our drama has had to keep us aware that *"when the fulness of the time was come, God sent forth His Son"* (Galatians 4:4).

Now, however, times have changed and moved on; we are nearer the second coming than our bride was. The end of our drama has a sudden and unique change in that reference to the *"roes and the hinds."* The passion and the hunger for her Beloved to come ends the drama in 8:14, where the bride says, "Make haste, my beloved, make haste. Come, come, come quickly. The world is now ripe, cups of iniquity are now full, Your people are now sealed, so there is really nothing standing in Your way. Make haste, make haste, make haste."

Similarly, the end of our message in Revelation 14:6-12 has a sudden and unique change. Another angel, a fourth one, comes down from heaven with great power, and the whole globe is enwrapped and engulfed in His glory (Revelation 18:1). This causes a surge of cries as wave after wave of God's love, justice, mercy reaches far out to all living upon the earth.

No longer does she tell her Beloved to flee to the mountains of Bether (Song 2:17) carrying the message of the gospel, and to do it until the day breaks, for the day has broken. The Son of Righteousness comes riding in His chariot with thousand of angels, ten thousand times ten thousand and thousands of thousands, each with his own task to fulfill until the clouds are awash with the saints of the Most High, all on their way to the New Jerusalem where the night is far past.

Parting Gem: *Even so, come, Lord Jesus. Make haste, my Beloved, make haste, make haste, make haste. Amen, and Amen, and again Amen."*

December 29 — *Review of Reviews #2* — 2 Timothy 1:12

Today's Thought: *"I am not ashamed: for I know whom I have believed, and am persuaded that he is able to keep that which I have committed unto him against that day."*

Whenever you now sing Song #511, "I Know Whom I Have Believed," remember this devotional on the drama called Song of Songs. For your information, this song just happens to be the author's favourite song.

We have spent the year launched out into the deep. We have let down our nets. We have surveyed a little, often confused book of the Bible. We have encountered several terms that have kept this book "in the dark." Looking at this drama as you have looked at it this year, look at this book as a parallel to the other prophetic books of Scripture. Let's review a few points of importance:

Song 2:1 declares that the bride is the rose of Sharon, the lily of the valleys, not Jesus Christ.

Three times the bride mentions, *"My beloved is mine, and I am his."* Should you look at other passages of Scripture, you would find similar words to confirm Solomon's. Jeremiah 30:22 states, *"And ye shall be my people, and I will be your God."* Jeremiah 31:33 states that as well.

The important one, the one the bride urges us to realize, and that we should be "proud" of are, her breasts. Embarrassing, maybe, but an important principle. Our doctrines are based on "the Word of God," depicted by the milk of the breasts, on the Old Testament and the New Testament, on Daniel and Revelation—the roes and the hinds; they are based on the wine of prophecy, the clusters of grapes, and they also inform us that a mature church has breasts and needs them for when she is spoken for at the coming of the Bridegroom. These breasts are out front, very attractive, uniform as in twins, prominent in presentation, and very noticeable; so also is the Word of God, the Holy Scriptures, the Bible and the Bible only.

Then the passion, desire, longing of both the Bridegroom and the bride is for them to get together. After everything is said and done, the whole Plan of Salvation was geared to reunite these two. Are you aware?

Parting Gem: *Take much time today to feast on the milk, meat, the wine.*

December 30 — *Appeal of Appeals* — Galatians 4:4

Today's Thought: *"But when the fulness of the time was come, God sent forth his Son."*

"The roe and the hart" in previous chapters in this drama of the Song of Songs have represented prophetic Scripture, particularly time-prophecies, like Daniel of the Old Testament and Revelation of the New Testament. Throughout this Song of Songs, that refrain or charge has consistently warned, *"by the roes, and the hinds of the field"* (time prophecies) not to stir up (or expect) nor awake my Beloved until He please. But suddenly, at the end of the song, there is a unique change in that reference to the *"roe and the hind of the field."* In the last verse, there is no longer a charge regarding a delay, but instead, an appeal that He *"make haste"* according to time prophecy. This indicates that the time has come for His appearing. Notice the difference:

Song of Songs 2:7 says, *"I charge you... by the roes, and by the hinds of the field, that ye stir not up, nor awake my love, till he please."* This refers to the time of 1,260 prophetic years of persecution, from AD 538 to AD 1798.

Song of Songs 3:5 says, *"I charge you... by the roes, and the hinds of the field, that ye stir not up, nor awake my love, till he please."* This is from 1844 in the Great Advent Movement, moving towards the great disappointment, the end of the 2,300 days.

Song of Songs 8:4 says, *"I charge you... that ye stir not up, nor awake my love, until he please."* This is from about 1888 and onward, where there is no more roes and hinds of the field, since all time-prophecies have been fulfilled.

Now, the very last verse switches gears and pleads, "Make haste, make haste, make haste, come quickly, quickly, quickly." Be like a roe or a young hart, a deer darting across the open field. Even so, come, Lord Jesus. Both our drama and Revelation close with the same appeal.

Parting Gem: *Be ye also ready for in an hour when you think not, the fullness of the time will have come. John wishes to say his appeal, "Even so, come, Lord Jesus" (Revelation 22:20).*

P.S. "Watch therefore: for ye know not what hour your Lord doth come... Therefore be ye also ready: for in such an hour as ye think not the Son of man cometh" (Matthew 24:42,44). Even so, come, Lord Jesus. Amen, amen, and again I say amen.

DECEMBER 31   *Summary of Twelve Summaries*   John 14:29

Today's Thought: *"And now I have told you before it come to pass, that, when it come to pass, ye might believe."*

God's people, that's you and me, have entered a new era of church history—an era where we see the closing of the judgment of the dead, and a switch to the opening of the judgment of the living. This point in time is heralded by the opening up of an entire book of the Bible—the Song of Solomon. [22]

The book, Song of Solomon, is framed in figurative language of prophetic symbolism. To be correctly understood and decoded, we have to let the Bible interpret itself by a cross-reference study of Scripture. This book is a drama depicting church history. It is Christ talking to His church (MB 34). The curtain opens of Act 1, Scene 1, in Chapter 1, Verse 1 on a hill called Mount Calvary, and the final curtain is pulled closed in Chapter 8, Verse 7 at the sealing of God's people. The last few verses are an epilogue where the actors, coming out onto centre stage, depict what events are soon to follow.

In this book, we saw God's people identified, God's church identified. In this book is a gift from the Bridegroom to His bride to prepare her for when He returns to claim her as His Bride. It is a gift to edify, encourage, uplift, and prepare you and me to "Behold the Bridegroom," for He *is* coming.

Therefore, was your mind, your heart prepared? Was your time arranged for this journey through the Song of Solomon? Was your heart gladdened by this festive mood of a wedding between a lover and His love, between my fair, my love and my Beloved? Did your hearts burn within you as you walked the "Emmaus Road" with my Beloved? Did you see the Great Advent Movement walk across the stage? Did you see the great disappointment of 1844 portrayed and the command to "prophecy again"?

This book has a strong parallelism with the book *The Great Controversy*, and one is encouraged to check this work with it. I would certainly encourage, yea urge, you to read *Testimonies to Minister*, from the bottom of page 409 to the top of page 410.

This year is over, the book has been read; I trust that your heart burned within you as you launched out into the deep and let your net down.

"Prepare to meet thy God, O Israel" (Amos 4:12).

---

[22] With slight alterations, this day's reading is a repeat of January 1's reading.

The Saga of the Second Coming

I saw off in the rising sun a small black cloud appear.
The saints look up in confidence; they know their Lord was here.
The wicked gaze with trembling stance as cold fear grips their hearts
That cloud grows large and brighter still, this cold fear stabs like darts.
The earth recoils, the heavens scream, the skies are all ablaze.
All people on this earth gaze up yet, most are in a daze.

Bright lightnings flash across the sky in thunderous fiery bolts.
Loud thunder cracks both far and near and shake with powerful jolts.
Black boisterous clouds clash back and forth as each cloud rocks and olls.
The earth reels like a drunken man, all seems way past control
Its surface ripped and torn apart; some islands disappear.
Those mountain chains of massive peaks are levelled neat and clear.

Huge ocean waves wipe cities down;   destruction's all around.
Hail stones as heavy talents pound down deep into the ground.
The globe convulses violently, heaves like some drunken drone
Yet tens of thousand angels stand around about the throne.
Upon that throne of glorious clouds sits One engulfed in fire.
The sky light up with thunderous light, caught in a new attire.

All eyes transfixed upon that cloud descending down the hall,
Fierce cries ring out from all about, some scream for rocks to fall.
While saints burst out in prayerful thanks, "This is our coming King
We've waited long, we've trusted Him to us salvation bring.
All praise to Him, our mighty God, this mighty Prince of Peace."
With eyes transfixed upon that cloud   from sin's strong power release.

The trumpets peal across all space blown by angelic host
When at the last the trumpets cease and angels man their post,
Christ upon that blazing cloud cries out from His great throne,
"Awake, awake, awake My saints, Your Father calls you home."
Countless angels wing their way to lift their saintly charge.
Up from their graves, their prison house, the swelling throngs enlarge.

From all across the earth they rise to meet their Lord in space.
From graves of dust, those prison cells, they see Christ face to face.
From waters deep, from ashes heap   and lots from mountain caves.
Unnumbered souls of risen saints rise up from ancient graves.
Those little babes laid in their graves to sleep away from harm,
Are carried high in angel's care and placed in mother's arms.

Two special groups rise up before that small black cloud appears;
For Christ had told accusers all, and them that used their spears,
That next they put their eyes on Him they would see Him in the skies.
An awful scene before their eyes as they from death arise.
Then some will even rise to see their hope materialize;
For they had died in special hope and kept God's Sabbath prize.

Then we alive and faithful yet, are changed so instantly;
This mortal clay takes on that state of Immortality.
Corruption in our bodies now puts incorruption on.
From glory now to glory then, a glorified new throng.
Seen rising up into that cloud to meet Christ in the air;
A joyful throng, triumphant group, one holy, pure and fair.

An awesome sight meets every eye as saints rise in the air,
Some giants tall, some pigmies small and skins of every fair.
Ascending now back into space that holy remnant rise;
The earth left void, the prison house of Satan and his hosts.
The Sea of Glass awaits those saints within the city gates,
The Tree of Life, the Saviour, all eternity awaits.

The Polishing of a Stone
(7T 264:3)

You may be a stone, sharp, rough and crude
    That needs to be squared, polished, smoothed.
Before into God's temple you can fit.
    But, once you're ready, that's really it.

Be not surprised, be not deceived,
    If hammer and chisel from God you receive,
To chip away roughness, to chisel you clean,
    To bring out God's glory, as yet unseen.

He chisels, He cuts, He polishes and grinds,
    Then when He's finished your place He will find.
He places you gently in a place that is yours,
    Or thrust you abruptly through all open doors.

The blows of His hammer, the cuts of His knife,
    Give you character, nobility, beauty and life.
The blows they may hurt you and you think not they'll heal,
    Yet not one is wasteful, each one is for real.

He knows of your frame, your hair and your clay,
    His work is to save you, though what a strange way.
His blows and His knife, His polishing grinds
    His view of your future is one hard to find.

A Poem That Can His Love Display

Poems are made by fools like me,
    But, only God can make a tree.
Yes, but let me be that lonely fool,
    If in God's hand I am His tool.

To tell of God's great love and care,
    And of His Presence just everywhere.
Like Paul of old I choose to be,
    A fool, a dude, whatever you see,

If in God's mighty hands I lay,
    A poem that can His love display.
If in some silly rhyme or verse,
    I can awaken some burning thirst,

Then praise to God for that silly gift,
    As His name, His power, His love, I lift.

Appendices

APPENDIX 1

Comparison of Song of Solomon with Revelation

Song of Solomon
    Old Testament

Revelation
    New Testament

Real Name:
    Song of Songs (1:1)

Real Name:
    Revelation of Jesus Christ.

History of God's children:
    N/A

History of God's children:
    7 Seals, 7 Churches

Wedding Invitation:
    Song of Songs 3:11

Wedding Invitation:
    Revelation 22:17

Great Disappointment Story:
    Chapters 4-6

Great Disappointment Story:
    Chapter 10

Warning:
    8:6 (*"Most hot flame."*)

Warning:
    Chapter 22:18, 14:10

Last Verses:
    "Make haste, My Beloved."

Last Verse:
    "Even so, come, Lord Jesus."

APPENDIX 2

What Happened Next Part A, Portion 1

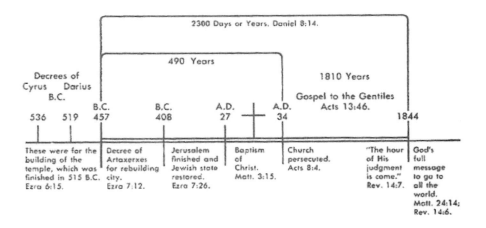

- **Daniel 9:24**—"*Seventy weeks are determined upon thy people and upon thy holy city, to finish the transgression, and to make an end of sins, and to make reconciliation for iniquity, and to bring in everlasting righteousness, and to seal up the vision and prophecy, and to anoint the most Holy.*"
- **Daniel 9:25**—"*Know therefore and understand, that from the going forth of the commandment to restore and to build Jerusalem unto the Messiah the Prince* **shall be seven weeks**, *and threescore and two weeks: the streets shall be built again, and the wall, even in troublous times*" (emphasis added).

(**7 prophetic weeks multiplied by 7 days per week = 49 prophetic days, or 49 literal years.**)

What happened after 49 literal years, which actually takes us from **457 BC,** when the decree went into effect, down to **408 BC**?

1. The City of Jerusalem was rebuilt: walls, streets, gates, temple, temples services. The Jewish economy was re-established, and *all* in very troublesome times.[23]
2. In **444 BC,** Nehemiah had himself appointed governor of Jerusalem in order to expedite the work, which was finished in **408 BC.**

457 BC	7 Prophetic Weeks	408 BC
Decree goes into effect.	*49 literal years (City of Jerusalem rebuilt).*	

Remember: This vision is used to seal up the vision and the prophecy.

What Happened Next
Part A, Portion 2

Daniel 9:25—*"Know therefore and understand... from the going forth of the commandment... unto the Messiah the Prince shall be...* **threescore and two weeks***..."* (emphasis added)

(62 prophetic weeks multiplied by 7 days per week = 434 literal years.)

What happened after another 434 literal years, which actually takes us down to **AD 27**?

1. John the Baptist was preaching repentance in the Jordan River area, preparing the way for the Messiah (John 1:1-37).
2. A 31-year-old Carpenter appears at the bank of the Jordan River.
3. John is forced to proclaim, *"Behold the Lamb of God, which taketh away the sin of*

---

[23] For further details of these troubles, read *Prophets and Kings* (Chapters 45-46), the Book of Ezra, the Book of Haggai, and the Book of Zechariah.

the world" (John 1:29).
4. John baptizes this Carpenter, Jesus of Nazareth (Matthew 3:15-16).
5. The heavens open and the Spirit of God, in the form of a DOVE, descends upon Christ (John 1:26).
6. Thunder breaks forth from the skies as a voice pronounces, *"This is my beloved Son, in whom I am well pleased"* (Matthew 3:17).
7. In the year **AD 27**, the anointing of the Most High Messiah takes place.

| 457 BC | 408 BC | 62 Prophetic Weeks
434 literal years. | AD 27 |

Remember: This prophecy is used to seal up the vision and the prophecy (which means that *if* the first part is correct, then the remainder of this prophecy must be true and accurate as well).

What Happened Next Part A, Portion 3

Daniel 9:26-27—*"And after threescore and two weeks shall Messiah be cut off, but not for himself… and he shall confirm… for one week: and in the midst of the week he shall cause the sacrifice and the oblation to cease."*

What happened that last and final prophetic week of the 70-week period, from **AD 27**, when Messiah was anointed, to **AD 34**, when the Jews officially rejected Christ? And specifically, what happened in the middle of the prophetic week, being **AD 31**, when Christ was crucified for us, not Himself (and after, as per Daniel 9:26)?

1. In the middle of the **prophetic week**, Christ was crucified in the spring of **AD 31.**
2. The Sanhedrin, the official council of the Jewish nation, voted to officially stone Stephen in **AD 34.**
3. Open persecution swept through the newly-formed church (Mark 1:15; GC 699:2).

4. James, the first of the twelve, was slain by Herod in **AD 44**.
5. The vineyard was let out to other husbandmen (Matthew 21:41; Isaiah 5:1-7; GC 328, 410).
6. Peter, directed by the Spirit, visited the Gentile Cornelius (Acts 11).
7. Saul of Tarsus is converted, becoming Paul, the apostle to the Gentiles. The dying testimony of Stephen was a factor.
8. The gospel continues to spread rapidly.
9. The temple and Jerusalem were destroyed by the Romans in **AD 70**.

457 BC	408 BC	AD 27	AD 31	AD 34
			Christ baptized.	Christ crucified.	Stephen stoned.

Remember: This prophecy is used to seal up the vision and prophecy. If the first part meets the prophecy, the rest will also.

What Happened Next Part B, The Remainder

What happened at the end of the prophecy, at the end of the 2,300 days (years), which actually brings us to **AD 1844**?

1. A Great Religious Awakening started in the 1830s.
2. William Miller, Joshua V Himes, Joshia Litch, and Charles Fitch were out front preaching the 2,300 day prophecy and Christ's coming in the United States.
3. George Irving, along with some three hundred preachers, covered England with the message of Christ's soon coming.
4. Joseph Wolff, "missionary to the world," a converted Jew, proclaimed the message in seventeen countries, fourteen languages, and the United States Congress.
5. Immanuel Lacunza, a South American Catholic priest, wrote and proclaimed the coming Messiah under the name "Rabbi Ben Ezra."
6. Child preachers under the influence of the Holy Spirit swarmed over the Scandinavian countries with this massage.
7. Boy preachers in Bohemia and other parts of the world were major

proclaimers of the second coming of Christ.
8. Great emphases were placed on this Second Coming of Christ.

457 BC   408 BC   AD 27   AD 31   AD 34   AD 1844

Remember: This prophecy was to confirm and seal the vision and the prophecy in its entirety.

Appendix 3

The Seven Churches of Revelation in the Light of Song of Song

Revelation 2:1-7 *"Unto the angel of the church of Ephesus write:"*
AD 31 to AD 100 (Apostolic Age)
Song of Songs 1:2-3
Rebuke: Revelation 2:4

Revelation 2:8-11 *"Unto the angel of the church in Smyrna write:"*
AD 100 to AD 323 (Age of Persecution)
Song of Songs 1:4
Rebuke: NONE

Revelation 2:12-17 *"To the angel of the church in Pergamos write:"*
AD 323 to AD 538 (Age of Compromise)
Song of Songs 1:5-6
Rebuke: Revelation 2:14

Revelation 2:18-29 *"Unto the angel of the church in Thyatira write:"*
AD 538 to AD 1563 (Age of Adversity or Papal Supremacy)
Flight INTO the wilderness for 1,260 years.
Song of Songs 1:7-2:7
Rebuke: Revelation 2:20

Revelation 3:1-6 *"Unto the angel of the church in Sardis write:"*
AD 1563 (Reformation) to AD 1798 (Age of Reformation)
Song of Songs 2:8-17
Rebuke: Revelation 3:2

Revelation 3:7-13 *"To the angel of the church in Philadelphia write:"*
AD 1798 to AD 1844 (Age of Great Second Advent Awakening)
Coming OUT of the wilderness
Song of Songs 3:1-5:6
Rebuke: NONE

Revelation 3:14-22 *"Unto the angel of the church of Laodicean write:"*
AD 1844 to Second Coming (Age of the Investigative Judgment)
Song of Songs 6:1-8:14
Rebuke: Revelation 3:15-19

APPENDIX 4

A Wedding Invitation

Give glory to Him
For the hour of His marriage (Judgment)
Is come.

You are cordially invited to leave the city of Babylon
To attend the wedding,
And to enjoy the reception wedding supper
In the city of
New Jerusalem.

As you travel,
Beware of the beast,
Because he is recovering
From his deadly wound.
In fact,

He is masquerading as the very Bridegroom,
And you must not receive his mark!
You will be identified at the
Door!
For
You must be wearing
The wedding garment.

(Berry, Textbook, p. 164)

APPENDIX 5

Recommended Books to Read

1. *Lest We Forget,* by George R. Knight.

2. *The Great Controversy,* by E.G. White.
   Follow the guideline set out in the Table of Contents.

3. *The Prophetic Song of Songs,* by Marion Berry.

4. *Sabbath School Quarterly,* by Marion Berry.

5. *Quarterly Textbook,* by Marion Berry.

6. *The Prophetic Faith of Our Fathers,* by Arthur Spalding.

7. *Early Writings,* by E.G. White.

Appendix 6

This Night of Nights

In "Night of Nights," May 13, it was stated, "Just in passing, that's the way it was from creation to the flood; there was no night there. Only after the flood when the sun and moon were affected did night and darkness come into existence."

Because of the fact that I have been challenged on this point to back it up, I wish to lay out for you my background data that brought that nugget to my attention. Whether I am correct or out in left field, the point remains that although one may not agree with me, this is still my "Nugget of Understanding." This is one reason I am proud to be a citizen of my country and a member of my church; we do have the privilege and the right to think for ourselves. Feel free to join me.

Allow me to start at the very end, the new earth, and work back towards creation.

Revelation 21:23,25 says, *"And the city had no need of the sun, neither of the moon, to shine in it: for the glory of God did lighten it, and the Lamb is the light thereof… And the gates of it shall not be shut at all by day: for there shall be no night there."*

Isaiah 60:19-20 says, *"The sun shall be no more thy light by day; neither for brightness shall the moon give light unto thee: but the Lord shall be unto thee an everlasting light, and thy God thy glory. The sun shall no more go down; neither shall thy moon withdraw itself: for the Lord shall be thine everlasting light, and the days of thy mourning shall be ended."*

Zechariah 14:6 says, *"And it shall come to pass in that day, that the light shall not be clear, nor dark: but it shall one day which will be known unto the Lord, not day, nor night: but it shall come to pass, that at evening time it shall be light."*

Isaiah 30:26 says, *"Moreover the light of the moon shall be as the light of the sun, and the light of the sun shall be sevenfold, as the light of seven days, in the day that the Lord bindeth up the breach of his people, and healeth the stroke of their wound."*

Isaiah here is talking about the restored heaven and earth and is saying that the sun will get back its original power and the moon will return to the sun as it is was before the flood, for that lesser light went out at the time of the flood. That sun will be as our present-day sun. The greater light needs enough power, heat, and light to reach out to its farthest family member, Pluto.

These are a few verses pertaining to the time after Christ comes and we enter the New Earth.

In Genesis 1:26-27, we read, *"And God said, Let us make man in our image, after our likeness: and let them have dominion over the fish of the sea, and over the fowl of the air… So God created man in his own image, in the image of God created he him; male and female created he them."*

Psalms 121:3-4 says, *"He will not suffer thy foot to be moved: he that keepeth thee will not slumber. Behold, he that keepeth Israel shall neither slumber nor sleep."*

Ecclesiastes 7:29 says, *"Lo, this only have I found, that God hath made man upright; but they have sought out many inventions."*

So because we are created in His image, after His likeness, and He never slumbers nor sleeps, let us accept that and apply it to those before the flood.

Should one look into the special gift God has given His church, he would notice many characteristics of the creation of Adam and Eve:

- He was created with more than twenty times the vital force of man today (3T 138-9).
- He was more than twice as tall as man now living (3SG 34), well-proportioned (3SG 84, 85) meaning their weight was heavy.
- He had power given to him akin to the Creator (Ed. 17).
- He was created with power similar to God (5T 311).

Check the Genesis record and notice that before the flood, man lived nearly a thousand years, while after the flood, their lifespans decreased rapidly. These antediluvians were well-proportioned, meaning that they were more than twice as tall as present-day man, and therefore would have had to weigh close to a ton each.

At the time of the flood, the earth went through such a tremendous violent upheaval that when it settled down, it was off of the original straight up and down axis it was originally given. The orbits of the sun and the moon were thrown askew in such a way as we have now. This switch in orbits brought on darkness as well as light.

At the time of the 2010 earthquake in Chile, the quake was so violent that it threw the earth off its axis some more and the length of our day actually changed by a millisecond. That quake lasted a short time, whereas the flood lasted forty days and forty nights. I wonder whether or not that Chile quake was "given" us to inform us that it happened first at the flood.

Appendix 7

A Synopsis of Our Drama (A Paraphrase)

This is the Song of Songs written by Solomon, king of Israel.

Let the kiss of reconciliation be given at Calvary, where the Agape love of Christ is better and more important than the wine of doctrine. This was the opening up of the first of the seven churches of Revelation 2-3—the Church at Ephesus.

During the Pergamos Church period, I, the bride-church, apostatized. The newly-formed Christian Church took over the vineyard of the Lord from the Jewish nation.

During the Thyatira and the Sardis Church period, I was forced to flee into the mountains of Italy, Switzerland, France, even as far away as Scotland, wherever there was some type of safety and seclusion so that I could worship my Beloved according to my conscience. I did this all because I refused to surrender my first love of my Beloved. I had to stay there, hidden, for 1,260 years, from AD 538 to AD 1798. Yet, during the Sardis Church period, we heard that the winter of persecution was past and the spring of the Reformation peeked over the mountains. We were encouraged to come away and join in that Reformation.

During my stay in the strongholds of the wilderness, My Beloved, Jesus Christ, describes me, His bride, with glowing words and phrases. I was His special charge.

In my study of Scripture, I knew the time had not yet come for my Beloved Jesus Christ to appear the second time. I stated that in Song 3:5.

Coming out of the wilderness as the Church of Philadelphia, I came out with no small fanfare. It was called the Great Second Advent Awakening. There were earthquakes, signs in the sun and the moon, as well as in the stars. It was awesomely magnificent. I was terrible as an army on the march under the bloodstained banner of Prince Emmanuel. One could even say that I was Satan's worst nightmare.

If a comparison can be drawn, it was like Jehovah God on Mount Sinai with fire, clouds, smoke, thunder—oh, the thunder—all in an attempt to get Israel's attention. So, when I came out of the wilderness, there were similar attention-getters. And like Israel of old, it worked.

There was a great earthquake in Lisbon, Portugal. There was a dark day with a corresponding blood-like moon that night; the stars fell like autumn leaves in a windstorm. It was awesome to behold. For three and a half years, from November 26, 1793 until June 17, 1797, there was this mighty French Revolution where all of France threw the Bible, both the Old and the New Testament, to the ground and trampled it. You can read about that attention-getter in Revelation 11:1-13.

Then in 1798, on February 10, General Berthier stormed into the Vatican and took Pope Pius IV captive, took him back to France where he died. Apparently the pope would not give Napoleon permission to rule the world. This really shook up the globe, for they realized that the deadly wound of Revelation had been inflicted upon the pope.

It just might be good to point out here that the next pope, who also took the name Pius, was also captured, but was later released when he agreed to give up control of the Papal States. These then became a part of the country of Italy. I have often wondered if these Papal States need to be returned to Vatican control in order for the deadly wound to be completely healed.

In various parts of the world, there were God-chosen warriors of the Word who arose to proclaim the near-coming of the Bridegroom. The world became aware that the deadly wound had been inflicted, without a doubt.

Things began to change then; new movements sprung up—movements like women's rights, healthful living, vegetarianism, children education. A great religious awakening took place and a burden for all of the heathen lands gripped the churches. Bible colleges sprang up; over time, these Bible colleges changed names and focus when they moved into university status. Then onto the stage of action came William Miller. He had taken a small book that was opened, but had previously been sealed, and ate it up over a six-year period of time. He came to the conclusion, among other things, that his Beloved, Jesus Christ, would come in about twenty-five years, or near 1843 or 1844.

He mistakenly believed, as was common in his day, that the sanctuary to be cleansed was the earth. Later, he and others discovered it to be the sanctuary in heaven, the sanctuary of the Most Holy Place.

When I opened the door to my Beloved, in Song 5:5-6, to come in the clouds, He didn't come as I expected, but He did come. He came to the Ancient of Days, for His espousal or marriage as in Song 3:11. The daughters of Jerusalem wanted to know in Song 6:1 where He had gone.

The misunderstanding of His not coming the second time was a most bitter disappointment to the waiting saints. It was so disappointing that of the estimated fifty to a hundred thousand Millerites who waited for Christ to come on October 22, 1844, less than one hundred survived and moved on to enter the Laodicean Church period, the Remnant Church. They named it the Seventh-day Adventist Church. The first part of the name, "Seventh-day," was a reference to the seventh-day Sabbath doctrine, and the last part of the name, "Adventist," was a reference to their belief of a soon-second coming. Their last-day, Present Truth Message is found in Revelation 14:6-12.

It may have been embarrassing, awkward, uncomfortable after October 22, when our Beloved did not come as we expected, but He did not leave us. One of our members saw an understanding of our disappointment, that it was the opening of the Investigative Judgment, not the Executive Judgment.

However, the other churches, and even some saints within my community, tore the veil from me. You know that the identifying mark of a bride is her veil. By tearing the veil from me, they were saying that I was not the expected bride of the Bridegroom. But I knew differently. I knew that I was His and He was mine, regardless of what other people said, thought, or taught. I wish to stress this point.

As far as my Beloved's coming was concerned, I tried several times to warn the world, the religious world, not to expect Him to come until He had done what He had to do. Yet, as strange as it may seem, either no one read nor heard me, or no one cared, or stranger yet, maybe Jehovah God orchestrated it to be the way it was (GC p. 401).

I found the message I was looking for, that of the Second Coming of the Bridegroom. I heard Him reach in to unlock the door, and when I went to open the door He was gone. He didn't come the second time like we expected, but instead to the Most Holy Part of the heavenly sanctuary. It was a bitter disappointment.

One mighty important fact I tried to stress in this drama is that the Bible and the Bible only is the rule of faith and conduct within this church. I tried using the symbolism of the grapes, deer, and milk, all connected in one way or another to the breasts. This has caused much embarrassment with people, but my reason for that worked.

Bibliography

Berry, Marion G. *The Prophetic Song of Songs, Quarterly.* Albia, Iowa: The Prophetic Song of Songs, Inc. 1969

_____. *The Prophetic Song of Songs, Resource Book.* Albia, Iowa: The Prophetic Song of Songs, Inc. 1969

Froom, LeRoy, E. *Prophetic Faith of Our Fathers.* Washington, D.C.: Review and Herald Publishing Association. 1950

George, Carl F. *Empty Pews, Empty Streets. Silver Springs, Maryland:* Columbia Union Conference of Seventh-day Adventist. 1988

Jemison, T. housel. *A Prophet Among You.* Mountain View, California: Pacific Press Publishing Association. 1955

Knight, George R. *From 1888 to Apostasy.* Washington, D.C.: Review and Herald Publishing Association. 2007

_____. *Lest We Forget.* Washington, D.C.: Review and Herald Publishing Association. 2008

Richards, H.M.S. Sr. *Walking Through the Bible With H.M.S. Richards.* Mountain View, California: Pacific Press Publishing Association. 1988

The Seventh-day Adventist Hymnal. Washington, D.C.: Review and Herald Publishing

Association. 1985

The Seventh-day Adventist Bible Dictionary. Washington, D.C.: Review and Herald Publishing Association. 1960

Smith, Uriah. *Daniel and Revelation.* Washington, D.C.: Review and Herald Publishing Association. 1955

Spaulding, Arthur W. *Christ's Last Legion.* Washington, D.C.: Review and Herald Publishing Association. 1965

_____. *Captain of the Hosts.* Washington, D.C.: Review and Herald Publishing Association. 1945

White, Ellen G. *Acts of the Apostles.* Washington, D.C.: Review and Herald Publishing Association. (abbreviation AA) 2005

_____. *Colporteur Ministry.* Washington D.C.: Review and Herald Publishing Association. (CM) 1953

_____. *Councils on Diets and Food.* Washington, D.C.: Review and Herald Publishing Association. (CD) 1946

_____. *Christ Object Lessons,* Washington, D.C.: Review and Herald Publishing Association. (COL) 1941

_____. *Desire of Ages.* Washington, D.C.: Review and Herald Publishing Association. (DA) 2005

_____. *Early Writings.* Washington, D.C.: Review and Herald Publishing Association. (EW) 1945

_____. *The Great Controversy.* Washington, D.C.: Review and Herald Publishing Association. (GC) 2005

_____. *Life Sketches.* Washington, D.C.: Review and Herald Publishing Association. (LS) 1943

_____. *Ministry of Healing*. Washington, D.C.: Review and Herald Publishing Association. (MH) 1942

_____. *Patriarchs and Prophets*. Washington, D.C.: Review and Herald Publishing Association. (PP) 2005

_____.*Selected Messages 1, 3*. Washington, D.C.: Review and Herald Publishing Association. (1SM)

_____. *Spiritual Gifts, Volume 3*. Washington, D.C.: Review and Herald Publishing Association. (3SG) 1986

_____. *Testimonies to the Church, Volumes 1, 4 - 7*. Washington, D.C.: Review and Herald Publishing Association. (1T, 4T, 5T, 6T, 7T) 1948

_____. *Testimonies to Ministers and Gospel Workers*. Washington, D.C.: Review and Herald Publishing Association. (TM) 1944

_____. *Thoughts From the Mount of Blessings*. Washington, D.C.: Review and Heralding Publishing Association. (TB)

Educational Bible Committee, *Witnesses for Jesus*. Mountain View, California: Pacific Press Publishing Association. 1952

Devotionals

In Heavenly Places. Washington, D.C.: Review and Herald Publishing Association. (IHP) 1986

Ye Shall Receive Power. Washington, D.C.: Review and Herald Publishing Association. (YSRP) 1996

The Upward Look. Washington, D.C.: Review and Herald Publishing Association. (UL) 1982

Gibbons, Cardinal. *Catholic Mirror*. December, 1893

NAD Adventist World. Washington, D.C.: Review and Herald Publishing Association... December, 2008